Phraseology and Multiword Expressions

Series editors

Agata Savary (University of Tours, Blois, France), Manfred Sailer (Goethe University Frankfurt a. M., Germany), Yannick Parmentier (University of Orléans, France), Victoria Rosén (University of Bergen, Norway), Mike Rosner (University of Malta, Malta).

In this series:

1. Manfred Sailer & Stella Markantonatou (eds.). Multiword expressions: Insights from a multilingual perspective.

Multiword expressions

Insights from a multi-lingual perspective

Edited by

Manfred Sailer

Stella Markantonatou

language
science
press

Manfred Sailer & Stella Markantonatou (eds.). 2018. *Multiword expressions: Insights from a multi-lingual perspective* (Phraseology and Multiword Expressions 1). Berlin: Language Science Press.

DOI:10.5281/zenodo.1182583
Source code available from www.github.com/langsci/184
Collaborative reading: paperhive.org/documents/remote?type=langsci&id=184

Cover and concept of design: Ulrike Harbort
Typesetting: Panagiotis Minos, Sebastian Nordhoff
Proofreading: Adrien Barbaresi, Alexandr Rosen, Andreas Hölzl, Andrew Spencer, Beatriz Sanchez Cardenas, Daniela Schröder, Eleni Koutso, Esther Yap, Ezekiel Bolaji, Gerald Delahunty, Guohua Zhang, Jeroen van de Weijer, Martin Haspelmath, Monika Czerepowicka, Plinio Barbosa, Rachele De Felice, Tamara Schmidt, Timm Lichte
Fonts: Linux Libertine, Arimo, DejaVu Sans Mono
Typesetting software: XƎLᴬTEX

Language Science Press
Unter den Linden 6
10099 Berlin, Germany
langsci-press.org

Storage and cataloguing done by FU Berlin

Freie Universität Berlin

Contents

Multiword Expressions: Insights from a multi-lingual perspective

Manfred Sailer

Goethe University Frankfurt/Main

Stella Markantonatou

Institute for Language and Speech Processing, Athena RIC, Greece

In this introductory chapter, we present the basic concept of the volume at hand. The central aspects of the individually contributed chapters are sketched and some of the relations among the chapters are pointed out.

1 Introduction

Multiword expressions (MWEs) are not only a challenge for natural language applications, they also present a challenge to linguistic theory. This is so because, for the vast majority of them, their structure can be predicted by the grammar rules of the language to which they belong while the semantics of a substantial subset of MWEs is unpredictable or fixed. Therefore, MWEs often defy the application of the machinery developed for free combinations where the default is that the meaning of an utterance can be predicted from its structure.

There is a rich body of primarily descriptive work on MWEs for many European languages but there is little comparative work in this area extending on descriptive, theoretical, and computational issues. This volume brings together MWE experts with individual languages as their background to explore the benefits of a multi-lingual perspective on MWEs, as regards all the dimensions of linguistic research: descriptive coverage, theoretical scrutiny, and computational exploitation.

Manfred Sailer & Stella Markantonatou. 2018. Multiword Expressions: Insights from a multi-lingual perspective. In Manfred Sailer & Stella Markantonatou (eds.), *Multiword expressions: Insights from a multi-lingual perspective*, iii–xxxi. Berlin: Language Science Press. DOI:10.5281/zenodo.1186597

We assume a broad concept of MWE in this volume, using MWE as the cover term for any kind of phraseological unit. As such, it comprises idioms, collocations, complex names, phraseological patterns, etc. We chose the term MWE as the default in this volume, but use its competitors interchangeably with it where no confusion arises. Each contribution will specify explicitly within which empirical sub-domain of phraseology it is located.

We hope that this introductory chapter will help the book to gain easier access to a wider audience and will place it within the current state of research in phraseology and on multiword expressions. We thought that two general issues about this book should be addressed here: the variety of linguistic formalisms used and the general research issues discussed.

The book contains contributions from various linguistic frameworks. Since the individual contributions are relatively short, we consider it useful to provide a brief overview over the frameworks.

We will identify some general research questions that we see either prominently emerging in the field or as topics that should be addressed in the future and will show how the contributions in this volume address some of these issues. The multi-lingual perspective will serve as a guiding principle in the choice of topics. Of course, our perspective may well be biased due to personal preferences and limitations.

Wherever it seems useful, we will point out links between the papers in this volume and show in which respect they point in the same direction or seem to reach mutually incompatible conclusions – a strong proof of the lively ongoing discussions in the MWE field!

It is a privilege for us that this book appears as one of the first volumes in the new Language Science Press series *Phraseology and Multiword Expressions*. We hope that it will pave the way for future books in this series that will take up some of the questions that are addressed here.

2 Topics in multi-lingual MWE research

In this section, we will briefly address three aspects that play an important role in the contributions to this volume: MWE classification, methods and issues in multi-lingual MWE research, and aspects of individual MWE types. In each of the following subsections, we will introduce the basic question and sketch how contributions in this volume address it.

2.1 Classifications of MWEs

The classification of MWEs is a challenge. Even more so, as there is no general consensus about what counts as an MWE. Burger (2015) characterises phraseological units by three properties: polylexicality, fixedness, and idiomaticity, where idiomaticity need not be present in all phraseological units. Fleischer (1997) views phraseology as a fuzzy concept with polylexicality as the only obligatorily present criterion. He assumes three further prototypical properties that define the fuzzy concept. As the term *prototypical* suggests, these properties can be present or absent to various degrees. These properties are fixedness, idiomaticity, and lexicalisation. Idioms of the type *kick the bucket* 'die' are the core cases of phrasemes, satisfying all three criteria. Collocations (*open the door*) may lack idiomaticity, phraseological patterns (*as goes X so goes Y*) may not be fully lexicalised.

The concept that an expression can be a gradually more or less typical representative of an MWE has been generalised to the extreme in most versions of Construction Grammar (Fillmore et al. 1988). This framework abandons the split between Lexicon and Grammar and replaces them with a Constructicon that consists of more or less general and complex constructions. In this view, traditional lexical entries are specific but simple constructions, and classical rules of grammar are general but complex constructions. MWEs, such as idioms, are found in a middle position of this continuum, being rather specific and, at the same time, quite complex constructions. Consequently, it is impossible to define MWEs in this framework – which has, of course, been a conscious design decision in Construction Grammar. Baldwin & Kim (2010) come from a different angle. For them, MWE-hood is in the eye of the beholder: we need to define what we assume to be the "rule" (at any level of linguistic description or language use), and anything that deviates from the rule in one way or another will be classified as an MWE. In this view, the degree of irregularity or idiosyncrasy of an MWE can be observed, but it will be a yes/no split as to what counts as an MWE and what does not.

So far, we have discussed three attempts to define the boundaries of the domain of MWE research. All of them have proven fruitful in research, and we do not see a point in choosing one over the other in abstracto. We can, however, understand the differences if we look at the underlying purpose of the definitions. Fleischer (1997) is in the tradition of the Soviet phraseological research. There, phraseology is considered the third pillar of linguistics, complementing the Lexicon and Grammar by looking at objects that have both lexical and phrasal properties. Fillmore et al. (1988) developed their theory in opposition to the very abstract universalist ideas in the Chomskyan paradigm. Finally, Baldwin & Kim (2010) have concrete computational applications in the back of their minds such as the extraction of MWEs. If there were no difference between MWEs and free combinations, it would be impossible (or meaningless) to build a database of MWEs. The insight that emerges from these considerations is that we need to clarify in which context and for which purpose a characterisation and, as we will see in a second, a classification of MWEs has been proposed. Rather than adopting or rejecting a proposal in general, we should examine critically how far a proposal is suitable relative to our own current framework and research question.

To be on the most inclusive side, let us assume that the domain of MWE research consists of any expression that contains more than one basic lexical element and that is lexicalised, fixed, idiomatic, or irregular in one way or the other. This results in a highly heterogeneous set of expressions. Consequently, we need to structure this huge empirical domain by imposing a classification on it. Just as before, however, there is no hope of finding a single classification or taxonomy of MWEs that can be used for all purposes. Nonetheless, some proposed classifications are better than others. This evaluation will need to take into account the purpose of the classification. Parsing, MWE extraction, cognitive representation, second language learning, machine translation, and many other purposes can be thought of. In all these domains, MWEs pose highly intriguing challenges, but it is unlikely that the same classification will be useful for all of them.

For illustration, we can look at a number of classificatory criteria that have been proposed in the literature and show that they are essential for some, but, probably, relatively useless for other purposes. Makai (1972) distinguishes between idioms of decoding and idioms of encoding. The first class of idioms contains expressions that can only be understood if they are known to the hearer. This is the case for expressions such as *kick the bucket* 'die', but less so for expressions like *answer the phone* or *brush one's teeth*. Idioms of encoding are expressions that need to be known in order to produce them. All three examples given would count as idioms of encoding, since it is an arbitrary convention that the idea of doing dental hygiene is expressed as brush one's teeth in English rather than as clean one's teeth. In German, it is the other way around, with *Zähne putzen* 'teeth clean' rather than *Zähne bürsten* 'teeth brush' being conventionalised, even though the instrument to brush your teeth with is called a *Zahnbürste* 'toothbrush' in German, just as it is in English.

The distinction between a decoding and an encoding perspective is clearly useful for parsing versus generation, but also for designing MWE collections for foreign language learners, who need both types of MWEs, in contrast to MWE collections for native speakers, which usually contain only idioms of decoding. For the purpose of a computational system for automatic MWE extraction, however, this distinction is completely immaterial; actually, it would be misguiding to evaluate an MWE extraction system with respect to its success in categorizing MWEs correctly as decoding or encoding MWEs.

Syntactic flexibility is a classificatory criterion that has been widely relied upon for retrieving, cataloguing, and parsing MWEs. Whether or not an MWE can appear in a number of different constructions, or, from a different point of view, can undergo some transformations, has been a central concern of treatments of idioms in Generative Grammar (see Fraser 1970, for example). One of the most cited works in the computationally oriented MWE literature, namely "Multiword Expressions: A pain in the neck for NLP" (Sag et al. 2002), is about the classification of MWEs in terms of syntactic flexibility. This criterion also plays a central role in the contributions to this volume by Kuiper, Laporte, Parra Escartín et al., Bargmann & Sailer, and Markantonatou & Samaridi – although the last two contributions are rather interested in the ability of MWEs to appear in different constructions and its theoretical ramifications than in classification per se. Syntactic flexibility remains a concern in classifications that are computationally oriented and rely on more criteria, for instance, classifications that draw on the syntactic function of MWEs: Parra Escartín et al. (2018 [this volume]) classify MWEs in terms of both syntactic flexibility and syntactic function (namely, whether an MWE functions as noun, verb or adjective/adverb).

Typically at least two degrees of flexibility are distinguished, telling apart *kick the bucket*-type expressions, which cannot undergo passivisation, from *spill the beans*-type MWEs, which can. This is a core distinction for formal theories of idioms such as the one in Generalized Phrase Structure Grammar (Gazdar et al. 1985) or in Nunberg et al. (1994). After all, passivisation has the status of a major diagnostic in linguistic theory. For instance, back in the early 80's, newborn Lexical Functional Grammar (LFG) relied on passivisation in order to advocate lexicalism and to define grammatical functions that are important axioms of the particular theory. Passivisation is discussed by several contributors to this volume, and opinions vary widely. Markantonatou & Samaridi (2018 [this volume]), who work within the LFG framework, draw on passivisation, as it seems to be able to split Greek MWE data nearly into two. Bargmann & Sailer (2018 [this volume]), on the other hand, argue that, in the right context, most/all English MWEs can passivise. Other languages, such as German, impose even fewer or no restrictions on MWE passivisation. It is on these grounds that, according to them, passivisation is neutralised as a universal classificatory diagnostic for MWEs, but it may be valid in individual languages.

Laporte (2018 [this volume]) argues explicitly that the flexibility criterion of classification is highly problematic because it actually points to an ensemble of syntactic behaviours and, to this moment, there has been no reliable research on exactly how this collective behaviour of diagnostics defines flexibility as a measurable property. It must be said, though, that Laporte does not so much claim that it is not possible to classify MWEs in terms of syntactic flexibility; rather, his argument is that, for the classification of MWEs in terms of a multi-dimensional feature such as syntactic flexibility, an important amount of data about different MWEs and the application of classification methods are required. These methods will apply over sets of features that receive binary values (+/−), that is, over categorical variables.

The approaches to syntactic flexibility we have discussed so far are categorical in nature. They ask whether an MWE can participate in a phenomenon or not, but they are not interested in the actual usage of the phenomenon. Of course, syntactic flexibility can be seen from the point of usage: an MWE that is frequently used with a structural "twist", even if it is the same "twist" most of the time, is it a syntactically flexible one or not? Hanks et al. (2018 [this volume]) argue for a quantitative definition of syntactic flexibility that takes into account the frequency of structural variations ("twists") of an MWE in a corpus and the reported first results suggest that there is little agreement between the "theoretically" and the "frequency" inspired notion of syntactic flexibility.

2.2 Multi-lingual studies of MWEs

Every multi-lingual or cross-lingual study of MWEs is confronted with a number of questions. First, in order to be able to compare a phenomenon across languages, some cross-linguistically, i.e. language-independent constant aspect has to be fixed. In this volume, this is achieved in different ways. In most papers, semantic aspects of the considered class of MWEs are kept constant in the comparison, usually together with some basic syntactic assumptions (such as looking at verbal MWEs).

Bargmann & Sailer (2018 [this volume]) concentrate on one particular type of MWEs, the so-called non-decomposable idioms. They identify this domain by semantic criteria that are independent of a particular language. Subsequently, they look at the way in which the languages they consider differ in the syntactic flexibility of these MWEs.

Fotopoulou & Giouli (2018 [this volume]) define their domain of study by semantic and syntactic criteria. They look at verbal MWEs that express emotions.

They use a semantic classification of emotion expressions with respect to the type of emotion and its intensity. On the formal side, they use a syntactic representation of MWEs that abstracts over some properties that are particular to individual languages. This allows them to identify comparable MWE classes in Modern Greek and French.

Hanks et al. (2018 [this volume]) discuss a particular method to extract MWEs from a corpus and to classify them automatically according to their syntactic flexibility. They present a case study of the English word *bite* and its primary French translation *mordre* by looking at an identical number of hits from standard general corpora of the two languages. They apply a Corpus Pattern Analysis (CPA) on this data set to identify the usage patterns of these two verbs, which include a number of MWEs. Using statistical collocation measures on the extracted patterns, they manage to determine the syntactic flexibility of each of these patterns. They show that their method can be applied to different languages and demonstrate that the extracted patterns of English and French can be used to study the cross-language correspondences as regards the patterns' literal and idiomatic meanings.

Osenova & Simov (2018 [this volume]) study MWEs in parallel corpora of Bulgarian and English. They discover that MWE translational equivalents, at least for the particular language pair, tend to be either MWEs themselves or just single words; interestingly, translating an MWE with a compositional phrase is a rare phenomenon in their data. In order to encode these correspondences in a way that can be useful to parsing, they employ catenæ (O'Grady 1998), which are argued to offer adequate expressivity for representing the structural and the semantic properties of MWEs.

Koeva et al. (2018 [this volume]) is the contribution that looks at the highest number of different languages. The authors compare named entities in five different languages from four language groups. The category of named entities is defined semantically as the names given to persons, locations, or organisations. The authors find that depending on the kind of named entity, a number of different semantic aspects may be included within a larger name – such as a title for a person's name, for example. They use these semantic categories to define language-neutral, abstract patterns. In a second step, they map these to syntactic patterns for individual languages and identify similarities and differences within the sample of languages they consider. As in the case of Fotopoulou & Giouli (2018 [this volume]), sticking to a clearly defined and relatively well-studied semantic domain can provide a very good basis for comparing the variation that is found in the morpho-syntax of the MWEs used in this domain.

Mititelu & Leseva (2018 [this volume]) consider a formal process, namely derivation of MWE parts in Romanian and Bulgarian. They use the same method of data sampling for the two languages: they extract MWEs from general dictionaries of idioms and collocations. Subsequently, they extract occurrences of these MWEs in corpora and classify the types of derivational morphology found in their data. The paper establishes that the productivity of MWEs in derivation is a general phenomenon that should be considered more systematically than it usually is. The use of two languages serves primarily two purposes: first, the authors can make a more general point than they could have when looking at just one language; second, they illustrate the fruitful applicability of their method across languages.

The general, cross-lingual insights made by the contributions in this volume comprise at least the following:

1. For well-defined and clearly understood semantic domains, it is possible to create a multi-lingual MWE sample. Once this semantically classified sample has been established, formal properties of the MWEs within the samples can be explored, including syntactic structure, flexibility, or morphological aspects. In a next step, we can seek for generalisations relating these language-specific[1] formal properties to the language-neutral semantic classification, both within and across the considered languages.

2. If there are comparable resources available (corpora, MWE collections, treebanks, or more advanced natural language processing tools), the methods of data sampling and data classification for MWEs can often be transferred from one language to another. This means that we will be able to use the same tools to study MWEs in one language and a parallel study of MWEs in another language. It does not mean, however, that we perform a comparison of MWEs in the two languages.

2.3 Special types of MWEs

Given the heterogeneity of MWEs, it is necessary to focus on individual types of MWEs. Remember that we defined MWEs here as complex expressions that show some sort of idiosyncrasy. Consequently, MWEs differ in their basic linguistic

---

[1]Throughout this chapter, we use *language-specific* or *language-independent* in the sense of "specific to one language" or "independent of a particular language", rather than in the sense of "specific/independent of language as such".

properties, but also in the types of idiosyncrasy they display. We have already seen in §2.2 that the limitation to a particular type of MWE is a necessary step for many cross-lingual considerations. In the present subsection, we will consider special types of MWEs, based on their morphological or syntactic structure or operations rather than on their semantics.

Focusing on special types of MWEs has been a useful method in any subdiscipline of linguistics. Here is a somewhat arbitrary collection of references to illustrate this point. To start with a negative example, the early Generative treatment of MWEs in Chomsky (1957) does not distinguish between MWEs of different degree of syntactic flexibility. This is the main reason for the validity of the critique of this approach brought forward in Chafe (1968).

The importance of looking at different MWE types separately was illustrated, for example, in Krenn (2000) and Gibbs et al. (1989). Krenn (2000) shows that automatic MWE extraction from corpora may require different methods for different types of MWEs. Gibbs et al. (1989) provide evidence that MWE types need to be carefully distinguished in psycholinguistic studies. Similarly, special MWE-types can be useful to address particular research questions: Hoeksema (2010), for example, looks at MWEs containing embedded clauses such as (1), to investigate how big a lexicalised linguistic unit can possibly be. Müller (1998) looks at binomials as in (2) to show that general rules of coordination in German interact with idiosyncratic lexical fillings in these constructions – in the present example, the law of growing members in co-ordination.

(1) *maken* [*dat* X *weg-kom-*] 'leave as soon as possible'
     We moeten maken dat we weg-komen!   (Dutch)
     we must make that we away-get
     'We need to leave!'

(2) *fix und fertig* / **fertig und fix*   (German)
     fast and ready   ready and fast
     'exhausted'

In this volume, three of such special types of MWEs have been addressed in some of the included chapters: MWEs and morphological derivation, patterns of Named Entities, and Light Verb Constructions. We will briefly summarise these contributions.

Mititelu & Leseva (2018 [this volume]) offer a rare contribution to the discussion about the derivation of MWEs from MWEs. Of course, there is a lot of work on derivational morphology, but it does not pay extra attention to the

productivity of idioms. Also, there is important work advocating that morphological derivation and MWEs should be represented with the same machinery,
namely that of Constructions (Riehemann 2001). However, derivation phenomena have hardly been explored within the domain of MWEs, although they are
wide-spread across languages. Below we use material from Mititelu & Leseva
(2018 [this volume]) and add some Modern Greek and Serbian data to illustrate
the variations of the phenomenon. In (3), the pairs of noun MWEs in three languages, namely Bulgarian, English and Modern Greek, can be analysed as standing in a derivation relation. In (4) and (5), an adjective MWE and a verb MWE
can be analysed as standing in a derivation relation (Modern Greek participles
function as adjectives). Lastly, in (6) and (7), we have adjective MWEs of the simile type that are derivationally related with verb MWEs (headed by de-adjectival
verbs), again of the simile type in two languages, namely Modern Greek and
Serbian.

(3)   a. *moden dizayn – moden dizayner*   (Bulgarian)

        b. *fashion design – fashion designer*   (English)

        c. *sχieδio moδas – sχieδiastis moδas*   (Modern Greek)

(4)   a. *svalyam   zvezdi*   (Bulgarian)
           take.down stars

           'to promise the moon'

        b. *svalyach na zvezdi*
           'one who promises the moon'

(5)   a. *pinao   sa likos*   (Modern Greek)
           I.am.hungry like wolf

           'being very hungry'

        b. *pinasmenos sa   likos*
           hungry   like wolf

           'very hungry'

(6)   a. *kokinos san paparuna*   (Modern Greek)
           red   as poppy

           'red (because of blushing)'

        b. *kokinizo   san paparuna*
           I.become.red as poppy

           'blushing a lot'

(7) a. *crven kao bulka*   (Serbian)
        red   as poppy
        'red (because of blushing)'
      b. *pocrveneo   kao bulka*
        I.become.red as poppy
        'blushing a lot'

Mititelu & Leseva (2018 [this volume]) map and contrast a wide range of deriva-tion types in Romanian and Bulgarian and, eventually, they reveal a rather com-plicated and promising field of study.

As already discussed in §2.2, Koeva et al. (2018 [this volume]) offer a strongly cross-linguistic account of the semantic and syntactic contexts where named en-tities occur. Named entities have often been treated as MWEs – naturally, only the named entities that are formed of more than one word are MWEs (indica-tively Downey et al. 2007; Vincze et al. 2011).

Named Entity Recognition is a widely discussed research topic in computa-tional linguistics. In this general context, Koeva et al., building on the fact that named entities come in patterns in all languages, have set the ambitious goal to enumerate the semantic and syntactic contexts in which named entities occur in a set of languages, namely Bulgarian, English, French, Modern Greek, and Ser-bian. The authors study named entities denoting persons, locations and organisa-tions and show that the semantic patterns could be language independent, while the syntactic patterns vary to some degree according to language specificities such as the existence of articles and cases along with word order preferences.

An impressive amount of literature has been dedicated to Light Verb Construc-tions (LVCs). Some relatively early approaches include Jespersen (1965), Gross (1998a), Butt (1995), Mel'čuk (1998). LVCs are structures that contain a verb that combines with another verb or a predicative noun to yield a monoclausal struc-ture in which the event described is not specified by the (first) verb but by the other predicates. In a sense, the (first) verb is considered to have lost some of its semantic weight and to have turned into a "light" verb. In the example be-low, which has been taken from Laporte (2018 [this volume]), two translation equivalent expressions are given in French and English. In these examples, the main verb *avoir/have* is not used with its proper (possessive) semantics while the described event is specified by the noun *conflit/conflict*. Consequently, the verb *avoir/have* is used as a light verb in (8).

(8) a. *Il a   eu un conflit avec sa famille.*   (French)
        he has had a   conflict with his family

b. *He had a conflict with his family.* (English)

LVCs occur in many languages and pose interesting questions about the theory of syntax and semantics. Not surprisingly, one question is how LVCs can be delineated from other types of verb MWEs and from compositional structures. Laporte (2018 [this volume]) offers a thorough discussion of the criteria used to set apart LVCs from other MWEs and from compositional structures. More on the descriptive side, Fotopoulou & Giouli (2018 [this volume]) include LVCs in their contrastive study of emotive MWEs in Modern Greek and French.

The individual types of MWEs considered in this volume constitute a representative subset of options. First, the studies include some frequently discussed structures, such as LVCs, but also structures that often remain unnoticed, such as derivation. Second, they include the question of what the internal structure of an MWE is (in its unmodified form), but also which types of operations (parts of) it can undergo. The paper on Named Entities by Koeva et al. (2018 [this volume]) clearly addresses the first type of question, whereas the discussion of derivation by Mititelu & Leseva (2018 [this volume]) is concerned with the second type of question. Related to these points is the question of whether an MWE instantiates a general pattern of the language, such as an "ordinary" verb-complement relation, or whether we are dealing with a particular pattern that is productively, though exclusively, realised by MWEs, such as, maybe, some of the Named Entity patterns or the LVCs addressed in some of the papers.

We are positive that the inclusion of MWEs in the linguistic discussion of particular structures or phenomena can lead to important insights both in our understanding of these phenomena and our understanding of MWEs. On the other hand, we consider it important to take a closer look at MWE-specific patterns and to identify in which way their properties relate to the more general phenomena of a language.

3 MWEs and linguistic theory

MWEs are situated at the overlap of the lexicon and grammar. This places them both at the centre and at the margins of linguistic theorizing. Theoretical discussions of MWEs typically take one of the following two questions as their starting point: Can the established tools of the lexicon or grammar be used to model MWEs? What insights can we get on the properties of words or grammatical processes from looking at MWEs? The first question starts from a given theory and applies it to MWEs, the second starts from observations on MWEs and uses them to modify the theory. Some of the papers in this volume are written from a particular theoretical perspective, including Generative Grammar (Kuiper's contribution), Lexicon-Grammar (Laporte and Fotopoulou & Giouli), Lexical Functional Grammar (Markantonatou & Samaridi), and Head-driven Phrase Structure Grammar (Bargmann & Sailer). In the present section, we will give a brief summary of the role MWEs have played in these theories and how the papers in this volume relate to this. There are, of course, important discussions on MWEs in many other frameworks, which we will have to leave aside here.[2]

3.1 Generative Grammar

Generative Grammar is a cover term for a diverse family of theories going back to Chomsky (1957). Since we will look separately at two "spin-off" theories, Lexical Functional Grammar and Head-driven Phrase Structure Grammar, we will limit ourselves here to the theoretical strand that could be called Chomskyan Generative Grammar whose current version is referred to as Minimalism (Chomsky 1995). In this tradition, the discussion of MWEs is very much focused on idiomatic, verbal MWEs. Kuiper (2004) provides an overview over the main developments in Generative Grammar and the role MWEs have played therein. Nunberg et al. (1994) give a detailed and critical evaluation of the use of MWEs in Generative syntactic argumentation.

From the first mentioning of MWEs in Chomsky (1965) on, the general analytic conception of MWEs has been that an MWE is inserted into the syntactic derivation as a single unit, though a unit with internal structure. An analytical challenge arises once this assumption is combined with the idea that non-canonical syntactic structures are derived from an underlying basic structure that is determined by argument selection, such as Deep Structure or the result of Merge. McCawley (1981) shows that these assumptions are incompatible with the data in (9): if the MWE *pull strings* is inserted as a unit, its parts cannot be spread over a relative clause and the noun it attaches to, as in (9a). If the head of the relative clause is generated inside the relative clause, (9a) would no longer be a problem, but, then, (9b) would be problematic, where the idiomatic noun *strings* is the head of a relative clause that does not contain the rest of the idiom.

(9) a. *The strings that Parky pulled to get me the job.* (McCawley 1981: 135)

   b. *Parky pulled the strings that got me the job.* (McCawley 1981: 137)

Only recently, the en bloc insertion approach to MWEs has been relaxed in some publications, such as Harley & Stone (2013) and Corver et al. (2016). Corver

---

[2]See the relevant overview chapters in Burger et al. (2007) for some more frameworks.

et al. integrate the distinction between decomposable and non-decomposable MWEs from Nunberg et al. (1994) into a Minimalist approach and assume distinct structural constraints for the two types of MWEs.

In Generative Grammar, MWEs have typically been used to test structural hypotheses, where two aspects of MWEs have received primary attention: first, their restricted yet not fully blocked syntactic flexibility, and second, their internal structure. For example, idioms provided a major piece of empirical evidence for the raising analysis in Government and Binding Theory (Chomsky 1986). As for the second point, over the years, the size of MWEs has often been taken as support for various syntactic notions: the perceived inexistence of MWEs including subjects was used as support for the existence of a VP in syntax. More recently, the size of MWEs has been claimed to correlate with phrases, i.e. structural domains that are assumed to be closed for a number of syntactic processes (Svenonius 2005).

In the present volume, Kuiper proposes an interesting new way of constructing syntactic arguments based on MWEs. Starting from the assumption that MWEs typically show some kind of irregularity, he formulates the following Law of Exception:

> Law of Exception: All formal properties of the grammar of a language are subject to exceptions manifested in idiosyncrasies in the lexical items of that language.

This approach allows him to derive support for a principle of grammar by showing that there are lexical items violating it.

3.2 Lexical Functional Grammar (LFG)

The generative, transformation free, phrase structure grammatical formalism of Lexical Functional Grammar (LFG) is:

- Unification based: information from the different components of an utterance is unified to form the overall linguistic information content; the linear order of the utterance components is not important.

- Lexicalistic: linguistic operations are divided into lexical and syntactic operations. For instance, valency changing operations are understood as lexical properties, while co-ordination is analysed as a syntactic phenomenon. The syntactic component of the grammar cannot affect the lexical one.

LFG develops different levels of analysis that stand in a mutually constraining relation to each other via well-defined mappings. Different formal means may be employed for the representations at the various levels of analysis such as the m-structure, where morphological information is represented, the c-structure, where phrasal structure information is represented, with a tree formalism, the f-structure, where functional relation information such as agreement, binding, and control are represented using attribute-value matrices (AVMs), and the s-structure, which is dedicated to semantic information. In particular, crucial features of the f-structure are the so-called Grammatical Functions (GFs) that stand for things like subject and object. LFG considers them as primitive notions and uses them to represent relations among the phrasal constituents. MWEs were first mentioned in the LFG literature when Bresnan (1982) used *to keep tabs on somebody* in order to construct an argument in favour of lexicalism. In this discussion, *tabs* heads a meaningless NP that instantiates the object of the structure or the OBJ(ect) GF in LFG parlance. When the passivisation lexical rule applies, *tabs* becomes the SUBJ(ect) of the passivised form *tabs were kept on somebody*. An idiomatic verb predicate *keep* is defined in the lexicon (10) that requires a subject, an object and an indirect argument dubbed ON OBJ. Also an idiomatic noun *tabs* is defined to be "semantically empty", which, in the LFG conception of grammar, entails that the noun does not introduce a predicate in the representation. Therefore, it does not have a PRED(icate) value and it only has a FORM value:

(10) keep V (↑ TENSE) = PRESS
       (↑ PRED) = 'observe<SUBJ,ON OBJ>'
       (↑ ON OBJ FORM) $=_c$ TABS

However, the semantically empty NP *tabs* should be prohibited from turning up as the object of other predicates. Andrews (1982) proposes a syntactic solution that draws on a reformulation of the Coherence Principle of LFG. Kaplan & Bresnan (1995: 67) note that in order to face the problem posed by semantically empty NPs "a separate condition of semantic completeness could easily be added to our grammaticality requirements, but such a restriction would be imposed independently by a semantic translation procedure. A separate syntactic stipulation is therefore unnecessary." Furthermore, Partee (2004: 158) points out that semantically empty NPs would be a problem for a Montague-like compositional approach to Semantics where NPs are assumed to contribute a predicate but that a possible solution would require a non-dispensable semantic translation level. This discussion highlights important aspects of the LFG approach to

MWEs. First, according to Bresnan (1982), MWEs that contain an idiomatic V NP component and passivise, can project an f-structure that contains an OBJ(ect) GF. Therefore, it is assumed that the syntax of MWEs is exactly like the syntax of compositional language in this respect, even when the fixed parts of an MWE are considered. The semantic component of the theory is expected to play an important role. Actually, state-of-the-art LFG has put emphasis on semantics and has offered interesting analyses of "idiomatic" constructions, such as the *way*-construction (11) (Asudeh et al. 2008: 30).

(11) *Sarah elbowed her way quickly through the crowd.*

It seems that the development of a semantic component questions the traditional conception of the syntactic component of the theory, for instance the so-called semantic forms (Lowe 2015). Semantic forms have been crucial for defining the coherence and completeness axioms of LFG that form a major part of the mechanism by which the grammar checks the grammaticality of strings. In a similar vein, several of the defining properties of Grammatical Functions reflect a set of behaviours that were considered syntactic, but now a lot of this burden may move to semantics, for instance, the conditions on the replacement of an NP by a clitic may be semantic in nature to some considerable degree (Arnold 2015). So far, passivisation has not received a semantic analysis in LFG and remains, so to speak, the identifier of "syntactic OBJecthoodness", therefore a discussion about the ability of MWEs to passivise could still be argued to be a syntactic discussion.

An applied approach to MWEs was offered by Attia (2006) embedded in an implemented LFG grammar of Arabic with a wide coverage. Attia has argued that MWEs should be disambiguated in a preprocessing step, i.e. before parsing. In his system, fixed and semi-fixed MWEs are processed by the morphological component that uses regular grammars (as opposed to the syntactic component that uses context-free grammars).

Such approaches open up theoretical issues, such as which is the part of speech that should be assigned to the fixed parts that are treated as words and, given the problems stemming from passivisation, how the LFG syntactic theory is affected by these novel words and their syntactic reflexes. These issues are a potential challenge for the generally accepted view that MWEs and compositional structures use exactly the same syntax. Markantonatou & Samaridi (2018 [this volume]) discuss exactly this question in the framework of LFG drawing on Modern Greek verb MWEs.

3.3 Head-driven Phrase Structure Grammar (HPSG)

Head-driven Phrase Structure Grammar (HPSG) has its origin in phrase structure grammar frameworks such as Generalized Phrase Structure Grammar (Gazdar et al. 1985), but has received a fundamentally different formal basis as a constraint-based feature structure grammar (Pollard 1999; Richter 2004). HPSG encodes all levels of linguistic analysis within one representation, a well-articulated notion of a Saussurian linguistic sign. The lexicon is of central importance for the theory, as all idiosyncratic information projects from the lexicon, and valence-alternation processes are expressed as lexical rules. The role of syntax is largely restricted to allowing lexical elements to combine in order to satisfy their valence requirements and, at the same time, to build up the phonological and the semantic representations of a sentence. All grammar rules are strictly local, i.e., referring only to a mother node and its immediate daughters. Since Sag (1997), a proliferation of grammar rules can be observed, which has been an attempt to connect HPSG and Construction Grammar more closely and, ultimately, led to the development of Sign-Based Construction Grammar (SBCG, Sag 2012).

There is no treatment of idioms or MWEs in Pollard & Sag (1987) or Pollard & Sag (1994), but at least since Krenn & Erbach (1994), there have been approaches to encode MWEs in HPSG. A basic obstacle to this task comes with the formalisation of HPSG: every node in a syntactic tree must be licensed by the grammar. This blocks every attempt to integrate idiosyncratic phrasal expressions as units. For this reason, HPSG researchers tend to promote lexical analyses of MWEs. This has been done in Krenn & Erbach (1994), who use the highly expressive selection mechanism of HPSG to account for the co-occurrence of idiom parts. The sign-based character of HPSG allows selection not only for syntactic category and semantic type, but for fine-grained syntactic and semantic properties as well, including the selection of a single lexeme. The discussion on MWEs has motivated a number of innovations in the theory, such as the use of underspecification in semantics, the introduction of lexeme identifiers in syntax, and the accessibility of specifiers of phrases from a higher node.

Many HPSG publications on MWEs have been written in the context of machine translation projects, which includes Krenn & Erbach (1994), Copestake et al. (1995) and Sag et al. (2002). An important drawback of the HPSG research on idioms is that it is almost exclusively restricted to the discussion of English and German examples, though there are recent approaches to Hebrew (Herzig Sheinfux et al. 2015) and Japanese (Haugereid & Bond 2011).

Recent approaches, such as Kay & Sag (2014) and Bargmann & Sailer (2018 [this volume]), propose such a lexical analysis for all idioms that have a regular syntactic shape. This generates a number of research questions: (i) Can the idiomatic reading be derived using the regular mechanism of semantic combinatorics? (ii) Can the attested differences in syntactic flexibility between idioms be captured? (iii) Can the co-occurrence of idiom parts be guaranteed and an idiom-external use of idiom components be blocked? In addition, syntactically irregular expressions still need to be captured by idiosyncratic grammar rules, and it is far from sure that the required rules satisfy HPSG's locality restriction that idiosyncrasy can only occur in local mother-daughter relations (see Sailer 2012). Given the constraint-based local nature of HPSG, the answer to (i) can only be positive However, mechanisms of semantic combinatorics have been proposed that are not compatible with standard, Montagovian, assumptions of compositionality, including underspecification and redundant semantic marking. Answers to question (ii) typically attempt to show that what seem to be idiosyncratic restrictions on the syntactic flexibility of MWEs follow from the general properties of the considered syntactic processes and the lexical properties of the stipulated idiomatic words. Kay & Sag (2014) and Bargmann & Sailer (2018 [this volume]) illustrate this strategy, which can be seen as a variant of the above-mentioned hypothesis in Nunberg et al. (1994) that the decomposability of an MWE is directly connected to its syntactic flexibility. As for question (iii), the selection mechanism is still the most popular means of ensuring the co-occurrence of idiom parts, while more flexible collocation mechanisms have been proposed as well (Sailer 2004; Soehn 2009). The final question of the analysis of syntactically irregular expressions and, in particular, the possible depth of syntactic idiosyncrasy has not been addressed systematically. Richter & Sailer (2014) and Kay & Sag (2014) look at MWEs with embedded clauses (such as *know on which side one's bread is buttered*), but all expressions they consider are syntactically regular.

3.4 Lexicon Grammar (LG)

A lot of pioneering and on-going work on MWEs has the Lexicon-Grammar (LG) framework as a reference point. LG is not a generative grammatical framework; rather, it strongly advocates a classification-based approach. LG relies on the classification of a large number of linguistic structures using as a linguistic unit not the word but the simple sentence that consists of a verb, its subject and two objects at maximum (Gross 1982a). Various structures are identified and used as classificatory properties for verbs, for instance the simple transitive active voice phrase (NP V NP for English) and the simple passive phrase (NP *be* V*ed by* NP for English) are listed as independent properties (and not as an ordered pair defining a transformation) that verb predicates such as *write* and *die* may or may not have, depending on whether the corresponding structures are attested. Matrices are developed for each class of the verbs that demonstrate similar behaviour with respect to these properties. The columns in the matrices are named for the properties and the rows for the various verb predicates; the symbols '+'/'−' are assigned to the cells depending on whether the predicate is found in the respective structure or not.

Classifications rely on empirically attested phenomena on the morphological and the syntactic level. Still, meaning seems to retain an important role in the definition of verb classes. For instance Gross (1975: 401–402) explains that the verb *dire* appears in structures that are not available to other verbs of "saying" and then notes:

> One might describe these restrictions by means of a standard transformational solution: the syntactic properties that have been observed for the verbs of /saying/ would only be attributed to the verb *dire*. All other verbs of /saying/, namely all verbs that indicate an emission of sound or of light, would be considered as intransitive verbs. (Gross 1975: 402)

In other words, because certain syntactic properties are observed with only one verb, namely with the representative verb *dire*, but not with the other verbs of the same class, a transformation is assumed that relates the syntactic properties of the representative verb *dire* with the syntactic properties of other members of the class; therefore, the verbs of "saying' do not share exactly the same syntactic properties, and they belong to the same class because they share the "emission" semantics and some syntactic properties. Things being so, the class is defined not by the morphosyntactic properties of its members but by their meaning.

Gross (1977) explains that LG assigns extreme importance to taxonomies because they pertain to the scientific nature of the linguistic quest. Taxonomies are a standard practice in biology whereby the use of the best representative of a species in experiments guarantees reproducibility of results. In the case of linguistics, the acceptability tests of linguistic structures by native speakers are considered experiments. Gross (1978) discusses the drawbacks of classification practices, namely that they result in disjoint classes of classified objects while in linguistic reality few clear-cut separating lines are observed. Still, he argues that it is worth paying the value of (probably vast) fragmentation into (not necessarily homogeneous) classes because this is the only known way of obtaining an organisation of linguistic data that guarantees reproducibility of linguistic experiments.

Early on, LG applied taxonomies on MWEs; LG prefers the term *fixed expressions* for MWEs (Gross 1982b; 1998a,b). The continuum from fully compositional structures to fully fixed expressions is recognised. The criteria developed set fixed expressions apart from terminology and professional or other sublanguages, from frequently used compositional structures and from "support constructions" (in §2.3 we encountered these constructions under the name "LVCs"). In this volume, the paper on Modern Greek and French emotive MWEs by Fotopoulou & Giouli studies a set of structures, including MWEs and support verb constructions, that denote emotions; these structures illustrate the aforementioned continuum between compositional and fixed language and an interesting cross-lingual result is obtained, namely that the degree of fixedness is related to the intensity of the emotion denoted.

MWE studies owe a lot to work conducted within LG. Laporte (2018 [this volume]) summarizes some of the work done on MWEs within LG, elaborates on its merits and compares the strongly data-based method of LG with the more hypothesis-driven approach of Generative Grammar.

4 What do we find important from here on?

All frameworks that are represented in this volume take a competence-oriented approach to MWEs, i.e., they attempt to model the possibilities rather than the usage of MWEs. However, with MWEs in particular, it is rather difficult to draw the line between what is a grammatically acceptable variation of an MWE and what is a variation that is licensed by some special rhetoric effect such as word play or what Egan (2008) calls "extended" uses of MWEs. Related to this, the rich literature on the discourse-constitutive effect of MWEs remains largely unexplored in its insights for the formal study of MWEs. This has direct repercussions on the formal modelling. First, most competence-oriented researchers agree that playful use of MWEs falls outside their empirical domain. They do not, however, necessarily agree on whether a particular lexical or structural variation of an MWE is an extended use or not. This has an influence on what set of data they aim to explain. While this is a general problem of competence-based approaches, it is particularly prominent in the study of MWEs. In the present volume, this contrast can be seen most clearly in the differences between the contributions by Laporte and Bargmann & Sailer: Laporte's data are based on simple sentence frames without context, whereas Bargmann & Sailer consider all MWE variations that they find in attested examples, taking into account their linguistic context though not the question of whether such examples would be considered rather unnatural by native speakers, even in the given context.

A second aspect that is usually left aside in the included frameworks is the inherent ambiguity of many MWEs. Given that idiomaticity, i.e., the presence of "compositional" or "literal" meaning next to an idiomatic meaning, is one of the three defining prototypical properties of MWEs, this is clearly a question that would deserve attention. Particularly intriguing are cases in which the idiomatic and the literal reading seem to be simultaneously present, as in (12), taken from Ernst (1981).

(12) *He bit his thirst-swollen tongue.*
       Reading: 'He bit his tongue & his tongue was thirst-swollen.'

Recent attempts to combine compositional and distributional semantics such as Gehrke & McNally (2016) can be considered a step towards a modelling of such co-existences of a literal and an idiomatic meaning.

While there are the above-mentioned similarities between the frameworks represented in this volume, there are also considerable differences. One major difference is the relative importance that they attribute to theoretical concepts and to data. Research in Generative Grammar is typically hypothesis driven. This has led to many hypotheses about MWEs. While most of them have been proven wrong by now, they were still useful in putting the focus of phraseological research on a particular aspect and led to an increase of knowledge in this domain. Lexicon Grammar, on the other hand, is rather data driven and has a relatively long tradition of systematic compilation and classification of data. While this led to the creation of rich resources on MWEs, it is less obvious which implications generalisations over the collected data should have for the theory. We have also seen how lexicalist theories such as LFG and HPSG attempt to develop tools to account for the more phrasal phenomena that we find in MWEs. The research questions in such frameworks are typically very specific and partly data-driven, partly hypothesis-driven.

The variety of analytic and methodological alternatives used in the theoretical descriptions of MWEs over the years is impressive and shows that this empirical domain has a lot to offer for theoretical linguistic research. We would be excited if the present volume stimulated more interaction and mutual reception across framework boundaries. There are still many types of MWEs that have not been described formally or for which no data have yet been collected systematically. Such studies can potentially corroborate or refute essential properties of a framework or at least motivate a small change in perspective.

Manfred Sailer & Stella Markantonatou

Acknowledgements

This book reflects a subset of the activities carried out in the ICT COST Action IC1207 *Parsing and multi-word expressions. Towards linguistic precision and computational efficiency in natural language processing (PARSEME)*, 2013–2017, in particular in the working group *Lexicon-Grammar Interface*. We are grateful to COST and to the co-ordinators of the action, in particular Agata Savary, for this opportunity of fruitful scientific exchange.

We would like to thank the reviewers of this volume:

- Doug Arnold

- Anastasia Christofidou

- Voula Gotsoulia

- Jack Hoeksema

- Gianina Iordăchioaia

- Koenraad Kuiper

- Cvetana Krstev

- Timm Lichte

- Johanna Monti

- Stefan Müller

- Petya Osenova

- Carlos Ramisch

- Agata Savary

- Alexandros Tantos

- Veronika Vincze

- Shuly Wintner

Thanks for providing detailed comments on the first versions of the chapters and for helping us, the editors, to decide which papers to include in this volume and for giving useful and informed feedback to our contributors.

We are also grateful to Agata Savary for being the member of the editorial board of *Phraseology and Multiword Expressions* who accompanied us from the (almost) final version of the manuscript to the real publication.

In his function as one of the main editors of Language Science Press, Stefan Müller has helped us getting started with this book project. We would like to thank him and Sebastian Nordhoff for their support concerning all practical and technical questions about the publication. We are grateful to the LangSci proof-readers. Yannick Parmentier has provided us with a version of the LangSci LaTex-style that was adjusted to this series, for which we are very grateful! Finally, we would like to thank Panagiotis Minos, who invested numberless hours in converting the individual chapters into a consistent format.

Abbreviations

GF	Grammatical Function	LG	Lexicon Grammar
HPSG	Head-Driven Phrase Structure Grammar	LVC	Light Verb Construction
		MWE	Multiword Expressions
LFG	Lexical Functional Grammar	SBCG	Sing-based Construction Grammar

References

Andrews, Avery D. 1982. Long distance agreement in Modern Icelandic. In Pauline Jacobson & Geoffrey K. Pullum (eds.), *The nature of syntactic representation*, 1–33. Dordrecht: D. Reidel.

Arnold, Doug. 2015. *A glue semantics for structurally regular MWEs.* http://typo.uni-konstanz.de/parseme/images/Meeting/2015-09-23-Iasi-meeting/WG1-ARNOLD-poster.pdf, accessed 2018-4-19. Poster at the 5th General Parseme Meeting, Iaşi, Romania, September 2015.

Asudeh, Ash, Mary Dalrymple & Ida Toivonen. 2008. Constructions with Lexical Integrity: Templates as the lexicon-syntax interface. In Miriam Butt & Tracy Holloway King (eds.), *Proceedings of the LFG08 Conference.* Stanford, CA: CSLI Publications. http://web.stanford.edu/group/cslipublications/cslipublications/LFG/13/papers/lfg08asudehetal.pdf, accessed 2018-5-8.

Attia, Mohammed A. 2006. Accommodating multiword expressions in an Arabic LFG Grammar. In Tapio Salakoski, Filip Ginter, Tapio Pahikkala & Tampo Pyysalo (eds.), *Advances in Natural Language Processing. Lecture Notes in Computer Science*, vol. 4139, 87–98. Berlin, Heidelberg: Springer.

Baldwin, Timothy & Su Nam Kim. 2010. Multiword expressions. In Nitin Indurkhya & Fred J. Damerau (eds.), *Handbook of Natural Language Processing*, 2nd edn., 267–292. Boca Raton: CRC Press.

Bargmann, Sascha & Manfred Sailer. 2018. The syntactic flexibility of semantically non-decomposable idioms. In Manfred Sailer & Stella Markantonatou (eds.), *Multiword expressions: Insights from a multi-lingual perspective*, 1–29. Berlin: Language Science Press. DOI:10.5281/zenodo.1182587

Bresnan, Joan. 1982. The passive in lexical theory. In Joan Bresnan (ed.), *The mental representation of grammatical relations*, 3–86. Cambridge, MA: MIT Press.

Burger, Harald. 2015. *Phraseologie: Eine Einführung am Beispiel des Deutschen.* 5th edn. Berlin: Erich Schmidt Verlag.

Burger, Harald, Dmitrij Dobrovol'skij, Peter Kühn & Neal R. Norrick. 2007. *Phraseologie/Phraseology.* Harald Burger, Dmitrij Dobrovol'skij, Peter Kühn & Neal R. Norrick (eds.). Vol. 2 (Ein internationales Handbuch der zeitgenössischen Forschung/An International Handbook of Contemporary Research). Berlin.

Butt, Miriam. 1995. *The structure of complex predicates in Urdu.* Stanford, CA: CSLI Publications.

Chafe, Wallace. 1968. Idiomaticity as an anomaly in the Chomskyan paradigm. *Foundations of Language* 4. 109–127.

Chomsky, Noam. 1957. *Syntactic structures.* The Hague: Mouton.

Chomsky, Noam. 1965. *Aspects of the theory of syntax.* Cambridge, MA: MIT Press.

Chomsky, Noam. 1986. *Barriers* (Linguistic Inquiry Monographs 13). Cambridge, MA: MIT-Press.

Chomsky, Noam. 1995. *The minimalist programm.* Cambridge, MA: MIT Press.

Copestake, Ann, Dan Flickinger, Robert Malouf, Susanne Riehemann & Ivan A. Sag. 1995. Translation using Minimal Recursion Semantics. In *Proceedings of The Sixth International Conference on Theoretical and Methodological Issues in Machine Translation (TMI-95).* Leuven.

Corver, Norbert, Jeroen van Craenenbroeck, Will Harwood, Marko Hladnik, Sterre Leufkens & Tanja Temmerman. 2016. *Idioms: Phrasehood and compositionality.* Leuven & Utrecht. http : / / static1 . squarespace . com / static /

5217e223e4b090faa01f8f2d / t / 5860d682579fb36de66fa84b / 1482741386255 / paper-idioms-phases.pdf, accessed 2018-4-19. Manuscript, Leuven and Utrecht.

Downey, Doug, Matthew Broadhead & Oren Etzioni. 2007. Locating complex named entities in web text. In *IJCAI'07 Proceedings of the 20th International Joint Conference on Artifical Intelligence*, 2733–2739. Hyderabad, India.

Egan, Andy. 2008. Pretense for the complete idiom. *Noûs* 42(3). 381–409.

Ernst, Thomas. 1981. Grist for the linguistic mill: Idioms and 'extra' adjectives. *Journal of Linguistic Research* 1. 51–68.

Fillmore, Charles J., Paul Kay & Mary Catherine O'Connor. 1988. Regularity and idiomaticity in grammatical constructions: The case of *let alone*. *Language* 64(3). 501–538.

Fleischer, Wolfgang. 1997. *Phraseologie der deutschen Gegenwartssprache*. 2nd edn. Tübingen: Niemeyer.

Fotopoulou, Aggeliki & Voula Giouli. 2018. MWEs and the Emotion Lexicon: Typological and cross-lingual considerations. In Manfred Sailer & Stella Markantonatou (eds.), *Multiword expressions: Insights from a multi-lingual perspective*, 63–91. Berlin: Language Science Press. DOI:10.5281/zenodo.1182591

Fraser, Bruce. 1970. Idioms within a transformational grammar. *Foundations of Language* 6. 22–42.

Gazdar, Gerald, Ewan Klein, Geoffrey Pullum & Ivan Sag. 1985. *Generalized phrase structure grammar*. Cambridge, MA: Harvard University Press.

Gehrke, Berit & Louise McNally. 2016. *Idioms and the syntax/semantics interface of descriptive content vs. reference.* Manuscript Paris and Barcelona.

Gibbs, Raymond W., Nandini P. Nayak, John L. Bolton & Melissa E. Keppel. 1989. Speakers assumptions about the lexical flexibility of idioms. *Memory and Cognition* 17(1). 58–68.

Gross, Maurice. 1975. On the relations between syntax and semantics. In Edward L. Keenan (ed.), *Formal semantics of natural language*, 389–405. Cambridge, UK: Cambridge University Press.

Gross, Maurice. 1977. Remarks on the separation between syntax and semantics. In *Studies in descriptive and historical linguistics. Festschrift for Winfred P. Lehmann*, 71–89. Benjamins.

Gross, Maurice. 1978. Taxonomy in syntax. *SMIL, Journal of Linguistic Calculus* (3–4). 73–96.

Gross, Maurice. 1982a. Simple sentences. Discussion of Fred W. Householder's paper (analysis, synthesis and improvisation). In Sture Allen (ed.), *Text processing. proceedings of Nobel Symposium 51*, 297–315. Stockholm: Almqvist & Wiksell International.

Gross, Maurice. 1982b. Une classification des phrases "figées"du français. *Revue Québécoise de Linguistique (RQL)* 11(2). 151–185.

Gross, Maurice. 1998a. Les limites de la phrase figée. *Langage* 90. 7–23.

Gross, Maurice. 1998b. Sur les phrases figées complexes du français. *Langue française* 77. 47–70.

Hanks, Patrick, Ismail El Marouf & Michael Oakes. 2018. Flexibility of multiword expressions and Corpus Pattern Analysis. In Manfred Sailer & Stella Markantonatou (eds.), *Multiword expressions: Insights from a multi-lingual perspective*, 93–119. Berlin: Language Science Press. DOI:10.5281/zenodo.1182593

Harley, Heidi & Megan Stone. 2013. The 'No Agent Idioms' hypothesis. In Raffaella Folli, Christina Sevdali & Robert Truswell (eds.), *Syntax and its limits*, 283–311. Oxford: Oxford University Press.

Haugereid, Petter & Francis Bond. 2011. Extracting transfer rules for multiword expressions from parallel corpora. In *Proceedings of the Workshop on Multiword Expressions (MWE 2011): From parsing and generation to the real world*, 92–100. Portland, Oregon: ACL. http://aclweb.org/anthology/W11-0814, accessed 2018-4-19.

Herzig Sheinfux, Livnat, Tali Arad Greshler, Nurit Melnik & Shuly Wintner. 2015. Hebrew verbal multi-word expression. In Stefan Müller (ed.), *Proceedings of the 22nd International Conference on Head-Driven Phrase Structure Grammar*, 122–135. Stanford, CA: CSLI Publications.

Hoeksema, Jack. 2010. De localiteit van idiomen. http://www.let.rug.nl/~hoeksema/localiteit, accessed 2018-4-19. Manuscript, University of Groningen.

Jespersen, Otto. 1965. *A modern English grammar on historical principles, Part VI, Morphology.* London: George Allen & Unwin Ltd.

Kaplan, Ronald M. & Joan Bresnan. 1995. The passive in Lexical Theory. In Mary Dalrymple, Ronald M. Kaplan, John T. Maxwell III & Annie Zaenen (eds.), *Formal issues in Lexical-Functional Grammar*, 20–130. Stanford, CA: CSLI Publications.

Kay, Paul & Ivan A. Sag. 2014. A lexical theory of phrasal idioms. http://www1.icsi.berkeley.edu/~kay/idioms-submitted.pdf, accessed 2018-4-19.

Koeva, Svetla, Cvetana Krstev, Duško Vitas, Tita Kyriacopoulou, Claude Martineau & Tsvetana Dimitrova. 2018. Semantic and syntactic patterns of multiword names: A cross-language study. In Manfred Sailer & Stella Markantonatou (eds.), *Multiword expressions: Insights from a multi-lingual perspective*, 31–62. Berlin: Language Science Press. DOI:10.5281/zenodo.1182589

Krenn, Brigitte. 2000. *The usual suspects. Data-oriented models for identification and representation of lexical collocations.* Vol. 7 (Saarbrücken Dissertations in Computational Linguistics and Language Technology). Saarbrücken: DFKI and Universität des Saarlandes. http://www.ofai.at/~brigitte.krenn/papers/diss.pdf.gz, accessed 2018-5-8.

Krenn, Brigitte & Gregor Erbach. 1994. Idioms and support verb constructions. In John Nerbonne, Klaus Netter & Carl Pollard (eds.), *German in Head-Driven Phrase Structure Grammar* (Lecture Notes 46), 365–396. Stanford, CA: CSLI Publications.

Kuiper, Koenraad. 2004. Phraseologie aus der Sicht der generativen Grammatik. In Kathrin Steyer (ed.), *Wortverbindungen – mehr oder weniger fest* (Institut für Deutsche Sprache, Jahrbuch 2003), 221–237. Berlin & New York: de Gruyter.

Kuiper, Koenraad. 2018. Multiword expressions and the Law of Exception. In Manfred Sailer & Stella Markantonatou (eds.), *Multiword expressions: Insights from a multi-lingual perspective*, 121–141. Berlin: Language Science Press. DOI:10.5281/zenodo.1182595

Laporte, Éric. 2018. Choosing features for classifying multiword expressions. In Manfred Sailer & Stella Markantonatou (eds.), *Multiword expressions: Insights from a multi-lingual perspective*, 143–186. Berlin: Language Science Press. DOI:10.5281/zenodo.1182597

Lowe, John. 2015. Complex predicates: an LFG+Glue analysis. *Journal of Language Modelling* 3(2). 413–462.

Makai, Adam. 1972. *Idiom structure in English.* The Hague: Mouton.

Markantonatou, Stella & Niki Samaridi. 2018. Revisiting the grammatical function "object" (OBJ and OBJ$_\theta$). In Manfred Sailer & Stella Markantonatou (eds.), *Multiword expressions: Insights from a multi-lingual perspective*, 187–213. Berlin: Language Science Press. DOI:10.5281/zenodo.1182599

McCawley, James D. 1981. The syntax and semantics of English relative clauses. *Lingua* 53. 99–149.

Mel'čuk, Igor. 1998. Collocations and lexical functions. In Anthony P. Cowie (ed.), *Phraseology: Theory, analysis and applications*, 23–54. Oxford: Oxford University Press.

Mititelu, Verginica Barbu & Svetlozara Leseva. 2018. Derivation in the domain of multiword expressions. In Manfred Sailer & Stella Markantonatou (eds.), *Multiword expressions: Insights from a multi-lingual perspective*, 215–246. Berlin: Language Science Press. DOI:10.5281/zenodo.1182601

Müller, Gereon. 1998. Beschränkungen für Binomialbildung im Deutschen. Ein Beitrag zur Interaktion von Phraseologie und Grammatik. *Zeitschrift für Sprachwissenschaft* 16(1/2). 5–51.

Nunberg, Geoffrey, Ivan A. Sag & Thomas Wasow. 1994. Idioms. *Language* 70(3). 491–538.

O'Grady, William. 1998. The syntax of idioms. *Natural Language and Linguistic Theory* 16. 279–312.

Osenova, Petya & Kiril Simov. 2018. Modeling multiword expressions in a parallel Bulgarian-English newsmedia corpus. In Manfred Sailer & Stella Markantonatou (eds.), *Multiword expressions: Insights from a multi-lingual perspective*, 247–269. Berlin: Language Science Press. DOI:10.5281/zenodo.1182603

Parra Escartín, Carla, Almudena Nevado Llopis & Eoghan Sánchez Martínez. 2018. Spanish multiword expressions: Looking for a taxonomy. In Manfred Sailer & Stella Markantonatou (eds.), *Multiword expressions: Insights from a multi-lingual perspective*, 271–323. Berlin: Language Science Press. DOI:10.5281/zenodo.1182605

Partee, Barbara H. 2004. *Compositionality in formal semantics: Selected papers of Barbara Partee*. Oxford: Blackwell Publishers.

Pollard, Carl. 1999. Strong generative capacity in HPSG. In Gert Webelhuth, Jean-Pierre Koenig & Andreas Kathol (eds.), *Lexical and constructional aspects of linguistic explanation*, 281–297. Stanford, CA: CSLI Publications.

Pollard, Carl & Ivan A. Sag. 1987. *Information based syntax and semantics. Vol.1: Fundamentals*. Stanford, CA: CSLI Publications. CSLI Lecture Notes 13.

Pollard, Carl & Ivan A. Sag. 1994. *Head-Driven Phrase Structure Grammar*. Chicago & London: University of Chicago Press.

Richter, Frank. 2004. *A mathematical formalism for linguistic theories with an application in Head-Driven Phrase Structure Grammar*. Universität Tübingen Philosophische Dissertation (2000). http://www.sfs.uni-tuebingen.de/hpsg/archive/bibliography/papers/richter_dissertation.ps, accessed 2018-4-19.

Richter, Frank & Manfred Sailer. 2014. Idiome mit phraseologisierten Teilsätzen: Eine Fallstudie zur Formalisierung von Konstruktionen im Rahmen der HPSG. In Alexander Lasch & Alexander Ziem (eds.), *Grammatik als Netzwerk von Konstruktionen*, 291–312. Berlin: de Gruyter.

Riehemann, Susanne. 2001. *A constructional approach to idioms and word formation*. Stanford University dissertation.

Sag, Ivan A. 1997. English relative clause constructions. *Journal of Linguistics* 33(2). 431–483.

Sag, Ivan A. 2012. Sign-Based Construction Grammar: an informal synopsis. In Hans C. Boas & Ivan A. Sag (eds.), *Sign-Based Construction Grammar*, 69–202. Stanford, CA: CSLI Publications.

Sag, Ivan A., Timothy Baldwin, Francis Bond, Ann Copestake & Dan Flickinger. 2002. Multiword expressions: A pain in the neck for NLP. In *Proceedings of the 3rd International Conference on Intelligent Text Processing and Computational Linguistics (CICLing-2002)*, 1–15.

Sailer, Manfred. 2004. Distributionsidiosynkrasien: korpuslinguistische Erfassung und grammatiktheoretische Deutung. In Kathrin Steyer (ed.), *Wortverbindungen – mehr oder weniger fest* (Institut für Deutsche Sprache, Jahrbuch 2003), 194–221. Berlin & New York: de Gruyter.

Sailer, Manfred. 2012. Phraseologie und Syntax (Head-Driven Phrase Structure Grammar). In Michael Prinz & Ulrike Richter-Vapaatalo (eds.), *Idiome, Konstruktionen, "verblümte rede". Beiträge zur Geschichte der germanistischen Phraseologieforschung* (Beiträge zur Geschichte der Germanistik 3), 241–262. Stuttgart: S. Hirzel Verlag.

Soehn, Jan-Philipp. 2009. *Lexical licensing in formal grammar*. Universität Tübingen. http://nbn-resolving.de/urn:nbn:de:bsz:21-opus-42035, accessed 2018-4-19.

Svenonius, Peter. 2005. Extending the extension condition to discontinuous idioms. In *Linguistic variation yearbook*, vol. 5, 227–263.

Vincze, Veronika, Istvan Nagy T. & Gábor Berend. 2011. Multiword expressions and named entities in the Wiki50 Corpus. In *Proceedings of Recent Advances in Natural Language Processing*, 289–295. Hissar, Bulgaria.

Chapter 1

The syntactic flexibility of semantically non-decomposable idioms

Sascha Bargmann
Goethe University Frankfurt/Main, Germany

Manfred Sailer
Goethe University Frankfurt/Main, Germany

Nunberg et al. (1994) caused a shift in perspective from a monolithic view of all idioms towards a word-level approach for semantically decomposable idioms. We take that idea one step further and argue that a semantically non-decomposable idiom of syntactically regular shape can also be analyzed in terms of individual word-level lexical entries. We suggest that these entries combine according to the standard rules of syntax and that the restrictions on the syntactic flexibility of a semantically non-decomposable idiom follow exclusively from the interaction of the special semantics of these entries with the semantic and pragmatic constraints of the relevant syntactic constructions in a particular language. In our analysis, the words constituting a non-decomposable idiom make partially identical semantic contributions. We formulate our analysis in Lexical Resource Semantics (Richter & Sailer 2004).

1 Introduction

In this paper, we make a theoretical point for loosening the close ties that Nunberg et al. (1994) claim exist between the semantic decomposability and the syntactic structure of idioms. We argue for a more uniform syntactic treatment of idioms within and across languages, saying that semantically non-decomposable idioms (henceforth abbreviated as SNDIs) like *kick the bucket* can and should be analyzed as consisting of individual word-level lexical entries that combine ac-

Sascha Bargmann & Manfred Sailer. 2018. The syntactic flexibility of semantically non-decomposable idioms. In Manfred Sailer & Stella Markantonatou (eds.), *Multiword expressions: Insights from a multi-lingual perspective*, 1–29. Berlin: Language Science Press. DOI:10.5281/zenodo.1182587

cording to the standard rules of syntax and contribute a piece of the meaning of the idiom.

We mainly base our case on the contrast between English and German when it comes to verb placement, constituent fronting, and passivization (§2 and §3). Our findings suggest that the differences in the syntactic flexibility of idioms might be due to differences among the semantic and pragmatic constraints that hold for the involved syntactic constructions in a particular language, rather than to differences in the syntactic encoding of the idioms themselves.

The central aspect of our analysis (§4) is that SNDIs are syntactically analyzed as combinations of individual words, and that these words can make identical semantic contributions to the overall meaning of the idiom. We formulate our analysis in Lexical Resource Semantics (Richter & Sailer 2004).

Before we conclude the paper (§6), we give a short outlook on the behavior of SNDIs in Estonian and French (§5), which provides further evidence for our argument.

2 Some data and a former approach

In this section, we will describe the behavior and architecture of SNDIs as perceived by Nunberg et al. (1994). We will look at their analysis of English data and challenging data from (mostly) German.

2.1 English SNDIs in Nunberg, Sag & Wasow (1994)

Nunberg et al. (1994), henceforth NSW, divide English idioms into two categories: Idiomatically Combining Expressions (ICEs) and Idiomatic Phrases (IPs).

ICEs, exemplified here by *pull strings*, consist of individual word-level lexical entries (*pull* and *strings*), each of which contributes a piece of the meaning of the idiom as a whole (*pull* ≈ 'use' and *strings* ≈ 'connections').

IPs, exemplified here by *kick the bucket*, are syntactically and semantically monolithic, i.e. the phrase as a whole is stored in the lexicon and coupled with the overall idiomatic meaning (*kick the bucket* ≈ 'die'). In other words: NSW do not assume the meaning of an IP to be distributed over individual parts, as there are none in their opinion, not even in those cases where a division into syntactic constituents seems highly plausible because the idiom appears to have a regular syntactic structure (as is the case with *kick the bucket*).

NSW base this bifold classification on the empirical observation that many English idioms (those that they then categorize as ICEs) are syntactically flexible to a certain degree, whereas some others (those that they then categorize as IPs) seem to be syntactically frozen. None of the sentences in (1) can normally be understood in the idiomatic sense.

(1) a. * *Alex kicked the cruel bucket.*   (additional adjective)

  b. * *Alex kicked a bucket.*   (determiner variation)

  c. * *The bucket (that) Alex kicked was cruel.*   (restrictive relative clause)

  d. * *The bucket was kicked.*   (passive)

  e. * *The bucket, Alex kicked.*   (NP-fronting)

  f. * *It was the bucket that Alex kicked.*   (*it*-cleft)

  g. * *What bucket did Alex kick?*   (*wh*-interrogative)

According to NSW, it is the syntactic monolithicity of IPs that explains their non-compatibility with the syntactic constructions in (1). All the parts of an IP must be given in the exact same linear sequence provided by its phrasal lexical entry. Any disruption of that sequence results in ungrammaticality.

This syntactic monolithicity of IPs, they say, stems from their meaning not being distributed over individual parts. ICEs like *pull strings*, on the other hand, allow for variations that affect the meaning of their individual components. For example, the meaning of the complement-NP's head noun can be restrictively modified or quantified over. IPs, in contrast, do not allow for any of these semantic operations, which is the reason for the ungrammaticality of (1a)–(1c).

All things considered, NSW observe a strong correlation between the semantic non-decomposability and the syntactic fixedness of IPs, which induces them to conclude that there exists a conditional dependency between the two. If an idiom is semantically non-decomposable, so they argue, it is syntactically fixed and hence to be analyzed in terms of a phrasal lexical entry, i.e. a monolithic syntactic block.

2.2 Challenging data for Nunberg, Sag & Wasow (1994)

NSW discuss the observations made for German in earlier versions of Schenk (1995) and Webelhuth & Ackerman (1999) that SNDIs like *den Löffel abgeben* 'die' (lit.: 'pass on the spoon') or *ins Gras beißen* 'die' (lit.: 'bite in the grass') can undergo syntactic processes. These include the dislocation of the finite verb to the second position (V2), see (2), and the dislocation of idiom chunks to the initial position (the *Vorfeld*), see (3a). The example in (3a) is taken from Trotzke & Zwart (2014: 138), example (3b) is a corpus example.[1]

(2) *Dann gab   Alex den Löffel ab.*
     then passed Alex the spoon on
     'Then Alex died.'

(3) a. *Den Löffel hat er ab-gegeben.*
         the spoon has he on-passed
         'He died.'

     b. *Den Löffel habe er noch nicht ab-geben wollen, ...*
         the spoon has he still not on-pass want
         'He didn't want to die yet, ...'[2]

NSW briefly explore a purely linearization-based/phonological explanation of data like those in (2). However, SNDIs also allow for passivization, see (4), a syntactic operation that cannot be analyzed as a simple word-order alternation, as it involves adding, inflecting, and often also deleting material.

(4) *Hier wurde der Löffel ab-gegeben.*
     here was   the spoon on-passed
     'Someone died here.'

These data suggest that an IP-like analysis is less attractive for German than for English, as there seem to be no syntactic restrictions in German that correlate with semantic non-decomposability.[3]

It is worth noting that English SNDIs are not necessarily fully fixed either. We will list three commonly mentioned types of data that support this (see, for example, Baldwin & Kim 2010) and add a fourth one. First, many English SNDIs have the same syntactic structure as any regular English V-NP combination, which sets SNDIs apart from syntactically irregular expressions like *kingdom come* 'paradise'. Second, English SNDIs show full morphological flexibility on their verbal heads, see (5).

---

[1]We will not provide a full morphological glossing for German, but only indicate the parts that are relevant for the discussion at hand.

[2]IDS corpora: N92/JAN.03243 Salzburger Nachrichten, 28.01.1992

[3]Soehn (2006) pursues an IP-analysis of German SNDIs. He accounts for the data in (2) and (4) by his formulation of quite abstract phrasal lexical entries that leave many syntactic relations underspecified. A disadvantage of this account is that the lexical representation of SNDIs differs dramatically from language to language, even for syntactically very similar idioms, such as those consisting of a verb and a direct object. Müller (2013b: 923) argues that an analysis that reflects cross-linguistic parallelism is generally to be preferred over one that does not.

(5) a. *Alex kicks/kicked the bucket.*

　　 b. *Kim's kicking the bucket caused great concern.*

Third, SNDIs allow for certain modifiers within the complement-NP, see (6).[4]

(6) *Alex kicked the political/proverbial/goddamn/golden bucket.*

Fourth, we even find passive examples of *kick the bucket*, see (7).

(7) *When you are dead, you don't have to worry about death anymore. ... The bucket will be kicked.*[5]

We will turn to such examples in §3.2. For the moment, it suffices to show that the postulated causal relation between semantic non-decomposability and syntactic fixedness loses much of its appeal in the light of these data.

We conclude that semantic non-decomposability and syntactic fixedness are not necessarily mutually dependent, i.e. an SNDI can show syntactic flexibility. This is rather obvious in German, but there are also some indications for English.

3 Construction-specific restrictions

In this section, we will look at German and English and point out the differences between these two closely-related languages when it comes to verb placement, constituent fronting, and the passive voice.

3.1 German

We will now go through the three mentioned syntactic processes in German and show that they impose no (or rather weak) semantic or pragmatic restrictions.

3.1.1 V2-Movement

In German, the position of the finite verb determines the clause type. In declarative main clauses, for example, the finite verb occurs in second position (V2), see (8a). In subordinate clauses, it typically occurs in final position (V-final), see (8b).

---

[4]Semantically, however, none of these modifiers seems to apply to the meaning of idiomatic *bucket.* For suggestions on how these additional adjectives should be interpreted, see Ernst (1981) and Potts (2005), among others.

[5]*The Single Man* by John Paschal & Mark Louis. 2000. Lincoln, NE: iUniverse. Page 195.

(8) a. *Alex hat gestern   einen Freund mit-gebracht.*
Alex has yesterday a   friend along-brought

'Alex brought along a friend yesterday.'

b. *dass Alex gestern   einen Freund mit-gebracht   hat*
that Alex yesterday a   friend along-brought has

'that Alex brought along a friend yesterday'

V-final is taken to be the basic position. V2 is taken to be derived. The dislocation of the finite verb from V-final to V2 is commonly referred to as V2-movement. There are only very few restrictions as to what verbs may occur in V2. All of these restrictions are either morphological or syntactic, never semantic or pragmatic (Schenk 1995: 262–263). As already mentioned, the fronted verb must be finite, compare (8a) above with (9).[6]

(9) * *Alex mit-gebracht   gestern   einen Freund hat.*
Alex along-brought yesterday a   friend has

If the fronted verb is a particle verb, the particle cannot be fronted together with the verb, see (10a) and (10b).[7]

---

[6]As pointed out to us by a reviewer, Haider (1997: 24) presents the example in (i.a) and suggests that some operators require the verb to be in final position to be in their semantic scope. This could be interpreted as a scopal effect of V2-movement, but Meinunger (2001) shows convincingly that the data should be analyzed as a syntactic ban on stranding these operators rather than as a semantic effect of V2-movement.

(i) a. *Der Wert hat sich weit mehr als   bloß   verdreifacht.*
the value has itself far   more than merely tripled

'The value has far more than merely tripled'

b. * *Der Wert verdreifachte sich weit mehr als bloß.*

[7]We are grateful to a reviewer for bringing up data in which a particle immediately precedes a fronted finite verb, see the example in (i) taken from Müller (2005: 14), and, therefore, could be mistaken as counterexamples to the generalization stated above. As Müller (2005) shows, however, these data are best analyzed with the particle inside the *Vorfeld* and, therefore, are compatible with the generalization.

(i) ... *gut   klar   komm ich nicht.*
good clear come I   not

'... I am not coping well.'

(10) a.   *Alex bringt morgen   einen Freund mit.*
             Alex brings tomorrow a   friend along

             'Alex will bring along a friend tomorrow.'

      b. * *Alex mit-bringt   morgen   einen Freund.*
             Alex along-brings tomorrow a   friend

3.1.2 *Vorfeld* placement

In a number of German clause types, including declarative main clauses, the fronted verb is preceded by a constituent. This constituent appears in the so-called *Vorfeld* 'prefield'. Frey (2006) argues that there are three ways that a constituent can end up in the *Vorfeld*.

1. *Formal movement*: The *Vorfeld*-constituent has the same intonational and pragmatic properties that it would have at the beginning of a V-final clause. This covers pragmatically unmarked subjects, including expletives as in (11a) and (11b), as well as aboutness topics. Formal movement is clause-bounded.

2. *Base generation*: This option is available for a small number of adverbials only. The *Vorfeld-es* in (11c) probably falls into this class.

3. *Ā-movement*: The *Vorfeld*-constituent is moved from one of a variety of positions. This movement is potentially unbounded. The moved constituent is stressed and receives a contrastive interpretation.

The *Vorfeld*-constituent can be of any syntactic category and grammatical function. Examples (11a) and (11b) illustrate that it can also be an expletive, i.e. it need not make an independent semantic contribution. Even the *Vorfeld-es*, an expletive that is not even a dependent of the clause, is allowed, see (11c) from Müller (2013a: 174).

(11) a. *Es hat geregnet.*
          it has rained

          'It rained.'

      b. *Es scheint, dass Alex schläft.*
          it seems that Alex sleeps

    c.   i. *Es kamen drei   Männer herein.*
           it came   three men   in

           'Three men came in.'

      ii. *dass (*es) drei   Männer herein-kamen*
           that (it) three men   in-came

Fanselow (2004) argues that German allows for what he calls *pars-pro-toto* movement, where only part of a contrastively interpreted constituent is moved into the *Vorfeld*. He provides the example in (12) (Fanselow 2004: 12) and argues that the question can equally well be answered by (12a) or (12b). In either case, the focus is on both the dative object and the verb, even though in (12a) it is only the dative object that occurs in the *Vorfeld*.

(12)   Was ist mit dem Buch passiert?   'What happened to the book?'

     a. *Meiner FREUNDIN hab   ich 's geschenkt.*
       my.DAT girlfriend have I   it given

       'I gave it to my girlfriend as a present.'

     b. [*Meiner Freundin geschenkt*] *hab ich's.*

3.1.3 Passive

Just like V2-movement and *Vorfeld*-placement, passivization has no effect on the truth conditions of a sentence. In contrast to the previous two, however, the passive does not mark the clause type. In German, just as in English, verbs that take an accusative complement usually passivize. The complement becomes the subject, and the subject becomes an optional oblique complement, see (13). In contrast to English, however, German also allows for the passivization of intransitive verbs, see (14a), and of verbs that take non-accusative complements, see (14b). All of these examples are taken from Müller (2013a: 287–288).

(13)   *Karl öffnet das Fenster.*   ⟶ *Das Fenster   wird (von Karl) geöffnet.*
      Karl opens the window   the window is   (by Karl) opened

      'Karl is opening the window.'   'The window is being opened (by Karl).'

(14)   a. *Hier wird getanzt.*
       here is   danced

       'People are dancing here.'

b. *Dem   Mann wird geholfen.*
the.DAT man is   helped

'The man is being helped.'

In German, passivization is only possible for verbs that have a *referential* subject. Consequently, verbs with an *expletive* subject, see (15) from Müller (2013a: 293), or no subject at all, see (16) from Müller (2013a: 295), do not passivize.

(15) * *Heute wurde geregnet.*
today was   rained

(16) a. *Dem   Student graut   vor der   Prüfung.*
the.DAT student is.terrified of the.DAT exam

'The student is terrified by the exam.'

b. * *Dem   Student wird (vom   Professor) vor der   Prüfung gegraut.*
the.DAT student is   (by.the professor) of the.DAT exam   terrified

Müller (2013a: 289) provides the example in (17) to show that unaccusative verbs usually do not passivize.[8]

(17) *Der Zug kam an.* ⟶ * *Hier wurde angekommen.*
the train came on   here was   arrived

'The train arrived.'

Overall, we follow Müller (2013a) and describe the German passive as demotion of a referential subject.

---

[8]In those cases where unaccusative verbs do passivize, a special pragmatic effect is achieved. Müller (2013a: 305) illustrates this point with the example in (i), which can be used to express a generally valid rule.

(i) *Hier wird nicht an-gekommen, sondern nur ab-gefahren.*
here is   not on-come   but   only away-driven

'One doesn't arrive here but only depart.'

This special pragmatic effect makes passivization possible in cases that otherwise seem completely out, such as with *haben* 'have':

(ii) *Hier wird keine Angst gehabt.*
here is   no   fear had

'Nobody is afraid here.' / 'You'd better not be afraid!'

3.2 English

We will now turn to parallel constructions in English and show that there are far stronger restrictions on fronted elements in English than in German. V2-like verb movement in English is restricted to auxiliaries. Since we do not know of any English SNDIs with an auxiliary, we will leave verb movement aside and focus on topicalization and passivization.[9]

3.2.1 Topicalization

Topicalization is illustrated in (18) from Ward & Birner (1994: 5).

(18)   GW: *Have you finished the article yet?*
        MR: *The conclusion I still have to do.*

Ward & Birner (1994) argue that, in English, one of the requirements of topicalization is that the meaning of the fronted constituent be (linked to) discourse-old information.

Contrary to German, English also lacks *pars-pro-toto* fronting. The English equivalent of (12a) is not a felicitous answer to a question like *What happened to the book?* because the fronted constituent is not linked to the previous context and English does not allow to interpret the fronted constituent just as a "pars" to a larger "toto" that would include the verb.

(19)   *What happened to the book?*   # *To my girlfriend, I gave it.*

Yet another observation is important for our purpose. Reflexive pronouns can only be fronted if they are used contrastively, as in (20a). The reflexive complement of an inherently-reflexive predicate such as *perjure* cannot be used to mark a contrast. Consequently, it cannot be fronted, see (20b).

(20)   a.   *Herself Alex watched in the mirror, not Chris.*
        b. * *Herself Alex perjured.*

---

[9]Another potentially relevant construction is locative inversion, see (i). It involves a fronted non-subject and a verb that precedes the subject:

   (i)   *Beneath the chin lap of the helmet sprouted black whiskers.* (Ward & Birner 1994: 7)

   Just as for subject-auxiliary inversion, there are very strong restrictions on the type of verb that may occur in this construction. In addition, there are strong discourse requirements. Again, we did not find an SNDI that would be a candidate for this construction, which is why we will not take it into consideration here.

We will interpret this as an indication that a topicalized constituent needs to make an independent contribution to the clause in which it is contained.[10]

3.2.2 Passivization

Kuno & Takami (2004: 127) argue that subjects of English passives are topics. Consequently, they need to be able to refer to entities in the discourse, ideally to entities that are either introduced in the previous discourse or can be inferred from it. Ward & Birner (2004) characterize passive subjects as being relatively discourse-old, i.e. at least not the discourse-newest element in the clause.

Kay & Sag (2014) provide the examples in (21) to show that expletives can occur as subjects of passive sentences.

(21)   a.   *There was believed to be another worker at the site besides the neighbors who witnessed the incident.*

        b.   *It was rumored that Great Britain, in apparent violation of the terms of the Clayton-Bulwer treaty, had taken possession of certain islands in the Bay of Honduras.*

If expletives have an empty semantics, this would contradict the observations

---

[10] A reviewer points out that fronting reflexive arguments of inherently-reflexive verbs is highly restricted in German as well. A bare reflexive complement of an inherently-reflexive verb cannot occur in the *Vorfeld*, see (i.a) from Müller (1999: 99–100), but if such a reflexive pronoun is contained in an argument-marking prepositional phrase, fronting is possible, see (i.b), which is parallel to an example from Müller. There is consensus, shared also by Müller (1999: 387), that the contrast in (i) is due to a prosodic constraint, namely that unstressable expressions cannot be moved to the *Vorfeld*. These do not only include bare inherently-reflexive pronouns but also accusative *es* 'it', see (i.c).

  (i)   a. * [NP: *Sich*]   *hat Peter geschämt.*
             himself has Peter be.ashamed.of

         Intended: 'Peter was ashamed of himself.'

      b. [PP: *Mit sich*]   *schleppt der junge Mann einen Korb* ...
             with himself drags   the young man a   basket

         'The young man is dragging a basket ...'
         https://filmchecker.wordpress.com/2013/12/13/filmreview-basket-case-1982. Accessed 2016-02-11.

      c. * *Es*   *haben die Kinder lesen müssen.*
          it.ACC have the children read must

         Intended: 'The children had to read it.'

from Kuno & Takami (2004) and Ward & Birner (2004). Kay & Sag (2014) do not provide any context, so we can only check on the observation from Ward & Birner (2004) that the subject is not the newest element in the sentence. We make the plausible assumption that the expletive subject is co-indexed with a post-verbal constituent, namely the NP *another worker* in (21a) and the extraposed *that*-clause in (21b). Consequently, the expletive is at best as discourse-new as the post-verbal constituent, which satisfies the constraint.

4 Analysis

We will first provide the basic idea of our analysis and then show that it allows us to derive the syntactic flexibility of SNDIs in a natural way.

4.1 A redundancy-based semantic analysis

The picture that emerged from the discussion in §2 was that the difference in the syntactic encoding of SNDIs and semantically decomposable idioms is questionable. We will propose an encoding of SNDIs in terms of individual word-level lexical entries and, based on the discussion in §3, derive the restrictions on their syntactic flexibility from the interaction of this encoding with the language-specific properties of the relevant syntactic constructions. This is also the position taken in Kay & Sag (2014), which, however, is exclusively based on English data.

There are at least two major challenges for any analysis of idioms in terms of individual word-level lexical entries. First, a mechanism is needed to ensure the co-occurrence of the idiom's components. We will call this the *collocational challenge*. Second, if the idiom's syntactic components combine according to the conventional rules of combinatorics, the idiom's semantics should equally emerge through the conventional mechanism of combinatorial semantics. We will call this the *compositional challenge*.

Any approach based on the insights of NSW has presented a solution to the collocational challenge. Within *Head-driven Phrase Structure Grammar*, for example, this is usually done by some sort of extended selectional mechanism (Krenn & Erbach 1994; Soehn & Sailer 2003; Sag 2007; Kay & Sag 2014), but more powerful collocational systems have also been used (Riehemann 2001; Sailer 2003; Soehn 2006). Common to all of these approaches is a proliferation of lexical entries. The word *kick*, for example, has lexical entries for its literal and for its idiomatic meanings. We will share this assumption and not elaborate on the collocational challenge any further – for such an elaboration, see, for example, the analysis of semantically decomposable idioms in Webelhuth et al. (to appear).

What we will focus on here is the compositional challenge, which has played a major role in making the phrasal analysis of SNDIs so attractive. If there is no evidence that parts of an SNDI make an individual meaning contribution, why not just assign the idiom meaning to the phrase instead of its words? In light of the data on the syntactic flexibility of SNDIs, however, such an analysis is not easily tenable.

Kay & Sag (2014) assign the entire meaning of an SNDI to its syntactic head. Such a suggestion is very natural within a head-driven syntax. To the other words within the idiom, Kay & Sag (2014) assign an empty semantic contribution.[11] They achieve this by working within *Minimal Recursion Semantics* (Copestake et al. 1995; 2005), where semantic representations are encoded as lists of simple predicate-argument expressions and subordination constraints among these. An empty semantic contribution is simply encoded as an empty list.

This analysis is sketched in (22). We distinguish the idiom-internal *kick* from its literal homonym by representing the former as $kick_{id}$. We proceed analogously for the other words. The semantic representation of $kick_{id}$ consists of the predicate $\mathbf{die_{id}}$, a situation s, and the index of the subject: x.

(22)   Semantic analysis of *kick the bucket* à la Kay & Sag (2014)
     a. $kick_{id}$: $\langle \mathbf{die_{id}}(s, x) \rangle$
     b. the_{id}: $\langle \rangle$
     c. $bucket_{id}$: $\langle \rangle$

Kay & Sag (2014) derive the right semantics for the idiom and thereby solve the compositional challenge. They also account for the absence of an internal modification reading, as the noun $bucket_{id}$ does not make any semantic contribution that could be modified. The semantic emptiness of $bucket_{id}$ is also made responsible for the fact that topicalization is not possible with *kick the bucket*, as topicalization requires the topicalized constituent to be non-empty.

In the light of the examples in (21), Kay & Sag (2014) do not impose a non-emptiness constraint on passive subjects. Instead, they classify the idiomatic verb $kick_{id}$ as belonging to a verb class that does not allow for passivization.

---

[11]The earliest reference to such an approach seems to be Ruhl (1975). Unfortunately, we could not get a copy of this paper. NSW explicitly reject this type of approach as failing to account for the syntactic fixedness of SNDIs.

While this analysis already goes a long way in what we consider the right direction, we think that a slightly different answer to the compositional challenge might get us even further. Instead of empty semantic contributions for the words *bucket_{id}* and *the_{id}*, we assume *redundant* semantic contributions and make use of *Lexical Resource Semantics* (LRS, Richter & Sailer 2004). Within this framework, Richter & Sailer (2001; 2006) argue that the co-occurrence of words that contribute the same semantic operator (such as question or negation) is common in the languages of the world and, therefore, should be analyzed that way. Sailer (2010) extends this argument to lexical semantic contributions in his analysis of the English cognate object construction. The semantic contributions of signs used in these works are list-based, just as in Kay & Sag (2014). In contrast to Kay & Sag (2014), however, the different lists may contain identical elements. Another difference is that the elements on the semantic contribution list need not be predicate-argument expressions but can be of any form.

Our analysis of *kick the bucket* is sketched in (23), where we indicate the lexical semantic contributions of the idiom's words.

(23) Redundancy-based semantic analysis of *kick the bucket*:
   a. *kick_{id}*: $\langle s, \textbf{die}_\textbf{id}, \textbf{die}_\textbf{id}(s, \alpha), \exists s(\beta) \rangle$
   b. *the_{id}*: $\langle s, \exists s(\beta) \rangle$
   c. *bucket_{id}*: $\langle s, \textbf{die}_\textbf{id}, \textbf{die}_\textbf{id}(s, \alpha) \rangle$

The verb *kick_{id}* contributes a situation s, the predicate $\textbf{die}_\textbf{id}$, and the formula that combines this predicate with its two arguments – one of them being the situation s. The second argument of $\textbf{die}_\textbf{id}$ is left underspecified, as its semantics will come from the subject. This underspecification is indicated with a lowercase Greek letter, here α, which is used as a meta-variable over expressions of our semantic representation language. The verb also contributes an existential quantification over the situational variable: $\exists s(\beta)$. The meta-variable β indicates that the scope of the quantifier is underspecified.

In other words, *kick_{id}* contributes the same kinds of elements as other verbs. Similarly, the semantic contribution of the determiner *the_{id}* is just like that of a normal determiner. It contributes a variable and a quantification over this variable. The noun *bucket_{id}*, just like other common nouns, contributes a referential variable and a predicate.

While the semantic contributions of the idiomatic words in (23) are analogous to those of non-idiomatic words, it can be seen that the contributions of *the$_{id}$* and *bucket$_{id}$* are contained in the contribution of *kick$_{id}$*.[12] This is what we refer to as *redundant marking*.

When words combine to form a phrase, their meaning contributions are collected, i.e. the list of semantic contributions of a phrase contains all the elements of its daughters' lists. For the sentence *Alex kicked$_{id}$ the$_{id}$ bucket$_{id}$*, the semantic contribution list will contain all the elements listed in (23) plus the contribution of the word *Alex*, which is just the constant **alex**.

At the sentence level, all the elements of this list must be combined into a single formula. To do this, each meta-variable must be assigned an element from the contribution list as its value. In our case, α would be assigned **alex**, which results in $\mathbf{die}_{id}(s, \mathbf{alex})$. This formula is taken as the value of the meta-variable β. This leads to the intended semantic representation of the sentence: $\exists s(\mathbf{die}_{id}(s, \mathbf{alex}))$. The constant **die$_{id}$** occurs only once in this logical form, even though it is contributed by two words in the sentence – *kick$_{id}$* and *bucket$_{id}$*.

The redundancy-based analysis of *kick the bucket* will directly carry over to other SNDIs, be it in English or in other languages. In our case, the same semantic contributions would be assumed for the words in the German idiom *den Löffel abgeben* 'die'.

In the next two subsections, we will look more closely at the syntactic flexibility of SNDIs. We will show that the attested behavior follows directly from the interaction of the proposed analysis of SNDIs and the construction-specific constraints presented in §3. We will also show some advantages of the redundancy-based approach over the one of Kay & Sag (2014).

4.2 Syntactic flexibility of German SNDIs

We will go through the three phenomena of German syntax discussed in §3.1 and look at them in the light of SNDIs.

4.2.1 German SNDIs and V2-movement

The restrictions on V2-movement are syntactic in nature and do not at all depend on the content of the verb. We hence expect that these constraints hold for the verbs in SNDIs. This is borne out. With *den Löffel abgeben*, for example, which contains a verb with the separable particle *ab*, a non-finite verb following the

---

[12]Technically, this effect can be achieved through selection. The selecting verb requires its complement to have the same index and to contribute the same constant: **die$_{id}$**.

Vorfeld is ungrammatical, see (24b), and so is fronting the finite verb together with the particle, see (25b).[13]

(24) a. *Alex hat den Löffel ab-gegeben.*
          Alex has the spoon on-passed

      b. * *Alex ab-gegeben den Löffel hat.*

(25) a. *Alex gab   den Löffel ab.*
          Alex passed the spoon on

          'Alex died.'

      b. * *Alex ab-gab den Löffel.*

4.2.2 German SNDIs and *Vorfeld* placement

As we saw in §3.1.2, there are three possibilities for a constituent to be licensed in the *Vorfeld*: formal movement, base generation, and Ā-movement for contrast. Fanselow (2004) provides examples of *Vorfeld* placement of constituents of SNDIs. One of his examples is given in (26) (from Fanselow 2004: 22), where the PP-constituent of the idiom *am Hungertuch nagen* 'be very poor' (lit.: 'gnaw at the hunger cloth') is fronted. The sentence has a contrastive interpretation; the alternatives are various degrees of poorness.

(26) *Am   Hunger-tuch müssen wir noch nicht nagen.*
       on.the hunger-cloth must   we yet not   gnaw

       'We are not down on our uppers, yet.'

---

[13]There are idioms where the verb must be in V2-position. Richter & Sailer (2009: 300) claim that the idiom in (i) has a fixed *Vorfeld* element followed by the finite form *tritt*. We think that this is due to the fact that this is an idiom with a "pragmatic point" (Fillmore et al. 1988) and, thus, a certain illocutionary force is part of the idiom, which is not compatible with a V-final clause.

(i) a. *Ich glaub, mich   tritt ein Pferd!*
         I   believe me.ACC kicks a   horse

         'I am very surprised.' / 'I can't believe this!'

     b. # *Ich glaub, dass mich ein Pferd tritt.*

When we apply these considerations to *den Löffel abgeben*, we see that in an active sentence, fronting the NP *den Löffel* should be unproblematic under a contrastive reading.[14]

This is shown in (27), where the alternatives are other consequences of serious illness.

(27) *Es sind zwar   viele schwer krank geworden, den Löffel hat aber noch*
      it are admittedly many heavy sick   become,   the spoon has but still

      niemand ab-gegeben.
      nobody on-passed

      'Though many got seriously sick, nobody has died yet.'

These contrastive cases clearly distinguish between our analysis and that of Kay & Sag (2014). Since the NP *den Löffel* contributes the same situational variable as the verb *abgeben*, it is easy to know to which larger "toto" the fronted "pars" belongs. In an analysis with an empty semantics of the NP, this would not be possible.

4.2.3 German SNDIs and the passive

We expect the passivizability of SNDIs to follow from the interaction between the above analysis and the general properties of the German passive discussed in in §3.1. The German passive voice demotes the subject of an active clause. In our analysis, a passive verb requires that there be a participant filling the thematic role of the active subject and that this subject have a non-redundant index.[15]

---

[14]For the non-contrastive case, we find clause-initial placement of the *Löffel*-NP in V-final clauses, at least in the passive. This shows that the idiom-internal NP can be fronted by formal movement.

  (i) Da ist nichts mehr zu machen. 'Nothing can be done anymore.'

    a. *Es sieht so aus, also ob [der Löffel jetzt endgültig   ab-gegeben ist].*
      it looks so out as   if the spoon now definitively on-passed is

      'It looks like it is definitely over now.'

    b. *Der Löffel ist jetzt endgültig ab-gegeben.*
      'It is definitely over now.'

[15]A bit more technically, the index of the active subject must not be identical with the index of the active verb or of any of the verb's arguments. This restriction does not seem to be valid for German only, but can be used to derive the ungrammaticality of *$Alex_i$ was shaved by himself$_i$*. A reviewer pointed out that a reflexive pronoun is possible in a *by*-phrase in a context that

There are additional restrictions on verbs that cannot be passivized or only with the special pragmatic effect mentioned in Footnote 8.

Dobrovol'skij (2000) argues that a VP-idiom, semantically decomposable or not, can never be passivized if the literal counterpart of the idiom's verb cannot be passivized. His example is the semantically decomposable idiom *einen Korb bekommen* 'get the brush-off' (lit.: 'receive a basket'), which can neither be passivized in its literal nor in its idiomatic reading.

Idioms with an expletive subject do not passivize either. An example is *Bindfäden regnen* 'rain heavily' (lit.: 'rain strings'), see (28).

(28) * *Hier werden/wird Bindfäden geregnet.*
        here are/is   strings   rained

This is expected under our analysis. The LRS analysis of expletives is redundancy-based. For weather verbs, Levine et al. (2014) assume that the expletive subject has the same index as the verb. Consequently, the sentence in (28) violates the constraint that the demoted subject must not have a redundant index.

A reviewer brought the example in (29a) to our attention. Müller (2002: 131) points out that if (29b) is the active counterpart of (29a), one is forced to allow the weather-*es* to be the underlying subject of a passive. This might undermine the explanation for blocking (28).

(29) a. *Die Stühle wurden nass geregnet.*
          the chairs were   wet rained

         'The rain caused the chairs to become wet.'

      b. *Es hat die Stühle nass geregnet.*
          it has the chairs wet rained

Our semantic-based constraint on passivization does not run into this problem. We give a very rough sketch of the logical form of (29) in (30). This formula can be paraphrased as in the following sentence. There are the eventualities s, s', and s'', such that s is a raining event, s' is a state with wet chairs, and s'' is a causation event in which the raining s causes the wetness s'.

(30) $\exists s \, \exists s' \, \exists s'' \, (\mathbf{rain}(s) \wedge \mathbf{wet}(s', \mathbf{the\text{-}chairs}) \wedge \mathbf{cause}(s'', s, s'))$

---

evokes alternatives to the reflexive pronoun, such as *Chris was shaved by Alex and Alex was shaved by himself.* This exception is clearly connected to a special semantics to which our non-redundant index requirement would need to be adapted.

Following the syntactic analysis in Müller (2002: 241), the resultative version of *regnen* comes about by a lexical rule that changes the verb's valence requirement and adds the semantic material required for the causation/result semantics. When one adapts this rule to LRS, it also changes the index of the verb from the raining event to the causation event. Consequently, resultative *regnen* in (29) has the index s'' in (30), whereas the raining – and, by redundancy, the expletive *es* – has the index s. Since the underlying active subject and the passivized verb have distinct indices under this analysis, the grammaticality of (29a) is predicted. Note that this analysis, again, is possible under a redundancy analysis of expletives but hard to implement if one assumes an empty semantics for expletives.

As for verbs allowing for passivization, Dobrovol'skij (2000: 561) distinguishes between idioms with idiom-external accusative objects, as in (31), and those with idiom-internal accusatives, as in his example in (32). For the former, there is no idiom-specific restriction on passivization.

(31) *etwas auf Eis legen* 'put something on hold'
      Das Projekt wurde auf Eis gelegt.
      the project was   on ice put

      'The project was put on hold.'

(32) *jemandem den Garaus machen* 'kill someone'
      ... den   lästigen Hausgenossen soll   nun ... der   Garaus
       the.DAT annoying housemates   should now   the.NOM Garaus
      gemacht werden ...
      made   be

      '... the annoying housemates should now be killed ...'

Dobrovol'skij (2000) assumes that the main function of the German passive is to promote an accusative complement. This promotion has the syntactic effect of realizing the underlying accusative complement as a subject and the semantic/pragmatic effect of assigning its referent the status of a topic. Based on these assumptions, he diagnoses a syntax-semantics mismatch in sentences like (32). Syntactically, he says, the idiom-internal NP is promoted, but semantically it is the idiom-external dative NP. In a subject-demotion approach, no such mismatch needs to be assumed for (32). We can derive the topicality of the dative NP from the fact that it occurs in a topic position – here, its appearance in the *Vorfeld* through formal movement (see §3.1.2).

Dobrovol'skij (2000) only considers passives of transitive verbs with an agentive meaning. Our approach does not have this limitation. We expect the passive to be possible with idioms having a non-agentive idiomatic meaning, such as *den Löffel abgeben*, for which we can indeed find examples, see (33).

(33) *Bei den Grünen   wird der politische Löffel schon   vor*
at the Green.party is   the political   spoon already before
Amtsabschied ab-gegeben.
resigning   on-passed
'In the Green Party, people die politically already before resigning from their office.'[16]

In this section, we argued that the restrictions on three syntactic processes of German (V2-movement, fronting, and passivization) are very weak and compatible with the syntactic, semantic, and pragmatic properties of an SNDI such as *den Löffel abgeben*. We therefore expect that the idiom can occur in all of them.

4.3 Syntactic flexibility of English SNDIs

We saw in §3.2 that English imposes semantic constraints on frontable constituents and on passive subjects. We will now explore the interaction of these constraints with our lexical encoding of SNDIs.

For topicalization, we saw in §3.2 that the topicalized constituent must be explicitly linked to the previous discourse, and that it must make an independent semantic contribution within its clause. In LRS, such a non-redundancy requirement can be expressed easily by saying that the semantic contribution of the topicalized constituent must not be properly included in the semantic contribution of the rest of the clause. In our analysis, the meaning of the NP *the bucket* is fully included in the meaning of the rest of the clause. Therefore, the ban on topicalization follows directly.

Matters are slightly more complicated when we look at the passive voice. The constraints on a passive subject have been shown to be weaker than those on a topicalized constituent. We saw above that a passive subject must refer to something that has been mentioned earlier in the discourse (or that can be inferred from such an element). This does not exclude the possibility of the subject making a semantic contribution that is contained in that of the rest of the sentence – as we saw in the cases of expletive passive subjects in (21).

---

[16]http://www.kontextwochenzeitung.de/politik/148/erst-schreien-wenn-etwas-geschafft-ist-1992.html. Accessed 2014-12-19.

Consequently, if the discourse conditions on passive subjects are met, even English SNDIs can be passivized. In (7), repeated in (34), *kick the bucket* is topical, only the tense and the result state are new.

(34)   *When you are dead, you don't have to worry about death anymore. ... The bucket will be kicked.*

The example in (34) is one out of admittedly few naturally occurring examples of the passive with this idiom.[17] The following examples show passives for other idioms that are classified as IPs in NSW, see (35), or do not pass the tests for semantic decomposability, see (36). Example (36) shows particularly clearly that the meaning of the idiom *have a cow* is discourse-old, as it is explicitly mentioned in the preceding clause.[18]

(35)   *saw logs* 'snore'
       I excitedly yet partially delusional turned to Alexandria to point out the sun as it set and all I see is eyelids and hear logs being sawed. *Come on! I can't say too much because I wasn't far behind as I was catching flies [= sleeping] about a minute later.*[19]

(36)   *have a cow* 'get angry'
       There was really no need for the police to have a cow, but a cow was had, *resulting in kettling, CS gas and 182 arrests.*[20]

An approach that assumes an empty semantics for the idiom-internal NP *the bucket* runs into severe problems. We saw above that passivization is possible for SNDIs if the strong discourse requirements are met. Thus, it would be wrong to categorically block the passivization of *kick$_{id}$*. Our approach correctly predicts the admittedly rare occurrence of passives with this idiom. Furthermore, an empty semantics for *the bucket* does not allow us to relate the NP's meaning to the preceding discourse. A redundancy-based account makes the required semantic information available at the clause-initial constituent.

---

[17] In a recent talk, Christiane Fellbaum presented two other naturally occurring examples of *kick-the-bucket* passives and passives of other English idioms that express the idea of "dying". In as far as context is included in her examples, they also satisfy the topicality requirement. See: http://www.crissp.be/wp-content/uploads/2015/04/Talk7-Fellbaum.pdf. Accessed 2015-08-27.

[18] Note that even though the examples in (35) and (36) may have a playful character, they do not blend the idiomatic and the non-idiomatic reading, as it would typically be the case in jokes or puns.

[19] http://5050experience.sportsblog.com/posts/1125677/feast.html. Accessed 2015-07-24.

[20] http://www.theguardian.com/commentisfree/2012/aug/01/cyclists-like-pedestrians-must-get-angry. Accessed 2015-08-24.

Let us conclude §4 with a brief summary of our analysis. We replaced NSW's causal relation between the semantic decomposability and the syntactic flexibility of idioms with an approach based on the interaction of the properties of idioms with the constraints on syntactic constructions. While, overall, our account is very similar to Kay & Sag (2014), an important difference is that we make use of redundant marking, a choice which we hope to have motivated above.

5 Extension to other languages

So far, we have only looked at English and German. These two closely-related languages already show considerable differences in their syntactic constructions, and these differences have far-reaching consequences for the flexibility of MWEs. In this section, we would like to briefly show that other languages have yet other constraints on similar syntactic operations and that these have a predictable effect on the flexibility of idioms.

5.1 Estonian

Muischnek & Kaalep (2010) name and describe a number of problems in applying an English-based classification of idioms to Estonian. Similar to German, Estonian allows for considerably more word-order flexibility than English. Muischnek & Kaalep (2010: 122) argue that Estonian has a passive-like construction whose function is to background a (usually human) subject, rather than to foreground an object. This is similar to the function of the passive in German. Consequently, passivizing intransitive verbs is possible, see (37).

(37) *Mees   jookseb*   ⟶   *Joostakse*
      man   run.PRESENT   run.IMPERS
      'The man is running.'   'Somebody is running.'

In order to emphasize its subject-backgrounding function, this construction is called *impersonal passive*. In contrast to German, there is no change in the morphological case of the active direct object, see (38). This leads us to expect that the lack of object foregrounding might be even stronger in Estonian than in German.[21]

---

[21]The differences between German passives and Estonian impersonal passives are discussed in detail in Blevins (2003).

(38) *Mees loeb   raamatut.* ⟶   *Loetakse   raamatut.*
      Man read.PRESENT book.PART   read.IMPERS book.PART

      'The man is reading a book.'   'A book is being read';
                                         'Somebody is reading a book.'

Muischnek & Kaalep (2010) state that the impersonal passive can be formed with all idioms, including SNDIs. The only condition is that the active subject be human. Kadri Muischnek (personal communication) kindly provided us with the example in (39).

(39) *Kas massiliselt heideti   hinge?*
      Q   massively threw.IMPERS soul.PART

      'Did they die massively?'[22]

5.2 French

In French, we see yet a different pattern. Abeillé (1995) lists French idioms that do not permit internal modification but do permit the passive voice, such as *faire un carton* 'hit the bull' (lit.: 'make a box'). These reported data suggest that French is more like German than like English when it comes to the passive. Lamiroy (1993) provides convincing arguments that this is indeed the case. Instead of promoting a non-subject argument, the French passive also primarily demotes a subject. French allows for the passivization of strictly intransitive verbs, see (40a) from Lamiroy (1993: 54), but not as productively as German, see (40b).

(40) a. *Il   a   été dormi dans mon lit.*
         it.EXPLETIVE has been slept in   my bed

         'Someone had been sleeping in my bed.'

      b. *Ils   courent.*   ⟶ * *Il est fréquemment couru ici.*
         they run   it is often   run   here

         'They are running.'   'There is often someone running here.'

We will leave the details of the passivizability of intransitive verbs in French aside. Gaatone (1993) gives examples of passivized French SNDIs, including the one in (41) (see Gaatone 1993: 47).[23]

---

[22]From the etTenTen corpus: http://www.keeleveeb.ee.

[23]The English counterpart *wear the pants* syntactically behaves like *kick the bucket*. The corresponding German expression *die Hosen an-haben* (lit.: 'have the pants on') cannot be passivized since the verb *haben* 'have' is unpassivizable in general.

(41) *porter la culotte* 'wear the pants'

Mme et	*M. Armand y*	*régnent paternellement, bien que*	*la*
Mrs	and Mr Armand there rule	paternally	even though the

culotte y	*soit portée par madame ...*
pants there is	worn by madam

      'Mrs and Mr Armand rule there paternally even though she is the
      dominant part'

In this section, we showed that our results of the German-English contrast carry over to other languages as well. Whether or not an SNDI can appear in a certain syntactic construction is dependent on the constraints on that construction in the particular language. Languages may differ significantly with regard to these constraints. For this reason, classical tests for classifying idioms, such as passivizability and fronting, cannot be easily applied across languages but need to be re-examined in each individual case.

6 Conclusion

Wasow et al. (1983) and Nunberg et al. (1994) have led to a shift in perspective from a monolithic, fully phrasal view of all idioms to a more lexical approach for semantically decomposable idioms. We agree with Kay & Sag (2014) in extending this lexical approach to SNDIs.[24] In order to provide a solid motivation for this step, it is essential to look at a larger set of languages, in particular languages that differ in the semantic and pragmatic properties of morphosyntactically similar constructions. The present paper made a first step in that direction and looked at verb fronting, topicalization, and passivization in German and English as well as the impersonal passive in Estonian and the passive in French. Whereas Nunberg et al. (1994) are forced to analyze English and German SNDIs in considerably different ways, the lexical analysis presented here provides a cross-linguistically uniform analysis.[25]

This type of analysis has consequences for the encoding of multiword expressions (MWE) in formal grammar in general. All MWEs that are of syntactically regular shape should receive a lexical encoding. The difference between semantically decomposable and semantically non-decomposable MWEs lies in the way

---

[24]Parallel treatments of SNDIs and semantically decomposable idioms have recently been proposed within other frameworks as well; see a short remark in Harley & Stone (2013: fn. 2) within a Minimalist approach and Lichte & Kallmeyer (2016) for Tree Adjoining Grammar.

[25]We side with Müller (2013b: 923), who states: "If we can choose between several theoretical approaches, ...we should take the one that can capture cross-linguistic generalizations."

in which the semantics of the MWE is distributed over the words constituting the MWE. Whereas the parts of a semantically decomposable MWE have an independent, i.e. non-redundant, meaning, the parts of a semantically non-decomposable MWE do not. Differences in the syntactic flexibility of semantically decomposable and semantically non-decomposable MWEs follow exclusively from the interaction between the language-specific constraints on a syntactic operation and the semantics of the MWE's constituents.

Acknowledgements

This paper profited from the feedback of numerous esteemed colleagues, many of whom were among the audiences at the PARSEME *1st Training School* in Prague, the *Computational Linguistics Research Colloquium* in Düsseldorf, the *16th Szklarska Poreba Workshop*, and the PARSEME *4th General Meeting* in Valletta. Special thanks go to Doug Arnold, Gisbert Fanselow, Christopher Götze, Timm Lichte, Stella Markantonatou, and Susanna Salem for their valuable questions, comments, and suggestions. We are also very grateful for the work of two anonymous reviewers and to the proofreaders of LangSci. All remaining errors are ours.

Abbreviations

DAT	dative	LRS	Lexical Resource Semantics
ICE	idiomatically combining expression	NSW	Nunberg et al. 1994
		PART	partitive case
IMPERS	impersonal passive	SNDI	semantically non-decomposable idiom
HPSG	Head-Driven Phrase Structure Grammar	V2	verb second
IP	idiomatic phrase		

References

Abeillé, Anne. 1995. The flexibility of French idioms: A representation with Lexical Tree Adjoining Grammar. In Martin Everaert, Eric-Jan van der Linden, André Schenk & Rob Schreuder (eds.), *Idioms. Structural and Psychological Perspectives*, 15–42. Hillsdale, NJ: Lawrence Erlbaum Associates.

Baldwin, Timothy & Su Nam Kim. 2010. Multiword expressions. In Nitin Indurkhya & Fred J. Damerau (eds.), *Handbook of Natural Language Processing*, 2nd edn., 267–292. Boca Raton: CRC Press.

Blevins, James P. 2003. Passives and impersonals. *Journal of Linguistics* 39(3). 473–520. DOI:10.1017/S0022226703002081

Copestake, Ann, Dan Flickinger, Robert Malouf, Susanne Riehemann & Ivan A. Sag. 1995. Translation using Minimal Recursion Semantics. In *Proceedings of The Sixth International Conference on Theoretical and Methodological Issues in Machine Translation (TMI-95)*. Leuven.

Copestake, Ann, Dan Flickinger, Carl Pollard & Ivan Sag. 2005. Minimal recursion semantics: An introduction. *Research on Language & Computation* 3(4). 281–332.

Dobrovol'skij, Dmitrij. 2000. Syntaktische Modifizierbarkeit von Idiomen aus lexikographischer Perspektive. In *EURALEX 2000 Proceedings*. http : / / www . euralex . org / elx _ proceedings / Euralex2000 / 064 _ Dmitrij % 20DOBROVOLSKIJ_Syntaktische%20Modifizierbarkeit%20von%20Idiomen% 20aus%20lexikographischer%20Perspektive.pdf, accessed 2018-4-19.

Ernst, Thomas. 1981. Grist for the linguistic mill: Idioms and 'extra' adjectives. *Journal of Linguistic Research* 1. 51–68.

Fanselow, Gisbert. 2004. Cyclic phonology-syntax interaction. Movement to first position in German. In Shinichiro Ishihara, Michaela Schmitz & Anne Schwarz (eds.), *Interdisciplinary studies on information structure* (Working Papers of the SFB 632 1), 1–42.

Fillmore, Charles J., Paul Kay & Mary Catherine O'Connor. 1988. Regularity and idiomaticity in grammatical constructions: The case of *let alone. Language* 64(3). 501–538.

Frey, Werner. 2006. Contrast and movement to the German prefield. In Valéria Molnár & Susanne Winkler (eds.), *The architecture of focus* (Studies in Generative Grammar 82), 235–264. Berlin & New York: Mouton de Gruyter.

Gaatone, David. 1993. Les locutions verbales et les deux passifs du français. *Langage* 27(109). 37–52.

Haider, Hubert. 1997. Typological implications of a directionality constraint on projections. In Artemis Alexiadou & Tracy Hall (eds.), *Studies on Universal Grammar and typological variation*, 17–33. Amsterdam: John Benjamins.

Harley, Heidi & Megan Stone. 2013. The 'No Agent Idioms' hypothesis. In Raffaella Folli, Christina Sevdali & Robert Truswell (eds.), *Syntax and its limits*, 283–311. Oxford: Oxford University Press.

Kay, Paul & Ivan A. Sag. 2014. A lexical theory of phrasal idioms. http://www1. icsi.berkeley.edu/~kay/idioms-submitted.pdf, accessed 2018-4-19.

Krenn, Brigitte & Gregor Erbach. 1994. Idioms and support verb constructions. In John Nerbonne, Klaus Netter & Carl Pollard (eds.), *German in Head-Driven Phrase Structure Grammar* (Lecture Notes 46), 365–396. Stanford, CA: CSLI Publications.

Kuno, Susumu & Ken-ichi Takami. 2004. *Functional constraints in grammar. On the unergative-unaccusative distinction.* Amsterdam, Philadelphia: Benjamins.

Lamiroy, Béatrice. 1993. Pourquoi il y a deux passifs. *Langage* 27(109). 53–72.

Levine, Robert D., Frank Richter & Manfred Sailer. 2014. *Formal semantics. An empirically grounded approach.* Manuscript Ohio State University and Goethe-University Frankfurt.

Lichte, Timm & Laura Kallmeyer. 2016. Same syntax, different semantics: A compositional approach to idiomaticity in multi-word expressions. In Christopher Pinon (ed.), *Empirical issues in syntax and semantics*, vol. 11, 111–140. http://www.cssp.cnrs.fr/eiss11/eiss11_lichte-and-kallmeyer.pdf, accessed 2018-4-19.

Meinunger, André. 2001. Restrictions on verb raising. *Linguistic Inquiry* 32(4). 732–740.

Muischnek, Kadri & Heiki-Jaan Kaalep. 2010. The variability of multi-word verbal expressions in Estonian. *Language Resources and Evaluation* 44(1–2). 115–135. DOI:10.1007/s10579-009-9096-x

Müller, Stefan. 1999. *Deutsche Syntax deklarativ: Head-Driven Phrase Structure Grammar für das Deutsche* (Linguistische Arbeiten 394). Tübingen: Max Niemeyer Verlag.

Müller, Stefan. 2002. *Complex predicates: Verbal complexes, resultative constructions, and particle verbs in German* (Studies in Constraint-Based Lexicalism 13). Stanford, CA: CSLI Publications.

Müller, Stefan. 2005. Zur Analyse der scheinbar mehrfachen Vorfeldbesetzung. *Linguistische Berichte* 203. 297–330.

Müller, Stefan. 2013a. *Head-Driven Phrase Structure Grammar: Eine Einführung.* 3rd, revised edn. Tübingen: Stauffenburg.

Müller, Stefan. 2013b. Unifying everything. *Language* 89(4). 920–950.

Nunberg, Geoffrey, Ivan A. Sag & Thomas Wasow. 1994. Idioms. *Language* 70(3). 491–538.

Potts, Christopher. 2005. *The logic of conventional implicatures* (Oxford Studies in Theoretical Linguistics). Oxford: Oxford University Press.

Richter, Frank & Manfred Sailer. 2001. On the left periphery of German finite sentences. In W. Detmar Meurers & Tibor Kiss (eds.), *Constraint-based approaches to Germanic syntax*, 257–300. Stanford, CA: CSLI Publications.

Richter, Frank & Manfred Sailer. 2004. Basic concepts of Lexical Resource Semantics. In Arne Beckmann & Norbert Preining (eds.), *ESSLLI 2003: Course material I* (Collegium Logicum 5), 87–143. Vienna: Kurt Gödel Society Wien.

Richter, Frank & Manfred Sailer. 2006. Modeling typological markedness in semantics. The case of negative concord. In Stefan Müller (ed.), *Proceedings of the 13th International Conference on Head-Driven Phrase Structure Grammar, Varna*, 305–325. Stanford, CA: CSLI Publications. http://cslipublications.stanford.edu/ HPSG/7/richter-sailer.pdf, accessed 2018-4-19.

Richter, Frank & Manfred Sailer. 2009. Phraseological clauses in constructional HPSG. In Stefan Müller (ed.), *Proceedings of the 16th international conference on Head-Driven Phrase Structure Grammar, Göttingen*, 297–317. Stanford, CA: CSLI Publications. http://cslipublications.stanford.edu/HPSG/2009/richter-sailer.pdf, accessed 2018-4-19.

Riehemann, Susanne. 2001. *A constructional approach to idioms and word formation*. Stanford University dissertation.

Ruhl, Charles. 1975. *Kick the bucket* is not an idiom. *Interfaces* 4. 2–4.

Sag, Ivan A. 2007. Remarks on locality. In Stefan Müller (ed.), *Proceedings of the 14th international conference on Head-Driven Phrase Structure Grammar, Stanford*, 394–414. Stanford, CA: CSLI Publications. http://cslipublications.stanford.edu/HPSG/2007/sag.pdf, accessed 2018-4-19.

Sailer, Manfred. 2003. *Combinatorial semantics and idiomatic expressions in Head-Driven Phrase Structure Grammar*. Philosophische Dissertation (2000). Arbeitspapiere des SFB 340. 161. Universität Tübingen. http://www.sfs.uni-tuebingen.de/hpsg/archive/bibliography/papers/sailer_dissertation03.ps, accessed 2018-4-19.

Sailer, Manfred. 2010. The family of English cognate object constructions. In Stefan Müller (ed.), *Proceedings of the 17th international conference on Head-Driven Phrase Structure Grammar, Paris*, 191–211. Stanford, CA: CSLI Publications. http://cslipublications.stanford.edu/HPSG/2010/sailer.pdf, accessed 2018-4-19.

Schenk, André. 1995. The syntactic behavior of idioms. In Martin Everaert, Eric-Jan van der Linden, André Schenk & Ron Schreuder (eds.), *Idioms. Structural and psychological perspectives*, 253–271. Hillsdale, NJ: Lawrence Erlbaum Associates.

Soehn, Jan-Philipp. 2006. *Über Bärendienste und erstaunte Bauklötze: Idiome ohne freie Lesart in der HPSG.* Frankfurt am Main: Peter Lang.

Soehn, Jan-Philipp & Manfred Sailer. 2003. At first blush on tenterhooks: About selectional restrictions imposed by nonheads. In Gerhard Jäger, Paola Monachesi, Gerald Penn & Shuly Wintner (eds.), *Proceedings of Formal Grammar 2003*, 149–161. Vienna.

Trotzke, Andreas & Jan-Wouter Zwart. 2014. The complexity of narrow syntax: Minimalism, representational economy, and simplest Merge. In Frederick J. Newmeyer & Laurel B. Preston (eds.), *Measuring grammatical complexity*, 128–147. Oxford: Oxford University Press.

Ward, Gregory & Betty J. Birner. 1994. A unified account of English fronting constructions. In *Penn working papers in linguistics*, vol. 1, 159–165. University Park: Penn State University Press.

Ward, Gregory & Betty J. Birner. 2004. Information structure and non-canonical syntax. In Laurence R. Horn & Gregory Ward (eds.), *The handbook of pragmatics*, 153–174. Malden, MA: Blackwell Publishing Ltd.

Wasow, Thomas, Ivan A. Sag & Geoffrey Nunberg. 1983. Idioms: An interim report. In Shirô Hattori & Kazuko Inoue (eds.), *Proceedings of the XIIIth International Congress of Linguistics*, 102–115.

Webelhuth, Gert & Farrell Ackerman. 1999. A lexical-functional analysis of predicate topicalization in German. *American Journal of Germanic Linguistics & Literatures* 11(1). 1–65.

Webelhuth, Gert, Sascha Bargmann & Christopher Götze. to appear. Idioms as evidence for the proper analysis of relative clauses. In Manfred Krifka, Rainer Ludwig & Mathias Schenner (eds.), *Reconstruction effects in relative clauses*. Berlin: Akademie Verlag.

Chapter 2

Semantic and syntactic patterns of multiword names: A cross-language study

Svetla Koeva
Institute for Bulgarian Language, Bulgarian Academy of Sciences

Cvetana Krstev
Faculty of Philology, University of Belgrade

Duško Vitas
Faculty of Mathematics, University of Belgrade

Tita Kyriacopoulou
Université Paris-Est Marne-la-Vallée

Claude Martineau
LIGM, Universite Paris-Est Marne-la-Vallée

Tsvetana Dimitrova
Institute for Bulgarian Language, Bulgarian Academy of Sciences

Named entities (NEs) constitute a great challenge for computational linguistics and one of the major research topics during the last decade. They can be divided in categories describing people, location, time, organization and others. In this paper we will restrict our discussion to proper names that belong to three main classes: personal, location and organization names, and that can be either single-word nouns or multiword expressions. First, we are going to define common (language-independent) semantic patterns for proper names and then we will present the cor-

Svetla Koeva, Cvetana Krstev, Duško Vitas, Tita Kyriacopoulou, Claude Martineau & Tsvetana Dimitrova. 2018. Semantic and syntactic patterns of multiword names: A cross-language study. In Manfred Sailer & Stella Markantonatou (eds.), *Multiword expressions: Insights from a multilingual perspective*, 31–62. Berlin: Language Science Press. DOI:10.5281/zenodo.1182589

responding syntactic patterns in English, Bulgarian, French, Greek, and Serbian. We will compare these patterns regarding grammatical categories of dependent constituents, definiteness, distribution of clitics, word order and various alternations. Our ultimate goal is to build a universal framework for Named Entity Recognition (NER).

1 Introduction

Proper names are usually defined as belonging to the following main classes: personal names, location names, and organization names, called also named entities (NEs). They can be single-word nouns or particular types of multiword expression (MWE).

The aim of this paper is to offer a common template for description and classification of proper names in different languages. Our objectives are: i) to formulate semantic patterns for personal, location and organization names that capture the general semantics and should be, to a great extent, language-neutral; ii) to describe language-specific syntactic patterns corresponding to a common semantic pattern. The syntactic patterns provide information about the grammatical class of the head and constituents; dependencies among the constituents; word order and contiguity; cliticisation (if applicable – for possessive pronoun and interrogative clitics).

This study is based on evidence gathered from five languages – English, Bulgarian, French, Greek, and Serbian – belonging to four different language groups (Germanic, Hellenic, Romance, and Slavic). The utility of language-neutral semantic patterns lies in the fact that they can be applied to new languages, thus paving the way towards more universal solutions for (rule-based) named entity recognition (NER). The set of language-specific syntactic patterns displays correspondences between morphological and syntactic language-specific characteristics, and they may serve as transformation rules in rule-based machine translation, cross-lingual information extraction and summarization.

2 Names: a general overview

In English (Huddleston 1988: 96), two different terms are often used: *proper noun* – referring to the part-of-speech of the word and comprising only single-word proper names, e.g., *John, London, Adidas,* and *proper name* – referring to the function of these words as referential elements and comprising single- and multiword proper names, as in *John, John Smith Junior, London, the United States of America,*

Nike, Microsoft Corporation. Following this distinction, proper names can be further specified as: proper nouns (*Anna, Asia, Google*), multiword expressions (*Jean-Pierre Deckles, New York, the United Nations*), and noun phrases (*Professor Deckles, New York City, the United Nations Organization*). Proper names – expressed either by proper nouns or by MWEs – show common semantic and syntactic behavior and we describe them in a uniform way.

Proper names do not "[d]escribe or specify characteristics of objects" but are "logically connected with characteristics of the object to which they refer" (Searle 1958: 173). For example, *Saint Petersburg* may refer to the second largest city in Russia (*They convened in Saint Petersburg*), a city in Florida, a city in Pennsylvania, the fictional hometown of Tom Sawyer and Huckleberry Finn, *St. Petersburg, Missouri*, but also to a college in Florida – *Saint Petersburg College*. A particular common noun (i.e., *city, street, president, actor*) specifies the object whose instances may be represented by a set of proper names; and such an object is always presupposed for a given proper name even if the common noun is not mentioned explicitly in the text. Furthermore, multiword names may comprise a category word (*square* in *Trafalgar Square*; *ocean* in *the Indian Ocean*), and in these cases, the category of the particular name is always explicitly shown (Carroll 1985: 144).

The relation between a proper name and its category object is reflected in WordNet where the relation between a concept and its instances is defined as an instant hypernym (instant hyponym) relation (Rodríguez et al. 1998). The instances (proper nouns) inherit characteristics from the concepts of the hierarchy to which they belong. For example, the name *Saint Petersburg* is an instance of a city, and the concept {city, metropolis, urban centre} links to the more general concept {region}, which, in its turn, links to an even more general concept {location}.

Different terms are used for common nouns that categorise the referents of proper names as members of different classes: descriptors, designators, category words (Carroll 1985), external evidence (McDonald 1996), triggers (Magnini et al. 2002), trigger words. To avoid confusion with the theory of reference, we will use the term *trigger*.

Triggers depend semantically on the referent of the personal name, and different names select different classes of triggers. In turn, triggers determine the characteristics of the object to which the name refers. For example, if we know that the word *Washington* is a family name, it can select the word *president* or the word *actor*. Further, the word *president* and the word *actor* are similar in the way they designate the concept for a person, and this determines the fact that both nouns can co-occur with adjectives denoting height, age, etc. The meaning of both words also implies that they may be specified by employing expressions for affiliation as complements (*the President of the USA, the actor at the Muppet Theatre*). However, not all words that are compatible with the first noun are compatible with the second (*stage actor* vs. **stage president*). Therefore, the notion of triggers is central for the classification of the semantic patterns of proper names and accordingly – for the description of the respective syntactic patterns.

3 Grammatical features of names in Bulgarian, English, French, Greek and Serbian: a brief overview

Personal names are singular and inherently definite (the same applies to location and organization names that cannot express definiteness). Some Bulgarian, English, French, Greek, and Serbian location and organization names are in singularia tantum or pluralia tantum, or marked for definiteness: with a definite article (English, French, Greek), with a definite article attached to the noun trigger with no pre-nominal modifiers or to the leftmost modifier in Bulgarian, and only with the definite form of adjectives in Serbian.

Bulgarian, French, Greek, and Serbian personal, location (apart from cities in French which usually do not express gender) and organization names are marked for grammatical noun gender – masculine or feminine, in contrast to the English ones. Location and organization names in Bulgarian, Greek and Serbian can be marked for neuter, as well. In Greek and Serbian, proper names have the nominative, accusative, genitive and vocative case. In Serbian, names can also be declined in the dative, locative and instrumental, while in Bulgarian vocative is observed only with some forenames.

Syntactically, proper nouns are heads of noun phrases but show restricted combinatorial properties compared to common nouns. For the five languages discussed in this paper, the forenames can be extended with one or more (rarely more than two) proper nouns: a nickname, a patronym and/or a family name. Agreement in gender and number is observed if they are of Slavic and Greek origin. For feminine surnames of Slavic origin in Serbian, the agreement in gender is allowed but not obligatory. Bulgarian, French, Greek and Serbian adjectives and Bulgarian, French and Serbian possessive pronouns change to agree in gender and number with the nouns they modify. Greek and Serbian adjectives and possessive pronouns agree in case with the head noun.

Compared to personal names, location names have a more diverse structure, while organization names show the highest complexity. Both location and organization names can be proper nouns or proper names, comprising proper and common nouns or noun phrases, which begin to function as names of geographical locations and organizations, respectively.

4 Names and multiword expressions

Many names are composed of more than one word and are classified as multiword names. They can comprise two or more proper nouns (*Ray Jackendoff, Merill Lynch*); common and proper nouns (Bulgarian: *Republika Bălgariya* 'Republic Bulgaria'); adjectives and a proper or a common noun (*International Monetary Fund, Upper Manhattan*); abbreviations (*Financial Advisors Ltd., John Smith Jr., Miami, FL*); numerals or numbers (*the Second Generative Grammar Conference; XX Generative Linguistics Conference*); verbs and adverbs with names of products such as books, movies, songs (*Someone to Watch over Me; Killing Me Softly*), etc.

Anderson (2007) provides a detailed classification of proper names, a subset of which is relevant for our study, as follows: simple opaque names (*John*); simple names that have a resemblance to a common word (*Prudence*); names based on other names (*Lincoln* – for a boulevard); names overtly derived from other names (Slavic family names); names based on compounds, some of them containing a name (*Queensland, Newtown*); names based on longer phrases – they may include another name (*the University of Queensland*) or not (*Long Island, Hen and Chicken Island*); and names based on sentences (as with titles of movies).

An important feature that systematically distinguishes location and organization names from personal names is that the TRIGGERS may be their integral part, constituting a MWE (Bulgarian: *Černo* MORE 'Black SEA',[1] English: PRESIDENT *Roosevelt Boulevard*, First Investment BANK, French: BANQUE *de France* 'BANK of France', Greek: Τράπεζα της Ελλάδος 'BANK of Greece', Serbian: *Jadransko* MORE 'Adriatic SEA', *Međunarodni* SUD *pravde* 'International COURT of Justice').

Carroll (1985) describes the non-classifying part of the location name as a name-stem (e. g., *Trafalgar* in *Trafalgar Square*) and explores rules according to which the name-stem can be used to stand for the whole name. Not only for some location names, but also for some organization names with internal triggers, the name-stem can replace the whole name, e.g., French: LA MAISON D'ÉDITION *Ha-*

---

[1]The translations in the paper are closer to literal translations than to proper ones, e.g., Bulgarian: *Republika Bălgariya* 'Republic Bulgaria' instead of 'Bulgarian Republic' or 'The Republic of Bulgaria', but Greek: ο Έλληνας Πρωθυπουργός 'the Greek PRIME MINISTER' (instead of 'premier', for example).

S. Koeva, C. Krstev, D. Vitas, T. Kyriacopoulou, C. Martineau & T. Dimitrova

chette 'the Hachette PUBLISHING COMPANY' or just *Hachette*, Greek: η Ολυμπιακή 'the Olympic' for Olympic AIRWAYS.

Further, a location name may feature a **personal name** specified by a PERSONAL TRIGGER (*SAN Jorge River*) that cannot be omitted without loss of the name function; similarly, an organization name may feature a **personal name** specified by a PERSONAL TRIGGER (*SAN Jose State University*) or a **location name** specified by a LOCATION TRIGGER (*Los Angeles CITY College*).

For the purposes of our study, we differentiate the names on the basis of their structure: i) whether the name is a MWE or a noun; ii) whether the multiword name obligatorily incorporates a trigger (an internal trigger); and iii) whether the name (either single or a MWE) is optionally specified by a trigger (an external trigger). The external triggers may be explicit or implicit, depending on the context (the City of New York, New York City vs. New York):

- Single-word personal name (*Arthur*).

- Multiword personal name (*Arthur Conan Doyle*).

- Multiword personal name, which incorporates an internal personal trigger. When people are famous, combinations with triggers such as holy, aristocratic and religious titles can be widely used and are stable (*POPE John Paul II*).

- Single-word personal name; it is specified by an external personal trigger (*UNCLE John*). Kinship terms are usually combined with a single-word personal name.

- Multiword personal name; it is specified by an external personal trigger (*PROFESSOR Steven Pinker*).

- Single-word location name (it can coincide or not with a personal name) (*Danube, Washington*).

- Multiword location name (it may - partially - coincide or not with a personal name) (*Little Rock, SAN Antonio*).

- Multiword location name, comprising an internal location trigger (*Rocky MOUNTAINS*). No additional location trigger of the same type can be added; being part of the name, the trigger cannot be omitted either. A multiword location name may include a personal name (and, rarely, an organization name) (*Cristina FORT*).

- Single-word location name; it is specified by an external location trigger (*River Nile*).

- Multiword location name; it is specified by an external location trigger (*volcano Klyučevskaya Sopka*).

- Single-word organization name (it may coincide or not with a personal name or a location name) (*Matalan, Poundland*).

- Multiword organization name (it may (partially) coincide or not with a personal or a location name) (*Mercedes Benz*).

- Multiword organization name, comprising an internal organization trigger as an integral part of the proper name. Another organization trigger of the same type cannot be added. The trigger, which is part of the name, cannot be omitted either. The multiword organization name may include a personal or a location name (*Princess Basma Youth Resource Center*, *Melbourne Grammar School*).

- Single-word organization name; it is specified by an external organization trigger (*Supermarket Galaxy*).

- Multiword organization name; it is specified by an external organization trigger (*the company Business Models Inc.*)

5 Semantic patterns for persons, locations and organizations

Names can be grouped into different semantic classes and subclasses with respect to the properties of their referents (explicated by triggers). A name from a given class (personal, location or organization) selects triggers from a particular set of semantic subclasses. For example, complex personal names are combined with triggers that define a legislative job title, executive job title, judicial position, academic position, academic title, military rank, and profession. The permissible combinations between types of names (proper nouns, MWEs), and semantic subclasses of triggers determine the semantic patterns applicable to the personal, location and organization names. The semantic patterns we propose show semantic compatibility valid for a particular semantic class and describe the permissible combinatory options. For example, a personal name can be extended with a kinship term (i.e., *the beautiful* STEP-DAUGHTER *of John from Paris,* **Anne Nicole**) and the kinship term can be specified in various ways and restricted for possessor and location, thus the respective semantic pattern is: (modifier: referent specification phrase) – trigger: kinship term – (complement: possessor phrase) – (complement: location phrase) – personal name.

As triggers refer to concepts, the semantic relations in which they are involved should be universal and must hold among the relevant concepts in any language. Thus, the semantic patterns describe language-neutral relations and can be regarded as universal structures with correlating language-specific syntactic patterns.

Following the detailed hierarchy employed by Giuliano (2009) for automatic classification of personal NEs, we can conclude that every common noun that determines the referent of a personal name can be a trigger, i.e., words such as *chess-player, singer, footballer,* etc. Magnini et al. (2002) use WordNet hierarchy for identification of large sets of triggers – hyponyms of high-level synsets such as {person}, {location}, {organization}. Some authors suggest verb triggers appearing in the local context of NEs (Zhang et al. 2004), e.g., for water bodies (like rivers) the verb *flooded* in *The Sava flooded the village* indicates that *Sava* is a river and not a person . There are detailed classifications of NEs (of more than 200 categories; cf. Sekine & Nobata 2004), while other classifications build shallow hierarchies with the major classes on the top and sets of subtypes with different granularity at the low levels (ACE 2018; Fleischman & Hovy 2002).

In our study, we distinguish the following semantic subclasses for person, location and organization names and their triggers:

- Persons and personal triggers –legislative job title: *prime minister*; executive job title: *executive officer*; judicial position: *judge*; academic position: *associate professor*; military rank: *major general*; profession: *engineer*; academic title: *Ph.D.*; true honorific: *Mister / Mr.*; aristocratic title: *Prince*; religious title: *Bishop*; kinship term: *sister*; holy title: *Saint.*

- Locations and location triggers –natural: *river*; public: *monument*; commercial: *restaurant*; infrastructure: *boulevard.*

- Organizations and organization triggers –business: *company*; political: *political party*; government: *ministry*; media: *publishing house*; human / non-government: *association.*

We classify proper names (persons, locations and organizations) in the patterns (A) to (I) below according to their shared features. Patterns are described in terms of the categories (a)-(d): (a) the semantic subclass of the trigger; (b) the type of the proper name that selects triggers; (c) obligatoriness / optionality of the trigger manifested by an internal or external trigger with respect to the name; (d) the semantic pattern that the proper name evokes.

5.1 Pattern A

(a) Semantic class of the trigger: legislative job title, executive job title, judicial position, academic position, academic title, military rank, profession. Specification of military ranks and top-level legislative, executive, and judicial triggers is not allowed: *prime minister of finance; lower level legislative triggers can be specified: engineer in automatics. (b) Type of the proper name: personal name extended or substituted by a family name. (c) External trigger. (d) Semantic pattern: (referent specification phrase) – trigger – (domain specification phrase) – (possessor phrase) – (affiliation phrase) – (location phrase).

Example: English: (*his* | *Stefan's*) (*new*) PROFESSOR (*of law*) (*at the University*) (*in Plovdiv*) **Ivan Ivanov.**

5.2 Pattern B

(a) Semantic class of the trigger: aristocratic title, religious title. (b) Type of the proper name: personal name or family name. Some aristocratic and religious titles are selected only by a personal name (POPE **Francis**), while others are selected by a family name (LORD **Orsini**). A trigger can also be part of a personal name (for distinguished persons) but no separate pattern is defined for this type of name. (c) External trigger. (d) Semantic pattern: (referent specification phrase) – TRIGGER – (affiliation phrase) – (location phrase).

Example: English: *the* (*new*) METROPOLITAN (*of the Church*) (*in San Francisco*) **Iona.**

5.3 Pattern C

(a) Semantic class of the trigger: kinship term. (b) Type of the proper name: personal name (rarely modified by family name(s)). (c) External trigger. (d) Semantic pattern: (referent specification phrase) – TRIGGER – (possessor phrase) – (location phrase).

Example: English: (*his* | *Ivan's*) (*blond*) STEP-BROTHER (*from Sofia*) **Stefan.**

5.4 Pattern D

(a) Semantic class of the trigger: holy title (a limited set of words). (b) Type of the proper name: personal name (rarely modified or substituted by a nickname). (c) External trigger. (d) Semantic pattern: (referent specification phrase) – TRIGGER – (location phrase).

Example: English: (*miraculous*) SAINT (*from Patara*) **Nicholas**.

5.5 Pattern E

(a) Semantic class of the trigger: true honorific. (b) Type of the proper name: personal name extended or substituted by a family name. (c) External trigger. (d) Semantic pattern: – trigger

Example: English: MONSIEUR **Ivan Ivanov**.

5.6 Pattern F

(a) Semantic class of the trigger: location. (b) Type of the proper name: location name. (c) External trigger. (d) Semantic pattern: (referent specification phrase) – TRIGGER – (specification phrase) – (possessor phrase) – (location phrase)

Example: English: *the* (*beautiful*) CITY (*near the big river*), **Plovdiv**.

5.7 Pattern G

(a) Semantic class of the trigger: location. (b) Type of the proper name: location name. (c) Internal trigger. (d) Semantic pattern: (referent specification phrase) – internal TRIGGER – (location phrase)

Example: English: *the* (*beautiful*) MOUNT **Fuji** (*in Japan*).

5.8 Pattern H

(a) Semantic class of the trigger: organization. (b) Type of the proper name: organization name. (c) External trigger. (d) Semantic pattern: (referent specification phrase) – TRIGGER – (domain specification phrase) – (possessor phrase) – (affiliation phrase) – (location phrase).

Example: English: *the* (*new*) COMPANY (*of his friends*) (*in Athens*), **Tetracom**.

5.9 Pattern I

(a) Semantic class of the trigger: organization. (b) Type of the proper name: organization name. (c) Internal trigger. (d) Semantic pattern: (referent specification phrase) – internal TRIGGER – (location phrase).

Example: English: *the (new)* **Hebros** BANK *(in Athens)*.

6 Language-specific syntactic patterns for persons, locations and organizations

We define the semantic patterns evoked by different types of proper names when combined with triggers, and the syntactic patterns that involve combinations of: modifiers, one or several, semantically restricted by the head proper noun and the trigger, and complements, semantically restricted by the trigger.

The syntactic patterns are language-specific and differ for personal, location and organization names. The syntactic patterns may involve combinations of adjectival modifiers in pre- or post-nominal position, one or several; pronoun modifiers in pre-nominal position (possessive and demonstrative); complements in post-nominal position, one or several; and a noun modifier in pre- or post-nominal position, alternating with a prepositional phrase.[2] Adjectival modifiers (that in Bulgarian, French, Greek and Serbian agree with the head noun in gender and number) may indicate physical shape, status, etc. Complements may indicate (domain) specification, affiliation, location, possessor, and may be prepositional or case complements, depending on the language structure.

Multiword names have the structure of a noun phrase and exhibit specific properties with respect to constituency of the head noun and the components, including various constraints on modifiers, complements, clitics (in Bulgarian and Greek), etc.

The syntactic patterns represent language-specific grammatical features and dependencies and how these features and dependencies are manifested in a particular language. One or more syntactic patterns from one or different languages may correspond to the same semantic pattern. The syntactic patterns, as they are presented in this paper, define constituency and reflect the morphological and syntactic structure of a particular language, although they do not strictly describe phrase structure and grammatical dependencies. However, the syntactic

---

[2]The *noun modifier – prepositional phrase* alternation is not described in the syntactic patterns.

patterns are formal enough to code the linguistic information correctly and to allow for the conversion to some formalism.

Syntactic patterns corresponding to the largely universal semantic patterns, described in §5, are formulated for English, Bulgarian, French, Greek, and Serbian. The generalizations for semantic patterns and respective syntactic patterns were constructed on the basis of observations and classifications made on dictionaries of NEs, annotated corpora of NEs and grammars for NE recognition developed so far (Krstev et al. 2013; Koeva & Dimitrova 2015).

6.1 Syntactic pattern A (single family name or multiword personal name)

Characteristics shared by the five languages[3]: i) Triggers are placed to the left of the personal name; a complex trigger phrase is likely to be an apposition[4]. Examples: English: *the new* PROFESSOR *of Sustainable Agriculture and Climate Change,* **Chris Smith** or **Chris Smith**, *the new* PROFESSOR *of Law at the University's Humanities Institute;* French: *Le nouveau* PROFESSEUR *de morale de l'Université de Fribourg,* **Thierry Collaud** 'the new PROFESSOR in ethics at the University of Fribourg, Thierry Collaud'or *Thierry Collaud, le nouveau* PROFESSEUR *de morale de l'Université de Fribourg* 'Thierry Collaud, the new PROFESSOR in ethics at the University of Fribourg'; ii) If no modifiers or complements exist, the trigger is indefinite (except for Greek where the article is obligatory); otherwise, it is definite. Examples: Bulgarian: MINISTĂR **Kuneva** 'MINISTER **Kuneva**' versus *noviyat* MINISTĂR *v pravitelstvoto* **Ivan Dimitrov** 'new-the MINISTER in government-the **Ivan Dimitrov**'; English: PROFESSOR **Chomsky** versus *the* PROFESSOR *of linguistics* **Noam Chomsky**; iii) personal names can be extended with one or more (rarely more than two) proper names: a nickname, a patronym and/or a family name, constituting a MWE. Example: Serbian: DR **Slavica Đukić-Dejanović**, PREDSED-NIK *Narodne skupštine* 'DR. **Slavica Đukić-Dejanović**, PRESIDENT of National Assembly'.[5]

---

[3]Language specific characteristics were also formulated but due to limitation of space they are represented only in the syntactic patterns.

[4]The restrictive apposition of a proper noun (whose omission changes the meaning of the sentence) is covered by the syntactic patterns (*the new* PROFESSOR *of Law,* **Chris Smith**). The non-restrictive apposition (**Chris Smith** , *the new* PROFESSOR *of Law*) is not included due to limitation of space. In this paper, the term apposition is used for the "non-restrictive apposition" only.

[5]The vertical bar – |, separates alternatives. The question mark indicates zero or one occurrences of the preceding element. The asterisk "*", indicates zero or more occurrences of the preceding element. Parentheses "()", are used to define the scope and precedence of the operators. The equality sign =, indicates the semantics of the prepositions and case phrases.

English: (((DefArt|GenDet|GPossPron) Adj* Trigger (PP *in*|*of*|*for* = *DomSpec*)? (PP *at* = *Aff*)* (PP *in* = *Loc*)?) | (DefArt Trigger (PP *in*|*of*|*for* = *DomSpec*)? (PP *at*|*of* = *Aff*)* (PP *in* = *Loc*)?) | IndefTrigger) **PerN**

Bulgarian: (((DefAdj (PossCL)?) | **DefPossPron**) Adj* Trigger (PP *po*|*na*|*za* = *Dom-Spec*)? (PP *na*|*pri*|*v*|*kăm*|*ot* = *Aff*)*) (PP *ot* = *Loc*)?) | (DefTrigger (PossCL)? (PP *po*|*na*|*za* = *DomSpec*)?   (PP *na*|*pri*|*v*|*kăm*|*ot* = *Aff*)*   (PP *ot* = *Loc*)?) | IndefTrigger) **PerN**

French: (((DefArt|PossPron) Adj* Trigger (PP *en*|*de* = *DomSpec*)? (PP *à* =*Aff*)* (PP *à* = *Loc*)?) | (DefArt Trigger Adj* (PP *en*|*de* = *DomSpec*)? (PP *à*|*de* = *Aff*)* (PP *à* = *Loc*)?) | IndefTrigger) **PerN**

Greek: ((DefArt Adj* (PossPron)? Trigger (GenP = *DomSpec*)? (PP σε = *Aff*)* (PP σε = *Loc*)?) | (DefArt Trigger (GenP = *DomSpec*)? (GenP = *Aff*)* (PP σε = *Loc*)?) | DefTrigger) **PerN**

Serbian: ((Adv | PossPron)? DefAdj* Trigger (PP *za*| GenP = *DomSpec*)? (PP *u*|*pri* | GenP = *Aff*)* (PP *u*|*za*|*iz* GenP = *Loc*)?) **PerN**

Table 1: Syntactic pattern A – an example translated in the five languages. The examples do not illustrate all variants.

English	Spain's SECRETARY of State for Foreign Affairs, **Gonzalo de Benito Secades**
Bulgarian	Dăržavniyat SEKRETAR na vănšnite raboti na Ispaniya, **Gonzalo de Benito Sekades**
French	le MINISTRE espagnol des Affaires Etrangères, **Gonzalo de Benito Secades**
Greek	ο Ισπανός Υπουργός Εξωτερικών, ***Gonzalo de Benito Secades***
Serbian	Državni SEKRETAR za spoljne poslove Španije, ***Gonzalo de Benito Sekades***

6.2 Syntactic pattern B (single- or multiword personal name)

Characteristics shared by the five languages: i) The trigger phrase is placed in front of the personal name but the appositive order can also be found, especially if the trigger phrase is complex. Examples: English: ***Venerable Dionysius,*** *the* ARCHIMANDRITE *of St Sergius' Monastery*; Serbian: *njegovo preosveštenstvo* EPISKOP *niški* **Irinej** 'His Grace Bɪsнop of-Niš **Irinej**'; ii) If no trigger modifiers or complements exist, the trigger is indefinite (except for Greek where the article is obligatory); otherwise, it is definite. Examples: Bulgarian: Pᴀᴛʀɪᴀʀʜ **Maksim** 'Pᴀᴛʀɪᴀʀᴄʜ **Maxim**'; French: *L'ᴀʀᴄʜᴇᴠÊQᴜᴇ de Paris, Monseigneur* **André Vingt-Trois** 'the Aʀᴄʜʙɪsʜop of Paris, Monsignor **André Vingt-Trois**'; *Le bienheureux* PÈʀᴇ **Brottier** 'the blessed ғᴀᴛʜᴇʀ **Brottier**'; iii) personal names can be extended with one or more (rarely more than two) proper names: a nickname, a patronym and/or a family name. These constituents form a complex name (MWE). Example: Greek: ο πρόσφατα χειροτονηθείς Σεβασμιότατος Μητροπολίτης Κεφαλληνίας, πατέρας **Γεώργιος Σαπουνάς** 'the newly appointed Most Reverend Bɪsʜop Mᴇᴛʀopoʟɪᴛᴀɴ of Kefalonia, ғᴀᴛʜᴇʀ **Georgios Sapounas**'.

English: ((DefArt Adj* Tʀɪɢɢᴇʀ (PP *of* = *Aff*)* (PP *in* = *Loc*)?) | (DefArt Tʀɪɢɢᴇʀ (PP *at/of* = *Aff*)* (PP *in* = *Loc*)?) | IɴᴅᴇғTʀɪɢɢᴇʀ) **PerN**

Bulgarian: (((DefAdj (PossCL)? | DefPossPron) Adj* Tʀɪɢɢᴇʀ (PP *na|pri|v|kăm| ot* = *Aff*)? (PP *ot* = *Loc*)?) | (DᴇғTʀɪɢɢᴇʀ (PP *na|pri|v|kăm|ot* = *Aff*)? (PP *ot* = *Loc*)?) | IɴᴅᴇғTʀɪɢɢᴇʀ) **PerN**

French: ((DefArt Adj* Tʀɪɢɢᴇʀ (PP *de* = *Aff*)* (PP *à|en* = *Loc*)?) | (DefArt Tʀɪɢɢᴇʀ* Adj* (PP *de* = *Aff*)* (PP *à|en* = *Loc*)?) | IɴᴅᴇғTʀɪɢɢᴇʀ) **PerN**

Greek: ((DefArt Adj* Tʀɪɢɢᴇʀ (GenP = *Aff*)* (GenP = *Loc*)?) | (DefArt Tʀɪɢɢᴇʀ (GenP = *Aff* | *Loc*)* (PP σε = *Loc*)?) | DᴇғTʀɪɢɢᴇʀ) **PerN**

Serbian: (((PossPron | PossAdj) Tʀɪɢɢᴇʀ) | (DefAdj* Tʀɪɢɢᴇʀ) | (Tʀɪɢɢᴇʀ DefAdj?)) (PP *u|za| GenP* = *Aff*)? (PP *u|za|iz GenP* = *Loc*)?) **PerN** DefAdj*

Table 2: Syntactic pattern B – an example translated in the five languages.

English	*the new* BISHOP *of the Christian Catholic Church of Switzerland,* Dʀ **Harald Rein**
Bulgarian	*noviyat* EPISKOP *na Hristiyanskata katoličeska cărkva v Šveycariya,* ᴅ-ʀ **Harald Rein**
French	*le nouvel* EVÊQUE *de l'Eglise catholique-chrétienne de la Suisse,* Dʀ **Harald Rein**
Greek	ο νέος Αρχιεπίσκοπος της Χριστιανικής Καθολικής Εκκλησίας της Ελβετίας, Δρ. **Harald Rein**
Serbian	*novoimenovani* BISKUP *Starokatoličke crkve Švajcarske,* ᴅʀ **Harald Rajn**

6.3 Syntactic pattern C (single- or, rarely, multiword personal name)

Characteristics shared by the five languages: i) The usual position of the trigger is in front of the personal name. The reverse order indicates apposition. Examples: Bulgarian: *moyata hubava* SESTRA **Ana** 'my-the beautiful SISTER **Anna**'; Greek: η αδερφή του Πέτρου, η **Μαρία** 'the SISTER of Peter, the **Maria**'; η **Μαρία**, η αδερφή του Πέτρου 'the **Maria**, the SISTER of Peter'. ii) The trigger is accompanied by modifiers or complements. Examples: English: *his older* STEP-BROTHER *from Paris,* **Stefan**; Serbian: *njegov rođeni* BRAT *četvorogodišnji* **Zoran** 'his birth BROTHER 4-year-old **Zoran**'; iii) The phrase headed by the trigger is definite. Examples: French: *la* SŒUR *de Marc,* **Marie** 'the SISTER of Marc, **Maria**' vs. *sa* SŒUR, **Marie** 'his SISTER, **Maria**'; *son* BEAU-FRÈRE *de Paris,* **Jean** 'his BROTHER-IN-LAW from Paris, **John**'.

English: (((DefArt | GenDet | PossPron) Adj* TRIGGER (PP *from* = Loc)?) | (DefArt Adj* TRIGGER (PP *of* = Poss[6])? (PP *from* = Loc)?)) **PerN**

Bulgarian: (((DefAdj (PossCL)?) | DefPossPron) Adj* TRIGGER (PP *ot* = Loc)?) | ((DefTRIGGER (PossCL)?) (PP *ot* = Loc)?) | (DefAdj Adj* TRIGGER (PP *na* = Poss)?) | (DefTRIGGER (PP *na* = Poss)?)) **PerN**

French: (DefArt | PossPron) Adj* TRIGGER ((PP *de* = PerN) | (PP *de* = Loc)?) **PerN**

Greek: (DefArt Adj* TRIGGER ((GenP = PerN) | (GenP = Poss))? (PP από DefArt = Loc)?) DefArt **PerN**

Serbian: (PerN* TRIGGER* (DefAdj* | (GenP = PerN))? (PP *iz* = Loc)?) **PerN** | (PossPron? DefAdj* TRIGGER* (PP *iz* = Loc)?) **PerN**

Table 3: Syntactic pattern C – an example translated in the five languages.

English	his beautiful SISTER-IN-LAW from Athens, **Maria**
Bulgarian	negovata krasiva SNAHA ot Atina, **Maria**
French	sa jolie BELLE-SOEUR d'Athènes, **Maria**
Greek	η όμορφη κουνιάδα του από την Αθήνα, η **Μαρία**
Serbian	njegova lepa SNAJA iz Atine, **Marija**

---

[6]The possessor phrase is shown only for the kinship terms.

6.4 Syntactic pattern D (single- and, rarely, multiword personal name)

Characteristics shared by the five languages: i) The trigger appears before the personal name but a complex trigger phrase often occurs in apposition. Examples: English: SAINT **Haralambos**, *the Holy* MARTYR *of Magnesia*; Serbian: SVETI *mučenik i arhiđakon* **Lavrentije** 'SAINT martyr and archdeacon **Lavrentije**'. ii) If no modifiers or complements exist, the trigger is indefinite (except for Greek where the article is obligatory); otherwise, it is definite. Examples: Bulgarian: SVETI **Nikola** 'SAINT **Nicholas**'; French: *le* SAINT *de l'Arcadie:* **Charles De Menou D'Aulnay** 'the SAINT of Arcadia: **Charles De Menou D'Aulnay**'.

English: (DefArt Adj* TRIGGER (PP *of*|*from* = *Loc*)? **PerN**) | (DefArt Adj* TRIGGER **PerN** (PP *of*|*from* = *Loc*)?) | (TRIGGER **PerN** (PP *of*|*from* = *Loc*)?)

Bulgarian: (((DefAdj (PossCL)? | DefPossPron) Adj* TRIGGER (PP *na*|*ot* = *Loc*)?) | (DefAdj Adj* TRIGGER (PP *na*|*ot* = *Loc*)?) | (DEFTRIGGER (PP *na*|*ot* = *Loc*)?) | INDEFTRIGGER) **PerN**

French: (DefArt Adj* TRIGGER (PP *de* = *Loc*)? **PerN**) | (TRIGGER Adj* **PerN** (PP *de* = *Loc*)?)

Greek: (DefArt Adj* TRIGGER (GenP = *Loc*)? **PerN**) | (DefArt TRIGGER **PerN** (GenP = *Loc*)?)

Serbian: (PossPron? DefAdj* TRIGGER ((PP *iz*|*u*|*sa* = *Loc*)? DefAdj? (N)?) **PerN** PossAdj? | **PerN** PossAdj? (PP *iz*|*u*|*sa* = *Loc*)?)

Table 4: Syntactic pattern D – an example translated in the five languages.

English	the Holy MARTYR **Chrysostomos** of Smyrna
Bulgarian	Svetiyat MĂČENIK **Hrisostom** ot Smirna
French	le Saint MARTYR **Chryssostomos** de Smyrne
Greek	ο Άγιος Ιερομάρτυρας **Χρυσόστομος** Σμύρνης
Serbian	Sveti MUČENIK **Hrizostom** Smirnski

6.5 Syntactic pattern E (family name or multiword personal name)

Characteristics shared by the five languages: i) The external trigger usually appears before the personal name, except for some triggers that can also appear after the personal name. Examples: English: *Mr. Smith*; Serbian: *Dušan Rašković*, DIPL. OEC.; ii) No modifiers and/or complements are allowed. Example: French: *M. Dupont* 'Mr. Dupont'; iii) If the trigger is indefinite, an article is not permissible (except for Greek where the article is obligatory). Example: English: *(the) Dr. Livingstone*; iv) personal names can be extended with one or more (rarely more than two) proper names: a nickname, a patronym and/or a family name that form a complex name (MWE). Example: Bulgarian: GOSPODIN *Ivan Ivanov* 'MISTER **Ivan Ivanov**'.

English: Bulgarian: French: INDEFTRIGGER **PerN**

Greek: DefArt TRIGGER **PerN**

Serbian: (TRIGGER **PerN**) | (**PerN** TRIGGER)

Table 5: Syntactic pattern E – an example translated in the five languages.

English	DR. *Mary Andrew Smith*
Bulgarian	D-R *Meri Andryu Smit*
French	DR *Mary Andrew Smith*
Greek	η Δρ. Μαίρη Άντριου Σμιθ
Serbian	DR *Meri Endru Smit*

6.6 Syntactic pattern F (single- or multiword location name)

Characteristics shared by the five languages: i) The trigger appears before the personal name. A heavy trigger phrase is often found in apposition. Examples: Greek: η όμορφη πόλη των Παρισίων / του Παρισιού 'the beautiful CITY of **Paris**'; η Σαντορίνη, το πιο όμορφο νησί της Ελλάδας 'the **Santorini**, the most beautiful ISLAND in Greece'. ii) The phrase headed by the trigger is definite. Examples: English: *the beautiful CITY of artists, **Plovdiv**; our beautiful CITY, **Plovdiv***; French: *la belle VILLE des mille fontaines, **Aix-en-Provence*** 'the beautiful CITY of thousand fountains, **Aix-en-Provence**'; iii) Location names can be MWEs. Examples: Bulgarian: HRAM-PAMETNIK *Sveti Aleksandăr Nevski* 'CATHEDRAL Saint **Alexander Nevski**'; Serbian: NADOŠLI *Beli Timok* 'RISING **Beli Timok**'.

English: (((DefArt | GenDet | PossPron) Adj* Trigger (PP *of = Spec*)? (PP *in = Loc*)?) | (DefArt Trigger (PP *of = Spec*)?) | IndefTrigger) **LocN**

Bulgarian: (((DefAdj (PossCL)? | DefPossPron) Adj* Trigger (PP *na = Spec*)? (PP *v|na|pri = Loc*)?) | (DefTrigger (PP *na = Spec*)? (PP *v|na|pri = Loc*)?) | IndefTrigger) **LocN**

French: (((DefArt | PossPron) Adj* Trigger (PP *de = Spec*)? (PP *de = Loc*)?) | (DefArt Trigger Adj* (PP *de = Spec*)?)) **LocN**

Greek: (((DefArt | PossPron) Adj* Trigger (GenP *= Spec*)? (PP σε *= Loc*)?) | (DefArt Trigger (GenP)?)) **LocN**

Serbian: ((PossPron | PossAdj)? DefAdj* Trigger (PP *u|na|pri|pod|u blizini| GenP = Loc*)?) **LocN**

Table 6: Syntactic pattern F – an example translated in the five languages.

English	the most romantic CITY in the world, **Paris**
Bulgarian	nay-romantičniyat GRAD v sveta, **Pariž**
French	la plus romantique VILLE dans le monde, **Paris**
Greek	η πιο ρομαντική πόλη του κόσμου, το **Παρίσι**
Serbian	najromantičniji GRAD na svetu, **Pariz**

6.7 Syntactic pattern G (multiword location name)

Characteristics shared by the five languages: i) The internal trigger is part of the location name, thus the location name is always a MWE. Examples: Bulgarian: *našiyat hubav* GRAD **Novi hAN** 'our-the beautiful CITY **Novi han**'; Greek: ο Ινδικός Ωκεανός 'the **Indian OCEAN**'; ii) A location name with an internal trigger is fixed, the order of constituents cannot be changed and insertions are not allowed. Examples: Bulgarian: *našata Stara* PLANINA 'our-the **Stara PLANINA**', **PLANINA stara*; French: *le célèbre* MONT *Blanc* 'the famous **MONT Blanc**', **Blanc* MONT. iii) The location name may contain a personal or a location name (rarely an organization name). Example: English: **Minnesota RIVER**; iv) The internal trigger may be specified by the same range of modifiers and complements permissible for the trigger.[7] Example: Bulgarian: *Černi* VRĂH 'Black PEAK'; v) External trigger can be added if different from the internal one. Example: English: CITY *of Colorado* SPRINGS; vi) Heavy trigger phrases often occur as appositions. Example: Serbian: *Novo Brdo, najveći rudarski* GRAD *u Srbiji i na celom Balkan- skom poluostrvu* 'New Hill, biggest mining TOWN in Serbia and on the entire Balkan Peninsula'.

English: ((DefArt | GenDet | PossPron) Adj* MWLocN (PP *in* = Loc)?) | (DefArt MWLocN (PP *in* = Loc)?) | MWLocN

Bulgarian: (((DefAdj (PossCL)?) | DefPossPron) Adj* MWLocN (PP *v|na|pri* = Loc)?) | (DefMWLocN (PP *v|na|pri* = Loc)?) | MWLocN

French: ((DefArt | PossPron) Adj* MWLocN (PP *de* = Loc)?) | (MWLocN (PP *de* = Loc)?) | MWLocN

Greek: ((DefArt | PossPron) Adj* MWLocN (GenP = Loc)?) | (DefMWLocN (GenP = Loc)?) | MWLocN

Serbian: ((PossPron | PossAdj)? DefAdj* (PP *u|na|pri|pod|u blizini* | GenP = Loc)?) MWLocN | GenP = Loc)?) | MWLocN

Table 7: Syntactic pattern G – an example translated in all five languages.

English	the vast **Great** PLAINS in the United States
Bulgarian	neobyatnite **Golemi** RAVNINI v Săedinenite štati
French	les **Grandes** PLAINES aux Etats-Unis
Greek	τα *Great* PLAINS της Αμερικής
Serbian	prostrane **Velike** RAVNICE u Sjedinjenim Državama

6.8 Syntactic pattern H (single- and multiword organization name)

Characteristics shared by the five languages: i) The trigger may either be placed before or after the organization name in case of apposition. Examples: Bulgarian: *hranitelnata* KOMPANIYA *"Danon"* 'nutritional-the COMPANY **Danone**'; English:

---

[7]For simplicity, not all variants are presented in the syntactic pattern (applicable also to Syntactic pattern I in §6.9).

Apache CORP. ii) The phrase headed by the trigger is definite. If the trigger is a single-word one or specified for domain, the trigger phrase may be indefinite (except for Greek where the article is obligatory). Examples: English: *the* COMPANY *of Buffett,* **Berkshire Hathaway**; Bulgarian: *investicionen* FOND *"Razvitie"* 'investment FUND **Razvitie**'; French: *la nouvelle* COMPAGNIE **Santus** 'the new COMPANY **Santus**', *notre nouvelle* COMPAGNIE **Santus** 'our new COMPANY **Santus**', *la nouvelle* COMPAGNIE *de Pierre,* **Santus** 'the new COMPANY of Pierre, **Santus**'; iii) The organization name can be a MWE – either a complex personal or location name or a fixed multiword organization name. Examples: Bulgarian: *novoto* UČILIŠTE *za deca s uvreden sluh v Sofiya* **"Prof. Dr. Dečo Denev"** 'new-the school for children with impaired hearing in Sofia **Prof. Dr. Dečo Denev**'; Greek: η μεταλλευτική εταιρία **Ελληνικός Χρυσός** 'the mining COMPANY **Hellas Gold**', η **Ελληνικός Χρυσός**, μεταλλευτική εταιρία 'the **Hellas Gold** mining COMPANY'; Serbian: FAB-RIKA *mašina* **"Ivo Lola Ribar"** 'Machine FACTORY **"Ivo Lola Ribar"**'.

English: (((DefArt | GenDet | PossPron) Adj* TRIGGER (PP *in*|*at* = DomSpec)? (PP *inat* = Loc)?) | (DefArt Adj* TRIGGER (PP *inat* = DomSpec)? (PP *in*|*at* = Loc)?) | TRIGGER) OrgN

Bulgarian: (((DefAdj (PossCL)?) | DefPossPron) Adj* TRIGGER (PP *po*|*na*|*za* = DomSpec)?   (PP *v*|*na*|*pri* = Loc)?) | ((DEFTRIGGER (PossCL)?) (PP *po*|*na*|*za* =DomSpec)? (PP *v*|*na*|*pri* = Loc)?) | TRIGGER) OrgN

French: (((DefArt | PossPron) Adj* TRIGGER (PP *de* = DomSpec)?) | (DefArt Adj* TRIGGER (PP *de* = PersN)?) | (DefArt TRIGGER)) (PP σε DefArt = **OrgN**)

Greek: ((DefArt Adj* TRIGGER (PossPron)? ((PP για = DomSpec?) | (Gen = DomSpec)?) | (DefArt Adj* TRIGGER (GenDet)?) | (DefArt TRIGGER)) (PP σε DefArt = **OrgN**)

Serbian: (PossPron? DefAdj* TRIGGER (PP *za* | GenP = DomSpec)? (PP *u*|*pri*| GenP = Aff)? (PP *iz*|*u*| GenP = Loc)? **OrgN**) | (OrgN TRIGGER)

Table 8: Syntactic pattern H – an example translated in the five languages.

English	China's investment BANK, **China International Capital Corporation Limited**
Bulgarian	**kitayskata** investicionna BANKA China International Capital Corporation Limited
French	la BANQUE d'Investissements en Chine, **China International Capital Corporation Limited**
Greek	η Τράπεζα Επενδύσεων της Κίνας, η *China International Capital Corporation Limited*
Serbian	kineska investiciona BANKA, **Kineska međunarodna kapitalna korporacija**

6.9 Syntactic pattern I (multiword organization name)

Characteristics shared by the five languages: i) The trigger is an integral part of the organization name, thus the organization name is always a MWE. Examples: English: *the European* BANK *for Reconstruction and Development in Serbia; the* ASSOCIATION *of Chartered Certified Accountants;* Greek: η Τράπεζα Εμπορίου και Ανάπτυξης της Μαύρης Θάλασσας 'the Black Sea Trade and Development BANK'. ii) Organization names containing an integral trigger are fixed, the order of constituents cannot be changed and insertions are not allowed. Examples: Bulgarian: *Evropeyska* BANKA *za văzstanovyavane i razvitie* 'European BANK for Reconstruction and Development'; *novosăzdadeniyat Evropeyski* FOND *za strategičeski investicii* 'newly-found-the European FUND for Strategic Investment'; iii) organization names with an integral trigger can contain a personal, location or organization name. Example: Serbian: *Memorijalni* CENTAR "*Josip Broz Tito*" 'Memorial CENTER "Josip Broz Tito"'; iv) The internal organization trigger can be specified by the same range of modifiers and complements permissible for it in a regular use. Example: French: L'ASSOCIATION *des Historiens* 'the ASSOCIATION of Historians'; v) Rarely, an organization trigger, different from the integral trigger, can specify the multiword organization name. Examples: Bulgarian: SĂYUZ *na tărgovcite v Bălgariya* 'UNION of traders-the in Bulgaria' ; ASOCIACIYA "SĂYUZ *na tărgovcite v Bălgariya*" 'ASSOCIATION UNION of traders-the in Bulgaria'.

English: (DefArt | PossPron) Adj* **MWOrgN** (PP *at|in = Loc*)?) | (**DefMWOrgN** (PP *at|in = Loc*)?) | **MWOrgN**

Bulgarian: (((DefAdj (PossCL)?) | DefPossPron) Adj* **MWOrgN** (PP *v|na|pri = Loc*)?) | (**DefMWOrgN** (PP *v|na|pri = Loc*)?) | **MWOrgN**

French: (DefArt | PossPron) Adj* **MWOrgN** (PP *à de = Loc*)?

Greek: ((DefArt | PossPron) Adj* **MWOrgN** (PP σε = *Loc*)?) | (DefArt **MWOrgN** (GenP = *Loc*)?) | **MWOrgN**

Serbian: (PossPron? DefAdj* **MWOrgN** (GenP = *Poss*)? (PP *iz|u| GenP = Loc*)?) | **MWOrgN**

Table 9: Syntactic pattern I – an example translated in all five languages.

English	World Association for Small and Medium Enterprises
Bulgarian	Svetovna asociaciya za malki i sredni predpriyatiya
French	Association Mondiale des Petites et Moyennes Entreprises
Greek	Διεθνής Σύνδεσμος Μικρομεσαίων Επιχειρήσεων
Serbian	Svetsko udruženje malih i srednjih preduzeća

7 Comparison of the five languages

At the semantic level, languages do not differ (significantly). The semantic patterns of proper names define the common semantics, regardless of the language in which it is realized: semantic patterns are language-neutral. Languages differ in lexical and phrasal categories, constituency, word order permutations and alterations. The differences in word order and alterations insert some nuances in the expressed meaning, i.e., the viewpoint of the speaker, but they do not alter the general meaning. The syntactic patterns of proper names show the correspondences among languages at the syntactic level: syntactic patterns are language-specific. A semantic pattern is a representation that can be linked with different syntactic frames in different languages and, vice versa, syntactic patterns from different languages may share a single semantic pattern. Thus, syntactic patterns make explicit the similarities and differences in the grammatical structure of the five languages.

The structure of the language-neutral semantic and language-specific syntactic patterns can be represented as a graph whose nodes are semantic and syntactic patterns while the arcs represent different languages. More than one language-specific syntactic pattern may be linked to one language-neutral semantic frame; in such a case, syntactic patterns are synonymous to the extent that they represent a common semantic structure. Through this type of representation, we offer an interlingual mapping of the syntactic structures of named entities in the five languages. Some of the most distinctive grammatical characteristics of NEs in English, Bulgarian, French, Greek and Serbian with respect to the single and multiword morphology and syntax will be outlined below.

7.1 Grammatical categories of dependent constituents

The syntactic patterns of English proper name triggers involve combinations of adjectival modifiers in pre-nominal position, one or several (they can be preceded by a definite article) ('*the great POET Burns*'); possessive pronoun modifiers in pre-nominal position ('*Welcome our new PROFESSOR, Jennifer S. Locke!*'); prepositional complements in post-nominal position; a noun modifier in pre-nominal position, alternating with a genitive determiner and a prepositional phrase, e.g., *the Grieg Piano* CONCERTO vs. *Grieg's Piano* CONCERTO vs. *the Piano* CONCERTO *by Grieg*.

In Bulgarian, the syntactic patterns for proper name triggers exhibit the following combinations: adjectival modifiers in pre-nominal position (*noviyat PRED-SEDATEL Petrov* 'new-the CHAIR Petrov'); possessive pronoun modifiers in pre-nominal position alternating with a possessive pronoun clitic in post-nominal position (*moyata sestra* Ana 'my-the SISTER Ana' vs. *SESTRA mi Ana* 'SISTER my.PossCL Ana'); prepositional complements in post-nominal position (*KOM-PANIYATA na Ivan* "Elit" 'COMPANY-THE of Ivan "Elit"'); and a noun modifier in pre-nominal position, alternating with a PP (*karate INSTRUKTORĂT Ivan* 'karate TRAINER-THE Ivan' vs. *INSTRUCTORĂT po karate Ivan* 'TRAINER-THE in karate Ivan').

In French, the phrase headed by a trigger is definite (with an alternation of the phrase with a definite article or possessive pronoun: *la belle VILLE des Mille Fontaines, Aix-en-Provence* 'the beautiful CITY of thousand fountains, Aix-en-Provence'; *notre belle VILLE, Paris* 'our beautiful CITY, Paris'). The proper name can be introduced by a preposition: *la belle VILLE de Paris* 'the beautiful CITY of Paris'; *notre belle VILLE de Paris* 'our beautiful CITY of Paris'.

In Greek, simple and multiword proper names are preceded by a definite article, e.g., το Παρίσι 'the Paris', οι Ηνωμένες Πολιτείες Αμερικής 'the United

States of America'. The phrase headed by the trigger is also definite: η όμορφη πόλη των καταρρακτών, **η Έδεσσα** 'the beautiful CITY of waterfalls, the **Edessa**'; η όμορφή μας πόλη, η Έδεσσα 'the beautiful our.PossCL CITY, the **Edessa**'. A location name can be put in the genitive case: η όμορφη πόλη του **Παρισιού** 'the beautiful CITY of **Paris**'. In that case, the use of the possessive pronoun clitic is not possible: *η όμορφή μας πόλη του **Παρισιού** 'the beautiful our.PossCL CITY of **Paris**'.

The syntactic patterns for Serbian names comprise combinations of adjectival modifiers in pre-nominal position (***Američka filmska*** AKADEMIJA 'American **Film** ACADEMY'); sometimes they can be found in post-nominal position (EPISKOP *niški* **Irinej** 'BISHOP of-Niš **Irinej**'); prepositional complements in post-nominal position (AZOTARA *u Pančevu* 'Fertilizer PLANT in Pančevo'); complements in genitive (alternating with a prepositional phrase) – DOM *zdravlja* 'HOUSE (of)-Health.Gen (Community Health Center)' and DIREKCIJA *za upravljanje oduze-tom imovinom* 'DIRECTORATE for Management of Seized Assets'.

Coordinated phrases are possible in all languages, e.g., Bulgarian: VICEPREMI-ERÄT *i* MINISTÄR *na obrazovanieto i naukata,* **Meglena Kuneva** 'Deputy PRIME MINISTER -THE and MINISTER of Education-the and Science-the, **Meglena Kuneva**'; French: ***Martin Vetterli***, PROFESSEUR *à l'Ecole polytechnique fédérale de Lausanne et* PRÉSI- DENT *du Conseil national de la recherche* '**Martin Vetterli**, PROFESSOR at the Federal Polytechnic School of Lausanne and PRESIDENT of the National Research Council'; Greek: ο πρωθυπουργός και πρόεδρος του ΣΥΡΙΖΑ Αλέξης Τσίπρας 'the PRIME MINISTER and HEAD of Syriza **Alexis Tsipras**'; Serbian: ***Hleb i kifle*** 'Bread and Rolls' (an organization name). Both triggers and proper names can appear in a coordinated construction (we do not encode coordination in the syntactic patterns).

7.2 Definiteness

Definiteness is expressed either by a morpheme as in Bulgarian and Serbian, or by an article as in English, French, and Greek. In English, French, and Greek, the definite article precedes the trigger, e.g., *le* PREMIER MINISTRE, **Justin Trudeau** 'the PRIME MINISTER, **Justin Trudeau**'. There are other means to express definiteness – i.e., the demonstrative pronouns, the possessive pronouns in English, French, and Serbian, e.g., French: *notre belle* VILLE, **Paris** 'our beautiful CITY, **Paris**'; Serbian: *njeno rodno* MESTO **Beograd** 'her native CITY **Belgrade**'.

With personal names in English, the definite article is obligatory when it is modified by an adjective and/or a PP complement: *the great* POET **Burns**, *the Scottish* POET **Burns**; *the* POET *from Kosovo,* **Fahredin Shehu**; *the* AUTHOR *of the*

Concerto, **Edvard Grieg**. The possessive pronoun, the article and the genitive determiner are in complementary distribution in English.

The definite form in Bulgarian is required when the trigger is modified by an adjective or a possessive pronoun (in this case the definite adjective is part of the first phrasal constituent: *noviyat* MINISTĂR **Valentin Dimitrov** 'new-the MINISTER **Valentin Dimitrov**', and / or a prepositional phrase; if there are no pre-nominal modifiers, the article is on the trigger word: MINISTĂRĂT *na finansite* **Valentin Dimitrov** 'MINISTER-THE of finance-the **Valentin Dimitrov**').

In Greek, all proper names are preceded by a definite article, e.g., η Μαρία 'the **Maria**', η Αθήνα 'the **Athens**', ο πρωθυπουργός Αλέξης Τσίπρας 'the PRIME MINISTER **Alexis Tsipras**'.

In Serbian, the definite article is not used; furthermore neither possessive pronouns nor adjectives are obligatory. However, when adjectives precede proper names, they are in definite form, e.g., *od izvesnog* **Stevice Miletića** vs. **od izvesna* **Stevice Miletića** 'from certain **Stevica Miletić**'.

7.3 Distribution of clitics in Bulgarian and Greek

The possessive pronoun clitics in Bulgarian are right-adjacent to the definite article, e.g., in the second position in the noun phrase (*noviyat ni* MINISTĂR **Valentin Dimitrov** 'new-the our.PossCL MINISTER **Valentin Dimitrov**' vs. MINISTĂRĂT *ni na finansite* **Valentin Dimitrov** 'MINISTER-THE our.PossCL of finance-the **Valentin Dimitrov**'). The possessive pronoun clitic in Bulgarian is also right-adjacent to an indefinite kinship term if used without an adjectival modifier as in MAYKA *mi* **Maria** 'MOTHER my.PossCL **Maria**'.

In Bulgarian the interrogative particle *li* (which is always a clitic) may appear after the first definite modifier (if not followed by a possessive pronoun clitic) or after the whole NP, as in: *noviyat li* DIREKTOR **Ivanov** 'new-the li.QuCL DIRECTOR **Ivanov**' and *noviyat* DIREKTOR **Ivanov** *li* 'new-the DIRECTOR **Ivanov** li.QuCL'). The above-stated rules for the definite article, possessive pronoun clitic and interrogative particle hold for the multiword names too, with the leftmost adjective being part of the proper name itself (**Bălgarskata narodna** BANKA 'Bulgarian-the National BANK').

Greek pronoun clitics are right-adjacent to the proper name, e.g., η Μαρία μου 'the **Maria** my.PossCL'. Once there is a trigger followed by the proper name, the possessive pronoun clitic is between the trigger and the proper name, e.g., ο καθηγητής μας Χρήστος Τσολάκης 'the PROFESSOR our.PossCL **Christos Tsolakis**'.

In Serbian, pronoun clitics can sometimes be used to express possession, as in *KOMŠIJA mi Asan* 'NEIGHBOR I.CL **Asan** (my neighbor Asan)'. However, these constructions are rarely used, being considered rather obsolete and non-standard and are therefore not included in the patterns.

7.4 Expression of semantic and grammatical dependencies

Prepositions are used to express semantic and grammatical dependencies, such as affiliation, domain specification, location in English, Bulgarian, French, Greek, and Serbian, and possession in English, Bulgarian, and French. Semantic and grammatical dependencies can be signified by cases in Greek and Serbian. In English, possession may also be expressed by a clitic –'s (marking the genitive determiner), and in Bulgarian by the derivational suffix of possessive adjectives.

7.5 Word order – position of the trigger with respect to the proper noun

In French, Greek and Serbian, word order permutations are common for personal names, as the first name and surname(s) can change places: French: ***Nicolas Sarkozy*** vs. ***Sarkozy Nicolas;*** Greek: **Γεώργιος Κοκκινόπουλος** 'Georgios Kokkinopoulos' vs. **Κοκκινόπουλος Γεώργιος** 'Kokkinopoulos Georgios'; Serbian: ***Marko Vitas*** vs. ***Vitas Marko***. In Serbian, a change of the order of the first name and the surname(s) of male persons results in a change of the syntactic properties, as in the former case both names inflect, while in the latter only the first name inflects, e.g., in the genitive ***Marka Vitasa*** vs. ***Vitas Marka***.

In all languages, the trigger can appear in pre- or post-nominal position: French: *le MINISTRE des Finances et des Comptes publics,* **Michel Sapin** 'the MINISTER of finance and of public accounts, **Michel Sapin**', or *Michel Sapin, MINISTRE des Finances et des Comptes publics* '**Michel Sapin**, MINISTER of finance and of public accounts'; Greek: ο Υπουργός Οικονομικών **Ευκλείδης Τσακαλώτος** 'the MINISTER of finance **Efkleidis Tsakalotos**', or ο **Ευκλείδης Τσακαλώτος**, Υπουργός Οικονομικών 'the **Efkleidis Tsakalotos**, MINISTER of finance'. Some abbreviations can appear only before or after the names, as in: Serbian: *JP "Srbijašume"* 'PC (Acronym for Public Company) Srbijašume' but *Takovo d.o.o.* 'Takovo (a place name) d.o.o.'.

In all languages, a complex trigger phrase is often in apposition (when the trigger appears as an apposition, it is always separated with a comma), e.g., English: ***Chris,** the new PROFESSOR of Agriculture and Forestry*; French: *le MINISTRE des Finances et des Comptes publics,* **Michel Sapin** 'the MINISTER of finance and of public accounts, **Michel Sapin**', or *Michel Sapin, ministre des Finances et des Comptes publics* 'Michel Sapin, Minister of finance and of public accounts'; Greek: ο Καθηγητής Γεώργιος Μπαμπινιώτης 'the Professor **Georgios Babiniotis**' or ο Γεώργιος Μπαμπινιώτης, Καθηγητής 'the **Georgios Babiniotis**, Professor'.

In all languages, the head personal name can be specified by more than one triggers in a preferred order of appearance: English: *Director General Prof. Smith*; Bulgarian: *generalniyat director prof. Smit* 'general-the Director Prof. Smith'; French: *Directeur général Prof. Smith* 'Director General Prof. Smith'; Greek: ο Γενικός Διευθυντής Καθηγητής Σμιθ 'the General Director Professor Smith'; Serbian: *Generalni director prof. Smit* 'General Director Prof. Smith'.

7.6 Alternations

In English, genitive determiners may alternate with a possessive prepositional phrase.

The possessive PP in Bulgarian may alternate with a possessive or relational adjective in pre-position (*stolicata na Italiya Rim* 'capital-the of Italy **Rome**', *italianskata stolica Rim* 'Italian-the capital **Rome**'). Alternations of possessive pronouns and possessive pronoun clitics in Bulgarian are also observed. A noun modifier in pre-nominal position can alternate with a prepositional phrase (*ski instruktorăt* 'ski instructor-the' vs. *instruktorăt po ski* 'instructor-the at ski').

In Greek, the genitive phrase may alternate with the preposition σε 'at' followed by accusative case, e.g., Γεώργιος Μπαμπινιώτης, Καθηγητής του Πανεπιστημίου Αθηνών '**Georgios Babiniotis**, Professor of the University of Athens' or Γεώργιος Μπαμπινιώτης, Καθηγητής στο Πανεπιστήμιο Αθηνών '**Georgios Babiniotis**, Professor at the University of Athens'. In this case, the two structures may convey a different meaning. The alternation is not possible for all proper names, e.g., Αλέξης Τσίπρας, Πρωθυπουργός της Ελλάδας '**Alexis Tsipras**, Prime Minister of the Greece', *Αλέξης Τσίπρας, Πρωθυπουργός στην Ελλάδα '**Alexis Tsipras**, Prime Minister in the Greece'. A location proper name describing residency at a continent, a country or a city may alternate as an adjective modifier or a PP complement attached to the trigger of a personal name (the same is true for English, Bulgarian, and Serbian), e.g., Greek: ο Πρωθυπουργός της Ελλάδας 'the Prime Minister of the Greece' or ο Έλληνας Πρωθυπουργός 'the Greek Prime Minister'; Serbian: *Ambasada Grčke* 'Embassy of Greece' vs. *Grčka ambasada* 'Greek Embassy' (while in French, the adjective follows the trigger: *le président français François Mitterrand* 'the president of-French.Adj **François Mitterrand**').

In French, we may have an alternation of the preposition *de* 'of' with the preposition *à* 'at', e.g., ***Martin Vetterli***, professeur *de l'École polytechnique fédérale de Lausanne* 'Martin Vetterli, professor of the Federal Polytechnic School of Lausanne' or ***Martin Vetterli***, professeur *à l'École polytechnique fédérale de Lausanne* 'Martin Veterli, professor at the Federal Polytechnic School of Lausanne'.

In Serbian, syntactic alternations are permissible, to some extent, with organization names: a complement in the genitive case instead of a PP complement (Ministarstvo *rada i socijalne politike* 'Ministry of Labor and Social Policy' instead of a Ministarstvo *za rad i socijalnu politiku* 'Ministry for Labor and Social Policy').

The features of the triggers in the five languages are summarized in Table 10.

8 Conclusion

The semantic classification and the syntactic patterns of single and multiword names in Bulgarian, English, French, Greek, and Serbian, may provide reliable data for rule-based Named Entity Recognition (NER).

Linguistic features and distribution facts are used to identify MWEs in NER tasks – both in handcrafted rule-based systems that rely heavily on linguistic knowledge, and in machine-learning techniques. In their research on the application of MWEs and NEs in keyphrase extraction, Nagy T. et al. (2011) conclude that previously known noun compounds are beneficial in NER, and that identified NEs enhance MWE detection, as noun compounds and multiword NEs are linguistically similar and sometimes it is not easy to distinguish between the two.

These arguments are further supported by the tagging practice where both compound nouns and multiword NEs are often tagged as nouns, as their linguistic behaviour is similar to that of single-word nouns (Vincze et al. 2011). Approaches such as that of Nagy T. et al. (2011) also use features involving NEs or pertaining to NEs (i.e., orthography and semantics of keyphrase candidates; positions of a token belonging to a specific NE class, as certain classes of NEs can be identified by their position in the beginning, in the middle or at the end of a keyphrase candidate). Galicia-Haro et al. (2004) discuss the (Spanish) composite NEs (titles of books, movies, songs, etc.) that are described in terms of syntactic and semantic features and of local context and consider discourse features such as introductory words, prepositions, redundancy; specific sets of names; etc.

Rule-based systems usually rely on large-scale lexical resources and grammars, often in the form of regular expressions or Finite State Transducers (Savary & Piskorski 2011; Maurel et al. 2011). Much work has been done on rule-based NER

Table 10: Comparison of the morphological and syntactic features of the five languages.

Features that concern the trigger	English	Bulgarian	French	Greek	Serbian
adjective in pre-position	+	+	+	+	+
adjective in post-position	-	-	+	-	+
PP in post-position	+	+	+	+	+
genitive phrase in post-position	-	-	-	+	+
genitive phrase in pre-position	-	-	-	+	-
genitive determiner in pre-position	+	-	-	-	-
definite article	+	-	+	+	-
definite morpheme	-	+	-	-	+
obligatory definiteness with modifier Adj/PP in a sentence	+	+	+	+	+
possessive pronoun clitic	-	+	-	+	-
dependencies expressed by prepositions	+	+	+	+	+
dependencies expressed by cases	-	-	-	+	+
analytically expressed dependencies	+	+	+	+	+
genitive determiner and PP alternation	+	-	-	-	-
genitive and PP alternation	-	-	-	+	+
poss. pronoun and possessive clitic alternation	-	+	-	-	-
noun modifier and PP alternation	+	+	-	+	+

Features that concern the whole NE	English	Bulgarian	French	Greek	Serbian
pre-position of the trigger	+	+	+	+	+
apposition	+	+	+	+	+
interrogative clitic	-	+	-	-	-

for the five languages discussed in this paper, although machine learning methods prevail. A set of general NER rules with reasonable accuracy has been developed for rule-based annotation of NEs in Bulgarian (Karagiozov et al. 2012), French (Maurel et al. 2011), Greek (Farmakiotou et al. 2000), and Serbian (Krstev et al. 2013). Vitas et al. (2007) discuss semantic and morphological (derivational and inflectional) properties of proper names in Serbian (plus French and English) taking into account the significance of regular derivation and the properties and function of possessive and relational adjectives produced from proper names. Koeva & Dimitrova (2015) discuss a strategy for a linguistic description and classification of Bulgarian NEs referring to persons, and their application in several resources (lexicons and an annotated corpus) for the definition and evaluation of a set of NER rules.

The syntactic patterns presented in this paper are formulated as rules comprising morphological characteristics and syntactic dependencies related to the semantic properties of personal, location and organization NEs in Bulgarian, English, French, Greek, and Serbian. We intend to further exploit the formally encoded linguistic information in rule-based NER approaches. Moreover, as the syntactic patterns for different languages are linked to the same semantic pattern, they can be considered equivalent at the conceptual level and may be applied to any task that involves multilingual processing: cross-lingual information extraction and text classification, multilingual summarization and machine translation. Last but not least, the presented approach contributes to comparative language studies and may be further extended to other word classes that show relatively regular morphological properties and syntactic dependencies.

Abbreviations

ADJ	adjective	GENP	(noun) phrase in genitive
ADV	adverb		
AFF	affiliation	INDEFTRIGGER	indefinite trigger
DEFART	definite article	INS	instrumental
DEFADJ	definite adjective	LIT.	literal translation
DEFPOSSPRON	definite possessive pronoun	LOC	location
		MWE	multiword expression
DEFTRIGGER	definite trigger		
(DOM)SPEC	(domain) specification	MWLOCN	multiword location name
GENDET	genitive determiner	MWORGN	multiword organization name

NE	named entity	POSSADJ	possessive adjective
QUCL	interrogative clitic	(POSS)CL	(possessive) pronoun clitic
NER	named entity recognition	POSSPRON	possessive pronoun
PERN	personal name	PP	prepositional phrase

References

ACE. 2018. *Automatic content extraction. English entity guidelines v6.6 15 2008.06.13*. ACE. https://www.ldc.upenn.edu/sites/www.ldc.upenn.edu/files/english-entities-guidelines-v6.6.pdf, accessed 2018-4-19.

Anderson, John. 2007. *On the grammar of names*. Oxford University Press.

Carroll, John. 1985. *What's in a name? An essay in the psychology of reference*. WH Freeman/Times Books/Henry Holt & Co.

Farmakiotou, Dimitra, Vangelis Karkaletsis, John Koutsias, George Sigletos, Constantine D. Spyropoulos & Panagiotis Stamatopoulos. 2000. Rule-based named entity recognition for Greek financial texts. In *Proceedings of the Workshop on Computational Lexicography and Multimedia Dictionaries (COMLEX 2000)*, 75–78.

Fleischman, Michael & Eduard Hovy. 2002. Fine grained classification of named entities. In *Proceedings of the 19th International Conference on Computational Linguistics*, vol. 1, 1–7.

Galicia-Haro, Sofía, Alexander Gelbukh & Igor Bolshakov. 2004. Recognition of named entities in Spanish texts. *MICAI 2004: Advances in Artificial Intelligence*. 420–429.

Giuliano, Claudio. 2009. Fine-grained classification of named entities exploiting latent semantic kernels. In *Proceedings of the Thirteenth Conference on Computational Natural Language Learning*, 201–209.

Huddleston, Rodney. 1988. *English grammar: An outline*. Cambridge University Press.

Karagiozov, Diman, Anelia Belogay, Dan Cristea, Svetla Koeva, Maciej Ogrodniczuk, Polivios Raxis, Emil Stoyanov & Cristina Vertan. 2012. I-Librarian—Free online library for European citizens. *INFOtheca* 13(1). 27–43.

Koeva, Svetla & Tsvetana Dimitrova. 2015. Rule-based person named entity recognition for Bulgarian. In *Slavic languages in the perspective of formal grammar (Proceedings of FDSL 10.5, Brno 2014)*, vol. 37 (Series Linguistik International), 121–139. Peter Lang.

Krstev, Cvetana, Ivan Obradović, Miloš Utvić & Duško Vitas. 2013. A system for named entity recognition based on local grammars. *Journal of Logic and Computation* 24(2). 473–489.

Magnini, Bernardo, Matteo Negri, Roberto Prevete & Hristo Tanev. 2002. A Word-Net-based approach to named entities recognition. In *Proceedings of the 2002 Workshop on Building and Using Semantic Networks*, vol. 11, 1–7. Stoudsburg: Association for Computational Linguistics.

Maurel, Denis, Nathalie Friburger, Jean-Yves Antoine, Iris Eshkol & Damien Nouvel. 2011. Cascades de transducteurs autour de la reconnaissance des entités nommées. *Traitement automatique des langues* 52(1). 69–96.

McDonald, David. 1996. Internal and external evidence in the identification and semantic categorization of proper names. *Corpus processing for lexical acquisition*. 21–39.

Nagy T., Istvan, Gábor Berend & Veronika Vincze. 2011. Noun compound and named entity recognition and their usability in keyphrase extraction. In *RANLP*, 162–169.

Rodríguez, Horacio, Salvador Climent, Piek Vossen, Laura Bloksma, Wim Peters, Antonietta Alonge, Francesca Bertagna & Adriana Roventini. 1998. The top-down strategy for building EuroWordNet: Vocabulary coverage, base concepts and top ontology. In *EuroWordNet: A multilingual database with lexical semantic networks*, 45–80. Springer.

Savary, Agata & Jakub Piskorski. 2011. Language resources for named entity annotation in the National Corpus of Polish. *Control and Cybernetics* 40. 361–391.

Searle, John R. 1958. Proper names. *Mind* 67(266). 16–173.

Sekine, Satoshi & Chikashi Nobata. 2004. Definition, dictionaries and tagger for Extended Named Entity Hierarchy. In *4th International Conference on Language Resources and Evaluation (LREC)*, 1977–1980. Lisbon, Portugal.

Vincze, Veronika, Istvan Nagy T. & Gábor Berend. 2011. Multiword expressions and named entities in the Wiki50 Corpus. In *Proceedings of Recent Advances in Natural Language Processing*, 289–295. Hissar, Bulgaria.

Vitas, Duško, Cvetana Krstev & Denis Maurel. 2007. A note on the semantic and morphological properties of proper names in the Prolex project. *Lingvisticae Investigationes* 30(1). 115–133.

Zhang, Jie, Dan Shen, Guodong Zhou, Jian Su & Chew-Lim Tan. 2004. Enhancing HMM-based biomedical named entity recognition by studying special phenomena. *Journal of biomedical informatics* 37(6). 411–422.

Chapter 3

MWEs and the Emotion Lexicon: Typological and cross-lingual considerations

Aggeliki Fotopoulou

Institute for Language and Speech Processing, Athena RIC, Greece

Voula Giouli

Institute for Language and Speech Processing, Athena RIC, Greece

The work presented in this paper is aimed at studying predicates that pertain to the semantic field of emotions, the focus being on Modern Greek verbal multiword expressions (verbal MWEs) and their counterparts in French. A core lexicon of verbal MWEs denoting emotion was extracted from existing Modern Greek lexical resources; the initial list was further extended and revised manually in view of corpus evidence. A classification of MWEs is proposed based on syntactic, selectional and semantic properties; an attempt to map the expressions identified onto their French counterparts was also made. The cross-linguistic study reveals similarities and discrepancies in the two languages, and highlights the interaction between MWEs structure and their underlying semantics, in that the intensity of the emotion denoted and the degree of fixedness of the relevant expressions seem to be highly correlated in both languages.

1 Introduction

The availability of user-generated content over the web and the increasing need to make the most out of it has brought about a shift of interest from factual information to the identification of subjective information (as opposed to facts) expressed by people or groups of people with respect to a specific topic. To this end, the task of determining the so-called *private states* (that is, beliefs, feelings,

Aggeliki Fotopoulou & Voula Giouli. 2018. MWEs and the Emotion Lexicon: Typological and cross-lingual considerations. In Manfred Sailer & Stella Markantonatou (eds.), *Multiword expressions: Insights from a multi-lingual perspective*, 63–91. Berlin: Language Science Press. DOI:10.5281/zenodo.1182591

and speculations) expressed in running text and the entities involved has been the focus of attention in the field of Natural Language Processing (NLP). Therefore, identification of expressions denoting emotion or emotional state in textual data and their classification is of paramount importance. In this respect, MWEs can hardly be overlooked since they constitute a significant proportion of the emotion lexicon.

We hereby present work aimed at treating verbal multi-word predicates that pertain to the *semantic field of emotions* from a cross-lingual perspective and systematising their lexical, syntactic and semantic properties. In this context, verbal MWEs in Modern Greek denoting emotion or emotional state were selected from existing language resources. Their lexico-semantic properties were also retrieved from these resources and new entries were encoded following the same principles. All MWEs were further assigned *semantic features* inherent to the semantic field. At the next stage, their mapping onto their counterparts in French was performed. The comparative study of Greek and French MWEs resulted in the identification of cross-lingual similarities and discrepancies. Moreover, correlations between lexical features and the underlying semantics of MWEs were also revealed. Our working hypothesis was that despite idiosyncrasies, MWEs that belong to a given semantic class share features that are characteristic for this class; moreover, these field-specific features are attested cross-linguistically. One step further, the (cross-lingual) treatment of MWEs might be useful not only from a purely linguistic point of view but also for NLP applications.

The paper is outlined as follows. An overview of background work on the study of the emotion lexicon and of MWEs is presented in §2, §3 outlines the methodological framework adopted, whereas the selection process of the lexical data is described in §4. The lexicon of emotion MWEs and the syntactic, selectional and semantic properties encoded are presented in §5; we discuss our findings in §6 and elaborate further on cross-lingual considerations in §7. Finally, our conclusions and prospects for future research are outlined in §8.

2 Background work

The seminal work at the syntax-semantics interface by Levin (1993) involves large-scale classification of English verbal predicates on the basis of shared meaning and syntactic properties. In this work, more than 3000 verbs were grouped into semantically coherent verb classes, each depicting a syntactic configuration that reflects verb meaning. A more fine-grained semantic classification of French verb and noun predicates denoting feeling, emotion and psychological states has also been performed (Mathieu 1999; 2005), aimed at a wide range of NLP applications. French nominal and verbal predicates denoting emotion and their lexicalised word combinations have been studied (Leeman 1991; Gross 1995; Balibar-Mrabti 1995; Tutin et al. 2006) from a different point of view. Finally, a comparative analysis of English and French single-word verbal predicates denoting emotion (Mathieu & Fellbaum 2010) reports on properties shared among the two languages on the grounds of syntax and semantics, unveiling at the same time the idiosyncrasies of each language.

As far as MWEs are concerned, a systematic treatment of French fixed expressions has been carried out (Gross 1982). In this work, the classification and the analysis of c. 20000 French verbal MWEs consists of the formal representation of their syntactic properties, selectional restrictions and the distinction between fixed and non-fixed constituents. Along the same lines, the classification of Greek fixed expressions (c. 6000 entries) has been performed based on the same formal principles and criteria (Fotopoulou 1993b; Mini 2009).

The present study is part of a larger effort aimed at developing lexical resources that encompass the Greek emotion lexicon, i.e., words and phrases that refer to emotional states and emotion-related mental events. Previous work involves treatment of nouns and verbs. In this context, 130 Greek noun predicates denoting emotion (*Nsent*) were identified and classified on the basis of the verbs' syntactic, semantic and distributional properties (Pantazara et al. 2008; Fotopoulou et al. 2009). In this context, support verbs (*Vsup*) and other verbs expressing diverse modalities (aspect, intensity, control, etc.) were identified and encoded as properties; these properties reveal the restrictions nouns impose on the lexical choice of verbs. Similarly, 339 Greek verbal predicates denoting emotion (*Vsent*) were classified into homogenous syntactico-semantic classes based on their syntactic, lexical and semantic properties (Giouli & Fotopoulou 2012); a number of syntactic features (i.e., argument structure, alternations), selectional restrictions imposed on the verbs' subject and object complements, emotion type, polarity and intensity were also defined and encoded formally.

In this respect, this work is further aimed at enriching the set of lexical resources pertaining to the semantic field of emotions with a lexicon that comprises verbal MWEs denoting emotion or emotional state. Moreover, the Greek MWEs were mapped onto their French counterparts. The ultimate goal was not only to develop a bi-lingual lexical resource, but also to test the hypothesis that, despite the idiosyncrasies that are inherent to MWEs in general, a certain degree of regularity (in terms of inherent properties) can be observed within a semantic class. To this end, we opted for reusing and extending existing lexical resources that encompass verb MWEs in Greek and French.

3 Methodological framework

The resources that form the basis of the present study have been developed using the Lexicon-Grammar (LG) methodological framework (Gross 1975). Being a model of syntax limited to the elementary sentences of a natural language, the theory argues that the unit of meaning is not located at the level of the word, but at the level of sentence of the form *Subject – Verb – Object*. Therefore, the elementary sentence is transformed to its predicate-argument structure, and the main complements (subject, one or more objects) are separated from other complements (adjuncts) on the basis of formal criteria. Distributional properties associated with words, i.e., types of prepositions, semantic features inherent to nouns in subject and object positions, etc. are also taken into account, resulting in a more fine-grained classification and in the creation of homogeneous word classes. Finally, transformation rules, construed as equivalence relations between sentences, generate additional equivalent structures. All this information (argument structure, distributional properties and permitted transformational rules) is formally encoded in the so-called *LG tables*.

Each table is defined by a set of distinct properties (syntactic, distributional, and semantic) and includes all the lexical items sharing these properties. Predicates with more than one usage or meaning are treated as separate lexical items possibly represented in different tables, and the syntactic and semantic properties are assigned to each entry as appropriate. In this sense, entries in one table are considered to form a homogeneous class. In an LG table, the set of properties that describe the entries are encoded as headers of the columns, whereas entries are listed at separate rows. At the intersection of a row corresponding to a lexical item (entry) and a column corresponding to a property, the cell is set to '+' if the property is valid for the given entry or '−' if it is not.

Similarly, MWEs are also treated as *elementary sentences* for which all possible fixed and non-fixed (or variable) arguments (if any) are consistently and uniformly encoded. The formalism provides the mechanism for encoding properties that are appropriate for the identification and processing of MWEs. More precisely, the MWE structure is represented as a Part-of-Speech sequence. According to the LG notation, N denotes a non-fixed nominal, whereas, C signifies a fixed one; numbers are used to represent the syntactic function of fixed or non-fixed constituents. In this sense, $N0$ is used to represent a non-fixed noun in subject position whereas, $C0$ denotes a fixed subject. Similarly, $N1, N2, N3$, etc., along with $C1, C2, C3$ etc. denote complements in object position (or complements of prepositional phrases), marked also for fixedness. It should be noted, however, that the internal structure of the noun phrase is not represented explicitly in general; patterns depict the elementary sentence or structure characterising each MWE class, whereas information regarding modifiers, determiners, etc. allowed for by certain expressions is provided in the form of *features* or *properties*. *Selectional restrictions* over the non-fixed or variable elements of MWEs as well as syntactic phenomena (e.g., passive alternation, etc.) – if any – are also encoded formally. Finally, other grammatical phenomena such as agreement features are accounted for.

For example, the MWE in (1) below comprises two fixed (or lexicalised) elements, a verb and a noun in subject position, and two variable elements, namely a nominal phrase in accusative and a possessive pronoun (*Poss*) that modifies the fixed nominal constituent. The variant nominal phrase is most often realised as a weak personal pronoun in pre-verbal position (*Ppv*); agreement in number and person between the two variable elements is mandatory:

(1) my devils catch me 'to become very angry'
     με πιάνουν τα διαόλια   μου / *σου / *του Γιάννη
     me pianun   ta δiaolia   mu / *su / *tu Γiani
     me catch.3PL the devils.NOM.PL.POSS my / your / the John.GEN

     'to become very angry'

In this case, a generic syntactic pattern like the one depicted in (2) below is used to describe a class in a LG table.

(2) a. Ppv V C0 Poss
     b. Ppv-1 V C0 Poss-1

The agreement attested between variable elements is then depicted via co-indexing as shown in (2b).

An example of MWE representation within the LG framework is illustrated in Table 1; the table comprises verbal MWEs with the underlying structure *N0 V Prep C1* (Fotopoulou 1993b).

It becomes evident, therefore, that the LG framework together with the requirement of substantial coverage leads to a *uniform* and *consistent* description of elementary sentences and the formal encoding of properties across languages in a comparable manner. In this respect, one of the main advantages of LG is that it allows comparisons between languages and facilitates the construction of *cross-language* resources.

Table 1: LG table of verbal MWEs (sample).

N0 =: +Hum	N0 =: -Hum	⟨E⟩					N1 =: Npc	N0V	N0 Vcmt N1 Prep C2	PhraseVsup
-	+	ακτινοβολώ	από	E	ευτυχία	E	-	+	-	-
+	-	αφρίζω	από	(E+τη)	λύσσα	(E+Poss-0)	-	-	-	-
+	-	βράζω	σε	το	ζουμί	Poss-0	-	-	-	-
+	-	γελάω	με	την	καρδιά	Poss-0	+	+	-	-
+	-	έρχομαι	σε	τα	λογικά	Poss-0	-	-	+	+
+	-	έρχομαι	σε	τα	συγκαλά	Poss-0	-	-	+	-
+	-	κάθομαι	σε	τα	αβγά	Poss-0	-	-	-	-
+	-	κάθομαι	σε	τα	αγκάθια	E	-	-	-	-
+	-	κιτρινίζω	από	τον	φόβο	Poss-0	-	+	-	-
+	-	λύνομαι	σε	τα	γέλια	E	-	-	-	-

4 Data selection

The initial list of Greek and French MWEs that pertain to the semantic field of emotions was manually compiled from data listed in existing LG tables for Greek (Fotopoulou 1993b; Mini 2009) and French (Gross 1982). The selection of the Greek MWEs was performed as a two-stage procedure: (a) manual identification of candidate MWEs that pertain to the semantic field emotion, and (b) validation of these candidate MWEs for inclusion or deletion on the basis of formal criteria besides intuitive judgments. The initial list of MWEs was further updated and extended, drawing on corpus evidence. More precisely, Greek MWEs were selected manually from a suite of specialised corpora (Giouli & Fotopoulou 2014) that were developed and annotated in view of guiding sentiment analysis. In this sense, our work is corpus-based and thus empirical rather than purely intuitive.

Since the scope of the current work is limited to clear instances of emotion denoting predicates (i.e., verbal MWEs), a formal distinction between direct and indirect affective expressions that correspond to emotion concepts was in order. For this reason, a set of lexical semantic tests (lexical substitution, paraphrasing, etc.) was adopted as a formal device guiding the selection of Greek verbal emotion predicates. Therefore, a candidate MWE is selected for inclusion in the lexicon if at least one of the following criteria is met:

Criterion 1: A candidate Emotion MWE is selected if it can be replaced by a sequence that comprises one of the verbs *feel* or *cause* and a *noun that denotes emotion (Nsent)*, that is, if there exists an *Nsent* that is related with the concept EMOTION via the IS-A relation, and the relation *MWE is semantically equivalent to "feel/cause Nsent"* is true. For example, the expression in (3) is semantically equivalent to an expression of the form *to feel* EMOTION, where EMOTION is *panic*:

(3) με πιάνει πανικός
    me piani panikos
    me catches panic.NOM
    'to panic'

Criterion 2: A candidate Emotion MWE is selected if it can be replaced by a verb predicate that denotes emotion (*Vsent*), that is, if there exists a *Vsent* defined as a conceptualization of a FEEL-EMOTION or CAUSE-FEEL-EMOTION event and the relation *MWE is semantically equivalent to "Vsent"* is true. For example, the expression in (4) is semantically equivalent with the *Vsent* φοβάμαι (fovame) 'to be frightened':

(4) πάγωσε το αίμα μου
    paγose to ema mu
    froze the blood.NOM my
    'I was terrified'

Criterion 3: A candidate Emotion MWE is selected if it can be replaced by the verb *to be* and an adjective that denotes emotion (*Asent*), that is, if there exists an *Asent* defined as conceptualizing an EXPERIENCER-EMOTION or TRIGGER-EMOTION entity, and the relation *MWE is semantically equivalent to "to be Asent"* is true. In the example (5) below, the expression is semantically equivalent to an expression of the form *to be Asent* – είμαι έκπληκτος (ime ekpliktos) 'to be surprised':

(5) μένω με το στόμα ανοικτό
    meno me to stoma anikto
    stay with the mouth open
    'to be aghast'

Finally, the selection of French MWEs denoting emotion and their mapping onto their Greek counterparts was performed manually. First, translations or translational equivalents of the Greek MWEs were either provided by human translators or extracted from standard mono- and bilingual lexicographic resources, such as the *Trésor de la Langue Française Informatisé*[1] and *WordReference.com*. In certain cases, translations were obtained using English as a pivot language. These translations were checked against entries in existing LG tables that define the typologies of French MWEs (Gross 1982). Once an expression was spotted, it was selected and aligned to its Greek counterpart(s).

The afore-mentioned process resulted in the identification of 607 Greek and 520 French MWEs that constitute the linguistic data of the current study. As one might expect, the numbers show that there is no 1:1 correspondence between Greek and French MWEs denoting emotion. In fact, the process of translating the list of Greek MWEs to the target language proved that the transition from one language to the other was not always straightforward. The outcome of this procedure can be summed as follows (see also §6.2):

- a Greek MWE is mapped onto a French MWE;

- more than one Greek MWEs are mapped onto a single French MWE;

- a single Greek MWE corresponds to more than one French MWEs;

- one or more Greek MWEs correspond to a single-word French verb rather than an MWE.

5 Description of the MWEs Emotion Lexicon

Data encoding was performed after data selection. The challenge of representing MWEs in lexical resources is to ensure that the variability along with extra features required by the different types of MWEs can be captured efficiently (Calzolari et al. 2002; Copestake et al. 2002). To this end, features and properties that are appropriate for the robust computational treatment of MWEs were retained from existing LG tables where applicable. MWEs extracted from corpora were encoded from scratch. Syntactic information includes the argument structure of the elementary sentence (by also depicting fixed and variable elements), modification information (if permitted), syntactic alternations, and selectional restrictions imposed over the variable elements of the MWE (often in subject and object(s) position). Additionally, all MWEs were coupled with information about

---

[1]The resources are available online (http://atilf.atilf.fr/tlf.htm; http://www.wordreference.com/).

their type in terms of compositionality, syntactic rigidity idiosyncrasies, and lexical choice. Moreover, semantic features that are relevant to the semantic field to which each of these predicates adheres are also encoded, namely: emotion type, polarity and intensity. In this way, the typologies of emotion MWEs in Greek and French were consolidated and cross-lingual analogies or discrepancies were identified. In the remainder, we will elaborate further on the encoding of verb MWEs. As we have already mentioned above, linguistic information is encoded formally in both the Greek and French tables, and this common representation facilitates the extraction of shared patterns – if any.

5.1 Emotion MWEs: fixed expressions – SVCs

In this section, we present the classification of verbal MWEs included in the emotion lexicon. Entries were assigned a value corresponding to the type they belong to, namely (a) fixed (or idiomatic) expressions and (b) support (or light) verb constructions (SVCs).

The identification of fixed expressions involves lexical, morphosyntactic and semantic criteria (Gross 1982; 1998b; Lamiroy 2003), to be taken into account, namely: *non-compositionality*,[2] i.e., the meaning of the expression cannot be computed from the meanings of its constituents; *non-substitutability*, i.e., at least one of the expression constituents does not enter in alternations at the paradigmatic axis; and *non-modifiability*, in that they enter in syntactically rigid structures, posing further constraints over modification, transformations, etc. To this end, linguistic tests were applied to all MWEs. The examples that follow conform to the criteria mentioned and are classified as *fixed expressions*:

(6) δαγκώνω τη λαμαρίνα
    ðagono ti lamarina
    bite   the panel.ACC
    'to be in love'

(7) *serrer   les dents*
    to.clench the teeth
    'to grit one's teeth/to be stressed or angry'

---

[2]We distinguish between *composability/decomposability* (Nunberg et al. 1994: 496) and *compositionality/non-compositionality*. Composability concerns the property of phrase elements to "[c]arry identifiable parts of the idiomatic meaning".

On the other hand, identification of SVCs for inclusion in the emotion lexicon is based on the following criteria:

SVCs Criterion 1: SVCs comprise a *support verb (Vsup)* and a *predicative noun denoting emotion (Nsent)*; support or light verbs of this type bear no meaning and are simply carriers of tense and person;

SVCs Criterion 2: SVCs comprise specific (modal) verbs expressing *diverse modalities* (aspect, intensity, control, etc.) and an *Nsent*. These verbs are considered as *Vsup variants*.

In this respect, SVCs are – to some extent – characterised by semantic transparency due to the fact that the predicative noun, which carries the predicative function within the SVC, is used in one of its literal senses. Basic support verbs are *έχω* (exo)/*avoir* 'to have', *είμαι Prep* (ime Prep)/*être Prep* 'be Prep', *κάνω* (kano)/*faire* 'to make', the operator verb *δίνω* (δino)/*donner* 'to give', and the causative verbs *προκαλώ* (prokalo)/*défier, provoquer* 'to cause', *προξενώ* (prokseno)/ *provoquer* 'to cause', *αφήνω* (afino)/*laisser* 'to leave', which have an effect on structures with the basic *Vsup*. In practice, however, SVCs are highly *idiosyncratic* and for this reason, it is quite difficult to predict which *Vsup* combines with a noun (Abeille 1988). In the case of emotion MWEs, a close inspection of the data, showed that domain-specific verbs assume the function of a basic *Vsup*. Greek SVCs in this semantic field usually select for the verbs *νιώθω* (nioθo) 'to feel' or *αισθάνομαι* (esθanome) 'to feel' (see (8)); similarly, their French counterparts select for the verbs *éprouver* 'to feel' and *ressentir* 'to feel', as shown in the example (9) below. These constructions are semantically equivalent with single-word verb predicates denoting emotion.

(8) νιώθω χαρά
     nioθo χara
     feel   joy.ACC
     'to feel joy'

(9) *ressentir de la joie*
     to.feel   of the joy
     'to feel joy'

Additionally, certain verbs selected by the *Nsent* predicates that function as *Vsup* variants may further denote the degree or intensity of the emotion. From a cross-linguistic perspective, these *Vsup* variants usually form a pair of translational equivalents in Greek and French as shown in the examples (10) and (11) respectively:

(10) πετάω από χαρά / τη χαρά μου
      petao apo χara / ti χara mu
      fly   from joy / the joy my
      'to be very happy'

(11) *sauter   de joie*
      to.jump of joy
      'to be very happy'

   Classification of MWEs as fixed expressions or SVCs is not always straightforward or clear-cut, as shown in §5.2.2 and §6.1. In fact, some expressions seem to comprise an intermediate class placed in between fixed expressions and SVCs. In other words, there seems to be a continuum between fixed expressions and SVCs (or between fixed and free expressions in other cases). These expressions may be considered (under syntactic and semantic conditions) as *semi-fixed*. A study of these expressions related to the *degree of fixedness* is currently in progress (Constant & Fotopoulou 2016).

5.2 Syntactic properties

Syntactic (and semantic) information is extracted from the LG tables for those MWEs that were accounted for in the past; new MWEs selected for the purposes of the current study were encoded as appropriate. Syntactic information in the LG tables comprises the *argument structure of each MWE, the syntactic alternations* defined for the particular MWE, and *selectional restrictions* imposed over the variable elements of the expressions. The encoding of modifiability specifically concerns the fixed modifiers of SVCs. In the next sections, we elaborate on these aspects.

5.2.1 Argument Structure

Verbal MWE expressions (fixed non-compositional and SVCs) that denote an emotion bear no syntactic idiomaticity, since they generally conform to the argument structure of the main verb and there is nothing exceptional in their syntactic behavior. This information is only implicitly encoded in the LG tables. In this respect, naming conventions of the initial tables correspond to specific configurations cross-linguistically, and this information can be easily and effectively retained in the current lexical resource. Information with respect to the underlying structure and the syntactic function of the (fixed and variable) constituent(s) further shows that verbal MWE predicates conform to the following patterns: (i) fixed subject MWEs, (ii) fixed complement MWEs, and (iii) any combination of the above. These types are presented in detail in the following paragraphs.

Fixed Subject MWEs comprise a verb and an *NP* in subject position; these are both lexicalised. Complements (if any) are represented as variant elements. According the LG notation, the generic syntactic pattern that describes MWEs of this type is *C0 V Ω*. The symbol $Ω^3$ is used to denote one or more complements a predicate subcategorises for, without further specifying their form. In the LG tables, however, the form and function of variable elements are further encoded. For example, the patterns *C0 V N1* and *C0 V Prep C1 N2gen*, used to describe Greek and French expressions in (12) and (13) below, further license a variable nominal phrase in object position or as the complement of a *PP* modifier respectively:

(12) cold sweat bathes me 'I am terrified'
  Κρύος ιδρώτας   έλουσε την Άννα.
  krios iδrotas   eluse   tin Ana
  cold   sweat.NOM.SBJ bathed the Anna.ACC.OBJ

  'Anna was terrified.'

(13) *La haine   niche dans le coeur de Anna.*
  the hate.SBJ nests in   the heart of Anna

  'Anna hates.'

It should be noted, however, that the variable complement is usually employed in its cliticised form as shown in (14); this property is also encoded in the LG tables.

(14) cold sweat baths me 'I am terrified'
  Την   έλουσε κρύος ιδρώτας.
  tin   eluse krios iδrotas
  her.OBJ bathed cold sweat.SBJ

  'She was terrified.'

Similarly, Greek SVCs may comprise an aspectual variant of a *Vsup* and a predicative noun denoting an emotion in subject position:

---

[3] We will not discuss the possible forms assumed by Ω in detail.

(15)   με πιάνει   πανικός
       me piani   panikos
       me catches panic.NOM.SBJ
       'to panic'

Fixed Complement MWEs. Verbal MWEs of this type comprise a verb and one lexicalised complement. Most often, this lexicalised complement is an *NP* in direct object position. The subject is represented as a variable argument of the elementary sentence; the generic syntactic pattern that describes fixed verbal MWEs of this type is *N0 V C1*, whereas the syntactic pattern of SVCs is *N0 Vsup Nsent*:

(16)   δαγκώνω τη λαμαρίνα
       δagono   ti lamarina
       bite   the panel.OBJ
       'to be in love'

(17)   *avoir   du chagrin*
       to.have of grief
       'to be sad'

Fixed PP Complement MWEs comprise a verb and a lexicalised prepositional phrase (*PP*) complement. The variable *NP* in subject position along with other non-fixed elements (if any) is also represented as appropriate. The generic pattern that describes this class is of the form *N0 V Prep C1*. In (18), the Greek MWE consists of the verb κάθομαι (kaθome) 'to sit' and the lexicalised *PP* στα καρφιά (sta karfia) 'on the nails'. Similarly, the French MWE in (19) consists of the verb *rire* 'to laugh' and the PP *aux larmes* 'to tears':

(18)   κάθομαι στα   καρφιά
       kaθome sta   karfia
       sit   to.the nails
       'to be anxious', 'to be on tenterhooks'

(19)   *rire   aux   larmes*
       to.laugh to.the tears
       'to roar with laughter'

Fixed Adjunct MWEs comprise a verb plus an adjunct (often adverb) that are both lexicalised. Other variable complements are depicted in the structure of the relative elementary sentence:

(20) *φέρω βαρέως*
      fero   vareos
      carry heavily
      'to be very sad'

(21) *Ils   s'   aiment comme deux tourtereaux*
      they REFL love   like   two   lovebirds
      'They are in love.'

Finally, a number of verbal MWEs have a *syntactic* structure that is a combination of the configurations presented. These structures are exhaustively represented in the resource:

(22) *μου   ανεβαίνει το αίμα   στο   κεφάλι*
      mu   aneveni   to ema   sto   kiefali
      me.GEN raises   the blood.NOM to.the head
      'to become very angry'

(23) *la moutarde monte au   nez*
      the mustard raises to.the nose
      'to become very angry'

(24) *avoir   froid dans le   dos*
      to.have cold in   the back
      'to be terrified'

5.2.2 Modification

Fixed non-compositional verbal expressions do not allow for any modification over the fixed constituents. On the contrary, SVCs are considered as syntactically more flexible constructions, and adjectival modification is allowed over the *Nsent*. However, constructions with a *Vsup* do not conform to a uniform pattern of modification (Moustaki et al. 2008). Adjectival modification within the MWE is found to be *free, semi-fixed* or even *fixed*. Modification in both languages involves *intensifiers* or – more generally – *grade indicators* like *μεγάλος* (meγalos)/*grand* 'big', *λίγος* (liγos)/*petit* 'few', *φοβερός* (foveros)/*intense* 'awful', *άκρατος* (akratos)/*intense* 'awful', etc..

(25) *Ο Γιάννης νιώθει ένα παθολογικό / υπαρξιακό / αόριστο / *δυνατό άγχος.*
      o Γianis nioθi ena παθoloγiko / iparksiako / aoristo / δinato anχos
      the John feels a pathological / existential / vague / strong anxiety

      'John feels a pathological / existential / vague / *strong anxiety.'

(26) *Jean éprouve une angoisse pathologique / vague / sourde / mortelle / de*
      John feels an anxiety pathological / vague / silent / deadly / of
      mort / existentielle.
      death / existential
      'John feels a pathological / vague / silent / deadly / existential anxiety.'

(27) *Με έπιασε μαύρη απελπισία   / *λύπη.*
      me epiase mavri apelpisia   / lipi
      me cought black dispair.NOM / sorrow.NOM
      'I was in total despair.'

(28) *J' ai eu une peur bleue / *tristesse bleue.*
      I have had a fear blue / sadness blue
      'I was terrified.'

The *fixed* modifiers, i.e., modifiers that seem to be idiosyncratic to a given *Nsent* cannot be employed productively. We note that in example (27) , the adjective μαύρη, mavri, 'black' is only used as a modifier of the nominal predicate απελπισία, apelpisia, 'despair', which cannot be described literally as being of black colour. Similarly, the French adjective *bleu* 'blue' in (28) is only used with the nominal predicates *peur* 'fear'. These expressions are also encoded as fixed in the LG tables. Actually, this is evidence of the existence of grey zones between SVCs and fixed expressions (cf. §5.1).

To conclude, Greek and French *Nsent* predicates in a SVC select from a variety of modifiers in an idiosyncratic manner. Moreover, the respective Greek and French expressions seem to present a variable degree of fixedness depending on the *Nsent* and the modifier selected. Free and semi-fixed modifiers are not encoded in the lexicon so far. On the contrary, fixed modifiers of the predicative noun are encoded as fixed elements of the expression.

5.2.3 Syntactic alternations

Information relative to syntactic alternations encoded in the LG tables was also kept in the lexical resource. The causative-inchoative alternation is a syntactic property that involves verbs (or pairs of verbs) which have an intransitive and a transitive usage. The inchoative form (intransitive) denotes a *change of state*, and the causative form (transitive) denotes a *bringing about of a change of state*. A number of emotive MWEs were found to enter this alternation. The following cases have been attested in the LG tables:

First case: a pair of two MWEs each one comprising a distinct verb, whereas all the other fixed elements are identical. The two verbs (which are often predicates denoting movement) normally enter (or signal) the transitive-intransitive alternation:

(29) to take one out of one's clothes 'to make someone angry'
    ο   Γιάννης την   **βγάζει** τη Μαρία   από τα ρούχα της. (CAUS)
    o   Gianis tin   vγazi   ti Maria   apo ta ruχa tis
    the John.SBJ her.OBJ takes.out the Maria.OBJ from the clothes hers
    'John makes Maria very angry.'

(30) to get out of one's clothes 'to be made angry'
    η   Μαρία   **βγήκε** από τα ρούχα της.   (INCHO)
    i   Maria   vγikie apo ta ruχa tis
    the Maria.SBJ went.out from the clothes hers
    'Maria was made very angry.'

(31) to send someone to the seventh sky 'to make someone happy'
    Eric **envoie** Léa au   septième ciel.   (CAUS)
    Eric sends   Lea to.the seventh sky
    'Eric makes Lea very happy.'

(32) to go up to the seventh sky 'to be happy'
    Léa **monte** au   septième ciel.   (INCHO)
    Lea goes-up to.the seventh sky
    'Lea is in the seventh heaven.'

Second case: MWEs that comprise a verb that enters the transitive-intransitive alternation (ergativity):

(33) to turn someone's lights on 'to make someone angry'
    ο   Γιάννης μου **άναψε**   τα λαμπάκια.   (CAUS)
    o   Gianis mu   anapse   ta labakia
    the John.SBJ I.GEN turned.on the lights.OBJ
    'John made me very angry.'

(34) my lights turn on 'I get angry'

Μου **άναψαν** τα λαμπάκια   (INCHO)

mu   anapsan   ta   labakia

I.GEN turned.on the lights.SBJ

'I got very angry.'

Similarly, other syntactic properties were encoded in the LG tables where applicable (i.e., passivisation, genitive-dative alternation, etc.).

5.2.4 Selectional restrictions

A number of *selectional restrictions* that are imposed on the *variable* elements of the MWEs (in subject and object(s) position) were encoded as properties in the LG tables. Like their single word counterparts, verbal MWEs denoting emotion select a nominal element that is obligatorily [+*human*]. Being at the heart of the syntax-semantics interface, this information relates to the participants of the emotion event. An emotion event generally involves an EXPERIENCER (that is, the individual experiencing the psychological state) and a THEME (that is, the content or object of the psychological state) or – occasionally – a CAUSE. These participants, however, are not realised in a uniform way in single word verbal predicates. In this respect, the distinction between *SubjectExperiencer* (SubjExp) and *ObjectExperiencer* (ObjExp) single word verbal predicates has been established (Belletti & Rizzi 1988) based on the syntactic distribution of the verbal arguments and the associated Semantic Roles. The former project the EXPERIENCER of the emotion as their structural subject and the THEME or the STIMULUS as their structural object; the latter realise the THEME or the STIMULUS as the subject and the EXPERIENCER as their object. This information is of relevance to a number of NLP applications, and although it has not been encoded in the LG tables, it can be deduced easily. In fact, as it has been shown (Giouli & Fotopoulou 2014) for the single-word verbal predicates denoting emotion, the *N0* or *N1* complements with the [+*human*] restriction can be mapped onto the EXPERIENCER participant in the emotion event.

This is true for MWEs too; here the EXPERIENCER is realised not as a structural subject but in object position. In this sense, the non-fixed element that bears the semantic restriction [+*human*] corresponds unambiguously to the EXPERIENCER of the emotion. In the following examples, the EXPERIENCER of the emotion is expressed by the subject of the Greek and French expressions as shown in (35) and (36) respectively, or by the direct object as depicted in (37) and (38) below:

(35) H Άννα   πετάει από χαρά.
      i   Ana   petai apo χara
      the Anna.SBJ.EXP flies of joy
      'Anna is very happy.'

(36) *Anna   rayonne de joie.*
      Anna.SBJ.EXP shines   of joy
      'Anna is very happy.'

(37) to take one out of one's clothes 'to make someone very angry'
      ο   Γιάννης με   έβγαλε   από τα ρούχα   μου.
      o   Γianis   me   evγale   apo ta ruχa   mu
      the John.SBJ me.OBJ.EXP took.out of   the clothes mine
      'John made me very angry.'

(38) *Ce film   m'   a ému   aux larmes.*
      this film.SBJ me.OBJ.EXP has touched in   tears
      'This film moved me to tears.'

Additionally, other *selectional restrictions* imposed on the variable elements of the verbal MWE are encoded. These restrictions further specify the type of complements (nominal, prepositional, sentential) that these predicates sub-categorise for. In this respect, prepositions selected by the MWE predicates are formally depicted and encoded.

5.3 Semantic classification

The semantic classification of the studied Greek and French MWEs was aimed at grouping them under pre-defined emotional concepts and at distinguishing semantically between expressions that are near synonyms. This was attempted following a schema defined for single-word Greek verbs denoting emotion (Giouli & Fotopoulou 2012) along three dimensions: (a) *emotion type* (b) *emotion polarity* (c) *emotion intensity* and (d) *aspect* of the emotion event. The semantic classification of verbal MWE predicates was performed separately by two experienced linguists in the form of primarily intuitive semantic grouping. At the next stage, discrepancies between the annotations thus obtained were discussed and resolved, whereas cases for which no agreement could be consolidated were left aside for future treatment. The outcome of this procedure was the definition of specifications that would be applicable for distinguishing between semantic classes.

Emotion is described as a set of two or more dimensions. The most common ones are *polarity*, i.e., *positive or negative connotation* of emotion and the *intensity* or strength of the emotion. The notion of semantic polarity, or the semantic orientation of words (whether they denote a positive or a negative emotion) has also been the focus of attention in many studies aimed at sentiment analysis (Esuli & Sebastiani 2006; Wilson et al. 2005) *inter alia*. In our approach, the encoding schema provides for the annotation of the *a priori polarity* of the emotion denoted, which subsumes one of the following values: (a) *positive*, i.e., predicates which express a pleasant feeling (b) *negative*, i.e., predicates which express an unpleasant feeling (c) *neutral*, i.e., predicates that denote an emotion that is neither positive not negative and (d) *ambiguous*, i.e., predicates expressing a feeling, the polarity of which is context-dependent (e.g., surprise).

Polarity identification results in a coarse – yet quite effective – classification of emotion expressions; a more fine-grained one was attempted on the basis of emotion types. Psychological considerations of sentiment claim that some emotions are more basic than others, therefore, they should be universal to all human languages. The identification of basic emotions is based upon specific functional and physiological criteria, yet languages are claimed to possess inventories that comprise a great number of emotion predicates that cannot be easily accommodated within such fairly straightforward schemes. To this end, different dimensions of emotion can be used to delineate senses. In the work presented here we adopted an extended version of the typological model defined by Plutchik (2001). The initial model comprises eight basic emotions: *anger, fear, sadness, disgust, surprise, anticipation, acceptance* and *joy*. On the basis of corpus evidence derived from a tri-lingual corpus (English, Greek, Spanish) annotated for sentiment (Giouli et al. 2013), the initial list of basic emotions was further extended with a set of complex emotions, such as *love* and *hate* or emotions of (self-)appraisal (e.g., *shame, respect*) that were not considered by Plutchik. To better account for the conceptual representation of the emotion vocabulary, the final set of emotion types includes 15 new classes, namely: *admiration, boredom, disappointment, envy, gratitude, hate, indifference, jealousy, love, relaxedness, remorse, resentment, respect,* and *shame*. Greek and French MWEs were assigned an emotion concept; this classification results in grouping Greek and French verbal MWEs under emotion concepts.

Moreover, to model the semantic distinction between near synonyms that occur within a semantic class such as φοβάμαι, fovame, 'to be scared', πανικοβάλλομαι, panikovalome, 'to panic', μου κόπηκαν τα ήπατα, mu kopikan ta ipata, 'to be very frightened', etc., entries were further coupled with the feature *inten-*

sity (or *strength*). The following values are provided for by the schema for the feature *strength: low, medium, high,* and *uncertain.* In fact, emotion verbal predicates have been shown to possess scalar qualities (Fellbaum & Mathieu 2012). In this respect, groups of verbs that were assigned the same emotion type were checked in order to identify different degrees of intensity of the same underlying emotion. In this respect, intuitive judgments of trained lexicographers were systematised and a number of linguistic tests were defined aimed at the consistent annotation and the ordering of predicates according to the intensity of the emotion they denote.

In both languages, intensity was proved to be dependent on the following aspects: (a) degree of fixedness (b) modifier selected (in SVCs) and (c) the *Vsup* selected. More precisely, the majority of verbal idioms were judged to express an emotional state or event of high intensity; these were further marked as not accepting any modifier. Similarly, the *Vsup* of an SVC seemed to have an impact on the value assigned to the feature intensity. Ultimately, a number of *Vsup* function as an intensifier of the emotion denoted. In this respect, the verbs *έχω* (exo)/*avoir* 'to have', *νιώθω* (nioθo)/*éprouver* 'feel' and *αισθάνομαι* (esθanome)/*ressentir* 'to feel' in Greek and French respectively usually denote an emotion that bears the value *medium* for the feature *intensity*; on the contrary, when the verbs *πετάω* (petao) 'fly' and *rayonner* 'shine' are employed instead, the entire expression is marked as denoting the same emotion, yet with an intensity marked as *high*. Modification of the Greek and French expressions is permitted only when the *Vsup* that evokes a *medium* intensity of an emotion is employed as shown in (39) and (41); when the *Vsup* denoting an emotional state of *high* intensity is employed, modification is blocked as in (40) and (42):

(39) *Η Άννα νιώθει χαρά / μεγάλη χαρά.*
      i   Ana nioθi χara / meγali χara
      the Anna feels joy / big   joy
      'Anna is happy / very happy.'

(40) *Η Άννα πετάει από χαρά / *μεγάλη χαρά.*
      i   Ana petai apo χara / *meγali χara
      the Anna flies of joy / big   joy
      'Anna is very happy.'

(41) *Anna éprouve de la joie / une grande joie.*
      Anna feels   of the joy / a   big   joy
      'Anna is happy / very happy.'

(42)   *Anna rayonne de joie / *rayonne d' une grande joie.*
       Anna shines   of joy / shines   of a   big   joy

       'Anna is very happy.'

Finally, the encoding schema also provides values for the feature *aspect*, i.e., the perspective taken on the internal temporal organization of the emotion event. Different values of *aspect* distinguish different ways of viewing the internal temporal constituency of the same event. The schema adopted provides the values *inchoativeAspect*, *terminativeAspect*, *durativeAspect* and *frequentiveAspect*. The encoding at this level, however, has been finalised only for the Greek MWEs.

6 Discussion

At the final stage of our study, an examination of the interplay between syntactic, semantic and lexical features of the studied MWEs was performed. Moreover, cross-lingual similarities and differences were identified. As has already been mentioned, our working hypothesis was that despite idiosyncrasies, MWEs that pertain to a given semantic class share features that are characteristic for this class; moreover, these features can be even attested cross-linguistically. As has already been mentioned in §5.1 above, MWE identification and classification employs lexical and morphosyntactic besides semantic criteria (Gross 1982; 1998a; Lamiroy 2003). However, they do not apply in all cases in a uniform way, and the variability attested brings about the notion *degree of fixedness* (Gross 1996). On the one hand, fixed expressions bear a meaning that cannot be computed based on the meaning of their constituents and the rules used to combine them. SVCs, on the other hand, have a rather transparent meaning due to the presence of the *Nsent* which retains its original sense. However, a number of problems are posed and the limits between SVCs and verbal fixed expressions (see also §5.1) are in some cases fuzzy: despite the semantic transparency entailed by the *Nsent*, the overall structure is often susceptible to a number of constraints as shown in examples (43) and (44) below:

(43)   *Φωτίστηκε το πρόσωπο του Νίκου από χαρά.*
       fotistikie to prosopo tu Niku apo χara
       was.lit.up the face.NOM the Nikos by happinesss

       'Nikos' face lit up with happiness.'

(44) * Φωτίστηκε ο   Νίκος   από χαρά.
     fotistikie o   Nikos   apo χara
     was.lit.up the Nikos.NOM by   hapiness

According to a study on verbal MWEs (Balibar-Mrabti 1995), expressions like the one depicted in (43) are defined as *semi-fixed* ones. In this respect, the verbal MWEs under study were found to be placed along the continuum *fixed, semi-fixed* and SVCs. Consequently, the class of semi-fixed expressions constitutes a grey zone, the intermediate mentioned in §5.1 and §5.2.2. However, in this work, we opted for classifying semi-fixed expressions that comprise a predicative noun *Nsent* as SVCs.

One step further, the correlation between the features *non-compositionality/fixedness* and the attributes *polarity* and *intensity* was examined. Our underlying assumption was that the degree of fixedness of the relevant expressions and the polarity/intensity of the emotion denoted are highly correlated. In this respect, the focus was placed on the values assigned for the feature *intensity* of the emotion denoted and their correlation to the aspects of MWE category (i.e., fixed expression or SVC). The majority of the considered Greek MWEs, that is 410 expressions, were attributed the value *Negative* for the feature *Polarity*, whereas only 169 were encoded as *Positive* and 133 as *Neutral*. Of these, 97 MWEs denote *anger*, 73 denote *fear*, and 105 denote *sadness*; 90 expressions were identified as expressing *joy* and 30 a *surprise* event. The remaining expressions are distributed across the remaining conceptual categories. Another interesting remark concerns verbal idiomatic *non-compositional* expressions; most of the expressions (260) that have been assigned the value *negative* for the feature *polarity* are also encoded as being of type *fixed* (as opposed to 150 expressions classified as SVCs). Additionally, fixed expressions were – in most cases – attributed a value *high* for the feature *intensity*. Of the approximately 300 *fixed* expressions, 210 are assigned the value *high* for the feature *intensity*. On the contrary, SVCs in both languages do not constitute a uniform class, and the overall emotion intensity denoted depends largely on the *Vsup* selected rather than the *Nsent* itself. Three cases are identified:

- The *Vsup* is selected by all *Nsent* predicates; these verbs[4] adhere to a productive and relatively open paradigmatic axis, and syntactic variability is allowed to some extent. In these cases, the *intensity* of the emotion denoted

---

[4]For example, *έχω* (eχo)/*avoir* 'to have', *νιώθω* (nioθo)/*éprouver* 'to feel' and *αισθάνομαι* (esθanome)/*resentir* 'to feel'.

is determined on the basis of the semantics of the *Nsent*; any possible modifier functions as an intensifier of the emotion denoted.

- The *Vsup* selection is subject to lexical restrictions, and syntactic variability is not allowed.[5] In this case, the *Vsup* contributes to the intensity and/or some aspectual meaning of the emotion denoted. The overall intensity of the emotion expression is determined on the basis of the semantics of the *Nsent*, and the *Vsup* functions as an intensifier.

- The *Vsup* selection is extremely limited or unique, and a strong lexicalization is attested; syntactic variability is not allowed and the *Vsup* is an intensive or aspectual variant that has a strong impact on the intensity of the emotion denoted:

(45) με τρώει η ζήλια   / *στενοχώρια / *λύπη
      me troi i   zilia   / stenoχoria   / lipi
      me eats the jealousy.NOM / worry.NOM / regret.NOM

      'to be devoured by jealousy'

(46) être rongé par la jalousie
      to.be gnawed by the jealousy

      'to be devoured by jealousy'

7 Cross-lingual considerations

Research on idioms reported in Villavicencio et al. (2004) shows that there is remarkable variation in MWEs across languages. Similar variations are attested in the data used in the current research. As one might expect, there is no one-to-one correspondence between syntactic patterns in the two languages. It is worth looking at SVCs and fixed expressions separately here.

Greek and French SVCs present a number of similarities in terms of the underlying syntax and semantics. In some cases, even a direct lexico-syntactic correspondence is observed for a cross-lingual MWE pair with similar semantics as illustrated in (47) and (48) below. Furthermore, semantic transparency in SVCs implies more correspondences at least at the level of syntactical patterns – we have demonstrated this with examples (8) and (9). As one might expect, differences between the Greek and French expressions are limited to basically those

---

[5]For example, *ανατριχιάζω* (anatriχiazo)/*frissoner* 'to shiver', *λάμπω* (labo)/*briller* 'to shine', *λιώνω* (liono)/*fondre* 'to dissolve', etc.

that exist in general between the two languages, i.e., usage of determiners and the indefinite article, case marking for NPs in subject and object position in Greek as opposed to PP complements in French, etc.

(47) to give to the nerves 'to cause anger'
      δίνω στα   νεύρα
      δino sta   nevra
      give to.the nerves

      'to cause anger'

(48) donner sur les nerfs

      to.give on the nerves
      'to cause anger'

In other cases, Greek and French SVCs share the same syntactic structure and underlying semantics, yet their lexical composition is different. The differences are attested both in the lexical choice of the *Vsup* and/or the overall structure of the verbal expression. For example, the French verb *nager* 'to swim' seems to be more productive than its Greek counterpart *πλέω* (pleo) 'to sail' as shown in (49) and (50) below. The latter is only employed in a rather fixed configuration and selects only one *Nsent*, showing, thus, a limited (or even fixed) distribution:

(49) *nager   dans le bonheur/ la joie/ l' optimisme/ l' amour*
      to.swim in   the happiness/ the joy/ the optimism/ the love

      'to be very happy/ happy/ very optimistic/ in love'

(50) *πλέω σε πελάγη ευτυχίας/   *στην ευτυχία/   *στην αισιοδοξία/ *στην*
      pleo se pelaɣi eftixias/   stin eftixia/   stin esioðoksia/ stin
      sail in seas   happiness.GEN/ in.the happiness/ in.the optimism/ in.the
      αγάπη
      aɣapi
      love

      'to be very happy/ happy/ optimistic/ full of love'

Being *conceptual metaphors* (usually obsolete), *fixed expressions* present in some cases considerable similarities in both lexical choice and structure cross-linguistically. Again, differences are limited to the usage of determiners, argument realization, selection of prepositions, etc. Often, the lexicalised nominal element (that assumes the function of the direct object) denotes a part of the body (*Npc*) as exemplified below. These expressions open a slot that is filled by a variable noun in genitive case in Greek and a PP complement in French (*à N* 'to N'). This element is usually realised as a cliticised pronoun – in both Greek (51) and French (52)) – and it designates the beneficiary of the event expressed by the predicate (Leclère 1976; Fotopoulou 1993a). This genitive (in Greek) and PP (in French) is a specific case with semantic and syntactic features; Leclère (1976) has offered the term *datif étendu*) for this genitive:

(51) μου κόβονται τα ήπατα 'my liver is cut'
  του κόπηκαν τα ήπατα
  tu kopikan ta ipata
  he.GEN cut the liver.PL.NOM
  'to be frightened'

(52) *lui casser les pieds*
  him to.break the feet
  'to get on one's nerves'

In some cases, similarities are attested in terms of argument structure. For example, the Greek verbal expression depicted in (53) and its French counterpart shown in (54) are encoded as entries in Greek and French tables. Each table features MWEs that share the same properties and lexico-syntactic constraints; this means that the resulting tables are to a large extent homogenous. Therefore, correspondences between homogenous LG tables in Greek and French can be obtained and mappings of MWEs from one language to the other are feasible.

(53) *βγαίνω από τα ρούχα μου*
  vɣieno apo ta ruχa mu
  get.out from the clothes mine
  'to be very angry'

(54) *sortir de ses gonds*
  to.get.out of one's pumps
  'to be very angry'

Additionally, there are many verbal idiomatic expressions which have no direct or precise equivalent in the other language and they correspond to a single word verbal predicate, as shown in the Greek example (55) which is attributed the French verb *gâcher* 'to spoil':

(55) to me he/she/it takes it out sour 'he/she/it makes it unpleasant to me'

     του   *το βγάζω* *ξινό*

     tu   to vɣazo ksino

     he.GEN it take.out sour

     'to make unpleasant'

Semantically almost equivalent expressions that still present differences in aspectual meaning and/or the intensity of the emotion have been identified in the Greek and (to a large extent) in the French data. Sense discrimination and the alignment of Greek and French MWEs can be enhanced on the basis of the values assigned to those emotion-related attributes: a set of MWEs are classified under the same emotion concept, yet sense discrimination is further enhanced on the basis of the values assigned to emotion-related attributes.

8 Conclusions and future research

MWEs pose challenges with respect to their identification, analysis and representation both to linguistic theory and to applications. In this study, we aimed at consolidating the typologies of emotion MWEs in Greek and French and at finding cross-lingual analogies and asymmetries. The syntactic, lexical and semantic properties of the Greek and French verbal constructions were systematically examined, by taking also into account the semantic properties of the semantic field, namely the features intensity and polarity of the emotion denoted. We have shown that, despite existing idiosyncrasies, in both languages the MWEs in the semantic field of emotion share properties. Moreover, syntactic, semantic and lexical features of emotion MWEs seem to have an impact on the semantics of the expression in terms of emotion-related features. Future work will be oriented towards (a) investigating the properties of semi-fixed expressions, taking into account the degree of fixedness (b) studying the aspectual variants of SVCs in both languages (c) revising the coding used in the emotion Lexicon according to new studies and data and (d) populating the lexical resource with new expressions.

Acknowledgements

The authors would like to thank the anonymous reviewers and the editors for their valuable comments that greatly contributed to improving the manuscript. They are especially grateful to Manfred Sailer for his constructive suggestions and support during the review process.

Abbreviations

ASENT	ajdective denoting emotion	NSENT	noun denoting emotion
CAUS	cause	PPV	pre-verbal position
EXP	experiencer	REFL	reflexive pronoun
INCHO	inchoative	SVC	support verb construction
E	zero element	VSENT	verb denoting emotion
LG	Lexicon-Grammar	VSUP	support verb

References

Balibar-Mrabti, Antoinette. 1995. Une étude de la combinatoire des noms de sentiment dans une grammaire locale. *Langue Française* 105. 88–97.

Belletti, Adriana & Luizi Rizzi. 1988. Psych-verbs and θ-theory. *Natural Language and Linguistic Theory* 6. 291–352.

Calzolari, Nicoletta, Charles J. Fillmore, Ralph Grishman, Nancy Ide, Alessandro Lenci, Catherine MacLeod & Antonio Zampolli. 2002. Towards best practice for multiword expressions in computational lexicons. In *Proceedings of the 3rd International Conference on Language Resources and Evaluation (LREC 2002)*. Las Palmas, Canary Islands.

Constant, Matthieu & Aggeliki Fotopoulou. 2016. *A systematic study on the fixedness degree of verbal multiword expressions: Application to Modern Greek and French*. Tech. rep. PARSEME's 6th general meeting in Struga, FYR Macedonia. Selected posters. 7-8 April 2016.

Copestake, Ann, Fabre Lambeau, Aline Villavicencio, Francis Bond, Timothy Baldwin, Ivan Andrew Sag & Dan Flickinger. 2002. Multiword expressions: Linguistic precision and reusability. In *Proceedings of the 3rd International Conference on Language Resources and Evaluation (LREC 2002)*. Las Palmas, Canary Islands: Association for Computational Linguistics.

Esuli, Andrea & Fabrizio Sebastiani. 2006. SENTIWORDNET: A publicly available lexical resource for opinion mining. In *Proceedings of the 5th International Conference on Language Resources and Evaluation (LREC 2006)*.

Fellbaum, Christiane & Yannick Yvette Mathieu. 2012. Scalar properties of emotion verbs and their representation in WordNet. In *Proceedings of the 6th International Conference of the Global WordNet Association (GWC-2012)*, 100–105. Matsue, Japan.

Fotopoulou, Aggeliki. 1993a. Traitement du cas génitif dans une classification des phrases à compléments figés du grec moderne. *Lingvisticae Investigationes* XVII(2). 259–280.

Fotopoulou, Aggeliki. 1993b. *Une classification des phrases à compléments figés en grec moderne. Étude morphosyntaxique des phrases figées.* Saint-Denis: Université Paris VIII dissertation.

Fotopoulou, Aggeliki, Marianna Mini, Mavina Pantazara & Argyro Moustaki. 2009. La combinatoire lexicale des noms de sentiments en grec moderne. In Iva Novacova & Agnes Tutin (eds.), *Le lexique des émotions*, 81–103. Grenoble: ELLUG.

Giouli, Voula & Aggeliki Fotopoulou. 2012. Emotion verbs in Greek. From Lexicon-Grammar tables to multi-purpose syntactic and semantic lexica. In *Proceedings of the XV Euralex International Congress (EURALEX 2012)*, 485–492. Oslo: University of Oslo.

Giouli, Voula & Aggeliki Fotopoulou. 2014. Linguistically motivated language resources for sentiment analysis. In *Proceedings of the Workshop for Lexical and Grammatical Resources for Language Processing. Collocated with the 25th International Conference on Computational Linguistics (COLING 2014)*, 39–46. Dublin: Dublin City University.

Gross, Maurice. 1975. *Méthodes en syntaxe. Régime des constructions complétives.* Paris: Hermann.

Gross, Maurice. 1982. Une classification des phrases "figées" du français. *Revue Québécoise de Linguistique (RQL)* 11(2). 151–185.

Gross, Maurice. 1995. Une grammaire locale de l'expression des sentiments. *Langue Française* 105. 70–87.

Gross, Maurice. 1996. Les formes *être Prép X* du français. *Lingvisticae Investigationes* 20(2). 217–270.

Gross, Maurice. 1998a. La fonction sémantique des verbes supports. *Travaux de linguistique* 37. 25–46.

Gross, Maurice. 1998b. Les limites de la phrase figée. *Langage* 90. 7–23.

Lamiroy, Béatrice. 2003. Les notions linguistiques de figement et de contrainte. *Lingvisticae Investigationes* 26(1). 1–14.

Leclère, Christian. 1976. Datifs syntaxiques et datif éthique. *Méthodes en grammaire française* 7396.

Leeman, Danielle. 1991. Hurler de rage, rayonner de bonheur: remarques sur une construction en de. *Langue française* (91). 80–101.

Levin, Beth. 1993. *English verb classes and alternations: A preliminary investigation.* Chicago: University of Chicago Press.

Mathieu, Yannick Yvette & Christiane Fellbaum. 2010. Verbs of emotion in French and English. In *Proceedings of the Fifth Global WordNet Conference.* Mumbai, India.

Mathieu, Yvette Yannick. 1999. Les prédicats de sentiment. *Langages* 136. 41–52.

Mathieu, Yvette Yannick. 2005. A computational semantic lexicon of French verbs of emotion. In James G. Shanahan, Yan Qu & Janyce Wiebe (eds.), *Computing attitude and affect in text*, 109–123. Dordrecht: Springer.

Mini, Marianna. 2009. *Linguistic and psycholinguistic study of fixed verbal expressions with fixed subject in Greek: A morphosyntactic analysis, lexicosemantic gradation and processing by elementary school children*. Patras, Greece: University of Patras dissertation.

Moustaki, Argyro, Mavina Pantazara, Aggeliki Fotopoulou & Marianna Mini. 2008. Comment traduire les noms d'émotion. Etude contrastive entre le grec moderne et le français. *Discours. Revue de linguistique, psycholinguistique et informatique. A journal of linguistics, psycholinguistics and computational linguistics* (3).

Nunberg, Geoffrey, Ivan A. Sag & Thomas Wasow. 1994. Idioms. *Language* 70(3). 491–538.

Pantazara, Mavina, Aggeliki Fotopoulou, Marianna Mini & Argyro Moustaki. 2008. La description des noms de sentiments du grec moderne. *Lingvisticae Investigationes* 31(2).

Plutchik, Robert. 2001. The nature of emotions. *American scientist* 89(4). 344–350.

Tutin, Agnès, Iva Novakova, Francis Grossmann & Cristelle Cavalla. 2006. Esquisse de typologie des noms d'affect à partir de leurs propriétés combinatoires. *Langue française* (2). 32–49.

Villavicencio, Aline, Timothy Baldwin & Benjamin Waldron. 2004. A multilingual database of idioms. In *Proceedings of the Fourth International Conference on Language Resources and Evaluation (LREC 2004)*, 1127–1130. Lisbon, Portugal.

Wilson, Theresa, Janyce Wiebe & Paul Hoffmann. 2005. Recognizing contextual polarity in phrase-level sentiment analysis. In *Proceedings of the Conference on Human Language Technology and Empirical Methods in Natural Language Processing*, 347–354.

Chapter 4

Flexibility of multiword expressions and Corpus Pattern Analysis

Patrick Hanks
RIILP, University of Wolverhampton, England

Ismail El Maarouf
Adarga Ltd., England

Michael Oakes
RIILP, University of Wolverhampton, England

This chapter is set in the context of Corpus Pattern Analysis (CPA), a technique developed by Patrick Hanks to map meaning onto word patterns found in corpora. The main output of CPA is the Pattern Dictionary of English Verbs (PDEV), currently describing patterns for over 1,600 verbs, many of which are acknowledged to be multiword expressions (MWEs) such as phrasal verbs or idioms. PDEV entries are manually produced by lexicographers, based on the analysis of a substantial sample of concordance lines from the corpus, so the construction of the resource is very time-consuming. The motivation for the work presented in this chapter is to speed up the discovery of these word patterns, using methods which can be transferred to other languages. This chapter explores the benefits of a detailed contrastive analysis of MWEs found in English and French corpora with a view on English-French translation. The comparative analysis is conducted through a case study of the pair (*bite*, *mordre*), to illustrate both CPA and the application of statistical measures for the automatic extraction of MWEs. The approach taken in this chapter takes its point of departure from the use of statistics developed initially by Church & Hanks (1989). Here we look at statistical measures which have not yet been tested for their ability to discover new collocates, but are useful for characterizing verbal MWEs already found. In particular we propose measures to characterize the mean span, rigidity, diversity, and idiomaticity of a given MWE.

Patrick Hanks, Ismail El Maarouf & Michael Oakes. 2018. Flexibility of multiword expressions and Corpus Pattern Analysis. In Manfred Sailer & Stella Markantonatou (eds.), *Multiword expressions: Insights from a multi-lingual perspective*, 93–119. Berlin: Language Science Press.
DOI:10.5281/zenodo.1182593

Patrick Hanks, Ismail El Maarouf & Michael Oakes

1 Introduction: phraseology and Multi-Word Expressions

Traditionally, people have long believed that each word has one or more meanings and that these meanings can be selected and put together, as if in a child's Lego set, to construct propositions, questions, etc. This belief is still widely (and unquestioningly, unthinkingly) held by many NLP (Natural Language Processing) researchers among others. This may indeed be a good way of accounting for basic *propositional logic,* but it accounts at best for only a very limited subset of natural language use. An alternative view is that logics are by-products of natural language. At the very least, we may say that the relationship between language and logic is not well understood. If the "Lego set" theory of meaning in language were tenable, it would not have been necessary for NLP and AI (Artificial Intelligence) researchers such as Ide & Wilks (2007), after many years of intensive (and expensive) effort, to declare that projects in Word Sense Disambiguation (WSD) have failed to achieve even their most basic goals.

> At present, WSD work is at a crossroads: systems have hit a reported ceiling of 70%+ accuracy (Kilgarriff et al. 2004), the source and kinds of sense inventories that should be used in WSD work is an issue of continued debate, and the usefulness of stand-alone WSD systems for current NLP applications is questionable. (Ide & Wilks 2007: 15).

The alternative view mentioned here is supported by lexicographers such as Atkins et al. (2001), Kilgarriff et al. (2004), and Hanks (2000). These lexicographers argue that much of the meaning of an utterance is carried by underlying patterns of co-selection of the words actually used, rather than by simple concatenations. These conclusions overlap to some extent with the tenets of Construction Grammar, though the methodologies are very different. In corpus linguistics, Sinclair declared, after a lifetime's empirical research into texts, corpora, and meaning, "Many if not most meanings require the presence of more than one word for their normal realisation" (Sinclair 1998: 4).

If these lexicographers and corpus linguists are right, it might appear that MWEs play a central role in the meaningful use of language. They are not merely an irritating set of exceptions, as used to be thought. According to this, MWEs are not exceptions to the rule; they are the rule. The exceptions, insofar as they exist in normal language use, are isolated meaningful uses of single words.

It has long been obvious that the meaning of MWEs such as *of course, a ballpark figure,* and *spill the beans* is not compositional. No courses, ball parks, or beans are invoked by someone deconstructing the meaning intended by a speaker who uses these expressions. However, extended analysis of large volumes of data leads to the somewhat unwelcome conclusion that the concept of a MWE may also be flawed, being nothing more than an attempt to extend the "Lego-set" theory to cover some so-called *fixed expressions* such as *spill the beans* and *kick the bucket*. Here, the choice of lexical items is fixed: one cannot talk meaningfully, except perhaps in jest, about *tipping over the haricots* or *booting the pail*. However, even in these very fixed MWEs, certain grammatical alternations, in particular verb inflections, are normal and unremarkable.

More to the point is the fact that many other expressions, that at first sight might be considered compositional, are associated with a limited phraseology. They do not vary freely, but employ selectional variations drawn from within a (usually quite small) lexical set. Such patterns are found for many expressions that intuitions alone might encourage us to classify as fixed. Corpus evidence shows that people not only grasp at straws, they also clutch at straws and even seize on straws. Moon (1998) observes that *shiver in one's shoes* (meaning 'to be afraid') may at first seem to be a fixed expression, but in fact corpus evidence shows that every lexical item in the expression allows a modicum of variation: people quake in their boots, shake in their sandals, and she even found a mention of policemen quaking in their size fourteens. (English policemen are supposed proverbially to have big feet.) The meaning of the idiom is the same in all cases; the cognitive values of the lexical items are so similar as to be virtually identical; and yet the actual words used to realize the expression can be different.

Conversely, when we examine the corpus evidence for an expression that might uncontroversially be classified as compositional, such as (1),

(1) *the wind was blowing from the north*

we find that the utterer of this unremarkable little sentence is in fact activating the meaning by drawing on a pattern containing a small but open-ended lexical set of items alternating with *wind: gale, blizzard, hurricane, typhoon, breeze, air,* not to mention adjectival subclassifications such as *a hot dry wind, a cold wind, strong winds, the fenland winds, a unidirectional wind.* To these can be added some much rarer lexical items such as *tempest, trades,* and *zephyr.* At the other end of the sentence forming the prototype or stereotype for this particular pattern, we find a very much larger set of expressions functioning as adverbials of direction: *from the north,* including *from the south, from the sea, over a cliff face, up the street, through a spider's web,* and so on.

These very conventional expressions are best classified as realizations of non-compositional patterns rather than as compositional concatenations for a variety of reasons. A prominent one is that the pattern so identified is contrastive: it is a set of stereotypical phrases that contrast with other uses of the words. For example, this pattern (see example 2) contrasts with other patterns having different meanings formed with the same verb, such as *to blow a whistle* and *to blow up a bridge*.

Another reason for seeking to identify patterns of verb use is that, once a pattern is established in the language or in the mind of a speaker, it can be exploited metaphorically and in other ways. Some typical exploitations of this pattern of the verb *blow*, found in the British National Corpus, are shown in examples (2)-(6).

(2) *Dennis Healey [a politician] wobbles about according to which way the wind is blowing.*

(3) *The winds of neo-liberalism are blowing a gale through Prague.*

(4) *Faint liberal breezes had been blowing through the Vatican since the second Vatican Council.*

(5) *...the winds of change that have blown through the energy business.*

(6) *The winds of fate blew for Jean Morris, winner of Middlesbrough Council's Captain Cook Birthday Balloon Race.*

Metaphorical exploitations bring in additional evidence that a pattern has become established. In the previous examples, the meaning can only be understood in relation to the *the wind blows* (not, say, *blowing up a bridge*), but cannot be confused with it, as there is no wind blowing literally.

The aim of this short introduction to MWEs was to set the study of MWEs in the broad context of phraseology, and stress the obstacles in the way of linguistic description. In order to understand and process meaning in text, it is necessary first to compile inventories of patterns of language use, which can be used as benchmarks against which actual utterances can be compared. The following section presents Corpus Pattern Analysis, a method for deriving patterns from corpora.

2 The Corpus Pattern Analysis framework

Corpus Pattern Analysis (CPA) is a research procedure designed to create empirically well-founded resources for NLP applications by combining interactively human data analysis and machine learning. It is based on the Theory of Norms and Exploitations (TNE, Hanks & Pustejovsky 2004; Hanks & Pustejovsky 2005;

Hanks 2013). TNE in turn is a theory that owes much to the work of Pustejovsky on the Generative Lexicon (Pustejovsky 1995), to Wilks (1975)'s theory of preference semantics, to Sinclair's work on corpus analysis and collocations (Sinclair 1966; 1987; 1991; 2004), to the Cobuild project in lexical computing (Sinclair 1987), and to the Hector project (Atkins 1992; Hanks 1994). CPA is also influenced by frame semantics (Fillmore & Atkins 1992). It is complementary to FrameNet. Where FrameNet offers an in-depth analysis of semantic frames, CPA offers a systematic analysis of the patterns of meaning and use of each verb. Each CPA pattern can in principle be plugged into a FrameNet semantic frame. Some work in American linguistics (Jackendoff 2002) has complained about the excessive "syntactocentrism" of American linguistics in the 20th century. TNE offers a lexicocentric approach, with opportunities for synthesis, which will go some way towards redressing the balance.

CPA starts from the observation that whereas most words are very ambiguous, most patterns have one and only one sense. Each word is associated with a number of patterns based on valency, which is comparatively stable, and one or more sets of preferred collocations, which are highly variable (Hanks 2012). In CPA, patterns of word use are associated with statements of meaning, called IM- PLICATURES. Each pattern has a primary implicature (the meaning of the pattern), and possibly a number of secondary implicatures (de Schryver 2010). To take a simple example, the word *blow* is multiply ambiguous. However, the expression *blow your nose* is unambiguous and contrasts with 60 or 70 other patterns of use of the same verb.

In the Pattern Dictionary of English Verbs (PDEV; http://pdev.org.uk), the main output of CPA, the sense of *blow your nose* is stored in the pattern "[[Human]] blow {nose}" while in the sense of "the wind blows" is represented by the pattern "[[Wind | Vapour | Dust]] blow [No object] [Adverbial of direction]". Patterns may combine various kinds of categories such as semantic types (Human, Wind, Vapour, Dust), grammatical categories (Adverbial of direction) and lexical items (*nose*). Semantic types are taken from the corpus-driven CPA Semantic Ontology available at http://pdev.org.uk/#onto. These categories may fill slots in the pattern template based on the SPOCA model, an acronym standing for the main clause roles that may be filled by arguments of a verb in a proposition: a Subject, a Predicator, an Object, a Complement, and an Adverbial (Halliday 1994). Each argument can in turn be further characterized if the pattern requires it, by filling information on the "subargumental cues" such as the nature of determiners, modifiers, quantifiers, prepositional phrases, and adverbs or particles.

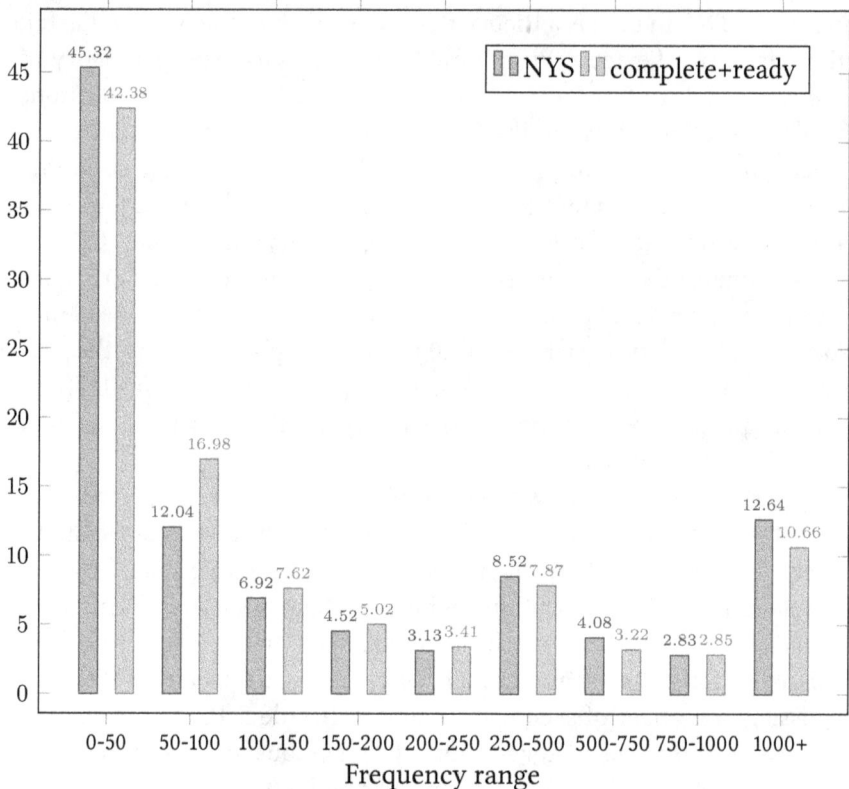

Figure 1: Proportion of NYS and complete and ready verbs w.r.t. frequency range in BNC50.

At the time of writing, PDEV covered 1,614 verbs for a total of 6,163 patterns, out of an estimated 5,500 total number of verbs in English (PDEV is therefore about 30% complete). PDEV is linked to a portion of the British National Corpus (BNC), BNC50, from which some of the statistics presented in this chapter are computed. BNC50 contains about 54 million tokens, and BNC, about 100 million. Figure 1 shows that the frequency distribution of complete verbs is very similar to that of NYS (Not Yet Started) verbs, e.g. that 40 to 45% of English verbs have a frequency lower than 50 in BNC50. For this reason, although PDEV is incomplete, it contains a representative sample of English verbs, large enough to warrant pilot studies. Results will need to be confirmed when PDEV is complete.

In PDEV, most verbs have a low number of patterns: the average number of patterns per verb is 3.8, and the verb with the greatest number of patterns is *break*, with 83 patterns. More than a quarter of verbs have only one pattern and

78% of verbs have five patterns or less. Verbs can also be contrasted in terms of qualitative characteristics. Particularly, some of them are used in idioms, others as phrasal verbs, and others combine with other lexical items in set phrases, that we propose to call lexically grounded patterns. Table 1 indicates the number of entries and patterns for these MWE-related categories of verbs.

Table 1: Number of verbs and of patterns for several MWE categories in PDEV.

MWE type	# verbs	# patterns	% patterns
Lexically grounded patterns	458	1,126	18.3
Phrasal verb patterns	198	512	8.3
Idiom patterns	200	453	7.3
MWE total	**548**	**1,649**	**26.7**

A *lexically grounded pattern* is a pattern which takes a lexical item or lexical set as an argument, either in subject, object, complement or adverbial position. For instance "[[Human]] take {responsibility} for [[Anything]]" is an example where a lexical item, *responsibility*, occupies the object position. In general the presence of lexical items is a strong sign of fixedness, so a significant portion of lexically grounded patterns overlap with idioms. All in all, there are 1,649 MWE patterns in PDEV, which accounts for 26.7% of PDEV patterns (about 34% of verbs). As each pattern is linked to a set of examples from the BNC, the whole MWE pattern set is connected to a total of 26,392 corpus examples (an estimated 84,836 over the whole BNC50, i.e. 1,545 per million).

PDEV *idioms* show very diverse statistical properties internally. For instance the estimated frequency in BNC ranges from 1 (e.g. *blowing off steam*) to 1,071 occurrences (for *as follows*) in BNC50, with an average frequency of 23.5 examples in BNC50 and a high standard deviation (67.2). 70% of idioms have 5 or more associated examples and 90% have less than 40 examples. The verb with the highest number of idioms is *throw*, with 24 idioms. Verbs with idioms on average have, for 64% of them, one idiom, for 19% of them, two idioms, and for 17%, three or more idioms.

3 A CPA study for English-French translation

The case study presented in this section focuses on *bite*, because it was found to encapsulate a large number of facts about English verbs, and particularly idiomatic structures. This verb is compared to the French *mordre*, which translates to 'bite' in its primary literal meaning: 'using teeth to cut'. We will observe how these verbs are used in each language, identify their common features and divergences by applying CPA to corpora. *Bite* was analysed using a sample of 500 lines from the BNC, and the same sample size was extracted from the Frtenten corpus (11 billion words; Jakubíček et al. 2013) for *mordre*.

Bite and *mordre* share interesting similarities in terms of their syntactic and semantic properties. Both verbs are mostly direct transitive, see examples (7) and (8), and can sometimes be accompanied with a locative adverbial, to indicate the [[Body Part]] bitten. Both verbs are also used in an intransitive pattern where the bitten entity, typically found in object position, is moved to a prepositional complement position, with *into* (*dans* in French) as preposition, see examples (9) and (10).

(7) *Those dogs bit the neighbours, the dustbin men, visiting aunts and each other.*

(8) *Le propriétaire ou le détenteur d'un chien qui a mordu une personne ou un autre animal a l'obligation de le déclarer au commissariat de son arrondissement.*

'The owner or the holder of the dog which has bitten a person or another animal is under the obligation of declaring it to the district police.'

(9) I'll wager that your salivary glands started pumping out liquid as you imagined yourself biting into the lemon.

(10) *Je mords dans une pêche : un goût d'eau sucrée accompagné d'un sentiment de vide.*

'I bite in a peach: a taste of sweet water together with a feeling of emptiness.'

These syntactic patterns are frequently employed in different situations which sometimes share very little in common with the literal meaning of the verb. To contrast these uses, CPA entries make use of semantic types which characterise the semantic properties shared by the collocates found in a given syntactic slot. In the literal sense of transitive patterns, *bite* and *mordre* typically collocate with [[Human]] (with the particular case of vampires) and [[Animal]] (e.g. *dogs*) as subjects, and with [[Human]], [[Animal]], and [[Body Part]] as objects. Other [[Physical Object]] nouns (e.g. *pillows, coins, pencils*) were found in English, but not in French, although they could be found in a larger sample. Transitive patterns of *bite* were also found to combine with [[Eventuality]] as subject and [[Human]] or [[Institution]] as objects, as in example (11).

(11)   *Provincial had been bitten by its own success.*

In this case, the pattern means "[[Eventuality]] adversely affect [[Human]] or [[Institution]]". The construction *bite + into* was also found with a metaphorical pattern expressed as "[[Event]] bites into [[Event]]", sharing the same meaning as the previous pattern (signaling an adverse effect). These metaphorical uses of *bite* seem to be English-specific: no such pattern was found in the French sample. This is because French typically uses *ronger* 'gnaw', as in example (12).

(12)   a.   *The recession is biting deeply into industry.*

     b.   *La recession ronge durement l'industrie.*

When English speakers use *bite* with direct objects such as *nails* or *fingers* to mean 'chewing at one's fingernails, biting the tips off', French speakers use *ronger* for *ongles* and *doigts* respectively. In this case, it is also considered as a distinct pattern in French. Other patterns were found, such as "[[Physical Object 1]] bite in|into [[Physical Object 2]]",[1] where the subject is neither [[Human]] nor [[Animal]]. This pattern can only be translated to French with *mordre* to cover uses where "[[Blade]] makes small cuts into [[Physical object]]". When the subject is *acid*, signalling the corroding effect the acid has on metal, French uses *ronger*. For other types of object nouns, such as *ploughs*, French would use the phrasal expression *se planter + dans*.

Semantic types can also help to contrast existing patterns from uses which combine with specific animals, e.g. [[Snake]], which was found both in French and English, and which refer to a different situation, defined as "[[Snake]] stabs [[Human]] or [[Animal]] with fangs, typically injecting poison under the skin". However, when considering [[Insect]] (e.g. *mosquitoes*) in subject position, the normal French verb is *piquer* (see example (13) below).[2]

(13)   a.   *The mosquitos came up and bit me in the dark.*

     b.   *Les moustiques sont venus et m'ont piqué dans le noir.*

However, *bite* does not collocate with nouns of other flying bugs such as *wasps*, *bees*, or *hornets*,[3] whereas these nouns can be used indifferently with *piquer*. This language-specific feature can be explained by the extra-linguistic fact that insects bite to feed, but bees, wasps, and hornets possess a specific device, positioned at

---

[1]English also uses patterns with the phrasal verb *eat away* for this meaning.

[2]Although *mordu par les moustiques* is acceptable.

[3]English uses the verb *sting*.

the bottom of their bodies, used to kill or in self-defence. This is the only pattern where *piquer* can be used as a translation of *bite*. The pattern "[[Human]] or [[Animal]] bite through [[Physical_Object]]" also has a literal meaning, but cannot be translated using *mordre*. The best translation equivalent appears to be *grignoter* (literally *nibble*), since it keeps the notion of 'using teeth', and correctly translates 'insects biting through leaves'. However this verb does not translate the fact that the bitten entity is filled with holes. The verb *bite* was only found in a single intransitive use, "[[Process]] bites", with the meaning "[have] a noticeable effect, usually an adverse effect", as in *the recession bit deeper*. This would be translated into French with the expression *se faire sentir* (literally 'to be felt'). The verb *mordre* was also found in metaphorical patterns which could not be translated with *bite*, namely "[[Building]] mord [[Area]]", as in (14), and "[[Vehicle]] mord la route", as in (15).

(14) *Certaines des constructions mordaient sur des terres privées.*

'Some of the buildings **encroached** on private lands.'

(15) *Quand vient le temps d'effectuer un dépassement, le véhicule mord la route.*

'When the time comes to pass the car in front, the vehicle **grips** the road.'

In addition to these patterns, 6 idioms were found for *mordre* (see Table 2), and 10 idioms for *bite* (see Table 3).

Table 2: Idiom CPA patterns for the verb *mordre*.

No	Pattern / *Implicature*	Frequency	%
4	[[[Human]] | le poisson] mord ([à l'hamecon | à l'appat]) [[Human]] *takes the bait (= is lured to do something that has bad consequences)*	10	2
7	[[Human]] mord {la vie à pleines dents} [[Human]] *enjoys life to the full [literally, *bites life with full teeth]*	6	1.2
9	[[Human]] se mord {les doigts} [[Human]] *experiences a bitter time [literally, *bites his/her fingers]*	21	4.2
11	[[Human 1]] fait mordre [la poussière] [à [[Human]]] [[Human 1]] *causes [[Human 2]] to bite the dust (= to die) or to lose a challenge [the latter sense only in French]*	6	1.2
12	[le serpent] se mord [la queue] [[Human]] *is stuck in a [[State of affairs]] and cannot find a way out [literally, *the snake bites his own tail]*	16	3.2
16	[[Human]] ne mord pas [NO OBJ]] [[Human]] *does not bite (= is harmless)*	6	1.2

Table 3: Idiom CPA patterns for the verb *bite*.

No	Pattern / *Implicature*	Frequency	%
13	Human 1 bites Human 2's head off	5	1.22
	Human 1 speaks sharply and unkindly to Human 2		
14	Human bites REFLDET lip	8	1.96
	Human grips his or her lip firmly with the teeth		
15	Human bites off more than [[Human]] can chew	4	0.98
	Human undertakes a task that is too difficult for him or her to *accomplish successfully*		
16	Human bites the hand that feeds [[Human]]	5	1.22
	Human attacks his or her benefactor		
17	Human or Institution bites the bullet	21	5.13
	Human or Institution decides to do something necessary but unpleasant		
18	Human is bitten by the [MOD] bug	7	1.71
	Human becomes very interested in [MOD]		
19	Human bites the dust	2	0.49
	Human dies suddenly and violently		
20	Entity or Process bites the dust	8	1.96
	Entity or Process comes to a sudden and unwelcome end		
21	Human bites REFLDET tongue	8	1.96
	Human makes a desperate effort not to say what is on his or her mind		
22	Once bitten twice shy	3	0.73
	An unpleasant experience causes someone to be more cautious in future		

These idioms share little in common (apart from the correspondence between patterns 11 in French and 19 in English) and do not involve the notion of 'teeth cutting'. Thus the correct French to English translation (and vice versa) required knowledge that is encoded in CPA patterns. Pattern 12, for instance, *le serpent se mord la queue*, is used to refer to situations where *serpents* 'snakes' are not involved, a phenomenon generally referred to as non-compositionality. In the next section we propose to measure this property as well as other important features, such as rigidity, using statistical measures. These measures will be applied to idioms which will be the focus of §4.

4 Statistical measures for the characterisation of MWEs

In this section, we will describe the use of statistical measures to automatically characterise the flexibility of MWEs. We feel that this is an important research topic, as it can contribute to describing in which respects MWEs are flexible and help to speed up their extraction from corpora.

4.1 Word association measures and lexicography: PMI

In psycholinguistics, *word association* means for example that subjects think of a term such as *nurse* more quickly after the stimulus of a related term such as *doctor*. Church & Hanks (1989) redefined *word association* in terms of objective statistical measures designed to show whether a pair of words are found together in text more frequently than one would expect by chance. PMI (Point-wise Mutual Information) between word x and word y is given by the formula

(16)
$$I(x,y) = log_2 P(x,y)/P(x).P(y)$$

where P(x,y) is the probability of the two words occurring in a common context (such as a window of 5 consecutive words), while $P(x)$ and $P(y)$ are the probabilities of finding words x and y respectively anywhere in the corpus. PMI is positive if the two words tend to co-occur, 0 if they occur together as often as one would expect by chance, and less than 0 if they are in complementary distribution (Church & Hanks 1989). PMI was used by Church & Hanks to examine the content word collocates of the verb *shower*, which were found to include *abuse, accolades, affection, applause, arrows* and *attention*. Human examination of these lists is needed to identify the *seed* members of categories with which the verb can occur, such as [[Speech Act]] and [[Physical Object]], giving at least two senses of the verb (Hanks 2012).

4.2 Span, rigidity, diversity and idiomaticity

Smadja (1993) recommends that collocations should not only be measured by their *strength*, such as by using the z-score, but also by their *flexibility*. We propose to characterise the flexibility of a multiword expression using four statistical measures, each focusing on a dimension of variation.

A MWE can be characterised by its mean span MEAN SPAN, that is, the stretch of text it is found to cover on average. This can be measured using the mean μ of the relative distances between two words making up the MWE, and computed as follows:

(17)
$$\mu(X,Y) = \frac{1}{n}\sum_{i=1}^{n} dist(X_i, Y_i)$$

A MWE can also be further characterised by its RIGIDITY. This can be measured using the standard deviation σ of the relative distances between the two words:

(18)
$$\sigma\left(X,Y\right) = \sqrt{\frac{1}{n}\sum_{i=1}^{n}\left(dist\left(X_i, Y_i\right) - \mu\left(X, Y\right)\right)^2}$$

For standard deviation, the minimum value when all the examples have identical span is 0, and there is no theoretical upper limit. Higher values would indicate a flexible or semantic, rather than a rigid, lexical collocation.

In a study of David Wyllie's English translation of Kafka's *Metamorphosis*, Oakes (2012) found that *stuck fast* and *office assistant* had mean inter-word distances of 1 with a standard deviation of 0. This showed that in this particular text, they were completely fixed collocations where the first word was always immediately followed by the second. Conversely, *collection* and *samples* had a mean distance of 2.5 with a standard deviation of 0.25. This collocation was a little more flexible, occurring both as *collection of samples* and *collection of textile samples*. *Mr. Samsa* had a mean distance of 1.17 and a standard deviation of 0.32. This is because it usually appeared as *Mr. Samsa* with no intervening words, but sometimes as *Mr. and Mrs. Samsa*.

Another way of looking at the flexibility of a collocation is by measuring the DIVERSITY of surface forms found for that collocation. A rigid collocation, where all found examples are identical in form and span, has very low diversity, while a collocation which has many surface forms has much higher diversity. One measure of diversity, popular in ecological studies, is Shannon's diversity index, which is equivalent to entropy in information theory, and given by the formula:

(19)
$$E = -\sum_{i=1}^{N} p_i \log_2 p_i$$

E is entropy, N is the number of different surface forms found for the collocation, i refers to each surface form in turn, and P_i is the proportion of all surface forms made up of the surface form currently under consideration. The choice of logarithms to the base 2 ensures that the units of diversity are bits. The minimum value of diversity (when all the examples of a MWE are identical) is 0, while the maximum value (when all the examples occur in different forms) is the logarithm to the base 2 of the number of examples found.

Finding statistical evidence for the flexibility of a sequence of words does not automatically entail that all the examples of the sequence belong to a MWE, and that the reading is non-literal. We therefore propose to measure the IDIOMATICITY of a MWE in context, by taking the ratio of the number of idiomatic occurrences of the expression divided by its total number of occurrences:

(20)

$$Idiomaticity\ (x,y) = \frac{number\ of\ idiomatic\ occurrences}{total\ number\ of\ occurrences}$$

A value of 1 would indicate that the MWE is always idiomatic, while a lower value would indicate that the MWE can be ambiguous with respect to its idiomatic reading. It must be borne in mind that this equation depends on a number of factors such as the overall frequency of the verb of a MWE in the specific language. The more frequent in everyday language the constituents of the MWE are, the more probable for them to be encountered in a corpus in their literal meaning. This is not related to the idiomaticity of the expression per se, which has to do with the opacity of the expression: the more opaque (as opposed to transparent) it is, the more idiomatic it is.

4.3 Worked out example

To illustrate how the values of each measure are computed, we propose a worked out example based on a pair of words used as boundaries, *bite* and *dog*, in a sample of 10 examples taken from pattern 1 of *bite*:

(21) "[Human 1 | Animal 1] bites [Animal 2 | Physical Object | Human 2]"

We chose this pair because it is a strong collocation (PMI = 7.7 in BNC). To apply our statistical measures, the first thing to do is to compute the distance between the boundary words. First, it is worth noting that we lump together alternative surface forms of the same boundary word, so we consider both *dogs* and *dog* as one word. Different decisions at this stage may lead to different results.

Figure 2 provides an example using signed distance (left or right): in the first example, *bite* is four words away to the left of *bite*, the distance is therefore -4. To compute the mean span, however, we recommend using the unsigned distance (i.e., 4 for the first example), but it is important to use the signed distance to compute the standard deviation, in order to capture word order variation. The unsigned text distances are therefore, in order of appearance of the examples, 4,4,3,2,4,1,3,2,1,2.

The mean μ characterises the mean span of an expression: *bite* and *dog* are 2.6 words apart.

(22)
$$\mu_{\{bite,dog\}} = \frac{4+4+3+2+4+1+3+2+1+2}{10} = 2.6$$

The standard deviation characterises the rigidity of an expression and makes use of the mean of the signed distances μ' computed as follows:

(23)
$$\mu'_{\{bite,dog\}} = \frac{(-4)+(-4)+3+(-2)+4+(-1)+3+(-2)+(-1)+(-2)}{10} = -0.6$$

The standard deviation can therefore be computed as:

(24)
$$\mu'_{\{bite,dog\}} = \sqrt{\frac{(-4-(-0.6))^2+(-4-(-0.6))^2++(-2-(-0.6))^2}{10}} = \sqrt{\frac{76.4}{10}} = 2.76$$

The score obtained for *bite* and *dog* is indicative of a low rigidity (2.76).

To compute diversity (entropy), we extract all the patterns of word forms between boundaries and count the frequency of each pattern class. Again, characters could also be used as the basic unit, but we use words; the string of the pattern can be characterised in various ways, we use word forms. A pattern is a full string between boundaries, with the null class accounting for cases where boundary words are adjacent. For X = {*dog,dogs*}, Y = {*bite,bites,bit,bitten*}, and i = {*that barks doesn't, that had been, another. In, to, by a police, {}, his pet, are, always*},

'A dog^{-4} that^{-3} barks^{-2} doesn't^{-1}	bite^0	1	,' replied Antonio Navarro,
of the $dogs^{-3}$ that^{-2} had been^{-1}	bitten^0	2	and strayed: scared that th
in saliva when one animal	bites^0	3	another^1. in^2 $dogs^3$, one of t
who had trained his dog^{-2} to^{-1}	bite^0	4	Arabs, and who informed
/p> He was chased and	bitten^0	5	by^1 a^2 police^3 dog^4 and then a
t was saved when her dog^{-1}	bit^0	6	him. The 22-year-
heltenham yesterday after	biting^0	7	his^1 pet^2 dog^3 , which was at
time by their own dog^{-2} are^{-1}	bitten^0	8	in the bedroom. In our bree
d. After that $dogs^{-1}$	bit^0	9	me on the feet. Blood came
/ herself that $dogs^{-2}$ always^{-1}	bite^0	10	people, especially them. T

Figure 2: Example of calculated distances for the pair (*bite, dog*) in concordance for *bite*.

P_i corresponds to the number of times the string is observed in the sample, divided by the total number of examples (in our case, 10). The entropy is computed as follows:

$$(25) \quad E_{\{bite,dog\}} = - \left(\left(\tfrac{1}{10} \log_2 \tfrac{1}{10} \right) + \left(\tfrac{1}{10} \log_2 \tfrac{1}{10} \right) + + \left(\tfrac{1}{10} \log_2 \tfrac{1}{10} \right) \right) = 3.12$$

The entropy is quite high as there is no particular pattern that dominates the sample: only the null pattern occurs twice, but the others, only once. Finally, no expression formed with *bite* and *dog* was found to have an idiomatic reading, therefore the idiomaticity is equal to 0.

The proposed measures are described for two variables. However, many idioms include more than two words, such as *let the cat out of the bag*. In such cases we take the span of the idiom as the distance from the first word to the last, which for this example would be 6 words.

5 A contrastive statistical analysis of idioms

In a pilot experiment on the annotated sample of the BNC corpus of *bite*, we found that the phrase *bite the bullet* was maximally rigid, as it occurred all 9 times in exactly that form. Thus the standard deviation of the collocation span was 0, and its diversity was also 0. In contrast, the phrase *bitten by the ...bug* was extremely flexible, occurring all 6 times in different forms such as *bitten by the travel bug*, *bitten by the London bug*, and *bitten by the bug of the ocean floor*. The standard deviation of spans was relatively small (0.48), reflecting that in all cases but one the variation consisted of the insertion of a single word, but the diversity index was at its maximum value for a set of 6 examples, log2(6) = 2.585.

The results for *bite* were borne out when the experiment was repeated on a larger corpus, the entire BNC. Table 4 shows the results obtained for English idioms. Idioms are represented by their boundary words and the table provides the scores using standard measures of collocational strength (PMI, t-score, and LogDice), along with the absolute frequency and our new measures: idiomaticity, entropy, mean span, and standard deviation.

In the full BNC, there were 19 occurrences of "[bite] by X the bug" altogether, where "[bite]" stands for any grammatical variant of *bite*, such as *bitten*, and "X" stands for any number (possibly zero) of intervening words. 16 of these were idiomatic, including 3 variants of the farewell *sleep tight, don't let the bed bugs bite*, and 3 were literal as in *I've been bitten by bugs in a hooker's bed*. This gave an idiomaticity of 16 / 19 = 0.842. Of the idiomatic examples, almost all were unique, such as *bitten by the travel bug* - the other *bugs* included *puppy love, acting, racing,*

Table 4: Summary of scores for some idioms of *bite*. SD: Standard Deviation

Idiom	Freq (total)	PMI	t-score	Log-Dice	Idioma-ticity	Entropy	Mean span	SD
[back] [bite]	87	5.914	10.380	5.549	0.989	0.338	1.057	0.277
[bullet] [bite]	36	10.484	6.477	8.561	1	1.069	2.055	0.404
[head] [bite] [off]	30	6.009	7.639	5.600	0.775	3.281	3.032	2.721
[dust] [bite]	26	8.918	5.088	7.438	1	0.235	2.03	0.192
[bug] [bite]	19	10.589	4.688	7.894	0.842	3.326	3.125	2.578

flower pressing and *showbiz*. On 3 of these occasions the nature of the bug did not appear between *bitten* and *bug*, which were simply connected as *bitten by the bug*. The Shannon diversity, resulting from pattern classes of 4, 3 and 3 members and 9 unique occurrences, had a very high value of 3.326. In terms of rigidity, the mean distance between *bite* and *bug* was 3.125, with a high standard deviation of 2.578. This was because cases such as *the acting bug really bit me* used the inchoative alternation, so *bug* appeared before *bit*. Also, influencing rigidity was the fact that even in the active voice, the number of intervening words[4] could vary.

The MWE *bite the bullet* occurred in 36 sentences altogether, there were no literal examples at all, but that MWE appeared as mentions of both a racehorse and a pop song. Of the other 34 examples, the vast majority (29) were exactly in the form "[bite] the bullet", the remainder being in the forms *bit the ideological bullet* (3), reversed as in a *harder bullet to bite* (1), and a statement by President Bush about an opponent: "I bite bullets, he bites nails". The idiom was rather rigid, with a mean span of 2.055, and a fairly low standard deviation of 0.404. Diversity was also low at 1.069.

The results on French idioms were obtained from the tagged sample from the Frtenten corpus. The results obtained here have taken only a part of the corpus into account. In the future, we will perform an exhaustive analysis of the remaining 196,500 examples. The scores are given in Table 5, using the same headers as Table 4.

The idiom *le poisson mord à l' hameçon* is a popular expression in French which means 'to take the bait' (see Table 2). As illustrated in Table 5, it was found in 3 different forms, which, despite varying mean span and frequency, were each

---

[4]Its French adjectival counterpart, *mordu de* is also diverse: *mordue des nuitées en famille sous la tente* 'fanatical about nights camping with the family', *mordus des jeux on ligne* 'addicted to on-line games' and *mordue d'esperanto* 'bitten by the Esperanto bug.'

Table 5: Summary of scores for some idioms of *mordre* (500 lines sample). SD: Standard Deviation

Idiom	Freq (total)	PMI	t-score	Log-Dice	Idioma-ticity	Entropy	Mean span	SD
[poisson] [mordre]	4	7.340	1.988	-2.222	0.75	0	1	0
[hameçon] [mordre]	4	12.259	2	2.664	0.75	0	3	0
[appât] [mordre]	2	10.475	1.413	0.894	1	0	3	0
[vie] [mordre]	6	4.434	2.523	-5.126	1	1.792	2.833	0.372
[doigt] [mordre]	21	9.387	4.789	-0.174	0.952	1.08	1.190	0.154
[poussière] [mordre]	6	9.360	2.446	-0.204	1	0	1	0
[queue] [mordre]	16	9.670	4.118	0.109	1	0.34	1.187	0.527
[serpent] [mordre]	13	11.022	3.604	1.457	1	1.7	1.846	0.591

found to be maximally fixed (standard deviation = 0) and minimally diverse (entropy = 0).

The pattern "[[Human]] se mord {les doigts}" rarely took its literal meaning in French, standing for 'a person experiencing a bitter time for his past actions' in 20 cases out of 21. It usually occurred in the corpus as *mordre les doigts*, but sometimes as *se mord encore les doigts* 'bites his fingers again', *mordrait un peu souvent les doigts* 'bit his fingers a bit often' and other variants. This gave a mean of 1.19, a standard deviation of 0.15, and an entropy of 1.08.

The idiom *mordre dans la vie à pleine dents* was also found as *mordre la vie à pleines dents*. Table 5 lists the scores when both variants are combined. If we consider *vie* as the boundary word (*à pleines dents* was only found once in a mention of a song), *mordre dans la vie* occurred 4 times with mean span of 3, while *mordre la vie* was found twice with mean span of 2.5. Since 5 out of 6 examples had a distance of 3 words, the standard deviation was quite low (0.372); however the idiom had a high entropy (2.833), as *mordre la vie* contributed 2 different unique pattern classes to the idiom.

If we compare English and French, the corresponding phrases *mordre la poussière* and *bite the dust* both have standard deviations for their spans of 0, since in the BNC and Frtenten corpora the verb is always exactly 2 words before the noun. However, as can be seen in Table 2, *mordre la poussière* can have the additional use 'losing a challenge' which was not found in English. The MWEs *bite one's fingers* and its apparent French translation *se mordre les doigts* are in stark idiomaticity contrast. While *bite one's fingers* was always found to be literal (5 cases), all instances of *se mordre les doigts* (21) were found to be idiomatic. It is worth noting that translation systems unaware of these facts will tend to make two mistakes (as can be checked with Google Translate): when translating from French to English, they will fail to translate the figurative meaning of *se mordre les doigts* with an equivalent idiom like *kick oneself*. From English to French, they will fail to translate the literal meaning of *bite one's fingers* and translate it with the frequent idiomatic sequence *se mordre les doigts*. For the verbs *mordre* and *bite*, we have shown that the measures of mean and standard deviation of span, Shannon Diversity, and idiomaticity give reasonable results as they reflect the flexibility of a MWE. We could also suggest a measure of constructional flexibility, which might be the ratio of times a MWE occurs in the active voice divided by the number of times the MWE occurs altogether, whether in the active or passive voice.

6 Generalization of statistical measures

Evaluating the applicability of statistical measures to different languages is one way to evaluate their validity. This section describes other methods to test the generalizability of measures.

6.1 Comparison with cognitively salient idioms

Hanks (2013: 5,21,214) makes a distinction between expressions that are cognitively salient (roughly equivalent to "easily called to mind") and socially salient (roughly equivalent to "frequently used"). He suggests that cognitive salience and social salience are independent variables, or may even be in an inverse relationship: that is, frequently used expressions are buried deep in the language user's subconscious mind and are not necessarily easily called to mind. The idioms *kick the bucket* and *spill the beans* are probably the most cognitively salient and most frequent idioms cited by linguists. Other idioms cited in this chapter are *grasping at straws, the way the wind blows,* or *shivering in one's boots*. These idioms, along with 4 idioms involving *bite*, make up the set of 10 idioms used for the experiments described in this section.

In the BNC, *kick the bucket* has 21 occurrences, although another 4 sentences containing both words were discounted as *kick* and *bucket* appeared in separate clauses. Another 8 were from a linguistic discussion of the phrase, as in "notice 'kick the bucket' appears as a verb phrase". Only 5 were idiomatic, in the sense of *to die*: 4 of these were in the exact form *kicked the bucket*, while the other had a sequence of 9 words between *kicked* and *bucket*, in *Arthur kicked the detonator of the bomb, and consequently the bucket.* This gave a mean separation of 3.5 words, a standard deviation of 1.870, and a modest diversity of 0.721. However, these results were biased by a small sample size and a single creative use of language. This left 8 literal examples of the phrase, as in *leaving his bucket to be kicked over by the cow.* Thus idiomaticity was 5/21 = 0.238.

In contrast, the phrase *spill the beans,* found 42 times overall in the BNC, was almost always (40 times) found in the idiomatic sense of 'reveal a secret'. The only exceptions were when the phrase was used as the title of a book, *A style guide to the New Age called spilling the beans,* and a television programme *Superchefs spill the beans,* where the phrase *spill the beans* takes both the literal and the figurative sense at the same time. The phrase was used just once in its purely literal sense, where a guest house owner was dreading *a dozen or more children spilling their beans, wetting the beds, hoarding old crusts.* Thus idiomaticity was very high: 40/42 = 0.952. Of the 40 idiomatic cases, the vast majority were in the exact form "[spill] the beans" (37); 2 were in the passive voice (*when the beans are spilled* and *the beans have been spilled*), and just one replaced *the* with *a few*: *he spilt a few beans.* The mean separation was 2.025, the rigidity as measured by the standard deviation was 0.987, and diversity as measured by entropy was a lowish value of 0.370. According to these results, *spill the beans* is more idiomatic, less flexible and slightly less diverse than *kick the bucket.* These findings are in stark contrast with reports that MWEs like *spill the beans* are more flexible than the relatively well behaved *kick the bucket.* Although *kick the bucket* is more idiomatic in the sense that it is fully opaque, it occurs more often in the text in its literal meaning because its literal meaning is more frequent in everyday language.

An idiom which stands out in Table 6 is *way the wind blows,* which was by far the strongest collocation according to the t-score and LogDice measures, and the lowest idiomaticity score (or having the greatest proportion of literally-intended examples). *bite ...bug* had highest entropy, as one can metaphorically be bitten by many kinds of bug. Finally *bite ...hand ...[benefit]* had the greatest mean span and standard deviation of span.

6.2 Inter-annotator agreement

Another way of demonstrating the validity of a statistical measure, such as MWE idiomaticity or mean span, is to determine the Inter-Annotator Agreement (or Inter-Rater Reliability, IRR). This is the degree to which two or more observers might concur on a classification or annotation task. A measure is only valid to the extent that humans can agree on the classification of the individual instances

Table 6: 10 English idioms retained for generalization experiments.
SD: Standard Deviation

Idiom	Freq (total)	PMI	t- score	Log- Dice	Idioma- ticity	Entropy	Mean span	SD
[back][bite]	87	5.914	10.380	5.549	0.989	0.338	1.057	0.277
[bullet][bite]	36	10.484	6.477	8.561	1	1.069	2.055	0.404
[head][bite][off]	30	6.009	7.639	5.600	0.775	3.281	3.032	2.721
[bug][bite]	19	10.589	4.688	7.894	0.842	3.326	3.125	2.578
[hand][bite] [BENEFIT]	15	5.584	7.639	5.196	1	2.463	5.933	5.842
[bean][spill]	40	10.947	6.705	8.917	0.952	0.370	2.025	0.987
[straw] [grasp/clutch]	33	9.865	6.077	8.172	0.892	2.213	3.485	1.623
[way][wind] [blows]	21	10.663	25.264	10.652	0.676	2.488	3.5	0.534
[shoe/boot] [quake/shiver /shake]	12	5.043	5.056	5.608	1	2.057	3.417	1.382
[bucket][kick]	5	8.647	4.349	7.004	0.238	0.721	3.500	1.870

which contribute to the measure. For example, do they agree on whether a MWE is being used in its idiomatic sense or not, and where it starts and ends? IRR falls in the range 0 for only random agreement to 1 for perfect agreement. As an illustration, we estimated the IRR, using Krippendorff's α measure,[5] between two native speakers of English as regards the span and idiomaticity of the phrase *kick the bucket*. There were 26 sentences in the British National Corpus containing both *kick* and *bucket*. An α value of 1 denotes perfect agreement among the annotators, and 0 shows that agreement occurred only by chance. The instructions given to each annotator were as follows:

For each sentence, choose one of the following:

1) the phrase *kick the bucket* (or a grammatical variant of it) does not appear in the sentence;

2) the phrase *kick the bucket* (or a grammatical variant of it) is idiomatic, and means 'to die';

---

[5]Krippendorff's α may be calculated using the 'irr' package in the R statistical programming language. The package 'irr' can be installed by the following command: install.packages("irr", repos = "http://cran.r-project.org")

The annotators' responses should be stored in a matrix, where each row corresponds to annotators' response values. The R command to create a matrix for three examples and 2 annotators is, for example: m = matrix(c(1,1,3,3,1,2), nrow=2).

3) the phrase *kick the bucket* (or a grammatical variant of it) is literal, and actually means to physically kick a bucket.

If you answered 2) or 3), use [to show where the phrase *kick the bucket* begins and] to show where it ends, as in the example: "I'm too young to [kick the bucket]".

In our experiment to find the agreement of the native speakers as to whether the phrase *kick the bucket* was absent, literal or idiomatic, Krippendorff's α was 0.745.[6] A value between 0.6 and 0.8 is said to be "good" agreement (Altmann 1991: 404).

This experiment was modified to consider only those cases where the annotators considered the phrase *kick the bucket* to be present:[7] we were looking at the agreement between the annotators in distinguishing literal and idiomatic uses, and Krippendorff's α was 0.635, still "good".

To look at the agreement with respect to the span of the idiom, the values in the matrix were replaced with the number of words between the square brackets marked by the annotators, or NA if they did not find the idiom in the sentence.[8] The annotators agreed in every case where they both marked off the start and end of the idiom (α = 1), showing that the limits of the idiom *kick the bucket* were clear-cut to these native speakers. Thus according to this small experiment, the measures of idiomaticity and mean span are valid for the expression *kick the bucket*.

6.3 Correlation and relatedness of measures

While the previous section illustrated techniques to test the validity of statistical measures, this section describes a final experiment focusing on the relatedness of different measures. To do this, we compared the values of our set of 10 idioms (see Table 6) according to 10 measures. These included the measures of mean and standard deviation of idiom span, Shannon Diversity and idiomaticity, compared with four standard measures for collocation strength: frequency of collocation, PMI, t-score and LogDice. Both the t-score and LogDice are used by the Sketch Engine lexicographers' tool (Rychlý 2008).

---

[6] Krippendorff's α is found by the following command: `irr:kripp.alpha(m,"nominal")`.

[7] The matrix was modified so that all the 1s (denoting absence of the phrase) were replaced by "NA" (not applicable).

[8] This type of numeric data is called "ratio" data, so the appropriate command to calculate Krippendorff's α is: irr:kripp.alpha(m,"ratio").

To determine whether these measures were independent of each other or whether one acts as a predictor for another, Spearman's rank correlation coefficient was computed for each pair of measures. This statistic was preferred to the Pearson correlation coefficient, as the sets of values for some of the individual measures were not normally distributed. The correlations between the measures are shown in Table 7. The most statistically significant correlation (p = 0.002, cor = 0.88) was between PMI and LogDice, suggesting that these measures of collocational strength agree with each other well. Another significant correlation was the inverse correlation between frequency and mean span (p = 0.008, cor = -0.78). Thus there was a tendency for more frequent idioms to be shorter (and to a lesser extent, not statistically significant) more rigid in their structures. There was no significant correlation between any of the measures in Table 4 and Table 5 with either of the measures of collocational strength, frequency and PMI.

Table 7: Correlations between scores in the 10 idiom study.
SD: Standard Deviation

Idiom	Freq (total)	PMI	t-score	Log-Dice	Idiom-aticity	En-tropy	Mean span	SD
Freq	1							
PMI	0.36	1						
t-score	0.51	0.03	1					
LogDice	0.24	0.88	-0.04	1				
Idiomaticity	0.23	-0.42	-0.09	-0.30	1			
Entropy	-0.39	0.08	0.01	0.01	-0.29	1		
Mean span	-0.78	-0.19	-0.15	-0.07	-0.25	0.43	1	
Standard deviation	-0.61	-0.27	-0.30	-0.44	-0.20	0.62	0.55	1

These results suggest that the new measures of idiomaticity, entropy, mean span and standard deviation of span may not be useful for discovering new MWE, but as we have shown, are useful for describing the characteristics of MWE once discovered.

7 Conclusions and perspectives

Sinclair (2004) wrote that the so-called "fixed phrases" are not in fact fixed: most phrases in English display some variety of form. "Variation gives the phrase its essential flexibility, so that it can fit into its surrounding context". Conversely, each word cannot be considered as a simple "Lego brick" which can be fitted in a slot-and-filler system, as corpus-based investigations reveal that each word preferentially selects other words, echoing J.R. Firth's maxim that "You should know a word by the company it keeps". In this context we have proposed to use Corpus Pattern Analysis as a technique to describe word patterns found in corpora, and have applied this technique to two verbs in French and English. CPA is a corpus-based technique to detect the lexical, syntactic, and semantic preferences of verbs, such as the fact that *bite* preferentially selects *mosquitoes* and *bugs* while *sting* normally selects *bees, wasps* and *hornets*. The application of the CPA methodology to a French corpus revealed however that *mordre*, the French translation of *bite* in examples such as *dogs bite*, was neither used with *mosquitoes* nor with *bees*: French speakers prefer to use *piquer* 'sting' for most kinds of "flying entity aggression". This suggested that patterns of words are more reliable units of translation than words in isolation, which opens up new research perspectives for using CPA in Translation studies and Machine Translation.

In this chapter, we proposed to use statistical measures which could be applied to any MWE in any language, by illustration on French and English. These new statistical measures characterise the flexibility of a MWE based on text distance: the mean span of MWEs, the standard deviation of the distance between their boundary words, their internal diversity, and their idiomaticity ratio. The results obtained by the application of these measures to *bite* and *mordre* revealed that each captured useful features of MWEs which compared favourably with intuitive notions of flexibility and compositionality. It is worth noting that the implementation of these measures required us to make a number of decisions explicitly, particularly deciding on a basic unit such as the word or character. Perspectives include testing these measures on other languages, particularly those with so-called free word order, and application to Machine Translation.

In his analysis of extended units of meaning, Sinclair (1991) noted, as we have done in our discussion of *bite* and *mordre*, that idioms can carry across to other languages. In his example, the Italian equivalent of *naked eye* is *a occhio nudo*. While this is true of many expressions, the contrastive analysis proposed in this chapter also suggests that the semantic space occupied by a single lexical item can be covered by several lexical items in another language. The MWE *naked eye* also exhibits a phenomenon we have not examined in this chapter: there is greater consistency of patterning to the left of the collocation than to the right. This suggests that we could use our measures to find the rigidity or diversity not only of the MWE itself, but of its context on either side. We could also look for the semantic prosody associated with MWE – for example, things seen with the naked eye tend to be difficult ("small", "weak" or "faint") to see.

Abbreviations

AI	Artificial Intelligence	PDEV	Pattern Dictionary of English Verbs
CPA	Corpus Pattern Analysis	PMI	Point-wise Mutual Information
IRR	inter-rater reliability	WSD	Word Sense Disambiguation

References

Altmann, Douglas G. 1991. *Practical statistics for medical research.* London: Chapman & Hall.

Atkins, Beryl T. 1992. Tools for computer-aided corpus lexicography: the Hector project. In Ferenc Kiefer, Gábor Kiss & Julia Pajsz (eds.), *Papers in Computational Lexicography: COMPLEX'92*, vol. 115, 1–60. Budapest: Hungarian Academy of Sciences.

Atkins, Beryl T., Núria Bel, Pierrette Bouillon, Thatsanee Charoenporn, Dafydd Gibbon, Ralph Grishman, Chu-Ren Huan, Asanee Kawtrakul, Nancy Ide, Hae-Yun Lee, Paul J. K. Li, Jock McNaught, Jan Odijk, Martha Palmer, Valeria Quochi, Ruth Reeves, Dipti Misra Sharma, Virach Sornlertlamvanich, Takenobu Tokunaga, Gregor Thurmair, Marta Villegas, Antonio Zampolli & Elizabeth Zeiton. 2001. *Standards and Best Practice for Multiligual Computational Lexicons. MILE (the Multilingual ISLE Lexical Entry) Deliverable D2.2-D3.2.* ISLE project: ISLE Computational Lexicon Working Group. http://www.w3.org/2001/sw/BestPractices/WNET/ISLE_D2.2-D3.2.pdf, accessed 2018-4-19.

Church, Kenneth Ward & Patrick Hanks. 1989. Word association norms, mutual information and lexicography. In *Proceedings of the 27th Association for Computational Linguistics Conference (ACL)*, 78–83.

de Schryver, Gilles-Maurice. 2010. Getting to the bottom of how language works. In *A way with words: Recent advances in lexical theory and analysis: a Festschrift for Patrick Hanks*, 3–34. Menha Publishers.

Fillmore, Charles J. & Beryl T. Atkins. 1992. Towards a frame-based organization of the lexicon: the semantics of RISK and its neighbors. In Adrienne Lehrer & Eva Feder Kittay (eds.), *Frames, fields, and contrasts: New essays in semantics and lexical organization*, 75–102. Hillsdale, NJ: Lawrence Erlbaum Associates.

Hanks, Patrick. 1994. Linguistic norms and pragmatic exploitations or, why lexicographers need Prototype Theory, and vice versa. In Ferenc Kiefer, Gabor Kiss & Julia Pajzs (eds.), *Papers in computational lexicography: COMPLEX'94*, vol. 94, 89–113. Hungarian Academy of Sciences.

Hanks, Patrick. 2000. Do word meanings exist? *Computers and the Humanities* 34(1). 205–215.

Hanks, Patrick. 2012. How people use words to make meanings: Semantic types meet valencies. In *Input, process and product: Developments in teaching and language corpora*, 54–69. Brno (CZ): Masaryk University Press Masaryk.

Hanks, Patrick. 2013. *Lexical analysis: Norms and exploitations*. MIT Press.

Hanks, Patrick & James Pustejovsky. 2004. Common sense about word meaning: Sense in context. In *Proceedings of text, Speech and Dialogue (TSD)*, 15–17. Brno, Czech Republic.

Hanks, Patrick & James Pustejovsky. 2005. A pattern dictionary for Natural Language Processing. *Revue Française de linguistique appliquée* 10(2). 63–82.

Ide, Nancy & Yorick Wilks. 2007. Making sense about sense. In Eneko Agirre & Philip Edmonds (eds.), *Algorithms and applications*, 47–73. Dordrecht, The Netherlands: Springer.

Jackendoff, Ray. 2002. *Foundations of language*. New York: Oxford University Press.

Jakubíček, Milos, Adam Kilgarriff, Vojtěch Kovvář, Pavel Rychlý & Vit Suchomel. 2013. The TenTen corpus fmily. In *7th International Conference on Corpus Linguistics (CL 2013)*. Lancaster.

Kilgarriff, Adam, Pavel Rychlý, Pavel Smrz & David Tugwell. 2004. The Sketch Engine. In *Proceedings of Euralex 2004*, 105–116. Lorient, France,

Moon, Rosamund. 1998. *Fixed expressions and idioms in English: A corpus-based approach*. Oxford University Press.

Oakes, Michael P. 2012. *Describing a translational corpus*. Michael Oakes & Meng Ji (eds.). Amsterdam/Philadelphia: John Benjamins. 115–148.

Pustejovsky, James. 1995. *The generative lexicon*. MIT press.

Rychlỳ, Pavel. 2008. A lexicographer-friendly association score. In *Proceedings of Recent Advances in Slavonic Natural Language Processing, RASLAN*, vol. 2008, 6–9.

Sinclair, John. 1966. Beginning the study of lexis. In Charles Ernest Bazell, John Cunnison Catford, Michael Alexander K. Halliday & Robert H. Robin (eds.), *In memory of J. R. Firth*, 410–430. London: Longman.

Sinclair, John. 1987. *The Collins Cobuild English Language Dictionary*. London: HarperCollins.

Sinclair, John. 1991. *Corpus, concordance, collocation*. Oxford: Oxford University Press.

Sinclair, John. 1998. The lexical item. In Edda Weigand (ed.), *Contrastive lexical semantics*, vol. 171 (Current Issues in Linguistic Theory), 1–24. John Benjamins.

Sinclair, John. 2004. The search for units of meaning. In John Sinclair & Ronald Carter (eds.), *Trust the text: language, corpus and discourse*, 24–48. London: HarperCollins.

Smadja, Frank. 1993. Retrieving collocations from text: Xtract. *Computational Linguistics* 19(1). 143–177.

Wilks, Yorick. 1975. A preferential, pattern-seeking, semantics for natural language inference. *Artificial Intelligence* 6(1). 53–74.

Chapter 5

Multiword expressions and the Law of Exceptions

Koenraad Kuiper
University of Canterbury, New Zealand

This chapter proposes the existence of a linguistic universal, the Law of Exceptions. It hypothesizes that a relationship exists between the grammar of a language and its lexicon such that all regularities expressed in the grammar of a language are matched by exceptions which are manifested in the lexicon of that language. It is also proposed that lexical idiosyncrasies are of two types. Type 1 idiosyncrasies are in the nature of arbitrary restrictions on options provided in the grammar while Type 2 idiosyncrasies involve breaches of the rules of the grammar. To test this law requires an initial examination of the linguistic domains where it might be tested. As a preliminary step to testing these ideas, this chapter is a scoping exercise looking chiefly at the structural properties of a subset of multiword expressions (MWE). It shows, following Barkema (1996), that many properties of MWEs cross-classify. The aim of the overview is then to examine domains of the morphosyntax of any language which might be analysed for sources of structural idiosyncrasy and thus to determine how individual languages might vary in this respect. Languages of exemplification are English, which has a relatively fixed word order and slight inflectional system, and, to a lesser extent Dutch and Māori, an Oceanic language.

1 Introduction

In the traditional grammar-lexicon model of human linguistic knowledge, the grammar accounts for the regularities in the language which a native speaker is taken to have acquired and thus the predictabilities in its sentences. The lexicon has traditionally been 'an appendix of the grammar, a list of basic irregularities,' (Bloomfield 1933: 274). While this distinction is increasingly contested, it will be maintained here. It is, in any case, an open question as to just where the

Koenraad Kuiper. 2018. Multiword expressions and the Law of Exceptions. In Manfred Sailer & Stella Markantonatou (eds.), *Multiword expressions: Insights from a multi-lingual perspective*, 121–141. Berlin: Language Science Press. DOI:10.5281/zenodo.1182595

boundary between the grammar and the lexicon lies and, more significantly for what follows, what kinds of 'basic irregularities' are possible; that is to say what kinds of idiosyncrasies can be expected to occur in the lexical items of a language.

Bloomfield's characterization raises the question as to the kinds of basic irregularities which might be found in the lexicon of a language. They appear to be of two types. Some irregularities are exceptional in cases where the grammar provides options but only one is taken in a particular lexical item. That does constitute an idiosyncrasy by way of arbitrary restriction but the rules of the grammar are not breached. Obligatory truncation is such a case as in (5) and (6). Phonetic truncation is an option the grammar provides but in (5) and (6) the MWEs are always truncated. Restricted collocations do not break any rules of the grammar. They provide arbitrary paradigmatic restrictions on linguistic choices when the grammar allows for a larger set of choices to be made. In such cases the grammar is permissive but the lexicon is restrictive. A second class of irregularities is the result of breaches of the grammar where the constraints imposed by the grammar do not provide alternatives. Here the grammar is restrictive but the lexicon is more permissive. Some borrowed words, for example, may breach the phonological constraints of a language. English phonotactics do not allow the onset sequence /ʃn/. But the dog breed of *schnauzer* is lexicalized in English with this initial cluster. Let us call exceptions of the first kind where they are manifest Type 1 idiosyncrasies and exceptions of the second kind Type 2 idiosyncrasies.

I now propose a hypothesis to link the grammar to its exceptions. The following hypothesis, the LAW OF EXCEPTIONS, is proposed as the strongest compatible with the distinction between the grammar and the lexicon.

> LAW OF EXCEPTIONS: All formal properties of the grammar of a language are subject to exceptions manifested in idiosyncrasies in the lexical items of that language.

The Law of Exceptions thus predicts that the lexicon of a language will contain lexical items which break every rule in the grammar of that language. This is in line with the view of Di Sciullo & Williams (1987) with the metaphor that the lexicon is like a prison in that its inmates have all broken one or other law (although Di Sciullo and Williams do not suggest all laws are broken by at least someone).

Note that it cannot be assumed that the Law of Exceptions is prima facie true. It might well be that there are areas of the grammar of a language and perhaps all languages where there are no exceptions, i.e. that there are laws that are never broken. Tensed verb second placement in main clauses of many Germanic languages is absolute as is suggested in the later discussion around examples (48)–(52). The verb second constraint in Dutch and German may be such an instance. The Law of Exceptions is therefore testable against all lexical items in the lexicon of a language.

This chapter focuses on the structural properties of a subset of lexical items, MWEs that have syntactic structure. Such lexical items may vary in many ways, so an account of the ways in which these properties can vary in general is useful, not least as a checklist for languages whose phraseology has not been documented. In the case of the languages of exemplification it will be shown that in every syntactic domain covered in this chapter, where there are regularities of both Type 1 and Type 2 in the grammar, there are exceptions in the lexicon.

Since the Law of Exceptions provides a relationship between the grammar of a language and its lexicon it is important initially to determine where exceptions cannot in principle be found. The prediction is that this will only be the case where a grammar has no regularities. For example, in the domain of morphology it is often considered that Chinese languages have no derivational morphology.[1] If that is the case, then the idiosyncratic properties manifested in the derivational morphology of derived words in other languages which do have derivational morphology are not in evidence in Chinese languages and so, obviously, are not available for analysis as to their idiosyncrasies. In the domain of syntax, since the syntax of a language determines what kinds of syntactic idiosyncrasies are possible, if the syntax of a language has antipassive voice, then there may be MWEs which exist only in the antipassive form or not in the antipassive form even when it is plausible that they should.[2] But, since only ergative languages have an antipassive voice, this syntactic property places a limit on the kinds of idiosyncrasies which can be expected in the lexical entries of lexical items in a particular language.

Since the Law of Exceptions applies to the current synchronic grammar, all MWEs which were historically unexceptional but are exceptions to the synchronic grammar fall under the Law of Exceptions. The reason for this is that native speakers of a language may be presumed to have internalized only the synchronic grammar of their native language (historical linguists excepted).

---

[1]But see Starosta et al. (1997) for a contrary view.

[2]It is likely that, at least for some grammatical rules, there is more than one way in which they may be violated. Take for example, the English passive. It may be that an MWE is only possible with a *get* auxiliary and not a *be* auxiliary or that the agent which is in an oblique position in a passive MWE cannot be deleted. The Law of Exceptions, therefore, needs to note in how many ways a grammatical rule might be breached. It is an open question whether all possible breaches have associated MWEs.

Turning now to MWEs, if we suppose following Sag et al. (2002) that MWEs are lexical units of more than one word, then in this chapter the analysis of the properties of MWEs will be restricted to those of the subset of phrasal vocabulary, i.e. MWEs having syntactic structure. The Law of Exceptions predicts that the lexicon of a human language will always contain an inventory of MWEs with grammatical structure since all languages have syntax. Such lexical items are in the mental lexicon because they have one or more idiosyncrasies, i.e. properties which cannot be predicted by the grammar of the language. That is why they are stored and retrieved rather than computed (Bresnan 1981).[3] Such lexical units are elsewhere termed, amongst other things, 'phrasemes' (Mel'čuk 2012) or are a subclass of 'morpheme equivalent units' (Wray 2008).

It follows that the structural properties of compound words will not be examined. This is because opportunities for structural variation in compounds are relatively slight (Selkirk 1982) while in the subset of MWEs with syntactic structure, opportunities for idiosyncratic variation of structural properties are considerable since the syntaxes of natural languages are complex and thus offer many opportunities for syntactic idiosyncrasy.

MWEs have two kinds of properties: digital properties such as having an obligatory plural in some instances, and gradable (analogue) properties such as their degree of semantic compositionality. Analogue properties can of two kinds: the MWE has a particular property to a greater or lesser degree or the MWE has the property some of the times it is uttered but not at other times.

Viewed diachronically, MWEs may exhibit idiosyncratic properties that were not idiosyncratic at some time in the past. Some of the many English MWEs which are originally quotations from Shakespeare and the King James bible translation, often termed 'winged words' in continental phraseological manuals (Gläser 1986) have such idiosyncrasies. They are not alone as can be seen by (1).

(1) *will he nill he*

    a. originally: *will he ne will he*
              will he not will he

    b. now truncated further to: *willy-nilly*[4]
        'regardless of what one might wish'

---

[3]That is not to say that they are unanalysable, as hybrid theories of speech production such as those of Cutting & Bock (1997), Titone & Connine (1999) and Sprenger et al. (2006) propose.

[4]Such archaisms have been noted in the inventory of MWEs for sources as various as Homeric epic (Lord 1960) and livestock auctions (Kuiper & Haggo 1984).

What general sources are there for the idiosyncratic properties of MWEs? The idiosyncratic properties of MWEs have three sources:

1. properties they have by virtue of being lexical items;

2. properties they have by virtue of being structurally complex;

3. properties they have by virtue of being phrases.[5]

The subset of MWEs which I will examine, as I have indicated above, may be defined on the basis of their structural properties, namely that they have syntactic structure. They may have other properties which may cross-classify. Sag et al. (2002) see idiomaticity as definitional for MWE. I do not regard semantic non-compositionality as a definitional criterion for MWE since it is shared with derived words (Jackendoff 2002) and, although many MWEs are idioms, many are not (Mel'čuk 2012). In example (2),

(2) *infidelity*

has a narrowed sense of 'marital infidelity'.

Having associated conditions of use is also a cross-classifying property since mono-morphemic words may also have associated conditions of use as in example (3).

(3) *Thanks!*

The property of being a restricted collocation is common to compounds and idioms. In a compound, since both constituents are lexicalized they must be restricted against one another.

That being the case an MWE can be a restricted collocation, semantically non-compositional, and have associated conditions of use as in example (4).

(4) *I declare the meeting open.*

Example (4) is an MWE. It is a restricted collocation. *Open* has a somewhat specialized sense and the whole expression is a formula used by the chair of a meeting to begin the formal proceedings of a meeting.

A classification of all lexical items on the basis of structural properties (which do not cross-classify) can be given as in Figure 1.[6]

---

[5]Here phrases are to be understood to include clauses and sentences, i.e. a sequence of words having syntactic structure.

[6]This is also the approach used by Fiedler (2007).

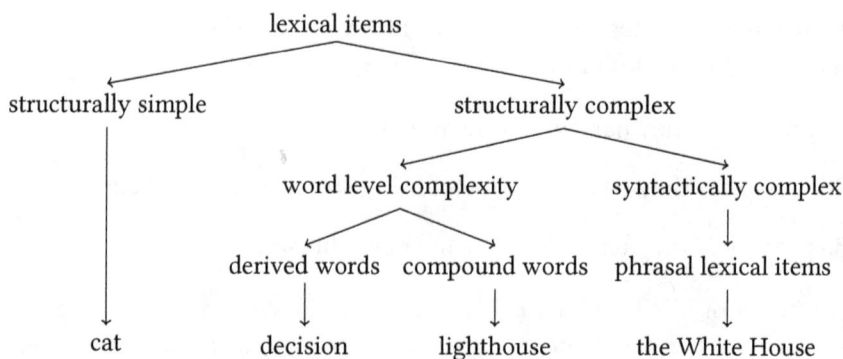

Figure 1: Structurally based classes of lexical items.

2 Idiosyncratic properties of MWEs

Many of the properties described below are described and exemplified for German by Burger (2010) and in Jaki (2014).

2.1 Idiosyncratic properties of MWEs which they have by virtue of being lexical items

Such properties are shared with structurally simple lexical items.

All MWEs may have phonological idiosyncrasies. This is probably a digital property. For example, MWEs may be lexicalized with idiosyncratic phonetic realizations, e.g. obligatory truncation as in (5). As noted above, this is a Type 1 idiosyncrasy.

(5)   *She'll be right.*
      #She will be right.

An Australian MWE indicating that there is nothing to be concerned about, and

(6)   *Good day.*

an Australian English greeting being conventionally realized as [gɪdei].

MWEs may also have idiosyncratic intonation contours, e.g. livestock auction formulæ (Kuiper & Haggo 1984), market cries and classroom greetings by elementary school children to their teacher in Australia and New Zealand which go at half normal articulation speed and have a distinctive tune on the formula as in (7).

(7)   *Good morning, Miss/Mrs/Mr X.*

Good morning, Mister Jones

Figure 2: Primary school greeting formula tune.

(8)   Māori
      Tihei   mauri ora
      sneeze spirit life
      'the sneeze of life'

(8) is used by a speaker when taking the floor during Māori oratory.

The formula has an intonationally raised and prosodically drawn out syllable on *hei* and a quicker than normal downward intonation contour on the remaining syllables of the phrase. This is also a Type 1 idiosyncrasy since such intonation contours are possible within the grammar.

Any lexical item may have conventional conditions of use such as (9)–(11). This is a digital Type 1 property since the grammar has nothing to say about the usage conditions of lexical items. Such lexical items are often termed formulae or routine formulae (Coulmas 1979).

(9)   *Sorry.*

a single word apology,

(10)   *Bullshit!*

a compound word exclamation of disbelief,

(11)   *If it please Your Honour.*

an MWE used by legal counsel seeking approval for a course of action of a presiding judge in a court

An example from Māori is the formula in (12).

(12) *kapiti hono,   tātai hono*
       join   connect recite connect

This is a bridging formula used to transition from the acknowledgement of the dead to greetings to the living in formal speechmaking.

While I have designated this property as digital, i.e. an MWE either does or does not have specific conditions of use, the specific conditions of use are themselves complex and not necessarily digital (Biber 1994). The contexts of use will also range from the general to the specific.

2.2 Idiosyncratic properties MWEs may have by virtue of their being structurally complex

Such properties are shared by structurally complex words.

It is possible for a MWE to exhibit morphological and/or morphosyntactic idiosyncrasy. The extent to which this is possible depends on the inflectional and derivational morphology of a language.[7] Languages with extensive inflectional morphology such as Turkish would be expected to exhibit inflectional idiosyncrasy in their MWEs. Chinese languages in the absence of inflectional morphology cannot. For example, in English an MWE may have an obligatory singular when a plural is semantically plausible as in (13) or an obligatory plural as in (14) when a singular is plausible. These are Type 1 idiosyncrasies.

(13) *give someone a hand*
       'assist someone'
       #*give someone a pair of hands*

(14) *as scarce as hens' teeth*
       'very scarce'
       #*as scarce as a hen's teeth*

MWEs may also have idiosyncratic derivational morphology. In the MWE in (15),

(15) *the use of undue force*
       or: *to use undue force*

---

[7]Note that it is rare for left hand constituents of English compounds to have inflections even when this is warranted semantically as in *head count* 'the counting of heads'. This restriction on the appearance of inflections appears to be a requirement of the word formation rules of English and thus not an idiosyncratic property of individual compounds.

this formula is used of police arrests in particular. The morphological idiosyncrasy is that there is no equivalent with *due force* (although there are no doubt situations where due force is applied).

In Māori, the expression

(16) *mā-na*   *(noa ake) te*   *kore e*   V *(o*   *NP)*
      PREP-3SG (just up) DET NEG TAM V (PREP NP)

      Lit. (His/they, …) not V-ing is (just) his fault.

      'NP is certain to V'

occurs in the example sentence in (17).

(17) *Mā-na*   *noa ake te*   *kore e*   *pai*   *o tā*   *tātou*   *rārangi*
      PREP-3.SG just up DET NEG TAM good of SG.A L.PL.INC line

      'Just because of him our lineout was no good.'[8]

This is from a piece of talk about rugby football in which lineouts are a set move.[9]

This MWE has the restriction that it always contains *māna*, with 3ʳᵈ person singular agreement, whatever the number of the subject NP. This is a case where the VP has a frozen morphology and agreement does not operate across the boundary between the open slot of the subject and the number inflection of the verb. Since the general rules of agreement do not operate in this case, this is a Type 2 idiosyncrasy.

An MWE may also retain as an idiosyncratic property an inflection which is no longer available in the current language. The Dutch MWE in (18)

(18) *des*   *duivels*
      the.GEN devil.GEN

      'to be very angry'

exhibits a genitive inflection on the article which is no longer current. This is a Type 2 idiosyncrasy since (18) exhibits a breach of the current rules of inflection.

It is also possible that an individual word may have different morphosyntactic properties in an MWE than it does elsewhere. An anonymous reviewer has given the following example from French. 'To cite from Grevisse (Bon Usage: 198) "*Orge* est féminin, sauf dans les deux expressions *orge mondé, orge perlé*."

---

[8]Detailed glosses: *Māna* 'for him/her'; *noa ake* 'just/merely'; *tā tātou* = 'ours (first person inclusive)', i.e., 'belonging to all of us'.

[9]Source: http://www.nzherald.co.nz/nz/news/article.cfm?c_id=1&objectid=10587508.

So a word may be feminine, except in certain fixed expressions.' Here presumably agreement with the gender of the noun would be un-idiosyncratic. This is a Type 1 idiosyncrasy since the grammar of French makes two genders available and the assignment of gender to individual words is (in part) arbitrary.

All structurally complex lexical items can have bound forms as constituents, derived words such as *agog*, compound words such as **ward***robe* (Richter et al. 2010). In MWEs the following examples show the presence of bound words:[10]

(19) Māori
      māngere **hōnia**
      lazy   very

      'very lazy'

(20) *be on* **tenterhooks**
      'to be in a state of agitation about a future event'

(21) *take* **umbrage** *at*
      'take offence at'

(22) **kith** *and kin*
      'relatives'

Being a bound word is a Type 1 idiosyncrasy since no rule of the grammar is breached by the fact that a word is bound within an MWE.

While this chapter will not specifically deal with the semantic idiosyncrasy of MWEs, it is useful to offer a few remarks on that property since it is shared with structurally complex lexical items such as derived and compound words. Semantic idiosyncrasy appears to be an analogue property.[11] Semantic idiosyncrasy can come about in a number of ways. As Jackendoff (1975) points out, many English derivational affixes are polysemous. In particular words, however, only one of the senses associated with the affix is part of the compositional reading of the word as a whole. Such selective compositionality occurs where not all the cross-product senses of affixes or words are part of the sense of the whole expression. In an MWE such as (23),

(23) BE *in stock*
      'be part of the current inventory of a shop or warehouse'

---

[10]In (19), *hōnia* is a bound form occurring only as a modifier of *māngere* 'lazy'.

[11]See Burger (2010) for a useful introductory discussion.

the word *stock* does not have the sense of 'liquid used for soups and sauces' but 'inventory'.[12] This is a Type 1 idiosyncrasy since such a reading is a possible reading but not the only possible one.

Non-compositionality can occur where the sense of a word in a lexical item does not occur when the word is used independently. This is not a matter of a breach of a grammatical or semantic rule. It would therefore be a Type 1 idiosyncrasy. It is manifest in a MWE such as (24).

(24) *without let or hindrance*
      'without any obstruction or interruption'

The noun *let* has a now defunct syntactic category and sense.[13]

A second kind of non-compositionality occurs when the rules of the semantics of the language are breached as in conventional figurative expressions such as (25). These are Type 2 idiosyncrasies. In such cases structurally complex lexical items also share the potential property of having analysable semantic representations. In (25), the phrase is figurative with the gloss 'accepting a difficult challenge or situation', *grasp* being 'accept' and the *nettle* being 'the difficult challenge or situation'.

(25) *grasp the nettle*

3 Idiosyncratic structural properties a MWE may have by virtue of being a phrase

In this section, I focus on those areas of potential structural idiosyncrasy which MWEs have but which they do not share with other structurally complex lexical items such as derived and compound words. Each relevant area will show that the Law of Exceptions appears to be corroborated.

All MWEs are associated with a phrase structural configuration. This is shown for one MWE in example (26), where the final NP is a slot (an open argument position).

(26) [VP[V *make*][NP[DET *the*][N *most*][PP[P *of*][NP]]]]
      'maximize the potential offered by ...'

---

[12] This selective compositionality may be the consequence of polysemy or homonymy. It can be difficult to separate these in particular instances.

[13] It also has this sense in the term *let* in tennis, namely an obstruction.

Having grammatical structure is a digital property. That is not to say that such structures are always permissible in the current synchronic grammar of the language as in (27).

(27) *be that as it may*
      'whatever the actual case may be'

Example (27) is in the subjunctive mood, a mood that no longer exists in the current synchronic grammar of English.[14] This is a Type 2 idiosyncrasy.

In (28), the syntax is calqued from a Chinese four character idiom (Kuiper & Tan 1989).

(28) *long time no see*
      'I haven't seen you for some time'

It can therefore be concluded that there are exceptions to the phrase structural regularities of the synchronic grammar. This is also a Type 2 idiosyncrasy.

The phrase structure of MWEs may be further constrained by general constraints that are lexicon internal in that not all the possible phrase structural configurations the grammar allows are to be found in MWEs. For example, grammars allow for recursive rules in their syntax. There is evidence of a degree of recursion in MWE as in (29).

(29) *a sight for sore eyes*
      'a welcome appearance'

In (29), there are two NPs one is the top NP while the other is embedded in a PP. However recursion is limited because MWEs are stored in a finite brain and so cannot be of indefinite length. How limited recursion in MWEs may be is an open question.[15] The Law of Exceptions is, however, corroborated as regards recursion in the grammar since this is a Type 2 idiosyncrasy albeit a general one since it is not just the property of a single lexical item.

O'Grady (1998) proposes that the citation form of idioms in the mental lexicon is in the form of lexical selection by heads of heads within their syntactic domains thus forming chains of heads. Some of these requirements are interesting in that, while phrases must have heads, it is not a necessary property of MWEs that the head position should dominate a lexical item or, in the case of functional projections, a specific functional head. This constraint may itself have exceptions,

---

[14]This is essentially a morphosyntactic property included here as a structural property.
[15]Hoeksema (2010), and Richter & Sailer (2009) discuss MWEs of clause length.

as suggested by an example from Māori as in (30), a formula expressing sympathy for someone's problem.

(30) *i*   *wāna nei*   *(hoki)*
      at/by/from his/her NEAR-SPEAKER EMPHATIC-PARTICLE

While *i* is the head of the PP, O'Grady's theory predicts that there must be a lexical head for *i* to select within the immediate domain of the PP, i.e. the head of the NP complement of *i*. *Hoki* is not a lexical head and is optional (therefore cannot be a lexical head). *Wāna* 'his/her' can be replaced by an appropriate possessive determiner, e.g. *wāu* 'your', *wā rātou* 'their'. There are however restrictions on the choice of possessives. The possessive pronoun always starts with *w*, a possible initial phoneme for these possessives otherwise, but many speakers use it only here. Normally the possessive determiners have *t-* for singular possessum, Ø- for plural, thus eg *tāna ~āna*. Some speakers allow *w-*, thus *wāna* for plural. However all speakers use only the *w*-forms in this MWE showing an idiosyncrasy typically associated with MWEs. Furthermore the possessive (taking possessive to be determiners) has no NP complement. The determiner position is also always a possessive, i.e., *i wōna nei* can not occur in this MWE. *I wōna nei* can certainly appear elsewhere given the right syntactic etc environment as in (31); just never in this MWE.

(31) *He nui ake   ōku waka i   wōna nei.*
      A big upwards my cars   than his   here'
      'My cars are bigger than his.'

Nei is obligatory. While in the morphosyntax of Māori there are three locative particles, one never finds either of the other locative particles: *nā*, 'near hearer' or *rā* 'over there' in this MWE. So there are no lexical heads within the domain of the head position of this MWE and the non-heads are idiosyncratic in various ways. Thus, unless one uses an analysis allowing functional heads to serve in O'Grady's head chain proposal in which *wāna* etc. are Determiners and thus functional heads, this MWE has no lexical head within the immediate domain of the head of the MWE.[16] This case therefore suggests that a strong form of O'Grady's proposal is falsified and the Law of Exceptions is corroborated.

---

[16] Ray Harlow (personal communication) provided this example and analysis. A case might be made for functional heads as well as lexical heads being predicted to be lexicalized in the case of possessives where the possessive marker could be regarded as a functional head of DP and where the NP within the possessive phrase is a slot.

The syntax of a language may require certain obligatory constituents, e.g. complements of transitive verbs or possessive NPs. In an MWE these may not be filled with lexicalized material as in (32) and (33). Where this is the case the idiosyncrasy is lexical and is not a breach of the rules of the syntax. It is an idiosyncrasy because, while *take* is transitive, it is an idiosyncratic feature of the MWE that the NP object of *take* in *take NP to task* is not lexically filled as it is in *take notice of*. Thus these are Type 1 idiosyncrasies.

(32)   *take* NP *to task*
       'hold someone responsible'

(33)   *get* NP*'s goat.*
       'annoy someone'

Such slots may be semantically restricted in idiosyncratic ways as in (34).

(34)   *drop in on* NP[+human]
       'visit someone unannounced'

Some MWEs have an optional but lexicalized constituent as in (35). Again this does not involve a syntactic irregularity since the rules of the syntax allow both configurations. In other words, while *drop* can have both human and non-human objects, *drop in on* can only have a human object. So these are also Type 1 idiosyncrasies.

(35)   (*keep* poss-NP) *fingers crossed*
       'hope for a good outcome'

Such optional constituents are either truncations as in (34) or they can be internal to the MWE as in (36).

(36)   *take* (*careful*) *note of* NP

In (36), *careful* is a highly preferred modifier and thus we can suppose that it is lexicalized but optional. Given that modifiers are permissible in general, this is a Type 1 idiosyncrasy.

The distinction between slots and optional constituents is that slots are lexically unspecified except for their syntactic category and are obligatory, optional constituents are lexically specified and optional while modifiable MWEs are optionally able to take any appropriate modifier.

Conversely, in some MWEs, internal modification having scope over an internal constituent is not permitted, for example in the case of (37).

(37)   *cut no ice*
       'have no impact'

This cannot be modified, as shown in (38),

(38)   *#cut no melting ice*

when the grammar would otherwise permit it.[17] This suggests that modifiability properties can sometimes be absolute such as cases where modifiability is impossible whereas for other MWEs it may be a preferred option with some highly favoured and other disfavoured modifiers.

The presence of a lexicalized optional modifier in (36) is idiosyncratic but it is not a grammatical irregularity. It is therefore a Type 1 idiosyncrasy. The restriction against modification in (37) could, by contrast, be regarded as a grammatical irregularity, i.e. a Type 2 idiosyncrasy. That such cases should exist is a prediction of the Law of Exceptions.

Where the syntax of a language allows a variety of related constructions for a similar argument structure, an MWE may only permit one or fewer than a full set of variations, e.g. double object constructions as in (39)–(42), passives as in (43) and (44). This is a Type 1 idiosyncrasy.

(39)   *give* NP *the sack*
       'terminate NP's employment'

(40)   *#give the sack to* NP

(41)   *#pay something attention*

(42)   *pay attention to something*
       'note or concentrate on something'

(43)   NP *cut off his/her nose to spite his/her face*
       'act in a way that is detrimental to oneself out of pique'

(44)   *#John's nose was cut off to spite his face.*

---

[17]The semantics of modifier constituents within MWEs is complex (Nicolas 1995). Nicolas suggests that a modifier placed internally to a MWE can have scope over the meaning of the whole expression. In (38) the internal modifier *melting* cannot be parsed as modifying *ice*. However there are other cases Nicolas regards essentially as adverbial in having scope over the metaphorical expression as a whole so that *cut no real ice* is parsed as 'really cut no ice' and *cut no empirical ice* is parsed as 'cut no ice empirically'. So the modification, while placed internally, is not semantically a modification of the constituent the modifier is predicted to modify in a compositional syntax. These cases are thus idiosyncratic. In that sense the placement of the modifier is structurally idiosyncratic.

Koenraad Kuiper

For each set of syntactic alternates of this kind there may be MWEs which are idiosyncratic in allowing only one of the two possibilities where the grammar would predict that both might occur. For example, a double object construction may be lexicalized in either one or other form as in (39)–(42), or both as in (45) and (46).

(45)   *give credit to* NP (*for*)
       'give positive acknowledgement to someone for something'
(46)   *give* NP *credit* (*for*)

Such distributions may well be matters of degree.[18]

In an MWE the antecedent of a pronominal or reflexive can be more restricted than the syntax of a language requires. Such cases can be seen as slots which are restricted to pronominals with additional slot restrictions as regards the antecedent of the pronominal. This is a Type 1 idiosyncrasy.

In (47), the antecedents of the possessives must be the agent arguments of *dig* as in (47a) and (47b).

(47)   *dig one's heels in*
       'resist'

    a.   *Jane dug her heels in.*
    b.   # *Jane dug Fred's heels in.*

An MWE can have argument structure which is different from that of its head verb as in (48). This again a Type 1 idiosyncrasy since the grammar allows for predicates to have various argument structures.

(48)   *raining cats and dogs*
       'raining heavily'

Rain is a zero place predicate but in (48) it is apparently a one place predicate.[19]

MWEs merge into the constructions of Construction Grammar. They are of two kinds: lexically motivated constructions, e.g. the *let alone* construction (Fillmore et al. 1988), and syntactically motivated constructions, e.g. irreversible binomials (Malkiel 1959). It is an open question whether the latter belong in the

---

[18] Fraser (1970) hypothesizes that there is a hierarchy of frozenness in construction types while Nunberg et al. (1994) propose that the degree of syntactic flexibility is related to the degree of compositionality of the MWE.

[19] This could be seen as a case of a lexicalized internal accusative such as one gets with *It snowed a blizzard.*

136

phrasal lexicon or in the grammar. The former clearly do belong in the lexicon given that they have lexical content.

As suggested above, the grammars of languages place limits on phraseological variation. Typologically different languages will therefore be predicted to give different ranges of idiosyncrasies for MWEs. One typological distinction, is that between what are termed free word order languages but are more accurately free phrase order languages such as Warlpiri and Latin.[20] Questions which are yet to be answered about such languages is what the underlying form of the syntactic representation of the MWEs of such languages might be. How flexible are their MWEs given that the languages themselves have relatively free phrase order? In turn what idiosyncrasies might their MWEs display in the relevant areas of the grammar?[21]

What of languages with the typological character of so called verb second (V2) languages such as Dutch and German where the canonical order – within a generative framework – in main clauses is I second but in subordinate clauses I last? German and Dutch phrasal dictionaries list VP idioms with the verb in VP final position although in main clauses the tensed verb will be in second position. For example, a Dutch MWE as in in (49) is verb last in subordinate clauses as in (50) but verb second as in (51).

(49) *van NP*   *houden*
      from someone/something hold
      'love someone/something'

(50) *Ik dacht   dat ik van mijn aapje   houden wou.*
      I thought that I from my little monkey hold   would.
      'I though that I would love my little monkey'

(51) *Ik hield van mijn aapje,*
      I held from my little monkey
      'I loved my little monkey'.

Verb second placement is also obligatory if the verb is the head of a VP MWE.[22]

---

[20]Ray Harlow (personal communication) indicates that no dictionary of phraseological units exists for Latin and Michael Walsh (personal communication) knows of no dictionaries of phrasal vocabulary for any aboriginal language.

[21]Michael Walsh and Maia Ponsonnet (personal communication) know of no studies that might assist in answering these questions.

[22]This phenomenon is also discussed by Schenk (1995), Nunberg et al. (1994) and Bargmann & Sailer (2018 [this volume]).

(52) *Ik dacht   dat ik het gewoon **uit mijn duim zuigen** kon.*
     I thought that I it just   out my   thumb suck   could
     'I though I could just make it up.'

(53) *Ik **zoog**   het gewoon **uit mijn duim.***
     I sucked it just   out my   thumb
     'I just made it up.'

What is the order in German and Dutch of the verb plus its complement for such MWEs in the mental lexicon? Is there an order at all or are there only dependencies? This is not a question of flexibility under movement. Verb second placement in main clauses is obligatory. Are there Type 2 idiosyncratic manifestations of these regularities in the MWEs of German and Dutch? The Law of Exceptions predicts that there should be cases in Dutch and German of MWEs which have main clauses where the tensed verb is not in second position.

Beyond the Law of Exceptions lies a further question as to the preponderance in the lexicon of a language of particular classes of exceptions. It is possible that different languages make different selective use of the parameters of variation noted above, e.g. some languages might have more bound words than others (Dobrovol'skij 1988).

4 Conclusion

The foregoing provides an outline of a set of structural properties of a grammar which have the potential to have exceptions and thus give rise to idiosyncratic structural properties of MWEs. It has been proposed that such exceptions are of two kinds: those which are 'basic irregularities', i.e. which are in breach of the rules of the grammar and which I have termed Type 2 idiosyncrasies, and idiosyncrasies which are the result of arbitrary restrictions on lexical items where the grammar makes no stipulation about such restrictions. Where such idiosyncrasies appear in lexical items, these have been termed Type 1 idiosyncrasies. By classifying idiosyncrasies on the basis I have, it also seems that Type 1 idiosyncrasies may be more common and diverse than Type 2 idiosyncrasies and that the lexicon is not as full of seriously lawless inmates as the prison metaphor in Di Sciullo & Williams (1987) suggests. Perhaps there is a maximum security wing for Type 2 inmates and a less secure set of cell blocks for Type 1 inmates whose deviance is by way of arbitrary restriction.

Acknowledgements

My considerable thanks to the editors of this chapter and its anonymous reviewers for numerous corrections and suggestions. I am grateful to Ray Harlow for the Māori examples. Note there has been no systematic study of the phraseology of Māori.

References

Bargmann, Sascha & Manfred Sailer. 2018. The syntactic flexibility of semantically non-decomposable idioms. In Manfred Sailer & Stella Markantonatou (eds.), *Multiword expressions: Insights from a multi-lingual perspective*, 1–29. Berlin: Language Science Press. DOI:10.5281/zenodo.1182587

Barkema, Henk. 1996. Idiomaticity and terminology. A multi-dimensional descriptive model. *Studia Linguistica* 50(2). 125–160.

Biber, Douglas. 1994. An analytic framework for register studies. In Douglas Biber & Edward Finegan (eds.), *Sociolinguistic perspectives on register*, 31–56. New York: Oxford University Press.

Bloomfield, Leonard. 1933. *Language*. New York: Holt, Rinehart & Winston.

Bresnan, Joan. 1981. A realistic transformational grammar. In Morris Halle, Joan Bresnan & George A. Miller (eds.), *Linguistic theory and psychological reality*, 1–59. Cambridge, MA: MIT Press.

Burger, Harald. 2010. *Phraseologie: Eine Einführung am Beispiel des Deutschen*. 4th edn. Berlin: Eric Schmidt Verlag.

Coulmas, Florian. 1979. On the sociolinguistic relevance of routine formulae. *Journal of Pragmatics* 3. 239–266.

Cutting, J. Cooper & Kathryn Bock. 1997. That's the way the cookie bounces: Syntactic and semantic components of experimentally controlled idiom blends. *Memory and Cognition* 25(1). 57–71.

Di Sciullo, Anna-Maria & Edwin Williams. 1987. *On the definition of word*. Cambridge, MA: MIT Press.

Dobrovol'skij, Dmitrij. 1988. *Phraseologie als Objekt der Universallinguistik*. Leipzig: Verlag Enzyklopädie.

Fiedler, Sabine. 2007. *English phraseology: A coursebook*. Tübingen: Gunther Narr.

Fillmore, Charles J., Paul Kay & Mary Catherine O'Connor. 1988. Regularity and idiomaticity in grammatical constructions: The case of *let alone. Language* 64(3). 501–538.

Fraser, Bruce. 1970. Idioms within a transformational grammar. *Foundations of Language* 6. 22–42.

Gläser, Rosemarie. 1986. *Phaseologie der Englischen Sprache.* Tübingen: Max Niemeyer Verlag.

Hoeksema, Jack. 2010. De localiteit van idiomen. http : / / www . let . rug . nl / ~hoeksema / localiteit, accessed 2018-4-19. Manuscript, University of Groningen.

Jackendoff, Ray. 1975. Morphological and semantic regularities in the lexicon. *Language* 51. 639–671.

Jackendoff, Ray. 2002. What's in the lexicon? In Sieb Nooteboom, Fred Weerman & Frank Wijnen (eds.), *Storage and computation in the language faculty*, 23–58. Dordrecht: Kluwer.

Jaki, Sylvia. 2014. *Phraseological substitutions in newspaper headlines: "More than meats the eye".* Amsterdam/Philadelphia: John Benjamins.

Kuiper, Koenraad & Douglas C. Haggo. 1984. Livestock auctions, oral poetry and ordinary language. *Language and Society* 13. 205–234.

Kuiper, Koenraad & Daphne Gek Lin Tan. 1989. Cultural congruence and conflict in the acquisition of formulae in a second language. In Ofelia Garcia & Ricardo Otheguy (eds.), *English across cultures. Cultures across English*, 281–304. Berlin: Mouton de Gruyter.

Lord, Albert Bates. 1960. *The singer of tales.* Cambridge, MA: Harvard University Press.

Malkiel, Yakov. 1959. Studies in irreversible binomials. *Lingua* 8. 113–160.

Mel'čuk, Igor. 2012. Phraseology in the language, in the dictionary, and in the computer. In Koenraad Kuiper (ed.), *Yearbook of Phraseology*, 31–56. Berlin: de Gruyter.

Nicolas, Tim. 1995. Semantics of idiom modification. In Martin Everaert, Erik-Jan van der Linden, André Schenk & Rob Schroeder (eds.), *Idioms: Structural and psychological perspectives*, 233–252. Hillsdale, NJ: Lawrence Erlbaum Associates.

Nunberg, Geoffrey, Ivan A. Sag & Thomas Wasow. 1994. Idioms. *Language* 70(3). 491–538.

O'Grady, William. 1998. The syntax of idioms. *Natural Language and Linguistic Theory* 16. 279–312.

Richter, Frank & Manfred Sailer. 2009. Phraseological clauses in constructional HPSG. In Stefan Müller (ed.), *Proceedings of the 16th international conference on Head-Driven Phrase Structure Grammar, Göttingen*, 297–317. Stanford, CA:

CSLI Publications. http://cslipublications.stanford.edu/HPSG/2009/richter-sailer.pdf, accessed 2018-4-19.

Richter, Frank, Manfred Sailer & Beata Trawiński. 2010. The collection of distributionally idiosyncratic items: An interface between data and theory. In Stefaniya Ptashnyk, Erla Hallsteinsdóttir & Noah Bubenhofer (eds.), *Corpora, web and databases: Computer-based methods in modern phraseology and lexicography*, 247–261. Schneider: Hohengehren.

Sag, Ivan A., Timothy Baldwin, Francis Bond, Ann Copestake & Dan Flickinger. 2002. Multiword expressions: A pain in the neck for NLP. In *Proceedings of the 3rd International Conference on Intelligent Text Processing and Computational Linguistics (CICLing-2002)*, 1–15.

Schenk, André. 1995. The syntactic behavior of idioms. In Martin Everaert, Eric-Jan van der Linden, André Schenk & Ron Schreuder (eds.), *Idioms. Structural and psychological perspectives*, 253–271. Hillsdale, NJ: Lawrence Erlbaum Associates.

Selkirk, Elizabeth. 1982. *The syntax of words*. Cambridge, MA: MIT Press.

Sprenger, Simone A., Willem J. M. Levelt & Gerard Kempen. 2006. Lexical access during the production of idiomatic phrases. *Journal of Memory and Language* 54. 161–184.

Starosta, Stanley, Koenraad Kuiper, Siew Ai Ng & Zhi-qian Wu. 1997. On defining the Chinese compound word: Headedness in Chinese compounding and Chinese VR compounds. In Jerome P. Packard (ed.), *New approaches to Chinese word formation: Morphology, phonology and the lexicon in Modern and Ancient Chinese*, 347–370. Berlin: Mouton de Gruyter.

Titone, Debora A. & Cynthia M. Connine. 1999. On the compositional and non-compositional nature of idiomatic expressions. *Journal of Pragmatics* 31. 1655–1674.

Wray, Alison. 2008. *Formulaic language: Pushing the boundaries*. Oxford: Oxford University Press.

Chapter 6

Choosing features for classifying multiword expressions

Éric Laporte
Université Paris-Est, Laboratoire d'informatique Gaspard-Monge CNRS, France

Multiword expressions (MWEs) are a heterogeneous set with a glaring need for classifications. Designing a satisfactory classification involves choosing features. In the case of MWEs, many features are a priori available. Not all features are equal in terms of how reliably MWEs can be assigned to classes. Accordingly, resulting classifications may be more or less fruitful for computational use. I outline an enhanced classification. In order to increase its suitability for many languages, I use previous works taking into account various languages.

1 Introduction

Multiword expressions range from idioms like *put pen to paper*, meaning 'undertake to write something', to multiword terms like *protein kinase* to support-verb constructions like *take a dip* 'bathe' and other types. Due to such diversity, there is a glaring need for classifications, if only for practical organization and for necessities of communication within the research community. Forty years after the first published comprehensive classifications of sets of MWEs, the community has not reached a satisfactory consensus on large classes or on the most relevant features. One outline of a classification (Sag et al. 2002), based on Nunberg et al. (1994), is influential, but some classes are fuzzily defined. The community is seeking to delineate the basic objects of the field. This uncertainty confuses computer scientists' main MWE-related activity, which is to recognise types of MWEs in

Éric Laporte. 2018. Choosing features for classifying multiword expressions. In Manfred Sailer & Stella Markantonatou (eds.), *Multiword expressions: Insights from a multi-lingual perspective*, 143–186. Berlin: Language Science Press. DOI:10.5281/zenodo.1182597

texts through statistical engineering: the community does not offer a consensual definition of types of MWEs.[1]

Classifications are a matter of features of the items to be classified. Which features should be used for classification, and therefore investigated in priority? Of course, linguistic relevance plays a prominent role in this selection, but my point in this paper is that many researchers overlook other important reasons for selecting or discarding some kinds of features. Some features are fuzzy and imprecise, that is, it is difficult to tell which MWEs have them. In resulting classifications, assignment of MWEs to classes is less reliable than it could be, and this is detrimental to computational use. Other features are more clear-cut and potentially more useful, but have not made their way to computational-linguistic literature yet. Another requirement for a convenient classification is that its outline be suitable for many languages. Accordingly, I use previous work taking into account various languages.

In §2, I exemplify and discuss the notion of a fuzzy feature. In §3 and §4, I investigate two connected topics: clusters of correlated features, and practical problems of observation. §5 advocates in favour of the practice of checking information against the lexicon. I outline an enhanced classification in §6.

2 Clear-cut or fuzzy features?

2.1 Examples

Some features are more clear-cut than others. For example, some MWEs select a preposition for a free slot/argument position,[2] as in *have pity on*:

(1)   *You could have pity on us.*

Nothing is totally definite in linguistics, but using *on* in this context is clearly appropriate.

In contrast, the semantic weight of verbs is a much fuzzier feature that lies in a continuum. The verb *have* in (1) is deemed "light", whereas it has full semantic weight in (2):

(2)   *They will have this machine in soon.*

    'This machine will soon be available for sale in their store.'

---

[1] However, there is a relative consensus on the delimitation of MWEs themselves. At least, many experts agree that this class includes collocations, multiword terms and support verb constructions. I will not address this issue in more detail for lack of space.

[2] Here, *free* means that the content of the slot, i.e. the noun phrase, is variable.

This is a basis to classify *have pity* in (1) as a support-verb construction, or light-verb construction, and *have in* in (2) as a phrasal verb. But, in *have a call* 'talk on the phone', or *have a goal*, or *make a joke*, intuition about the semantic weight of the verb in these expressions remains unsettled or depends on whom you ask.[3]

2.2 Related work

2.2.1 Earlier work on clear-cut features

All the main features for present classifications had already been proposed by 1995, so the historical background is worth reviewing.

The first research works on MWEs with extended classificatory results define classes and subclasses with relatively clear-cut features. For instance, Labelle (1974)'s study of French support-verb constructions with *avoir* 'have' assigns a class to expressions with an argument position introduced by the preposition *sur* 'on', as in:

(3)   *Lyon a un avantage sur Marseille.*

        'Lyon has an advantage over Marseille.'[4]

This kind of sharp distinction neatly separates classes. For example, *avoir un faible pour* 'have a taste for' definitely does not select *sur*, since sequences like (4) are rejected.[5]

(4)   * *J'ai un faible sur toi.*
        Lit. 'I have a taste on you.'

The other features used to define Labelle's classes are similar. Many features come down to applying elementary syntactic operations, one at a time, and judging the acceptability of the result, while watching out for unexpected meaning changes. The method used by Labelle, called Lexicon-Grammar (LG) by Guillet & La Fauci (1984), is briefly described by Gross (1994). It was applied to MWEs by

---

[3]Another fuzzy feature of MWEs is whether they belong to terminology. *Protein kinase* does, *smooth operator* 'persuasive person; manipulative person' does not; but *sore throat* 'inflammation of the throat' is somewhere in between, since it is used by professionals but mainly to communicate with non-professionals.

[4]For examples not in English, I do not provide glosses because they would not be useful for the reader. I provide a translation of the literal meaning when it is different from the non-literal meaning.

[5]Independently of that, *avoir un avantage* may also occur with other prepositions, maybe less clearly selected: *J'ai un avantage par rapport à toi.* 'I have an advantage as compared to you.'

other authors since then (Meunier 1977; Giry-Schneider 1978; Danlos 1980; Gross 1982; Freckleton 1985; Machonis 1985; Ranchhod 1990; etc., in English, Romance languages, Greek, etc.). All prefer clear-cut features such as:

- parts of speech (multiword nouns; verbal, adverbial and adjectival idioms)

- applicable syntactic operations, including optionality vs. compulsoriness of fixed constituents and free slots.[6]

Some examples of clear-cut features are less likely to occur at the top of a classification tree:

- phrase structure (e.g. number of fixed objects in a verbal idiom)

- number of free slots, their selected prepositions, restrictions on what may fill them

- compulsory coreference relations (e.g. in *think on one's feet* 'improvise a reaction quickly', between the free subject and the possessive)

Nothing is totally definite in linguistics, but the implicit rationale behind preference for clear-cut features is that it is unwise to place poorly understood features in a decision tree, especially at its top.

2.2.2 Earlier work on fuzzy features

However, outside this LG trend, clear-cut features are readily mixed with fuzzier ones, even when defining large classes. The clear-cut features are essentially the same as above. The fuzzier ones often involve semantics or psycholinguistics.[7]

Semantic weight is often used to define support-verb constructions, or light-verb constructions, such as *have pity, have a goal, take a dip*. This section will show that this definition relies entirely on fuzzy features, and so does the other naive definition.

---

[6] Fraser (1970: 39) also proposes a classification of verbal idioms based on applicable syntactic operations. But he tests it on a sample of 131 idioms only (p. 40–41). In addition, he hypothesizes entailments between operations: for instance, if an idiom accepts passivization, it would also accept permutation of complements. His classification presupposes the entailments: when some of them are wrong for an idiom, there is no class for it. This is the case for the French idioms *faire le jour sur* (lit. make the day on) 'shed light on' and *claquer la porte au nez de* (lit. slam the door to the nose of) 'slam the door in the face of', which accept passivization, but not permutation of complements.

[7] Wisely, current classifications of MWEs avoid using terminologicalness to define main classes.

Baldwin & Kim (2010: 276) define light-verb constructions by the fact that their verb is "semantically bleached or 'light', in the sense that [its] contribution to the meaning of the light-verb construction is relatively small in comparison with that of the noun complement," that is semantically weak. This definition dates back to Jespersen: "[s]uch everyday combinations as those illustrated in the following paragraphs after *have* and similar 'light' verbs (...) are in accordance with the general tendency of modern English to place an insignificant verb, to which the marks of person and tense are attached, before the really important idea (...) *I really must have a good stare at her.*" (Jespersen 1942: 117). But in many occurrences, verbs are felt to lie somewhere in a spectrum of intermediate stages between significant and insignificant. And, even though the feature is polar, it is not scalar: there is no metrics according to which it would be possible to measure how close an item is to the poles of the range.

Alternative views of support-verb constructions have been proposed. One of them is in terms of predicate-argument structure: "nouns that have characteristics of predicates" (Gross 1981: 32, my translation; Cattell 1984). By *predicate-argument structure*, I mean the concept borrowed from logic by linguists, who initially applied it (Tesnière 1959) to sentences such as:

(5)   *The wire connects the device to the socket.*

In this analysis, the predicate-argument structure of (5) is 'connect'('wire', 'device', 'socket'), where the predicate is 'connect' and the arguments are 'wire', 'device' and 'socket'. The predicate does not necessarily match with a verb:

(6)   *Everyone took a look at our project.*

Analysing (6) as 'take'('everyone', 'look') or 'take'('everyone', 'look', 'project') is not satisfactory, precisely because *take* is too weak to make sense as the core of a predicate-argument structure. If you analyse (6) as 'take_look'('everyone', 'project') instead, you consider that the predicate is *take a look* (or the noun *look*, which makes little difference, since *take* has features of a mere function word). Or, in other words, the noun *look* has valency two. On the basis of this type of analysis, support-verb constructions could be defined as those in which the predicate does not match with the main verb, but with a noun (a predicational noun, or noun that has valency) or another part of speech (PoS). Unfortunately, this definition still relies on a shaky semantic intuition: which part of a sentence matches best with the intuition of predicate? Take the following sentence:

(7)   *He made a joke.*

In (7), is the verb *make* to be analysed as a "performance" predicate, or is it so light that the sentence is equivalent to *He joked*?

Another alternative is suggested by examples from Jespersen (1942), which all involve deverbal nouns such as *stare*, and by the pairs of sentences explicitly pointed out by Harris (1964: 17–19):

(8) a. *He took a look at it.*

  b. *He looked at it.*

Could support-verb constructions be defined by the equivalence between the content verb (*looked*) and the support-verb followed by the deverbal noun (*took a look*)? This would be consistent with both previous definitions.[8] Unfortunately, the definition based on equivalence with a verb would exclude many expressions for which no equivalent verb is in use (Labelle 1974):

(9) a. *Il a eu un conflit avec sa famille.*
      'He had a conflict with his family.'

  b. * *Il s'est conflité avec sa famille.*
      Lit. He conflicted himself with his family.
      'He conflicted with his family.'

This is not desirable because (9a) otherwise behaves like a typical support-verb construction. It is syntactically and semantically similar, for example, to (10a), for which an equivalent verb is observed:

(10) a. *Il a eu une réconciliation avec sa famille.*
      'He had a reconciliation with his family.'

  b. *Il s'est réconcilié avec sa famille.*
      Lit. He reconciled himself with his family.
      'He was reconciled with his family.'

Here are parallel examples in English:

(11) a. *He has the goal of getting rich.*

  b. * *He goals to get rich.*

---

[8] As for the definition based on semantic weight, if *look* is equivalent to *take a look*, little is left for *take* to contribute to the meaning. Now for the definition referring to predicate-argument structure: if *looked* is the predicate in (8b), its equivalent *took a look* should logically be considered as the predicate in (8a).

(12) a. *He has the aim of getting rich.*

  b. *He aims to get rich.*

Reformulating, the property of equivalence with a content verb would not classify (9a) and (11a) as support-verb constructions, in spite of their striking similarity with (10a) and (12a).

Thus, we are left with the first two naive definitions of support-verb constructions: one with the semantic weight of the verb, and the other with predicate-argument structure. Both definitions rely on particularly fuzzy semantic intuitions. They situate the feature of being a support-verb construction in a continuum between two poles. A more precise definition will be reported in §2.2.3.

Gibbs & Nayak (1989: 104) define another loose feature, SEMANTIC DECOMPOSABILITY, as the "[contribution of] parts of idioms to their figurative interpretations as a whole [according to] speakers' assumptions". For example, the parts of *pull strings* 'covertly use one's influence on personal connections' would be *pull* 'exploit' and *strings* 'personal connections'. This is a continuously graded intuition: "People's intuitions about the decomposability of any idiom can vary along some continuum of semantic decomposition" (Gibbs & Nayak 1989: 67); "in general, idiom phrases exist on a continuum of analyzability ranging from those idioms that appear to be highly decomposable (e.g., *pop the question*) to those that can be viewed as semantically nondecomposable (e.g., *kick the bucket*)" (Gibbs & Nayak 1989: 107). Nunberg et al. (1994: 497, 508) reterm this feature SEMANTIC ANALYSABILITY and redefine it as the fact that the "idiomatic interpretation [can] be distributed over [the] parts of the [expression]". The wording is different, but it comes to the same thing, since the only source to know the distribution of the idiomatic interpretation over the parts of the expression is speakers' assumptions.[9] Nunberg et al. (1994: 520–523) cite an uncertain case: they represent *take advantage of* with two lexical entries, one of which is semantically analysable while the other is not, although they "know of no evidence that the two entries might be semantically different". This case where the same idiom, in the same sense, both is and is not analysable implicitly situates it at some intermediate stage. Although analysability is imprecise, Sag et al. (2002) and Baldwin & Kim (2010: 270) adopt this feature, going back to the term of SEMANTIC DECOMPOSABILITY,[10] to distinguish two of their major classes of MWEs: semi-fixed expressions and syntactically-flexible expressions.

---

[9]Nunberg et al. (1994: 496–497) contrast semantic analysability with *transparency*, which is about speakers' ability to guess why an expression with some literal meaning is used to convey a given non-literal meaning.

[10]Baldwin & Kim (2010: 270) equate their notion of decomposability to Nunberg et al. (1994: 496)'s semantic analysability.

Thus, reputed classifications use fuzzy features as liberally as clear-cut ones, even at the top of their classification trees.

2.2.3 Clear-cut features and lexical inventorying

There is something more to be learned from early work on MWEs: extensive practice of lexical description leads researchers to discover clear-cut features and adopt them in their classifications.

Recall that Labelle (1974) and other LG authors cited in §2.2.1 prefer clear-cut features. This specificity is connected to their practice of inventorying lexical items: they delimit a set of phrases on the basis of features, systematically record phrases belonging to the set, obtain comprehensive lists and study them in order to reach well-documented conclusions. The papers and PhDs of these linguists either include a comprehensive list of members of each class proposed, or at least were published after the completion of such lists.[11] For example, Freckleton (1985) lists 8000 English verbal idioms; by 1987, Gross' laboratory[12] had studied 12700 entries of French predicational nouns used with support verbs (Tolone 2011: 144).

This labour-intensive method contrasts with common practice of that time. Nunberg et al. (1994: 498), for example, do not challenge the LG approach or the resulting classifications,[13] but base most of their research on sporadically picked examples: the only sizable lists reproduced in their paper (p. 532–534) answer empirically one of the many issues they address. When they claim that the number of MWEs with anomalous morphosyntactic structure, like *every which way* 'in all directions; in complete disorder', is "not so small" (Nunberg et al. 1994: 515), as a reply to Chomsky (1980: 149) who claims such expressions are not "typical", they do not compare numbers of lexical entries in comprehensive dictionaries. (Tables of MWEs settle this dispute in favour of Chomsky: morphosyntactically anomalous MWEs are really a small minority.)

Sag et al. (2002) and Baldwin & Kim (2010) share the same weaknesses. In no language did any research group assign semantic (un)analysability to com-

---

[11] The lists still exist. They describe features for all entries and take the form of tables of features, which are easy to use. Many of these tables are freely available, e.g. at http://infolingu.univ-mlv. fr/ for French. They remain to be diffused so that they reach out to the mainstream community.

[12] Laboratoire d'automatique documentaire et linguistique (LADL), a part of Université Paris 7 and of CNRS.

[13] Nunberg et al. (1994: 498)'s divergence from Machonis (1985) is terminological: they call *conventionality* what Machonis (1985: 306) and Danlos & Gross (1988: 128–129) call *lack of compositionality*, that is impossibility of predicting the meaning or use of the MWE on the basis of *only* a knowledge of the rules that determine the meaning and use of its parts when they occur separately.

prehensive classes of MWEs. Bond et al. (2015: 64) encode this property in 421 English idioms, but this is a small sample, not a comprehensive lexical inventory; in contrast, Grégoire's study of 5000 Dutch MWEs led her to give up categorizing them as analysable or not (Grégoire 2010: 31–32).

But what is the connection between clear-cut features and extensive lexical description? When the description of a feature gives clear-cut results throughout the inventory of expressions, authors understandably tend to consider these results particularly reliable, and to prefer this feature over others, all else being equal.

This is how Gross and his followers in the 1970s came across formal features of support-verb constructions which are still used as criteria to recognise them (Langer 2005). They systematically scanned the lexicon of French nouns, studied their syntactic constructions and worked out criteria of recognition of predicational nouns for dubious cases. One of these criteria is a formal property of determiners and adjuncts (Gross 1976: 109) which is also observed in English. In (13a), if possessive determiners, phrases with *of* and genitives are inserted around *joke*, they cannot refer to anything else than the subject:

(13)   a.   *He made a joke.*
       b.   *He made his joke.*
       c.   * *He made your joke.*
       d.   * *He made Ann's joke.*

How does this criterion correlate with the intuitive notion of predicate (cf. §2.2.2)? In other sentences where the core of the intuition-identified predicate is a noun, like (8a) *He took a look at it* or (11a) *He has the goal of getting rich*, this constraint is also observed. But when the intuitive predicate is a verb, the constraint is not observed:

(14)   a.   *He made your car.*
       b.   *He made Ann's car.*

(15)   a.   *He reported your joke.*
       b.   *He reported Ann's joke.*

This formal test is a reason for analysing (13a) as 'joke'('he'), but (14a) as 'make'('he', 'car') and (15b) as 'report'('he', 'joke'('Ann')), in spite of their apparently similar structure.

This property, when used as a criterion to distinguish support-verb constructions from full-verb constructions, gives more precise results than those I mentioned in §2.2.2. It does not help with the distinction between support-verb constructions and verbal idioms. Some verbal idioms behave as (13):

(16) a. *He thought on his feet.*

          'He improvised a reaction quickly.'

      b. * *He thought on Ann's feet.*

Others behave as (14) and (15):

(17) a. *He melted your heart.*

          'He made you feel sympathy.'

      b. *He melted Ann's heart.*

But a similar property (Gross 1979: 865–866, Footnote 6), which is used in a forth-
coming compendium on French grammar (Abeillé & Vivès 2011: 16), contributes
to making more definite the distinction between support-verb constructions and
verbal idioms. Take the following construction with the support verb *make*:

(18) *The quake made damage to the area.*

A syntactic operation applied to (19a) produces a variant (19b) where *make* is
absent:

(19) a. *The damage to the area made by the quake (is described in the diary).*

      b. *The damage to the area by the quake (is described in the diary).*

This criterion classifies *have the back of,* meaning 'back, support', as a verbal
idiom, not as a support-verb construction, because it has no variant in which
have would be absent. Take the following sentence:

(20) *The president has the back of our children.*

A banal syntactic operation on (20) would produce the subject of the following
sentence:

(21) * *The president's back of our children (is manifested by real actions).*

But (21) is not in use.

This criterion applies to all support-verb constructions. The syntactic operations that remove the support verb are not the same for all support-verb constructions, even in a given language: (19) exemplifies one of them for English, (20)–(21) another. Applying the criterion may involve knowing all operations and testing them, because the criterion rules out the support-verb construction analysis only if none applies, e.g. for *have the back of*.[14] In Italian (De Angelis 1989), Portuguese (Ranchhod 1990, Rassi et al. 2014), Korean (Han 2000), Greek (Kyriacopoulou & Sfetsiou 2003) and other languages, LG authors selected analogous technical criteria and definitions.

The larger linguistic and NLP community was not receptive to LG in the 1980s and 1990s, and access to publications was difficult. Cattell (1984), though he did not explicitly challenge the LG syntactic criteria, stuck to definitions based on semantic intuition, and so did many linguists. Since then, both traditions, that is intuitive vs. technical definitions of support-verb constructions, have continued in parallel.[15] Thus, support-verb constructions provide an example of a feature that can be defined either as clear-cut or as fuzzy. The notion itself is basically the same, but some definitions ensure more definite membership than others.

This review of earlier work showed that researchers engaged in projects of extensive lexical description tend to discover more clear-cut features and adopt them in their classifications, but that recent literature does not make a difference between clear-cut and fuzzy features. Recent classifications are derived indifferently from both.

---

[14]This criterion also rules out the support-verb construction analysis for *take advantage of*:

    (i) *The bank takes advantage of deposit slip errors.*

The syntactic operation of (19) does not apply:

    (ii) *The advantage taken by the bank of deposit slip errors (has been revealed).*

    (iii) **The advantage by the bank of deposit slip errors (has been revealed).*

Neither does that of (20)–(21):

    (iv) *The advantage the bank takes of deposit slip errors (has been revealed).*

    (v) **The bank's advantage of deposit slip errors (has been revealed).*

[15]The use of *light verb* is loosely correlated with the intuitive approach and *support verb* with the technical approach. Gross (1981: 12) adopts the term of *support verb*, with the idea that, for example, *make* "supports" a predicational noun in (13a).

2.3 Discussion

I could not find in the literature any discussion of whether the use of these fuzzy features is an issue at all, or if their relevance compensates for their drawbacks. Even NLP literature does not care more than corpus linguistics or the philological or generative traditions.

Fuzzy features can be less technical. For example, as opposed to the definition of support-verb constructions based on the semantic weight of the verb, a concern for definiteness leads one to adopt formal criteria that involve applying detailed syntactic operations, as in (13c) *He made your joke*, and assessing the result. It is not just that this complexity can be seen as a drawback: it also makes precise features more likely to be language-dependent. The criteria illustrated by (13) for English need to be adapted when they are applied to, say, Italian or Korean, due to differences in syntactic constructions. Decisive criteria for support-verb constructions have been found in many languages, but they are not exactly the same. Butt (2010) also draws this conclusion on the basis of a review of typological and diachronic literature. In contrast, the fuzzy definition based on the semantic weight of the verb is language-independent.

But the price to be paid for language independence is that you cannot tell if an item satisfies the definition or not. Then, to which class does it belong? In practice, in order to avoid fuzzy membership of classes, and uncertain inclusions between classes, fuzzy features must be replaced by clear-cut, binary models of them.

Proponents of fuzzy features rarely claim these might be useful for computer applications. Semantic analysability/decomposability, for instance, is relevant to the mental lexicon, maybe to first language acquisition, but probably not to computational applications. If, in the future, information is attached to parts of idioms in formal semantic representations, can it be exploited computationally? Nunberg et al. (1994: 501) cite a variation on *tilt at windmills* 'fight against imaginary or invincible opponents':

(22)   *tilting at the federal windmill*

One can imagine that a parser that would handle a semantic representation of *tilt at windmills* composed of separate structures for the parts *tilt* and *windmill* might interpret (22) more correctly than a parser with an atomic semantic representation of the idiom. But, as of 2018, both types of parsers are hypothetical, since few parsers interpret idioms. The challenge of identifying even their least creative variants, such as *tilt bravely at windmills*, is probably a priority as compared to that of unlexicalized, playful variations like *tilt at a federal windmill*.

Besides this remote perspective, computational applications of analysability are elusive. Bond et al. (2015) do not say that the analysability encoded in the dictionary is used by the English HPSG grammar to check restrictions on the form of idioms.

No clear use has been found either for another fuzzy feature, which consists in the fact that native speakers that don't know the MWE can guess its sense or not when they hear it in an uninformative context. For example, according to Osherson & Fellbaum (2010: 3), the sense of *rest on one's laurels* 'keep from making effort out of self-satisfaction from prior achievements' is easily guessed, but that of *walk on eggshells* 'be very cautious' is not.[16] This feature is relatively fuzzy: "the classification suggested above is only approximate, a number of idioms (…) cannot be straightforwardly fit into any one category"; they do not claim any computational use of this feature, and it is hard to imagine a realistic one.

In contrast, many clear-cut features are straightforwardly exploitable in language processing, especially those that directly determine the possibility of occurrence of actual forms, such as selected prepositions or applicability of syntactic operations. Clear-cut features of MWEs, as described in LGs, have been used early and recently in Tree-Adjoining Grammars (Abeillé 1988), symbolic machine translation (Danlos 1992), finite-state parsers (Senellart 1998), symbolic dependency parsers (Tolone 2011) and statistical parsers (Constant et al. 2013).

Clear-cut features have significant methodological and practical advantages. When fuzzy features are used instead, it is worth checking carefully that their linguistic relevance motivates this choice.

3 Correlated features

3.1 An example

In some cases, it is easy to replace a single fuzzy feature with a bundle of clear-cut ones. For example, the syntactic operations applicable to verbal idioms, instead

---

[16]This feature is the more restrictive of the two features that Nunberg et al. (1994: 495) call *conventionality*. Osherson & Fellbaum term it *non-compositionality*, but it is quite different from *lack of compositionality* (cf. Footnote 13) in Danlos & Gross (1988: 128–129): when speakers that don't know *rest on one's laurels* figure out what it means, they don't base their guesses only on a knowledge of the rules that determine the meaning and use of the parts when they occur separately, but also on their imagination and cultural familiarity with classical antiquity. Nunberg et al. (1994: 496–497)'s *transparency* (speakers' ability to guess why an expression with some literal meaning is used to convey a given non-literal meaning) is less restrictive: even if speakers can't figure out the non-literal meaning of an unknown idiom, they may be able to guess the motivation of this meaning once they are informed of it.

of being collectively considered as a single (fuzzy) feature, are better dealt with separately from one another.

Here are a few examples of syntactic operations.

- Optionality of fixed constituents:

  (23)   a.   *John bearded the lion in his den.*
             'John faced the danger directly.'
         b.   *John bearded the lion.*

- Optionality of free slots:

  (24)   a.   *John bears comparison to Magritte.*
             'John is similar enough to Magritte to be likened to him.'
         b.   *John bears comparison.*

- Insertion of free adjuncts:

  (25)   a.   *This dealt a blow to my hopes.*
         b.   *This dealt a strong blow to my hopes.*

- Topicalisation:

  (26)   a.   *He would not deal such a blow to you.*
         b.   *Such a blow, he would not deal to you.*

- Dative shift:

  (27)   a.   *This dealt a blow to my hopes.*
         b.   *This dealt my hopes a blow.*

- Reduction in a repeated occurrence:

  (28)   a.   *I changed my mind about China.*
         b.   *You changed yours about India.*

- Pseudocleft construction:

(29)   a.   *John fights fire with fire.*
           'John uses the same arms as his opponents.'
      b.   *The way John fights fire is with fire.*

- Passivization:

(30)   a.   *The price of the coffee caught John short of change.*
           'Given the price of the coffee, John had no change.'
      b.   *John was caught short of change by the price of the coffee.*

Not all operations are applicable to the same idioms. For example, *bear comparison to* admits the removal of its prepositional free slot, but not passivization:

(31)   * Comparison to Magritte is borne by John.

Fraser (1970: 34) is aware of these differences between features. The straightforward model for syntactic flexibility is a multidimensional space of variation, since there are independent features. Nunberg et al. (1994: 509) claim that some large range of syntactic operations is "loosely correlated". Contrasts such as (24a) vs. (31) show that such correlation, if it exists, is not 100%. Since correlation is a statistical notion, only statistical evidence could support Nunberg et al. (1994)'s claim. This could be done by measuring the correlation with extensive lexical data. For example, Freckleton (1985)'s table C1P2, which contains *beard the lion in his den*, shows a positive but loose correlation between optionality of the prepositional object and passivizability: the Pearson's correlation coefficient, computed with these data, is 0.13.

Sag et al. (2002: 6), Baldwin & Kim (2010: 278) cluster all syntactic operations into SYNTACTIC FLEXIBILITY. Syntactic flexibility is an imprecise feature, since idioms that undergo only some of the known syntactic operations are intermediate cases, "syntactically flexible to some degree", as Sag et al. (2002) put it. But they do not measure the correlation either. Even so, both Sag et al. (2002: 3) and Baldwin & Kim (2010: 279) derive some of their major classes from "the" feature of syntactic flexibility. Baldwin & Kim (2010) subdivide verbal idioms into two subclasses: one of non-decomposable idioms "with hard restrictions on word order and composition", i.e. no application of syntactic operations, and another of decomposable, syntactically flexible idioms. They leave open the question of where intermediate cases should belong in practice: when some syntactic operations apply and others don't, they cross-classify, i.e. they assign the same lexical item to different classes. None of these authors shows the benefit for NLP or linguistics of using a unidimensional scale as a model for a multidimensional variation space.

These models artificially create fuzzy features and the associated problems. Their authors do not explain what motivates this innovation, nor do they state a position on previous classifications that avoid equating distinct syntactic operations.

3.2 Discussion

Syntactic flexibility is a cluster of loosely correlated features and should not be used as if it were a single feature, especially when defining major classes: such definitions are imprecise. If a lexical database registers *bear comparison to* in a class of syntactically flexible idioms, this signals that this idiom admits at least some syntactic operations, but users cannot be certain about any specific operation, for example the removal of its prepositional free slot: (24b) *John bears comparison.* Reversely, if it is in a class of non-syntactically-flexible idioms, it does not admit all the possible operations, but users cannot safely deduce that it does not admit, say, passivization: (31) **Comparison to Magritte is borne by John.* This compromises computational usage: a major function of a classification is to ensure that the members of each class have the corresponding defining features.

Thus, as long as all properties are not securely established for all entries, it is a good practice to specify each criterion accurately. This leads to individuating a number of features, and to specifying which entries have which features, like in LG tables, which show that syntactic operations are not visibly more correlated in French (Gross 1982), Italian (Vietri 2011) or Greek (Fotopoulou 1993) than in English (Freckleton 1985).

A correlation between features may give a sense that they are particularly relevant to classification, because they might stem from a hidden, underlying, fundamental property. Moreover, if these features are used jointly for classification, assigning an entry to a class will implicitly specify all features at the same time, killing two birds with one stone. However, the temptation should be resisted until a systematic investigation assesses how correlated the features are. If intuition overestimates the degree of correlation, which often happens, and if a classification equates loosely correlated features, assigning an entry to a class does not specify any of the features, failing to kill any of the proverbial birds.

Fundamental scientific progress has often been achieved by elaborating a distinction between two notions that are easy to confuse, e.g. weight and mass in physics. In their model, Sag et al. (2002) and Baldwin & Kim (2010) do the reverse: they replace a set of relatively precise features, which are objectively distinct and had been treated as such before, with an imprecise one, which is therefore more difficult to handle. Their model adds artificial uncertainty.

Thus, merging a cluster of loosely correlated features into an "aggregate" feature decreases the accuracy of the model and weakens its information content.

4 Reproducibility of observation of features

4.1 Examples

Even without any excess of optimism about correlations, some features are more clear-cut than others for another reason: reproducibility. Reproducible observations are those inherently susceptible to high inter-judge agreement. This notion may sound technical and is often ignored, but my point in this part is that it has considerable practical significance for projects with realistic goals.

Features are not equal in terms of inter-judge agreement. For example, the compulsoriness of a coreference relation in an MWE, e.g. in *think on one's feet* 'improvise a reaction quickly', between the subject and the possessive, is judged by checking the grammaticality or acceptability[17] of some sentences, which is relatively factual, as in (16) cited here as (32):

(32) a. *He thought on his feet.*
      b. * *He thought on Ann's feet.*

With *melt someone's heart* 'make someone feel sympathy', such coreference is not compulsory, as shown in (17a) *He melted your heart.* Few native speakers will disagree with such observations. Consequently, this feature can be recorded in a lexical database in a relatively reliable way. Similarly, the applicability of syntactic operations to MWEs is tested by applying the operations, as in (16), (17) and (23)–(31), while judging the acceptability of the result and the conservation of the meaning. Therefore, in most cases, it is also reproducibly observable.

---

[17]By *grammatical* we mean that a sentence may be used to convey some information in some situation and in some context. This is consistent with how *grammatical* is used by most linguists, and identical to what Harris (1957: 293) means by *acceptable* (Ross 1979: 161). In fact, we will use *acceptable*, to avoid confusion with Chomsky's use of *grammatical* (Chomsky 1957: 15), which is in principle divergent since some nonsense sequences may be grammatical in his sense.

In contrast, semantic analysability/decomposability in the sense of Gibbs & Nayak (1989), Nunberg et al. (1994: 508), Sag et al. (2002) and Baldwin & Kim (2010) has no other empirical ground than pure semantic impressions. "There are no well-defined procedures for specifying whether a given idiom is semantically decomposable or not." (Gibbs & Nayak 1989: 106). Nunberg et al. (1994: 523–524)'s intuitions about the analysability of *take advantage of* are unstable (cf. §2.2). They cite *take stock* 'take the time to think' as analysable and *take hold* 'grasp' as non-analysable, but other speakers' introspection is not sure to reproduce this contrast. According to them, *take stock* "can be roughly paraphrased as 'make an assessment', with the noun *stock* semantically approximating 'assessment'." But in the same vein, *take hold* can be paraphrased as 'voluntarily acquire a grasp', where *take* would denote the 'voluntary acquiring' and *hold* the 'grasp'. Acceptability is judged by introspection too, but is more factual and can be backed by corpus attestations in some cases. Joint use of introspection and corpus attestation is more and more recognized as a valid source of empirical data on acceptability (Johansson 1991: 313;[18] Fillmore 1992: 58; 2001: 1;[19] McEnery & Wilson 1996: 16;[20] Kepser & Reis 2005;[21] Gries 2011: 87[22]). *Roll one's eyes*, in its idiomatic meaning, denotes a 'feeling of surprise and rejection for something stupid or strange', and often also an actual eye movement that expresses this feeling, but this physical element of meaning is perhaps not necessarily present in all occurrences of the idiom:

---

[18] "The corpus remains *one* of the linguist's tools, to be used together with introspection and elicitation techniques. Wise linguists, like experienced craftsmen, sharpen their tools and recognize their appropriate uses."

[19] "One [cannot have] success in the language business without using both resources: any corpus offers riches that introspecting linguists will never come upon if left to their meditations; and at the same time, every native speaker has solid knowledge about facts of their language that no amount of corpus evidence, taken by itself, could support or contradict."

[20] "Why move from one extreme of only natural data to another of only artificial data? Both have known weaknesses. Why not use a combination of both, and rely on the strengths of each to the exclusion of their weaknesses? A corpus and an introspection-based approach to linguistics are not mutually exclusive. In a very real sense they can be gainfully viewed as being complementary."

[21] "It is one of the main aims of this volume to overcome the corpus data versus introspective data opposition and to argue for a view that values and employs different types of linguistic evidence each in their own right."

[22] "It is obvious that corpus linguists need to make subjective decisions all the time, and they need to document their subjective choices very clearly in their publications. However, in spite of these undoubtedly subjective decisions, many advantages over armchair linguistics remain: the data points that are coded are not made-up, their frequency distributions are based on natural data, and these data points force us to include inconvenient or highly unlikely examples that armchair linguists may 'overlook'."

(33)   *We've all rolled our eyes at a particularly catchy headline.*

Many idioms share this property (Burger 1998: 44). In their meaning, the feeling part is rather non-analysable, whereas the physical movement part is rather analysable. When compromising between these intuitions, not all speakers are likely to obtain the same result. It is not just that the semantic analysis of the feeling part is funny: more importantly, there is no reason why different observers would assign the idiom to the same class.

The contrast between more or less reproducibly observable features is also observed in French, in Italian, and presumably in any language. Take this French idiom:

(34)   *se mettre le doigt dans l'œil*
       Lit. put one's finger in one's eye

       'have a mistaken understanding'

My own impressions in terms of analysability are precarious: does *le doigt* (lit. one's finger) really stand for an element of meaning like 'understanding(x)', *mettre* (lit. put) for 'choose' and *dans l'œil* (lit. in one's eye) for 'wrong'?

Semantic analysability poses recurrent problems of reproducibility of observation. This makes it a fuzzy feature.

4.2 Related work

Reproducibility of observation is not a new requirement. It is a central concern for American structuralists such as Bloomfield and Harris, who typically improve it by adjusting the definition of features under analysis, and in particular, by resorting to FORMAL OR SYNTACTIC CRITERIA, as in (16b) *He thought on Ann's feet*, avoiding to rely directly on pure semantic intuition. This tradition focuses on selecting knowledge that can be reproducibly observed, as part of a quest for scientificity in linguistics. In the observation of semantic features, DIFFERENTIAL SEMANTIC EVALUATION is more reproducible than absolute semantic evaluation (Gross 1975: 391–392).[23] For example, take the following French support-verb construction:

---

[23]"Pairs of sentences that are candidates for being related by a transformation are judged to be synonymous or not. Thus, meaning is only involved in comparisons, and *differences* in meaning are detected in this manner. In the physical sciences, it is well-known that *absolute* evaluations of a variable (e.g. temperature) lead always to rather crude results, when compared to *differential* evaluations of the same variable. The situation appears to be the same in linguistics with respect to meaning. Attributing absolute terms to forms is quite problematic, and anyway, has proved to be rather unsuccessful, while comparing the meanings of similar forms may bring to light subtle differences that may be hard to detect directly."

(35)   *Le mur a de la couleur.*
        Lit. The wall has colour.
        'The wall is colourful.'

Far from all interviewed speakers agree that (35) denotes intensiveness; in other words, this observation is little reproducible. Now take the following variant:

(36)   *Le mur a une couleur.*
        'The wall has a colour on it.'

When asked if (35) is more intensive than (36), much more speakers share this perception, agreeing that (36) is more neutral. The differential observation is more reproducible than the absolute one.[24] Reproducibility decreases back if you compare phrases, for example *de la couleur* vs. *une couleur,* instead of complete sentences. The LG method is much about such practical techniques of elaborating the procedures of observation or the definition of features, in order to improve reproducibility. When you ask the right question, it is easier to agree on an answer. In practice, performers of LG work are trained to be systematically watchful of their own dubious or instable judgments, and to compare these judgments to those of their peers. This measurement of reproducibility is subjective, but peer controlled, in order that subjectivity does not affect the quality of the results. It is performed right from the beginning of the project, and separately for each feature, to detect which features raise reproducibility problems. Such detection leads to two types of decisions:

(i) give up the study of "bad" features, that is those that cannot be observed with reasonable reproducibility

(ii) look for "good" features for which methodological precautions ensure reasonable reproducibility

A reproducibility issue often causes a shift from an intuition-defined feature to one or several new criterion-defined ones. The latter may be a little different, but they have an advantage: it is clearer what they are. Such decisions refine or shift the target of the description and, of course, eventually affect the classifications based on the features.

There are few ongoing debates about such practices in linguistics, and even less in research on MWEs. Reproducibility is alien to Baldwin & Kim (2010)'s

---

[24]Here are two other examples of definite semantic differences: (35) denotes more of a favourable subjective judgment than (36), and (35) may evoke one or several colours, whereas (36) evokes one.

concerns, except for an allusion in connection with interpretation of nominal compounds (Baldwin & Kim 2010: 275).[25] In current practices beyond LG, measurement of reproducibility is more objective: it takes the form of inter-judge agreement statistics. But these statistics either focus on a small sample of features deemed representative, or handle features collectively, not individually (Palmer et al. 2005: 86 is an exception): in both cases, they don't help to tell the "good" features from the "bad". The inter-judge agreement approach tests how a team of descriptive linguists fare as regard reproducibility, it does not assess the potential of each feature. It views reproducibility as a behavioral problem only, not as a syntactic or lexicological problem, and disregards the fact that the problem is different for each feature.

In addition, current practices usually take into account only small samples of prototypical MWEs deemed representative.[26] But many reproducibility issues stem from the diversity of lexical entries: their detection requires comprehensive scrutiny of the lexicon.[27]

Globally, with the shift from subjective to objective procedures, quality of measurement has deteriorated. It is worse than that: now, reproducibility assessment is rarely used for feedback on the aims of the description or on its practical procedures. First, such feedback would require differential assessment on individual features. Second, inter-judge agreement is usually computed at the end of the descriptive phase (Meyers et al. (2004: 803) is an exception), when it is too late for feedback. Reproducibility assessment is only regarded as a quality indicator: researchers are content with measuring the symptoms and rarely attempt to cure them.[28]

---

[25] Anyway, in the case of analysability, no such improvements of the definition seem to be at hand.

[26] Gibbs et al. (1989: 60) assess the consistency of undergraduates' judgments of semantic decomposability of a sample of 36 idioms.

[27] The complexity of the assessment of reproducibility has three dimensions: the number of features, the number of lexical entries and the number of judges. Informal LG practices deal with all three dimensions. But objective measurement of inter-judge agreement is costly, which leads to limiting its ambition in terms of two of the three dimensions: the number of features and of lexical entries. Thus, the operation loses its essential benefits.

[28] Another way of improving the resources has emerged: automating error detection targeted at specific error types in resources. For example, Meyers et al. (2004) automatically check formal and heuristic properties of dictionary entries; Cohen et al. (2011) check a constraint that the occurrences of dictionary entries in a corpus are supposed to fulfill. These a posteriori checks are celebrated as contributing to "quality assurance" and to "the development of a true science of annotation" (Cohen et al. 2011: 82), but they are hardly relevant to the present discussion, since they do not target features with reproducibility issues. In addition, they do not contribute to refining the target of description, as a priori vigilance about reproducibility does.

LG also contributes to reproducibility indirectly, by supporting the publication of results in readable formats. LG tables display readably which entries have which features. Their well-known tabular format is theory-, framework-, formalism- and implementation-independent and allows for explicit negative information, e.g. the fact that *bear comparison to* has no passive. Publishing LG tables in scientific publications and web sites indirectly tends to increase reproducibility, since peers can easily check if they agree with the recorded information. Kaalep & Muischnek (2008) adopt a readable tabular format too, but do not individuate columns for individual features. LG tables are used as source code, i.e. for manual edition; they usually need to be automatically translated into application-dependent formats (Tolone & Sagot 2011; Constant & Tolone 2010), and this is their main flaw for computational linguists (Hathout & Namer 1998; Gardent et al. 2005).[29] However, other formats are less readable: the DuELME Grégoire (2010: 34–36) and Lefff (Tolone & Sagot 2011) formats contain lists of features without explicit negative information: to check that an entry does *not* have a given feature *f*, you have to verify that none of the features it has is *f*.

4.3 Discussion

Reproducibility is an epistemological requirement for scientificity. Low reproducibility casts a doubt on what exactly a feature is, since different observers perceive the feature differently. Gross (1981: 14) even says about traditional semantic classification of prepositional adjuncts: "Perception of such distinctions depends a lot on individuals; therefore, they might be of no interest" (my translation). Features with high reproducibility of observation are essential when lexical entries are described manually, and provide a good basis for a classification with an ambition of stability and scientificity. In addition, many of these features are factual, and therefore informative for further research, no matter the linguistic theory adopted. Factual features are available for language processing, especially when they determine the possibility of occurrence of actual forms, as in (16), (17) and (23)–(31): this is essential to automatically recognizing such MWEs.

LG authors' experience on a number of languages proves that the requirement of reproducibility does not drastically limit the diversity of features to be studied. Their tables of MWEs contain a large collection of useful features. For instance, the study of prepositional-phrase idioms compatible with *be* in English by Machonis (1987) showed that many of them admit a syntactic operation that inserts

---

[29]Tolone (2011) improved part of the LG in that regard: she homogenized the mnemonic identifiers of properties, encoded properties common to whole classes and created a user documentation in English.

verbs such as *get* or *throw* and a causative or agentive subject, as *be in a jam* 'be in trouble':

(37)   a.   *Kathy was in a jam.*

     b.   *An unfortunate situation had (got + thrown) Kathy into a jam.*[30]

But some idioms don't admit this operation with the same verbs, as *be in the wrong* 'be morally or legally wrong':

(38)   a.   *The cyclist is in the wrong.*

     b.   *Slapping the pedestrian (got + *threw) the cyclist in the wrong.*

Features related to this little-known causative construction, usually classified in recent literature under the large category of "lexical variation", are decisive for the automatic parsing of sentences such as (37b).

4.4 A more detailed example

Semantic features such as analysability are rare in LG descriptions: they are difficult to define with sufficient rigour. I will exemplify this difficulty with a new semantic feature which is interesting for NLP, but requires a precise definition before it can be encoded in LG tables.

The French law term *citer un témoin* (lit. 'quote a witness') 'call somebody as a witness' is an MWE because the verb *citer* has this meaning only with the noun *témoin*. Still, the meaning of this noun in the idiom is the same as a meaning this noun can also have, as a (lexicalized) law term, when *citer* is not present at all in the context. Even in the idiom, it usually refers to a specific person. It can belong to a chain of coreferring expressions, no matter whether it is the first element of the chain, as in (39), or not, as in (40).

(39)   *La défense a cité un témoin. Il vient de s'exprimer.*
     Lit. The defence quoted a witness. He has just expressed himself.

     'The defence called a witness. He has just spoken.'

In (39), *un témoin* 'a witness' and *il* 'he' refer to the same person.

---

[30]The notation *(got + thrown)* serves to refer to several variants, here both *had got Kathy into a jam* and *had thrown Kathy into a jam*. This notation inspired from algebra and commonly used in LG is more informative than the notation *got/thrown*, since the parentheses delimit precisely where each variant begins and ends.

(40)   *Ils avaient un autre témoin, mais finalement ils ne l'ont pas cité.*
       Lit. They had another witness, but finally they did not quote him.

'They had another witness, but they ended up not calling him.'

In (40), *un témoin* in the idiom is replaced by the pronoun *l'* 'him', which refers to the same person as *un autre témoin* 'another witness'. In a chain of coreferring expressions like those of (39) and (40), the syntactic markers of the coreference such as determiners, pronouns, etc., follow the same rules as when the noun is not part of an idiom. For example, in (39), *il* 'he' has the same form as when *un témoin* 'a witness', but not the rest of the idiom, is present in the context:

(41)   *La défense a un témoin. Il vient de s'exprimer.*
       'The defence has a witness. He has just spoken.'

The feature that I wish to single out, and which *témoin* 'witness' in (39) shares with many other idiom components, is a combination of three properties:

(i) The component, when used in the idiom, has mandatorily a meaning that it can also have (as a lexicalised meaning) when the rest of the idiom is not present at all, not even in the context, as opposed to *feet* in *think on one's feet* 'improvise a reaction quickly', or to *eyes* in *roll one's eyes*, where *eyes* doesn't always refer to eyes. [31]

(ii) The component can be the first in a chain of coreferring expressions, and then the syntactic markers of the coreference: determiners, pronouns, etc., follow the same rules as when the noun is not part of the idiom. This does not happen, for instance, with *posture* in the French idiom of (42):

(42)   *Kathy était en mauvaise posture.*
       Lit. Kathy was in bad posture.

'Kathy was in trouble.'

To refer to the trouble after they have used this idiom, speakers use another noun:

[31]Property (i) matches what Burger (2007: 96) calls *partly idiomatic* expressions. It is more restrictive than analysability/decomposability: for instance, in *pull strings* 'covertly use one's influence on personal connections', the noun *string* does not keep any of the lexicalized meanings it has when *pull* is not present at all. As a consequence, the feature that I am defining is different from analysability too.

(43)   *Kathy était en mauvaise posture. Ces difficultés auraient pu être évitées.*
       Lit. Kathy was in bad posture. This trouble could have been avoided.

       'Kathy was in trouble. This trouble could have been avoided.'

Without this idiom, they can use the same noun:

(44)   *Kathy avait une posture fière. Cette posture a été commentée.*

       'Kathy had a proud posture. This posture has been commented.'

But if the first expression referring to the trouble is part of the idiom of (42), speakers do not use the same noun for other coreferring expressions:

(45)   * *Kathy était en mauvaise posture. Cette posture aurait pu être évitée.*
       Lit. Kathy was in bad posture. This posture could have been avoided.

       'Kathy was in trouble. This trouble could have been avoided.'[32]

(iii) The component can occur in a chain of coreferring expressions without being the first, and then the syntactic markers of the coreference such as determiners, pronouns, etc., follow the same rules as when the noun is not part of the idiom. This does not happen, for example, with *strings* in *pull strings* 'covertly use one's influence on personal connections'. When speakers refer to the connections before using this idiom, the coreference between the first mention of the connections and the idiom component is not explicitly marked:

(46)   *I needed connections to make myself known, and John could pull strings for me.*

In this form, *strings* has the same form as if there were no mention of it before. Without the idiom, we observe a syntactic marker of coreference:

(47)   *I needed connections to make myself known, and John provided them to me.*

---

[32]Example (45) is not entirely parallel to (39): (39) involves pronouns and (45) involves determiners and nouns. Studying feature (ii) requires taking into account diverse syntactic markers of coreference. This feature is connected with pronominalizability, but not only.

Speakers do not use this marker if the second mention of the connections is part of the idiom:

(48)   * *I needed strings to make myself known, and John could pull them for me.*

But why get interested in the combination of features (i)–(iii),[33] which has never been studied or named? Because it is shared by many other terminological idioms, for example the French term of geometry *abaisser une perpendiculaire à* 'drop a perpendicular on to' (lit. move down a perpendicular to).[34] The idiom component that has the feature, like *témoin* 'witness', is often a technical term too, and is able to denote a referent in a clear and specific way. In such case, these idioms are meaningful elements of technical texts, a realistic target for future improvements to the automated understanding of natural language texts.

My definition is based on properties (i)–(iii), which are relatively formal.[35] Even so, this feature is probably not ready for encoding, that is for production of a satisfactory list of the idioms with this feature: only large-coverage encoding experiments would tell if this definition ensures sufficient reproducibility of observation.

In this section, all the examples above focus on nouns that are parts of verbal idioms. How does the feature extend to other PoS? Here are two noteworthy features closely related to this one.

In a large proportion of multiword nouns, the head noun keeps all the grammatical and semantic behaviour it has as an independently existing lexical entry.

---

[33] It is not an "aggregate" of features (i)–(iii) as in §3 above: it is specifically a conjunction of these independent features, in the sense that an idiom has it if and only if it has simultaneously (i), (ii) and (iii). Alternatively, features (i)–(iii) might be studied separately, but they are likely to be less useful than their conjunction.

[34] *Abaisser* has this meaning only with *perpendiculaire* and *parallèle* 'parallel', which keep their autonomous terminological meaning and ability to be referred to anaphorically:

(i)   *On abaisse une perpendiculaire de A à BC. Cette droite est parallèle à CD.*
       'A perpendicular is dropped from A on to BC. This line is parallel to CD.'

[35] My definition does not include another striking property of *témoin* 'witness' in (39): it can refer to a specific entity, as opposed to *fire* in (29a) *John fights fire with fire*, which alludes to ways of fighting in general. The semantic distinction between specific and generic reference is a matter of pure intuition. As such, its reproducibility of observation can be low, for example in the case of *bread* in *They will take the bread from our mouths* 'They will divert money from us': in this sentence, does *the bread* refer to material goods in general, or to a specific instance of income?

This is the case of *red wine*: it is a (terminological) MWE because *red* has this meaning only with *wine*, but *wine* can be equated with the independent lexical entry *wine*, with the same properties (i)–(iii) as above. With multiword nouns, this is related to another test: *red* can usually be inserted in sentences with *wine* or removed from them, without unexpected changes in acceptability or meaning:

(49) a. *They have an interest in wine.*

     b. *They have an interest in red wine.*

(50) a. *Is red wine healthy and worth the calories?*

     b. *Is wine healthy and worth the calories?*

This test uses differential semantic assessment. *Smooth operator* 'persuasive person; manipulative person' doesn't share this feature, as the meaning changes in (51)–(52) show:

(51) a. *Ask the operator to dial.*
       'Ask the switchboard operator to dial.'

     b. *Ask the smooth operator to dial.*

       'Ask the persuasive person to dial.'; 'Ask the manipulative person to dial.'

(52) a. *Any lady I've dated will tell you I'm no smooth operator.*

       'Any lady I've dated will tell you I'm not manipulative.'

     b. *Any lady I've dated will tell you I'm no operator.*

       'Any lady I've dated will tell you I'm not a switchboard operator'

Some adverbs are specific to one or a few verbs, which nevertheless keep all their behaviour. Here are two examples in French from the tables of multiword adverbs by Gross (1986):

(53) a. *(chanter + crier + rire) à gorge déployée*
       Lit. (sing + shout + laugh) at opened-out throat

       '(sing + shout + laugh) out loud'

     b. N_0 *aller à* N_1 *comme un tablier à une vache*
       Lit. N_0 fit N_1 as an apron does a cow

       'N_0 fit N_1 supremely badly'

As opposed to the preceding examples, these have no terminological value.

Care for reproducibility in observation of linguistic facts characterizes a conception of humanities in which scholars not only share insights and deepen their intuition, but also gather reliable factual knowledge, paying attention to practical techniques that improve the quality of their description. In this conception, descriptive work, and in particular lexical description, is fundamental. For instance, assessing reproducibility of observation is a practical matter: it involves scanning through the lexicon while trying to describe which entries have a feature and which don't. Thus, preferring features that can be observed by humans in a reproducible way is good practice.

5 Checking information against the lexicon

5.1 Discussion

Checking information against the lexicon is still alien to a large part of MWE research. Baldwin & Kim (2010) do not cite studies using intensive lexical description of MWEs, except for Estonian MWEs. The companion website to their paper cites corpora and tools, but no NLP dictionaries.[36] Among the tools, it even omits those based on dictionaries. Current descriptive research is not eager to achieve large lexical coverages. FrameNet has a small coverage of MWEs (Hartmann & Gurevych 2013), and so do, among NLP dictionaries, VerbNet, WordNet and Meaning-Text. Bond et al. (2015) encode for HPSG a sample of English idioms with a possessive coreferent with the subject, like *roll one's eyes*, but here is how the size of the result compares with previous efforts: Freckleton (1985)'s classes C1A and C11 contain 538 verbal idioms with such a possessive, while Bond et al. (2015: 64)'s four classes that correspond to C1A and C11 total 168 ones. Aside from LGs, sizable lexical databases of MWEs are few. The NomLex-Plus and Nom-Bank dictionaries of English nouns with predicate-argument structure list 8000 entries (Meyers 2007). Kaalep & Muischnek (2008)'s database lists 13000 Estonian MWEs. The DuELME dictionary of Dutch MWEs totals 5000 expressions (Grégoire 2010).[37]

My point in this part is that information on MWEs is worth checking against the lexicon. Reluctance against lexical description is rarely explicit, and when it is, it is not motivated by sound reasons.[38]

---

[36] http://handbookofnlp.cse.unsw.edu.au/?n=Chapter12 was looked up in August 2016.

[37] The SemLex Dictionary of Czech MWEs is still little documented in publications (Bejček & Straňák 2010).

[38] "Again, in itself this type of approach [interviews, surveys, statistics] is neither good nor bad. The question is whether it leads to the discovery of principles that are significant. We are back

Sure, intensive investigation into the lexicon is costly. For example, the construction of LG tables of MWEs, which are comprehensive repositories with representation of individual features (cf. §2.2.1), has always involved considerable work. But the objective of a satisfactory processing of MWEs is worth cost and effort. (The reason one enjoys Dostoyevsky is not because he is easy to read.) And the tables are available for several languages, which shows that this work is realistic.

The reluctance towards intensive lexical description might come from a feeling that it is deemed an unskilled, low-grade occupation. But such a feeling is unfounded: in projects of construction of large lexical databases of MWEs, linguists are obviously engaged in highly skilled labour.

The reluctance may be directed towards manual work. As computer science is about automating information processing, many computational linguists may understandably feel excited about devising "knowledge-free" solutions that avoid the need of *any* labour-intensive activity, be it in preliminary operations. But, in the case of MWE-related NLP, relying on this only hope is adventurous: the goal of fully automating acquisition of knowledge about all MWEs has been giving hard times to the community for more than 15 years.

No dictionary is 100% complete or 100% error-free, but this does not make them useless.

And manual lexical description has several advantages. The resulting data allows for more well-documented studies and is likely to be useful for making successful rules or devising successful machine learning experiments. When linguists scrutinize 10 features on a comprehensive part of a 1000-item class, what they find out is worth taking a look. It provides examples and counter-examples which are useful to test predictions, proposals and hypothetical rules or generalities. LG tables, as large repositories of factual features, are a source of examples for further research, no matter the theory, framework or implementation to be used. Creativity of language is a major obstacle to its scientific study, and it lies, among other things, in the combinatorics of lexical items and grammat-

---

to the difference between natural history and natural science. In natural history, whatever you do is fine. If you like to collect stones, you can classify them according to their color, their shape, and so forth. Everything is of equal value, because you are not looking for principles. You are amusing yourself, and nobody can object to that. But in the natural sciences, it is altogether different. There the search is for the discovery of intelligible structure and for explanatory principles. In the natural sciences, the facts have no interest in themselves, but only to the degree to which they have bearing on explanatory principles or on hidden structures that have some intellectual interest." (Chomsky 1979: 58–59) Beyond the depreciative rhetoric of this passage, Chomsky actually suggests skipping factual observation when it involves extensive description.

ical constructions: systematic investigation in the lexicon is therefore a way of addressing this problem.

Intensive lexical description is crucial to selecting features for classification, and therefore to the quality of classification. The construction of the NomLex-Plus and NomBank dictionaries of English nouns with predicate-argument structure involved an unprecedented investigation into support-verb constructions in English and into features to recognize and classify them (Meyers 2007). The study of idioms that take the form of a prepositional phrase in Romance languages (Danlos 1980; Ranchhod 1990; Gross 1996; Vietri 1996), English (Machonis 1988) and Greek (Moustaki 1995) singled out a particularly useful feature for the top of MWE classifications. Some of these idioms are compatible with *be* or the equivalent copula in other languages and may appear in predicative position, as in (54b):

(54) a.   *John will reach the end on time.*

     b.   *John will be on time.*

Others may not:

(55) a.   *The crisis has a demographic cause in the final analysis.*

       'The crisis has a demographic cause, when everything has been considered.'

     b. * *The cause is in the final analysis.*

Those compatible with *be*, like *on time* 'punctually; punctual' in (54), *on vacation* and *on the spot* 'immediately; in the same place; in trouble', usually pose a problem of PoS: are they closer to adjectives or to adverbs?[39] In contrast, those like *in the final analysis* in (55a) and *for instance* are clearly adverbial expressions. Compatibility with *be*, that is the contrast between (54) and (55), provides a relatively sharp division in a large number of cases where PoS distinction would otherwise be particularly uncertain. Applying this criterion requires investigating into the syntactic contexts of idioms in sentences, but this is the usual price to be paid to resolve PoS issues,[40] and PoS are key to a general classification of MWEs. So, this criterion is more relevant than the presence vs. absence of a determiner, retained by Baldwin & Kim (2010: 278) at the top of their classification, a criterion that only uses the internal structure of idioms.

---

[39] Lexicalized MWEs are lexical items, so they may have a PoS like single-word lexical items do.

[40] The most appropriate definition of each PoS is based on its possible syntactic contexts in sentences. For example, in English, a noun is to be recognized by its ability to be preceded by determiners and adjuncts, followed by adjuncts, etc.

Lexical data deepens knowledge of how correlated two features are. It does so by providing reliable statistics on lexical entries: how many entries with feature *f* also have feature *g*? For example, the causative construction of (37b), with a prepositional-phrase idiom and *get, throw* or other verbs like *keep*, is observed only when the idiom is compatible with *be*:

(56) a. *John will be on time.*

  b. *This gift will keep John on time.*

(57) a. * *The cause is in the final analysis.*

  b. * *This point keeps the cause in the final analysis.*

Such specific grammatical information allows for measuring correlations accurately.

  Intensive lexical description tends to make researchers more cognizant of variation, including less frequent variations and variations of less frequent items. As such, it is complementary to corpus annotation, which rather makes them aware of context-related issues.

  Lexical description also provides means of separating homonymous entries, for example the various interpretations of *on the spot*: 'immediately'; 'in the same place'; 'in trouble'. Such separation, in turn, is essential to construct cross-lingual tables (Ranchhod & De Gioia 1996).

  All these benefits of lexical description make it *a priori* useful for applications. There is still little significative feedback from the NLP use of any comprehensive dictionary of MWEs, but this may come from the complexity of the problem and the interdependence of all subproblems of symbolic syntactic parsing.

5.2 Predicted vs. checked features

Gibbs & Nayak (1989: 104) hypothesize that semantic analysability/decomposability "determines the syntactic behavior of idioms". In this section, I examine the present and potential consequences of this conjecture.

  With Nunberg et al. (1994), the hypothesis becomes two claims. First, the analysability of an expression predicts syntactic operations are applicable to it: "the syntactic properties of idioms [that is the applicability of syntactic operations] are largely predictable from the semantically based analysis of idioms we are proposing [i.e. their analysability]." (Nunberg et al. 1994: 507). In parallel, the unanalysability of an expression predicts syntactic operations are not applicable to it: "we (...) explain a variety of 'transformational deficiencies' of idioms by positing a bifurcation between [unanalysable] and [analysable] expressions, with only the latter type permitting those processes" (Nunberg et al. 1994: 508).

After these claims, analysability became popular in the community and was used to define some of the major classes of MWEs. The two predictions give a sense that analysability is an underlying, fundamental property, and that its use in classification implements a strategy of parsimony, since assigning an entry to a class automatically specifies all the predicted features. Sag et al. (2002: 4) retain only the second prediction: "due to their opaque semantics, non-decomposable idioms are not subject to syntactic variability, e.g. in the form of internal modification (#*kick the great bucket in the sky*) or passivization (**the breeze was shot*)."[41]

However, Nunberg et al. (1994) do not check the claims, either on available data or on original data. A general claim requires systematic verifications, which they mention as a perspective for future work: "testing this prediction systematically is a nontrivial project" (Nunberg et al. 1994: 531). Therefore, both claims remain hypotheses.

When authors check the predicted syntactic features, they readily find out counter-examples to both predictions (Abeillé 1995; Stathi 2007). Here are three more that I picked from the lists of French verbal idioms by Gross (1982):

(58)   *rater un éléphant dans un couloir*
        Lit. miss an elephant in a corridor

        'be unable to hit the broad side of a barn; have poor aim; be unable to reach targets'

Example (58) seems analysable as *miss(x, easy-target)*, but does not admit syntactic variations, not even omission of the prepositional complement.

(59)   *trouver chaussure à son pied*
        Lit. find shoe to one's foot

        'find the perfect match for oneself'

Example (59) seems analysable as something like *find(x, partner)*, but does not admit syntactic variations either. Conversely, (60) is hardly semantically analysable:

(60)   *mettre toutes les chances de son côté*
        Lit. put all the chances on one's side

        'not take any chances'

---

[41] *Shoot the breeze* means 'talk casually'.

But it admits the passive form:

(61)   *Toutes les chances sont mises de votre côté.*
       Lit. all the chances are put on your side

       'You are not taking any chances.'

Nunberg et al. (1994: 512) extend their claims in the case when an idiom is analysable: "the syntactic versatility of an idiom is a function of how the meanings of its parts are related to one another and to their literal meanings". In other words, details of the semantic structure of analysable idioms would predict which syntactic operations are applicable.

It is particularly difficult to give credit to this hypothesis. Its authors do not check it any more than the previous one; the alleged rules of prediction are unknown. Formalizing them would be a challenge that no one has taken up since. Instead, Riehemann (2001) finds that which types of syntactic variation a given idiom can undergo is highly unpredictable.

Baldwin & Kim (2010: 280) adopt Nunberg, Sag & Wasow's 1994 hypothesis as their own: "the exact form of syntactic variation [of verbal idioms] is predicted by the nature of their semantic decomposability". But they do not provide any evidence to support it. Even worse, their formulation suggests that, instead of describing the syntactic variation of verbal idioms, one might infer it automatically from a description of their analysability. But recall that syntactic variation is more reproducibly observable than analysability: thus, the suggested proposal comes down to inferring several factual features from a property that poses problems of definition and observation (cf. §3.2). Such a process would hardly be effectual.

Predicting features might seem a clever move. But it necessarily begins as a hypothesis, which needs to be checked to get any scientific value. So, predicting features does not allow for bypassing the verification step.

6 An adapted classification

I propose in Figure 1 a decision tree adapted from Baldwin & Kim (2010: 279), but which avoids the flaws discussed above, and in particular features that are too fuzzy or difficult to observe. It uses all the MWE-related LG work, including the studies on English, Romance languages, Greek, Korean and other languages, cited in §2.2.1, §2.2.3, §3.2 and §5.1. Much of this work was conducted in parallel and cross-linguistic comparisons showed that, even though the details of formal criteria depend on the languages (§2.3), the notions they define are similar. For example, the typology of French support verbs by Gross (1998) is transferred to the English FrameNet by Ruppenhofer et al. (2006: 37–38) without any modification. The classification in Figure 1 is in terms of notions defined by criteria mentioned in the text of this chapter, but the criteria are not repeated in the figure. Thus, it is formulated for English and easily adaptable to many other languages: to adapt it to French, substitute *être* for *be.*

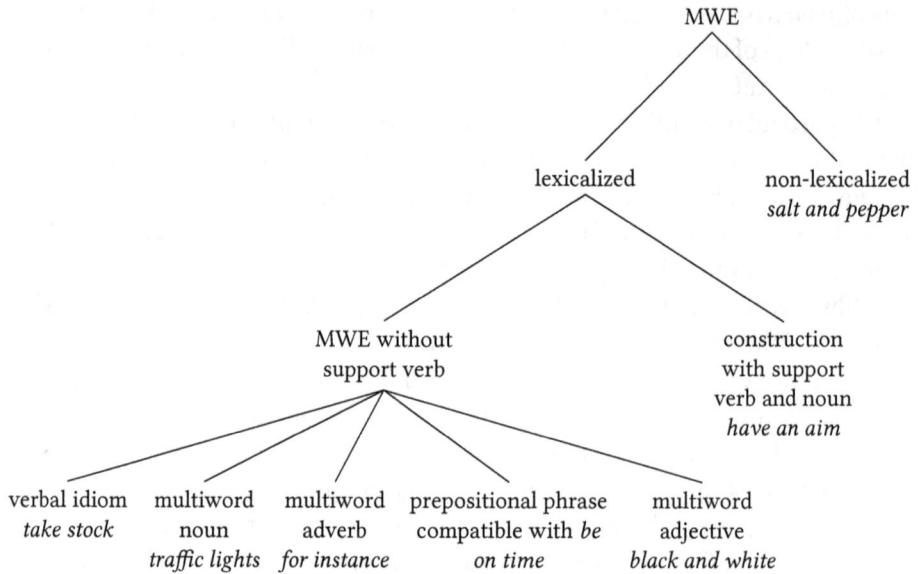

Figure 1: Classification of MWEs.

The top distinction is between lexicalized and non-lexicalized expressions. By non-lexicalized expressions, I mean those that are fully compositional but in which a statistical preference for an element is not explained by extra-linguistic facts. For example, the preference for *sell a house* over *sell a wall* is explained by cultural habits, so we don't need to describe it as a linguistic property; therefore, *sell a house* is not an MWE. In contrast, the preference for the French phrases *tondre la pelouse* 'mow the lawn' and *couper l'herbe* 'cut the grass' over *tondre l'herbe* 'mow the grass' and *couper la pelouse* 'cut the lawn' is a purely linguistic fact. This suggests *tondre la pelouse* and *couper l'herbe* are MWEs, but they are not lexicalized, since the other two are in use. The term *black and white* 'composed of shades of black or of a single colour' is lexicalized. If it were fully compositional, speakers would be able to interpret *white and black* the same way as *black and white,* which they aren't. The same holds for *traffic lights*: if it were fully compositional, speakers would be able to interpret it as another type of light connected with traffic.

The second distinction in Figure 1 relies on the notion of support-verb construction. This is not an easy distinction, but the literature shows that trained linguists are able to make it on the basis of formal criteria that ensure sufficient reproducibility of observation: these criteria are outlined in §2.2.3. Support-verb constructions are a significant class because they are numerous both in texts and in a dictionary: out of the 62,100 MWE entries of the French LG, 12,700 (20%) are support-verb constructions (Tolone 2011). Support-verb constructions have in common a crucial property which is a good reason to place them so close to the top of the classification: the construction with the verb, for example *have a passion*, and the construction without the verb, which is usually a predicational noun, here *passion*, are not adequately described by two distinct lexical entries. For example, the arguments of *have a passion* are exactly the same as those of *passion*, including the preposition of the complement (*for*) and the restrictions on what may fill both slots (the subject contains a human noun; the complement may contain a human, concrete or abstract noun or an infinitival clause). Moreover, occurrences without the support verb are usually more frequent in texts than occurrences with it (Laporte et al. 2008).

The third distinction in Figure 1 is based on PoS.[42] It conflates adverbs with prepositions and conjunctions, with the view that a multiword preposition like *in spite of* or a multiword conjunction like *in case that* may also be analysed as a multiword adverb with a free prepositional or clausal slot.[43] This lowest level of the tree includes an additional "PoS", namely "prepositional phrase compatible with *be*", such as *on time* and *on vacation*, in order to sort out partially the problem of assigning a PoS to idioms taking the form of prepositional phrases: are they adverbs or adjectives? The compatibility with *be* provides a relatively sharp division in a large number of cases where PoS distinction is particularly uncertain (cf. (54)–(55), §5.1). The multiword adjective category is meant for expressions that do not take the form of prepositional phrases, for example *black and white* 'composed of shades of black or of a single colour' or *safe and sound* 'unharmed'. In Figure 1, the distinction between support-verb constructions or not is just above the decision about PoS. It could also be the other way round, which would make the support-verb-construction class a brother of the verbal-

---

[42]The appropriate definition of each PoS in this context is based on its possible syntactic contexts in sentences (cf. §5.1, footnote 40).

[43]Here, *free* means that the content of the slot, that is the noun phrase or the embedded clause, is variable.

idiom class. This variant would give prominence to PoS, which are always key information, well-known classes and often clear-cut features.

In Figure 2, I propose an alternative classification that may bewilder many researchers. But those that take seriously the notion of support-verb construction will probably find it more consistent than Figure 1. From Gross (1981: 34), Ranchhod (1983) and Cattell (1984), the notion of support-verb construction includes constructions like *be angry* or *get loose*, where the support verb is *be* or one of its variants (Meyers 2007: 123). With this view, phrases like *be angry* or *be a genius* become support-verb constructions and therefore MWEs. Another consequence is that, in a support-verb construction, the core of the predicate may be an adjective or even a prepositional phrase (e.g. *be on time*) instead of a noun. Few computational linguists are familiar with these two ideas. But analysing all these expressions as support-verb constructions is consistent. They undergo semantic and syntactic phenomena observed with other support verb constructions:

(i) Syntactic operations produce constructs where the core of the predicate occurs without the verb, with the same meaning. For example, in the same way as *have* disappears in the alternance between *the habit the customer had* and *the customer's habit*, the verb *be* also disappears between *a customer who was angry* and *an angry customer*.

(ii) Other verbs can replace *be*, causing an aspectual or stylistic effect: compare *The customer was angry* with *The customer got angry*. This pair is parallel to *The customer had a habit / The customer gained a habit*.

(iii) There exist constructs with an additional causative or agentive subject and another verb, as in (37) or in *The team was confident / Football made the team confident*. Such pairs are parallel to *The team had a goal / Football gave the team a goal*.

Figure 2 adopts this view and considers the copula (a linguistic term for *be* or its equivalent introducing a predicate) as a part of a support-verb construction. Prepositional phrases compatible with *be* shift to support-verb constructions. Since more expressions are considered MWEs than in Figure 1 and support-verb constructions become more diverse, they are divided in subclasses too, taking into account the PoS of the core of the predicate.[44] The core of the predicate may

---

[44] The exact list of PoS under support-verb constructions and non-support-verb constructions depends on languages: in Arabic, Chinese or Korean, among others, predicational adjectives are used without a copula, and the class of copulative constructions with a predicational adjective is irrelevant for them.

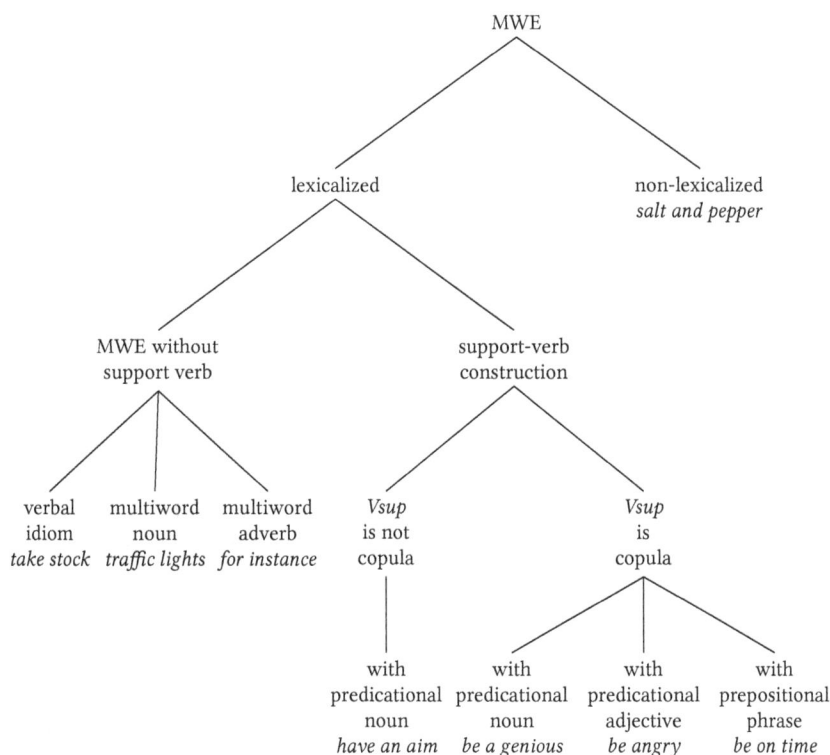

Figure 2: Classification of MWEs where copula is considered a support verb.

be either a word (*have an aim, be a genius, be angry*) or multiword (*have a point of view, be a smooth operator, be safe and sound, be on time*). There are two new categories: copulative constructions with a predicational adjective, for example *be angry, be safe and sound,*[45] and with a predicational noun, for example *be a genius, be a smooth operator.*

In Figure 2, the distinction between support-verb constructions or not is just above the decision about PoS. In addition, the PoS-based classification of support-verb constructions takes into account the PoS of the core of the predicate: noun (*aim, point of view, genius, smooth operator*), adjective (*angry, safe and sound*) or prepositional phrase (*on time*). This is an essential element of the diversity of these constructions. We can shift the PoS level of the decision tree above the

---

[45]Non-predicational adjectives are those compulsorily attributive, for example *prime* in *This is John's prime role:* **This is John's role that is prime.* Another sense of *prime* corresponds to a predicational adjective: *21 is not prime.*

support-verb-construction level, but then the tree will classify all support-verb constructions as verbal MWEs, and it will be desirable to add a second PoS level below, to take into account the PoS of the core of the predicate. Thus, the decision tree will have one more level than Figure 2 to define the same classes.

7 Conclusion

Something is to be learned from the experience of the last 20 years in respect of choosing features for classifying MWEs. Current practice routinely uses fuzzy features, or features defined in an imprecise way. On many occasions, a cluster of loosely correlated features is considered as a single feature. The choice of features with such flaws is likely to lead to classifications less fruitful for computational use. For example, describing the analysability/decomposability of verbal idioms is much less feasible and useful than describing their syntactic variation.

Selecting more appropriate features is not an easy task. It requires prioritizing good practices when studying MWEs. One of them consists in systematically assessing the reproducibility of observation of each feature, in order to obtain reliable repositories of lexical data. Another good practice is to check facts and predictions against the lexicon. It is understandable that some researchers try to avoid the patient examination of thousands of lexical entries for dozens of individual features, in the hope to reach the same results through other means. But it turns out that the laborious descriptive work they wish to elude is required not only to check hypotheses, but also to come across valid hypotheses: researchers that ignored large-coverage data constructed unverifiable hypotheses that won the attention of the community and resulted in loss of time.

The LG approach implements these good practices in descriptive and analytical work. On the basis of the results of such work carried out on several languages in parallel, I outlined an enhanced classification of MWEs.

Acknowledgements

Thanks to the anonymous reviewers, to the scientific editors and to Alexis Neme, for their comments, suggestions and questions that considerably enriched this paper. Only I am responsible for its content.

Abbreviations

HPSG	Head-driven Phrase Structure Grammar	NLP	Natural Language Processing
LG	Lexicon Grammar	POS	part of speech

References

Abeillé, Anne. 1988. Light verb constructions and extraction out of NP in a Tree Adjoining Grammar. In *Papers of the 24th Regional Meeting of the Chicago Linguistics Society*, 1–15.

Abeillé, Anne. 1995. The flexibility of French idioms: A representation with Lexical Tree Adjoining Grammar. In Martin Everaert, Eric-Jan van der Linden, André Schenk & Rob Schreuder (eds.), *Idioms. Structural and Psychological Perspectives*, 15–42. Hillsdale, NJ: Lawrence Erlbaum Associates.

Abeillé, Anne & Robert Vivès. 2011. Les constructions à verbe support dans la Grande Grammaire du français. In *International Conference Lexis and Grammar. Abstracts*, 13–20. University of Cyprus.

Baldwin, Timothy & Su Nam Kim. 2010. Multiword expressions. In Nitin Indurkhya & Fred J. Damerau (eds.), *Handbook of Natural Language Processing*, 2nd edn., 267–292. Boca Raton: CRC Press.

Bejček, Eduard & Pavel Straňák. 2010. Annotation of multiword expressions in the Prague dependency treebank. *Language Resources and Evaluation* 44(1-2). 7–21.

Bond, Francis, Jia Qian Ho & Dan Flickinger. 2015. Feeling our way to an analysis of English possessed idioms. In Stefan Müller (ed.), *Proceedings of the 22nd International Conference on Head-Driven Phrase Structure Grammar, Nanyang Technological University (NTU)*, 61–74. Stanford, CA: CSLI Publications. http://cslipublications.stanford.edu/HPSG/2015/bhf.pdf, accessed 2018-4-19.

Burger, Harald. 1998. *Phraseologie: Eine Einführung am Beispiel des Deutschen*. Berlin: Erich Schmidt Verlag.

Burger, Harald. 2007. Semantic aspects of phrasemes. In Harald Burger, Dmitrij Dobrovol'skij, Peter Kühn & Neal R. Norrick (eds.), *Phraseologie/Phraseology*, vol. 1 (An International Handbook of Contemporary Research), 90–109. Berlin & New York: de Gruyter.

Butt, Miriam. 2010. The light verb jungle: Still hacking away. In Mengistu Amberber, Brett Baker & Mark Harvey (eds.), *Complex predicates: Cross-linguistic perspective on event structure*, 48–78. Cambridge, UK: Cambridge University Press.

Cattell, Ray. 1984. *Composite predicates in English.* Sydney: Academic Press.

Chomsky, Noam. 1957. *Syntactic structures.* The Hague: Mouton.

Chomsky, Noam. 1979. *Language and responsibility: Based on conversations with Mitsou Ronat.* New York: Pantheon books.

Chomsky, Noam. 1980. *Rules and representations.* Oxford: Basil Blackwell.

Cohen, K. Bretonnel, Lawrence E. Hunter & Martha Palmer. 2011. A scaleable automated quality assurance technique for semantic representations and proposition banks. In *Proceedings of the Fifth Linguistic Annotation Workshop*, 82–91. Portland.

Constant, Matthieu, Anthony Sigogne & Joseph Le Roux. 2013. Combining compound recognition and PCFG-LA parsing with word lattices and conditional random fields. In *ACM Transactions on Speech and Language Processing (TSLP)*, vol. 10, 8.1–8.24.

Constant, Matthieu & Elsa Tolone. 2010. A generic tool to generate a lexicon for NLP from Lexicon-Grammar tables. In Michele De Gioia (ed.), *Actes du 27e Colloque international sur le lexique et la grammaire, Seconde partie*, 79–93. Rome: Aracne.

Danlos, Laurence. 1980. *Représentations d'informations linguistiques: Constructions N être Prép X.* Université Paris 7 dissertation.

Danlos, Laurence. 1992. Support verb constructions: Linguistic properties, representation, translation. *Journal of French Language Studies* 2(1). 1–32.

Danlos, Laurence & Maurice Gross. 1988. Building electronic dictionaries for Natural Language Processing. In Kazuhiro Fuchi & Laurent Kott (eds.), *Programming of future generation computers II*, 123–131. Amsterdam: Elsevier.

De Angelis, Angela. 1989. Nominalisations with Italian support verb *avere*. *Lingvisticae Investigationes* 13(2). 223–237.

Fillmore, Charles J. 1992. Corpus linguistics or computer-aided armchair linguistics. In Jan Svartik (ed.), *Directions in corpus linguistics: Proceedings of Nobel Symposium 82, Stockholm, 4-8 August 1991*, 35–60. Berlin: Mouton de Gruyter.

Fillmore, Charles J. 2001. Armchair linguistics vs. corpus linguistics revisited. In Sylvie De Cock, Gaëtanelle Gilquin, Sylvia Granger & Stéphanie Petch-Tyson (eds.), *Proceedings of ICAME. Future challenges in corpus linguistics.* Université Catholique de Louvain.

Fotopoulou, Aggeliki. 1993. *Une classification des phrases à compléments figés en grec moderne. Étude morphosyntaxique des phrases figées.* Saint-Denis: Université Paris VIII dissertation.

Fraser, Bruce. 1970. Idioms within a transformational grammar. *Foundations of Language* 6. 22–42.

Freckleton, Peter. 1985. Sentence idioms in English. In *Working Papers in Linguistics*, 153–168 + appendix (196 p.) University of Melbourne.

Gardent, Claire, Bruno Guillaume, Guy Perrier & Ingrid Falk. 2005. Maurice Gross' grammar lexicon and natural language processing. In Zygmunt Vetulani (ed.), *Proceedings of the 2nd Language and Technology Conference*, 120–123.

Gibbs, Raymond W. & Nandini P. Nayak. 1989. Psycholinguistic studies on the syntactic behavior of idioms. *Cognitive Psychology* 21(1). 100–138.

Gibbs, Raymond W., Nandini P. Nayak, John L. Bolton & Melissa E. Keppel. 1989. Speakers assumptions about the lexical flexibility of idioms. *Memory and Cognition* 17(1). 58–68.

Giry-Schneider, Jacqueline. 1978. Syntax and lexicon: *blessure* 'wound', *nœud* 'knot', *caresse* 'caress'. *SMIL, Journal of Linguistic Calculus* 1978(3-4). 55–72.

Grégoire, Nicole. 2010. DuELME: a Dutch electronic lexicon of multiword expressions. *Language Resources and Evaluation* 44(1-2). 23–39.

Gries, Stephan T. 2011. Methodological and interdisciplinary stance in corpus linguistics. In Vander Viana, Sonia Zyngier & Geoff Barnbrook (eds.), *Perspectives on corpus linguistics*, 81–98. Amsterdam: John Benjamins.

Gross, Maurice. 1975. On the relations between syntax and semantics. In Edward L. Keenan (ed.), *Formal semantics of natural language*, 389–405. Cambridge, UK: Cambridge University Press.

Gross, Maurice. 1976. Sur quelques groupes nominaux complexes. In Jean-Claude Chevalier & Maurice Gross (eds.), *Méthodes en grammaire française*, 97–119. Paris: Klincksieck.

Gross, Maurice. 1979. On the failure of generative grammar. *Language* 55(4). 859–885.

Gross, Maurice. 1981. Les bases empiriques de la notion de prédicat sémantique. *Langages* 63. 7–52, 127–128.

Gross, Maurice. 1982. Une classification des phrases "figées"du français. *Revue Québécoise de Linguistique (RQL)* 11(2). 151–185.

Gross, Maurice. 1986. *Grammaire transformationnelle du français. Vol. 3. Syntaxe de l'adverbe*. Paris: ASSTRIL.

Gross, Maurice. 1994. The lexicon-grammar of a language: Application to French. In Ronald Asher (ed.), *The Encyclopaedia of language and linguistics*, vol. 4, 2195–2205. Oxford: Pergamon.

Gross, Maurice. 1996. Les formes *être Prép X* du français. *Lingvisticae Investigationes* 20(2). 217–270.

Gross, Maurice. 1998. La fonction sémantique des verbes supports. *Travaux de linguistique* 37. 25–46.

Guillet, Alain & Nunzio La Fauci. 1984. *Lexique-grammaire des langues romanes. Actes du 1er Colloque Européen sur la grammaire et le lexique comparés des langues romanes* (Lingvisticae Investigationes Supplementa 9). Amsterdam: John Benjamins.

Han, Sun-Hae. 2000. *Les prédicats nominaux en coréen: Constructions à verbe support hata.* Champs-sur-Marne : Université de Marne-la-Vallée dissertation.

Harris, Zellig. 1957. Co-occurrence and transformation in linguistic structure. *Language* 33(3). 283–340.

Harris, Zellig. 1964. *The elementary transformations* (Transformations and Discourse Analysis Papers 54). University of Pennsylvania.

Hartmann, Silvana & Iryna Gurevych. 2013. *Acquisition of multiword lexical units for FrameNet: Presentation at The International FrameNet Workshop 2013.* Berkeley, CA, USA.

Hathout, Nabil & Fiammetta Namer. 1998. Automatic construction and validation of French large lexical resources. Reuse of verb theoretical linguistic descriptions. In *Proceedings of the Language Resources and Evaluation Conference*, 627–636. Granada.

Jespersen, Otto. 1942. *A Modern English Grammar on Historical Principles. Part VI. Morphology.* Copenhagen: Ejnar Munksgaard.

Johansson, Stig. 1991. Times change, and so do corpora. In Karin Aijmer & Bengt Altenberg (eds.), *English corpus linguistics*, 305–314. London: Longman.

Kaalep, Heiki-Jaan & Kadri Muischnek. 2008. Multi-word verbs of Estonian: a database and a corpus. In *Proceedings of the LREC Workshop Towards a Shared Task for Multiword Expressions*, 23–26. Marrakech.

Kepser, Stephan & Marga Reis. 2005. Evidence in Linguistics. In Stephan Kepser & Marga Reis (eds.), *Linguistic evidence: Empirical, theoretical, and computational perspectives*, 1–6. Berlin: Mouton de Gruyter.

Kyriacopoulou, Tita & Vasso Sfetsiou. 2003. Les constructions nominales à verbe support en grec moderne. *Linguistic Insights: Studies in Language and Communication* 5(1). 163–181.

Labelle, Jacques. 1974. *Étude de constructions avec opérateur avoir (nominalisations et extensions).* Paris: Université Paris 7 dissertation.

Langer, Stefan. 2005. A linguistic test battery for support verb constructions. *Lingvisticae Investigationes* 27(2). 171–184.

Laporte, Éric, Elisabete Ranchhod & Anastasia Yannacopoulou. 2008. Syntactic variation of support-verb constructions. *Lingvisticae Investigationes* 31(2). 173–185.

Machonis, Peter A. 1985. Transformations of verb phrase idioms: passivization, particle movement, dative shift. *American Speech* 60(4). 291–308.

Machonis, Peter A. 1987. The Lexicon-Grammar of English: Support and operator verbs. In Werner Bahner, Joachim Schildt & Dieter Viehweger (eds.), *Proceedings of the 14th International Congress of Linguists*, 992–995. Akademie-Verlag.

Machonis, Peter A. 1988. Support verbs: an analysis of *be Prep X* idioms. *The SECOL Review* 122. 95–125.

McEnery, Tony & Andrew Wilson. 1996. *Corpus linguistics.* Edinburgh University Press.

Meunier, Annie. 1977. Sur les bases syntaxiques de la morphologie dérivationnelle. *Lingvisticae Investigationes* 1(2). 287–331.

Meyers, Adam. 2007. *Annotation guidelines for NomBank: Noun argument structure for PropBank.* Tech. rep. https://nlp.cs.nyu.edu/meyers/nombank/nombank-specs-2007.pdf (Accessed January 2016). Unpublished manuscript.

Meyers, Adam, Ruth Reeves, Catherine Macleod, Rachel Szekely, Veronika Zielinska, Brian Young & Ralph Grishman. 2004. Annotating noun argument structure for NomBank. In *Proceedings of the Language Resources and Evaluation Conference*, 803–806. Lisbon.

Moustaki, Argyro. 1995. *Les expressions figées être prép C W en grec moderne.* Paris: Université Paris VIII dissertation.

Nunberg, Geoffrey, Ivan A. Sag & Thomas Wasow. 1994. Idioms. *Language* 70(3). 491–538.

Osherson, Anne & Christiane Fellbaum. 2010. The representation of idioms in WordNet. In *Proceedings of the Fifth Global WordNet Conference.* Mumbai, India.

Palmer, Martha, Daniel Guildea & Paul Kingsbury. 2005. The Proposition Bank: an annotated corpus of semantic roles. *Computational Linguistics* 31(1). 71–106.

Ranchhod, Elisabete. 1983. On the support verbs *ser* and *estar* in Portuguese. *Lingvisticae Investigationes* 7(2). 317–353.

Ranchhod, Elisabete. 1990. *Sintaxe dos predicados nominais com estar* (Linguística 12). Lisboa: Instituto Nacional de Investigação Científica.

Ranchhod, Elisabete & Michele De Gioia. 1996. Comparative Romance syntax. Frozen adverbs in Italian and in Portuguese. *Lingvisticae Investigationes* 20(1). 33–85.

Rassi, Amanda, Cristina Santos-Turati, Jorge Baptista, Nuno Mamede & Oto Vale. 2014. The fuzzy boundaries of operator verb and support verb constructions with *dar* 'give' and *ter* 'have' in Brazilian Portuguese. In *Proceedings of the*

Workshop on Lexical and Grammatical Resources for Language Processing, 92–101.

Riehemann, Susanne. 2001. *A constructional approach to idioms and word formation*. Stanford University dissertation.

Ross, John Robert. 1979. Where's English? In Charles Fillmore, Daniel Kempler & William Wang (eds.), *Individual differences in language ability and language behavior*, 127–163. New York: Academic Press.

Ruppenhofer, Josef, Michael Ellsworth, Miriam R. L. Petruck, Christopher R. Johnson & Jan Scheffczyk. 2006. *FrameNet II: Extended theory and practice*. Berkeley, CA: International Computer Science Institute.

Sag, Ivan A., Timothy Baldwin, Francis Bond, Ann Copestake & Dan Flickinger. 2002. Multiword expressions: A pain in the neck for NLP. In *Proceedings of the 3rd International Conference on Intelligent Text Processing and Computational Linguistics (CICLing-2002)*, 1–15.

Senellart, Jean. 1998. Reconnaissance automatique des entrées du lexique-grammaire des phrases figées. *Travaux de linguistique* 37. 109–121.

Stathi, Katerina. 2007. A corpus-based analysis of adjectival modification in German idioms. In Christiane Fellbaum (ed.), *Idioms and collocations. Corpus-based linguistic and lexicographic studies*, 81–108. London: Continuum.

Tesnière, Lucien. 1959. *Éléments de syntaxe structurale*. Paris: Klincksieck.

Tolone, Elsa. 2011. *Analyse syntaxique à l'aide des tables du Lexique-Grammaire du français*. Champs-sur-Marne: Université Paris-Est dissertation.

Tolone, Elsa & Benoît Sagot. 2011. Using Lexicon-Grammar Tables for French verbs in a Large-Coverage Parser. In Zygmunt Vetulani (ed.), *Human Language Technology. Challenges for computer science and linguistics: 4th Language and Technology Conference, LTC 2009, Revised Selected Papers*, 183–191. Poznan, Poland: Springer.

Vietri, Simonetta. 1996. The syntax of the Italian verb *Essere Prep*. *Lingvisticæ Investigationes* 20(2). 287–363.

Vietri, Simonetta. 2011. On a class of Italian frozen sentences. *Lingvisticæ Investigationes* 34(2). 228–267.

Chapter 7

Revisiting the grammatical function "object" (OBJ and OBJ$_\theta$)

Stella Markantonatou

Institute for Language and Speech Processing, Athena RIC, Greece

Niki Samaridi

Faculty of Philology, National and Kapodistrian University of Athens

Free subject verb multiword expressions (MWEs) of Modern Greek and English provide data that challenge the theoretical status of the syntactic notion OBJECT. We compare the syntactic reflexes of three types of verbal complement: objects of typical monotransitive verbs, indirect objects of ditransitive verbs and fixed accusative noun phrases (NPs) that occur as direct complements of verbs in MWEs. Passivisation, clitic replacement, object optionality and distribution present themselves as syntactic reflexes that draw relatively clear cut lines across these three classes of verbal complements and suggest that the Grammatical Functions OBJ(ect) and OBJ(ect)$_\theta$ of LFG should not be assigned to the fixed accusative NPs that occur in verb MWEs; rather a new Grammatical Function should be defined for this purpose.

1 OBJ and OBJ$_\theta$

1.1 OBJ and OBJ$_\theta$ in Modern Greek and English

It is widely claimed that the grammatical behavior of MWEs can be captured with the same machinery that is used for compositional structures (Gross 1998a,b; Kay & Sag 2014) and Bargmann & Sailer 2018 [this volume]. We will present evidence from Modern Greek and English that possibly challenges this claim at the level of Grammatical Functions (GFs), more particularly the notion of syntactic object. GFs are primitive concepts for Lexical Functional Grammar (LFG) that is

Stella Markantonatou & Niki Samaridi. 2018. Revisiting the grammatical function "object" (OBJ and OBJ$_\theta$). In Manfred Sailer & Stella Markantonatou (eds.), *Multiword expressions: Insights from a multi-lingual perspective*, 187–213. Berlin: Language Science Press. DOI:10.5281/zenodo.1182599

the theoretical framework of our discussion. Other linguistic theories, such as transformational grammar (Baker 2001) and HPSG (Pollard & Sag 1994) use GFs implicitly through appropriate structural interpretations.

LFG distinguishes between two objects, the OBJ and the OBJ$_\theta$ (Bresnan & Moshi 1990; Dalrymple 2001). OBJ combines with prototypically transitive verbs. According to existing wisdom on syntax and semantics, the NP *τον κώδικα των Ναζί* (ton kοδika ton Nazi) 'the Nazi code' (1) is the object of the transitive verb: it is marked with the accusative case while the semantics of the eventuality of code breaking assigns it the Proto-Patient role (Dowty 1990).

(1)   *Τιούριγκ: ο   κρυπτογράφος που έσπασε τον κώδικα   των Ναζί.*
      Turing: o   kriptoγrafos   pu   espase ton kοδika   ton Nazi.
      Turing: the cryptographer who broke   the code.ACC the Nazi

      'Turing: the cryptographer who broke the Nazi code.'

OBJ$_\theta$ (Bresnan & Moshi 1990) always co-occurs with an OBJ in the environment of an active predicate. Its distribution is restricted to the so-called ditransitive verbs. In (2) the NP *a book* instantiates the OBJ$_\theta$ GF and the NP *Sue* instantiates the OBJ. The NP *Sue* becomes the subject of the passivised verb in (3).

(2)   *Helen gave Sue a book.*

(3)   *Sue was given a book.*

Modern Greek has a relatively small number of ditransitive verbs, such as the verb *διδάσκω* (δiδasko) 'teach' (4)-(7), that subcategorise for OBJ$_\theta$ (Kordoni 2004). Examples (5)-(7) show that Modern Greek passive ditransitive verbs pattern with standard English passive verbs (3): the NP *ιστορία* (istoria) 'history' that instantiates the OBJ$_\theta$ does become the subject of the passive form of the verb (6).

(4)   a.   *Ο   Πέτρος διδάσκει στη   Μαρία ιστορία.*
          O   Petros δiδaski sti   Maria istoria.
          the Petros teaches to.the Maria history.ACC

          'Petros teaches history to Maria.'

      b.   *Ο   Πέτρος διδάσκει τη   Μαρία   ιστορία.*
          O   Petros δiδaski ti   Maria   istoria.
          the Petros teaches   the Maria.ACC history.ACC

          'Petros teaches Maria history.'

(5) H   Μαρία διδάσκεται ιστορία   από τον Πέτρο.
     I   Maria διδaskiete istoria   apo ton Petro.
     the Maria is.taught   history.ACC by the Petros

     'Mary is taught history by Petros.'

(6) * Ιστορία διδάσκεται τη Μαρία   από τον Πέτρο.
       Istoria διδaskiete ti   Maria   apo ton Petro.
       history is.taught   the Maria.ACC by the Petros

(7) Ιστορία διδάσκεται στη   Μαρία από τον Πέτρο.
     Istoria διδaskiete sti   Maria apo ton Petro.
     history is.taught   to.the Maria by the Petros

     'History is taught to Mary by Petros.'

But are OBJ and OBJ$_\theta$ that have been modeled on compositional data enough to capture MWE behavior? This is how the original question, namely whether "compositional" syntax is appropriate for MWEs, may be couched in an LFG framework. The discussion in the remainder of this paper is structured as follows: at the second part of §1 we present the diagnostics for distinguishing between the two types of object that are available in LFG, namely the OBJ and the OBJ$_\theta$. In §2 we apply the classical constituency diagnostics on MWEs in order to identify the constituents that will instantiate the GFs. In §3, we apply the objecthood diagnostics on the constituents identified within MWEs and compare the results with the ones received from the application of the same diagnostics on compositional structures. Passives are discussed in §4. In §5 we discuss the results of the application of objecthood diagnostics on MWEs, the pros and the cons of four different answers to our original question and argue in favor of the adoption of a new GF, which we call FIX. Finally, in §6 we show that a variety of MWEs can be modeled with FIX. We conclude with a set of questions open to future research.

1.2 Diagnostics for distinguishing between OBJ and OBJ$_\theta$

Hudson (1992) has discussed the following 11 diagnostics for distinguishing between English direct and indirect objects, OBJ and OBJ$_\theta$ respectively in LFG terms: passivisation, extraction, placement after a particle, participation in heavy-NP shift, accusative case in a true case system, lexical subcategorisation, bearing the same semantic role as the prototypical direct object, animacy, existence of idioms with the same verb head, being the extractee of an infinitival complement, controlling a depictive predicate. Although some of these diagnostics have been shown to be disputable (Thomas 2012), they still provide an excellent starting point that we will adapt to the needs of Modern Greek. Modern Greek hardly uses any verb+particle constructs and has no infinitivals. Of the remaining diagnostics lexical subcategorisation, heavy NP shift, animacy and control of a depictive predicate do not apply to MWEs that have fixed structures and non-compositional semantics. The idiom-based diagnostic is left out because fixed expressions are idioms. Lastly, the extraction diagnostic will be used as a diagnostic of constituency.

We will not use semantic roles as a diagnostic because of their inherent fuzziness (Dowty 1990) and because MWEs have non-compositional semantics. LFG assumes that OBJ can bear any or no thematic role at all since expletives can also materialize objects. It is generally accepted that Modern Greek has no overt expletives (Kotzoglou 2001). OBJ$_\theta$, on the other hand, has been restricted to "themes'" (Bresnan & Moshi 1990).

The NP that instantiates an OBJ$_\theta$ never turns up as the subject in passives (6) while the NP that instantiates an OBJ does (5), (7).

The case diagnostic yields ambiguous results in Modern Greek because direct and indirect objects and a range of adjuncts denoting time and place are instantiated with accusative NPs: of the two accusative NPs in (8), the NP *ένα γράμμα* (ena γrama) 'a letter' functions as an object while the NP *την Παρασκευή* (tin Paraskievi) 'on Friday' is an adjunct that can be questioned with *πότε* (pote) 'when'.

(8)   Θα γράψω   ένα γράμμα   στον Κώστα την Παρασκευή.
      Θα γrapso   ena γrama   ston Kosta tin Paraskievi.
      will write.1SG a   letter.ACC to.the Kostas the Friday.ACC

      'I will write a letter to Kostas on Friday.'

Other diagnostics found in the literature seem to be language specific (Shi-Ching 2008). One of them is the position of the object in the sentence. In Modern Greek, normally both OBJ and OBJ$_\theta$ follow the verb. Modern Greek is a language with relatively free word order. Adjuncts can appear anywhere in the sentence between constituents (the exact positions depend on the type of the adjunct).

We will enrich our collection of diagnostics with various types of pronominalisation including relativisation (9), *Who/What*-questions (10), (11) and clitic replacement (12). Pronominalisation has been used as a constituency diagnostic (Radford 1988). In certain languages relativisation has been used as a diagnostic for distinguishing between OBJ and OBJ$_\theta$: in Cantonese (Shi-Ching 2008), the OBJ of monotransitive verbs and the OBJ$_\theta$ in ditransitive constructions are relativised with a gap while the OBJ of ditransitive constructions is relativised with a resumptive pronoun. Modern Greek does not have similar pronominalisation phenomena but we will see that relativisation is of some interest. We will also use *Which*-questioning (10), which has been adopted by Shi-Ching (2008) in her discussion of OBJ/OBJ$_\theta$ in Cantonese and has been briefly discussed in Kay & Sag (2014), as well as clitic replacement (12).

(9) *Ο κώδικας των Ναζί τον οποίο έσπασε ο Άλαν Τιούργικ...*
     O kοδikas ton Nazi ton opio espase o Alan Turing...
     'The Nazi code that Alan Turing broke ...'

(10) *Ποιον κώδικα έσπασε ο Άλαν Τιούριγκ;*
     Pion koδika espase o Alan Turing?
     'Which code did Alan Turing break?'

(11) *Τί έσπασε ο Άλαν Τιούργικ;*
     Ti espase o Alan Turing?
     'What did Alan Turing break?'

(12) *Τον έσπασε   ο   Άλαν   Τιούριγκ.*
     Ton espase   o   Alan   Turing.
     him broke.3SG the Alan.NOM Turing.NOM
     'Alan Turing broke it.'

We will adopt the standard assumption that Modern Greek OBJ/OBJ$_\theta$ are materialized as phrasal constituents when they are not materialized by weak pronouns (clitics). Modern Greek widely uses pre-verbal clitics, which have been analysed both as NPs and as affixes (Joseph 1989). We do not think that the phrasal status of clitics bears on the issues examined here.

2 Multiwords

Word order permutations, adverb placement and control phenomena indicate the presence of phrasal constituents in Modern Greek MWEs. Drawing on Kay & Sag (2014) and Samaridi & Markantonatou (2014), we assume that Modern Greek free subject verb MWEs contain an idiomatic verb predicate that selects for a free subject and a number (including zero) of (possibly) idiomatic complements.

2.1 Constituency diagnostics

Radford (1988) mentions preposing, postposing and adverb interpolation as distributional diagnostics of phrasal constituents. We will use the term WORD ORDER

PERMUTATIONS to collectively refer to preposing and postposing.

Because we are working with MWEs that contain postverbal NPs –often of some complexity– we note that in Modern Greek, postnominal genitive NPs or weak pronouns denoting possession or some property and postnominal PPs cannot be extracted from the matrix NP (13b), (14b). The matrix NP[1] participates in word order permutations (13c), (14c).

(13) a. *Ο Γιάννης φοράει τα παπούτσια του   Γιώργου.*
          O Γianis forai [ta paputsia tu   Γioryu].
          the John   wears the shoes   the.GEN George.GEN
          'John wears George's shoes.'

     b. * *Του Γιώργου φοράει ο Γιάννης τα παπούτσια.*
          Tu Γioryu   forai o Γianis   ta paputsia.

     c. *Τα παπούτσια του Γιώργου φοράει ο Γιάννης.*
          [Ta paputsia   tu Γioryu] forai o Γianis.

(14) a. *Η Ελένη αγόρασε ένα ταψί για γλυκά.*
          I   Eleni ayorase [ena tapsi yia ylika].
          the Eleni bought   a   tin   for cakes
          'Eleni bought a tin for cakes.'

     b. * *Για γλυκά αγόρασε η Ελένη ένα ταψί.*
          Γia ylika ayorase i Eleni ena tapsi.

     c. *Ένα ταψί για γλυκά αγόρασε η Ελένη.*
          [Ena tapsi yia ylika] ayorase i Eleni.

Furthermore, a temporal adverb may occur between the verb and its NP complement (15a), (16a) but it cannot occur within the NP (15b), (16b):

(15) a. *Ο Γιάννης φόρεσε χθές   τα παπούτσια του Γιώργου.*
          O Γianis forese χθes   [ta paputsia tu Γioryu].
          the John   wore yesterday the shoes   the George.GEN
          'John wore George's shoes yesterday.'

     b. * *Ο Γιάννης φόρεσε τα παπούτσια χθες του Γιώργου.*
          O Γianis   forese ta paputsia χθes tu Γioryu.

---

[1]The matrix NP is placed in brackets '[]' in the examples (13)-(16).

(16)   a.   *H   Ελένη αγόρασε χθες   ένα ταψί για γλυκά.*
            I   Eleni ayorase χθes   [ena tapsi yia ylika].
            the Eleni bought yesterday a   tin for cakes

       'Eleni bought a tin for cakes yesterday.'

       b.   * *H Ελένη αγόρασε ένα ταψί χθες για γλυκά.*
            I Eleni ayorase ena tapsi χθes yia ylika.

Radford (1988) notes that pronouns such as 'what' can be used to question NP constituents irrespectively of their syntactic function, namely whether they are subjects (17), objects (18) or complements of prepositions (19), as well as a range of sentential complements.

(17)   *Tí   ήρθε το πρωί;   Το τραίνο.*
       Ti   irθe to proi?   To treno.
       what.NOM came the morning the train

       'What came in the morning? The train did.'

(18)   *Tí   φοράει ο   Γιάννης; Τα παπούτσια του.*
       Ti   forai o   Γianis?   Ta paputsia tu.
       what.ACC wears the John.NOM the shoes   his

       'What does John wear? His shoes.'

(19)   *Από τί   κρύωσε   η   Ελένη;   Από τον αέρα.*
       Apo ti   kriose   i   Eleni?   Apo ton aera.
       from what caught.cold the Eleni.NOM from the wind

       'What gave a cold to Eleni? The wind.'

We will use these diagnostics to identify phrasal constituents in MWEs.

2.2 MWE constituents

Below we will use two types of verb MWE that admit a free subject (not a fixed one):

1. The first type is represented with the verb MWE (20) and contains an accusative NP that is an independent nominal MWE. We know that it is independent because it can combine with several verbs and it is synonymous with the noun *permission*. We will use the label NP_MWE to refer to this type of nominal MWEs.

(20) *Έδωσε το πράσινο   φως   για το Erasmus+.*
Edose to prasino   fos   yia to Erasmus+.
gave   the green.ACC light.ACC for the Erasmus+

'S/He gave the green light for Erasmus+.'

2. The second type contains fixed accusative NPs that do not form independent NP_MWEs. We will use the label Fixed_NP to denote this type of NP that here is represented with three verb MWEs admitting a free subject. Two of them involve the Fixed_NP *τα μούτρα* POSS (ta mutra POSS) where the obligatory POSS anaphor is bound by the subject (22), (23). The noun *μούτρα* (mutra) 'face' is a colloquial word (21). Within the MWEs, the Fixed_NP *τα μούτρα* POSS (ta mutra POSS) does not have the meaning 'POSS face'.

(21) *Πλύνε   τα μούτρα σου   που είναι μες τη βρώμα.*
Pline   ta mutra   su   pu ine mes ti   vroma.
wash.IMP the face.ACC yours.GEN that is   in   the dirt

'Wash your face that is very dirty.'

(22) *Ρίχνω   τα μούτρα   μου.*
Riχno   ta mutra   mu.
drop.1sg the face.ACC mine.GEN

'I suppress my dignity.'

(23) *Κοιτώ   τα μούτρα   μου.*
Kito   ta mutra   mu.
look.1sg the face.ACC mine.GEN

'I look at myself.'

Word order permutations (24a)-(24b), adverb interpolation (25a)-(25b) and *What*-questioning (26a)-(26b) establish that the NP *τα μούτρα* POSS (ta mutra POSS) is a constituent of the respective MWEs:

(24) a. *Τα μούτρα   σου   να ρίξεις.*
Ta mutra   su   na riksis.
the face.ACC yours.GEN to drop.2SG

'It is your dignity that you should suppress.'

b. *Τα μούτρα σου κοίτα.*
   Ta mutra su kita.
   the face.ACC yours.GEN look.2SG.IMP
   'Look at yourself.'

(25) a. *Ο Γιάννης έριξε τότε τα μούτρα του.*
     O Γianis erikse tote ta mutra tu.
     the John dropped then the face his
     'Then John suppressed his dignity.'

   b. *Η Ελένη κοίταξε τότε τα μούτρα της.*
      I Eleni kitakse tote ta mutra tis.
      the Eleni looked then the face hers
      'Eleni looked at herself for once.'

(26) a. *Έριξε τότε τα μούτρα του. Τί έριξε;*
     Erikse tote ta mutra tu. Ti erikse?
     dropped then the face his what dropped
     'He suppressed his dignity for once. What did he do?'

   b. *Η Ελένη κοίταξε τα μούτρα της. Τί κοίταξε;*
      I Eleni kitakse ta mutra tis. Ti kitakse?
      the Eleni looked the face hers what looked
      'Eleni looked at herself. What did she do?'

3 OBJ, OBJ$_\theta$: Syntactic reflexes

3.1 Objecthood diagnostics and the Fixed_NP

Constituency diagnostics seem to set apart structures with an NP_MWE from structures with a Fixed_NP.

The passivisation diagnostic returns a range of results: (20) has a passive counterpart (27a) but (23) and (24) do not (examples (27b) and (27c) respectively):

(27) a. *Δόθηκε το πράσινο φως για τη δόση.*
     Δοθikie to prasino fos γia ti δosi.
     was.given the green.NOM light.NOM for the instalment
     'Permission for the instalment was given.'

b. * *Τα μούτρα μου κοιτάχτηκαν (από εμένα).*
Ta mutra mu kitaxtikan (apo emena).
the face mine was.looked.at by me
'I looked at myself.'

c. * *Να ριχτούν τα μούτρα σου (από εσένα).*
Na rixtun ta mutra su (apo esena).
to be.dropped the face yours by you
'It is your dignity that you should suppress.'

The relativisation diagnostic yields similar results: (20) does not block relative clauses targeting the NP_MWE (28) while (22) and (23) block relative clauses with the Fixed_NP as a target (29).

(28) *το πράσινο φως το οποίο έδωσε η ΕΕ στους αγρότες*
to prasino fos to opio eδose i EE stus aγrotes
the green light the that gave the EU to.the farmers
'the green light that EU gave to the farmers'

(29) * *Τα μούτρα σου, που έριξες τότε, να τα ξαναρίξεις.*
Ta mutra su, pu erikses tote, na ta ksanariksis.
the face yours that dropped.2SG then to them re.drop.2SG
'You suppressed your dignity then and you should suppress it again.'

The *Which*-questions diagnostic returns similar results: NP_MWEs (20a) allow for which-questions (30) but Fixed_NP (22),(23) do not (31).

(30) ? *Ποιο πράσινο φως έδωσε η Ευρωπαϊκή Ένωση;*
Pio prasino fos eδose i Evropaiki Enosi?
which green light gave the European Union
'Which permission did the EU give?'

(31) is a piece of dialogue that was evaluated by 6 native speakers who were instructed to choose one of the following three labels: "joke", "description of an event", "other". All speakers chose the label "joke". The joke, irony or pun effects seem to be due to the fact that the question *ποιο χέρι* (pio χieri) 'which hand' is unexpected in the context of the MWE. The MWE does not imply that someone actually put his/her hand in the fire while the question *ποιο χέρι* (pio χieri) shifts discourse to the literal meaning of *χέρι* (χieri) 'hand'. Raskin (1985) argues that jokes arise from the violation of the Gricean conversational maxims that require information-bearing and serious and sincere communication.

(31) *Βάζω το χέρι μου στη   φωτιά ότι ο Κώστας ζει. Ποιο χέρι;*
      Vazo to χieri mu sti   fotia oti o   Kostas zi.   Pio   χieri?
      put   the hand my in.the fire   that the Kostas lives which hand

      'I am absolutely sure that Kostas is alive. Which hand?'

The replacement with a clitic in discourse with the same MWE produces an interesting effect: as expected, (20) allows for cliticisation of the NP MWE within the same expression (32), however, definite Fixed_NPs also allow for cliticisation with the same MWE (33):

(32) *Έδωσε το πράσινο φως για το Erasmus+; Ναι, το έδωσε.*
      Eδose to prasino fos γia to Erasmus+? Ne, to eδose.
      gave   the green   light for the Erasmus+? yes, it gave

      'Did s/he give the green light for Erasmus+? Yes, s/he did.'

(33) was also evaluated by 6 speakers who were instructed to choose one of the following three labels: "joke", "description of an event", "other". They all chose the label "description of an event". Therefore, the clitic *τα* (ta) 'them' can be used to replace objects in the context of the same MWE.

(33) *Θα ρίξω τα μούτρα μου. Εγώ δεν τα   ρίχνω.*
      Θa rikso ta mutra mu. Eγo δen ta   riχno.
      will drop the face.PL$_j$ mine I   not them$_j$ drop

      'I will suppress my dignity. I will not.'

Tsimpli & Mastropavlou (2007) following work by Cardinaletti & Starke (1999) and Tsimpli & Stavrakaki (1999) argue that Modern Greek third person clitics are "clusters of agreement and case features" and that they lack a referential index –a fact that explains their need of an antecedent. We can safely assume that cross-reference across same MWEs satisfies agreement and case features and makes sure that semantics is identical across structures.

Indefinite Fixed_NP cannot be replaced by a clitic even in the context of the same MWE (35). Compositional structures (34) allow for clitic replacement of indefinite objects, even across different predications.

(34) *Ο Γιώργος έταξε   στην Ελένη διακοπές. Τις   σχεδιάζει καιρό.*
      O Γioryos etakse   stin Eleni δiakopes. Tis   sχieδiazi kiero.
      the George promised to.the Eleni holidays them plans   time

      'George has promised a holiday to Eleni. He has been planning it for some time.'

(35)   to promise hares with stoles 'to make unrealistic promises'
Έταζε   λαγούς με   πετραχήλια. *Τους έταζε   παντού.
Etaze   laɣus me petraχilia. *Tus etaze   pantu.
promised hares$_j$ with stoles   them$_j$ promised everywhere

'He made unrealistic promises. He made these promises to everyone.'

Ariel (2001), in the context of Accessibility Theory, argues that "referring expressions code a specific and (different) degree of mental accessibility" where "mental accessibility" is meant as a shorthand of "accessibility of mental representations that are available to the addressee in the discourse". Referential expressions are accessibility markers guiding the addressee how to retrieve appropriate mental representations. Drawing on distributional findings, Ariel suggests an ordering of referential expressions from low to high accessibility markers. On this ordering, definite expressions are situated on the edge of low accessibility marking and 3rd person clitics on the edge of high accessibility marking. This means that the addressee perceives definiteness as a signal that an entity has just been introduced to the discourse and the existence of a clitic as a signal that she has to look for an entity that has been introduced to the discourse sometime ago. Therefore, definiteness should "attract", so to say, clitics. Perhaps, definiteness is the reason why (only) definite Fixed_NP can be replaced with a clitic. The reader should keep in mind that replacement of a Fixed_NP with a clitic is allowed only in the strict context of the same MWE and that indefinite Fixed_NP cannot be replaced (35).

Lastly, discourse collapses if cross-reference is required across different MWEs (36) and across MWEs and compositional structures (37) (compositional structures allow for cross-reference across different predications). (36) and (37) below sound absurd. At best, (37) produces a joke/irony effect – an effect that was observed with *Which*-questions as well.

(36)   * Ο   Πέτρος έριξε   τα μούτρα του και μετά τα   κοίταξε.
       O Petros erikse   ta mutra tu kie meta ta   kitakse.
       the Petros dropped the face.PL$_j$ his and then them$_j$ looked

'Petros suppressed his dignity and then he looked at himself.'

(37)   * Έριξα   τα μούτρα μου. Τα   είχα καλύψει πριν.
       Eriksa   ta mutra mu. Ta   iχa kalipsi prin.
       dropped the face.PL$_j$ mine. them$_j$ had covered before

'I suppressed my dignity. I had covered my face in advance.'

English MWEs present a picture similar to the Modern Greek one. Kay & Sag (2014) discuss the case of the English verb MWE *to kick the bucket* and apply similar diagnostics. The MWE *to kick the bucket* resists passivization. Furthermore, relativisation, *Which*-questioning and replacement of *the bucket* with *it*[2] are not possible (38a)–(38c).

(38) a. * *the bucket that the peasant kicked ...*
    b. * *Which bucket did the peasant kick?*
    c. *The peasant kicked the bucket.* *Also, his wife kicked it.*

3.2 Application of objecthood diagnostics on OBJ$_\theta$

The accusative NP την ελληνική ιστορία, tin eliniki istoria, 'the Greek history' in (39) instantiates an OBJ and responds positively to all constituency diagnostics.[3] In (40) the definite NP *την ελληνική ιστορία* (tin eliniki istoria) instantiates an OBJ$_\theta$.

(39) *Ο   Πέτρος διδάσκει στην   κοπέλα την ελληνική   ιστορία.*
    O   Petros διδaski stin   kopela tin eliniki   istoria.
    the Petros teaches to.the girl   the Greek.ACC history.ACC
    'Petros teaches the Greek history to the girl.'

(40) *Ο   Πέτρος διδάσκει την κοπέλα   την ελληνική   ιστορία.*
    O   Petros διδaski tin kopela   tin eliniki   istoria.
    the Peter   teaches the girl.ACC the Greek.ACC history.ACC
    'Peter teaches the girl the Greek history.'

We have already illustrated with examples (5)-(7) that the Modern Greek OBJ$_\theta$ patterns with the English OBJ$_\theta$ as regards passivisation.

Relativisation is somehow unwelcome with an OBJ$_\theta$: (41a), (41b) were accepted as grammatical by 50% of the speakers.

(41) a. *η   κοπέλα   που   διδάσκει ο   Πέτρος την ελληνική ιστορία*
      i   kopela   pu   διδaski o   Petros tin eliniki   istoria
      the girl.NOM who teaches the Petros the Greek   history.ACC
      'the girl to whom Petros teaches the Greek history'

---

[2] *It* is the nearest English equivalent of Modern Greek clitics.
[3] However, it must be noted that 5 out of the 7 speakers who commented on (39) and especially (40) thought them acceptable but somewhat clumsy.

b. η   ελληνική ιστορία   που διδάσκει ο   Πέτρος την κοπέλα
   i   eliniki   istoria   pu διδaski ο   Petros ti   kopela
   the Greek   history.NOM that teaches the Petros the girl.ACC

'the Greek history that Petros teaches to the girl'

The *Which*-questions diagnostic returns a variety of results: (42a) was rejected by all the speakers while (42b) was accepted as grammatical by a 50% of the speakers.

(42) a. * Ποια   κοπέλα διδάσκει ο   Πέτρος την ελληνική ιστορία;
        Pia   kopela διδaski o   Petros tin eliniki   istoria?
        which girl   teaches the Petros the Greek   history.ACC

    b. Ποια   ιστορία διδάσκει ο   Πέτρος την κοπέλα;
        Pia   istoria διδaski o   Petros tin kopela?
        which history teaches the Petros the girl?

While OBJ can be replaced with a clitic (43a), replacement of OBJ$_\theta$ with a clitic is not possible in discourse with the same predication (43b).

(43) a. Ο Πέτρος **την**   διδάσκει την ελληνική ιστορία.
        O Petros **tin**('girl') διδaski tin eliniki   istoria.
        the Petros her   teaches the Greek   history

       'Petros teaches her the Greek history.'

    b. * Ο Πέτρος την   διδάσκει την κοπέλα.
        O Petros tin('history') διδaski tin kopela.
        the Petros it   teaches the girl

Replacement of an OBJ$_\theta$ with a clitic is possible in a discourse with a different predication. In (44), the clitic *την* (tin) 'her' may refer to either an NP instantiating an OBJ (*την Μαρία* (tin Maria) 'Maria') or to the complement of a P (*στην Μαρία* (stin Maria) 'to Maria'). Furthermore, the clitic *την* (tin) 'her' in the second clause refers to the NP *την ελληνική ιστορία* (tin eliniki istoria) 'the Greek history' that instantiates the OBJ$_\theta$.

(44) Ο Πέτρος διδάσκει στη   Μαρία / τη Μαρία την ελληνική ιστορία. Την
    O Petros διδaski sti   Maria / ti Maria tin eliniki   istoria. Tin
    the Petros teaches to.the Maria / the Maria the Greek   history her
    έχει κάνει να την αγαπήσει.
    eχi kani na tin aγapisi.
    has made to it   like

    'Petros teaches Maria the Greek history. He has made her love it.'

Similar results are received if the same diagnostics are applied on English OBJ$_\theta$ (Thomas 2012): the English OBJ$_\theta$ cannot be replaced by *it* (45).

(45)   * *John gave Mary it.*

3.3 The overall syntactic behavior of OBJ, OBJ$_\theta$ and of the (yet unknown) GF assigned to Fixed_NP

The results of the application of the diagnostics on the GF assigned to Fixed_NP, OBJ, OBJ$_\theta$ and ADJ instantiated with accusative NPs including optionality, case marking and position in the sentence are summarized in Table 1. We have not provided detailed data for the application of the diagnostics on ADJ.

Direct objects can be optional in Modern Greek (Anastasopoulos et al. 2013). Kordoni (2004) presents Modern Greek data where OBJ$_\theta$ is omitted. MWEs, on the other hand, hardly allow for constituent omission.

Table 1: The overall syntactic behavior of OBJ, OBJ$_\theta$, ADJ, and the GF assigned to F(ixed)_NP according to the objecthood diagnostics.[a]

| Phenomenon | F_NP | F_NP | OBJ | OBJ$_\theta$ | OBJ$_\theta$ | NP adj |
Language	EL	EN	EL	EL	EN	EL
Optionality	N	N	Y	Y	N	Y
Relativisation	N	N	Y	?Y	Y	Y
Which-questions	N	N	Y	?Y	Y	Y
Clitic—same MWE	Y	N*	Y	N	N*	N
Clitic-different MWE	N	N*	Y	Y	N*	N
Clitic-compositional	N	N*	Y	Y	N*	N
Accusative Postverbal	Y	Y	Y	Y	Y	Y/N
Passivisation	N	N	Y#	N	N	N

[a]Clarifications on Table 1:

1. F_NP: it stands for Fixed_NP.

2. N*: English has no clitics. We refer to the usage of the pronoun *it* - see (38c) and (45).

3. Y#: Not all transitive verbs have passive counterparts in Modern Greek.

4. ?Y: Speakers responses were not unanimous.

5. Y/N: Modern Greek accusative NP adjuncts can appear in both pre- and post- verbal positions.

The feature "accusative postverbal" takes the same value for all the examined categories and has no discriminating role, therefore it will not be taken into account in the remainder of this discussion. Furthermore, ADJ, OBJ and OBJ$_\theta$ respond positively to relativisation and *Which*-questions, indicating that the two diagnostics are sensitive to the semantics of the NPs rather than their syntactic function (Kay & Sag 2014). These diagnostics will not be used as objecthood diagnostics for Modern Greek or English.

A more detailed picture of the situation with passivisation in our collection of Modern Greek verb MWEs is given in the next section.

4 A more detailed picture of passivisation in Modern Greek MWEs

Out of a collection of 1120 verb MWEs[4] a percentage of 57,5% are formed with verbs that have a passive counterpart. The remaining 42,5% are formed with verbs that have no passive counterpart. Of the MWEs that are formed with verbs that have a passive counterpart in the general language, only 53 have a passive MWE counterpart. Among the passivisable MWEs, 24 contain a free accusative NP that becomes the subject of the passive form (46), 6 contain an NP_MWE (27) and 23 contain a Fixed_NP. Of the MWEs that are formed with passivisable verbs but do not have a passive MWE counterpart, 76 contain a free accusative NP, 24 contain an accusative NP_MWE and 221 contain a Fixed_NP. Percentages in Table 2 are calculated over the whole data set (1120 MWEs).

(46) O   όρος κοινότητα   ... αφέθηκε στην ιστορική ησυχία του.
      O   oros kinotita   ... afeθikie stin istoriki isiçia tu.
      the term community ... was-left to.the historical peace its

    'The term community was left alone in its historical peace.'
    http://commonsfest.info/2015/i-istoria-ton-kinon-ston-elliniko-choro/

Several of the passivisable MWEs contain Fixed_NP whose head nouns seem to instantiate senses different from the nouns' literal ones. For instance, the noun *μέτρα* (metra) 'meters', is used with the sense 'measures' in (47). Such senses are used widely in compositional structures. Along with idioms, the collection used also includes collocations.

---

[4]http://users.sch.gr/samaridi/attachments/article/3/LexicalResources.pdf

Table 2: Passives in the dataset of Modern Greek free subject verb MWEs

Verbs	Total	MWE	Total	Complement	Total
passive	644 (57,5%)	passive	53 (4,7%)	Free NP	24 (2,1%)
				NP_MWE	6 (0,54%)
				Fixed_NP	23 (2%)
		no passive	591 (52,7%)	Free NP	76 (6,8%)
				NP_MWE	24 (2,1%)
				Fixed_NP	221 (19,7%)
no passive	426 (42,5%)				
Total	1120				

(47) *Αυτά είναι τα μέτρα   που κατέθεσε η ελληνική κυβέρνηση.*
      Afta ine ta metra   pu kateθese i   eliniki kivernisi.
      these are the measures that submitted the Greek   government
      'These are the measures that the Greek government submitted.'

If these collocations are put aside, only a percentage of 1% corresponds to passivisable MWEs with a Fixed_NP. In (48) the Fixed_NP *μεγάλα λόγια* (meγala loγia) 'big words' is the subject of the passive form of the MWE *λέω μεγάλα λόγια* (leo meγala loγia) 'to make big promises'.

(48) *Είναι σύνηθες να λέγονται μεγάλα λόγια από μικρούς πολιτικούς.*
      Ine siniθes   na leγonte meγala loγia apo mikrus politikus.
      is   common to say.PASS big   words by small   politicians
      'Often unimportant politicians make big promises.'

The collection we have used is of relatively medium size but clearly shows that Modern Greek MWEs do not prefer passivisation: passivisable MWEs (both fixed ones and collocations) account only for the 4,7% of the total number of MWEs.

5 OBJ, OBJ$_\theta$ or some NEW GF?

We are turning now to our main question, namely whether OBJ or OBJ$_\theta$ can be assigned to Fixed_NP or whether a new GF (LFG) should be defined. In what follows we will use the collective term "meaning preserving NPs" for Fixed_NP with heads with independent, non literal senses, accusative NP_MWE and, of course, for free accusative NPs. The picture that has emerged so far reveals three groups of verb MWE:

Group 1: The group of passivisable verb MWEs that contain meaning preserving NPs and satisfy objecthood diagnostics; it comprises the majority of passivisable Modern Greek MWEs.

Group 2: The group of non passivisable verb MWEs containing both meaning preserving NPs and Fixed_NP.

Group 3: The rather small group (1%) of passivisable verb MWEs that contain Fixed_NP.

We can safely say that Group 1 contains verb MWEs whose verbal head selects for an OBJ because all obejcthood diagnostics are satisfied. In LFG, passivisation is modeled with a lexical rule that takes as input an active transitive predicate and maps the active OBJ on the SUBJ of the output passive predicate and the active SUBJ on an adjunct of the passive predicate. We assume that the LFG lexical rule for passivisation that requires an OBJ applies normally on these MWEs. Furthermore, an OBJ function can be assigned to passivisable verb MWEs with a Fixed_NP that constitute Group 3; the set of such verb MWEs is very small and it will be harmless to consider them as idiosyncratic (further research might reveal interesting aspects of these Fixed_NP).

Group 2 comprises verb MWEs that do not passivise but contain both meaning preserving NPs that satisfy objecthood diagnostics except for passivisation, and Fixed_NP that satisfy only clitic replacement in the same MWE context provided they are definite.

Kay & Sag (2014) discuss a similar distribution of English MWEs. In order to model the dichotomy introduced by passivisable versus non-passivisable MWEs, they split verbs into real transitive and pseudo-transitive ones.[5] Real transitive verbs correspond to Group 1 above. The class of pseudo transitive verbs of Kay and Sag includes verbs of measurement such as *cost, weigh, measure* and MWEs with Fixed_NP such as *to kick the bucket*, therefore pseudo-transitive verbs can be considered a superset of Group 2. By definition then, pseudo-transitive verbs do not select real objects therefore they do not passivise. Furthermore, Kay and

---

[5]In the revised version of the manuscript http://www1.icsi.berkeley.edu/ kay/idiom-pdflatex.11-13-15.pdf the transitive/pseudo-transivite dichotomy has been replaced with the distinction between meaningful and meaningless idiomatic complements of idiomatic verb predicates, the assumption being that passivisation applies on meaningful objects. Of course, in compositional language there are several verbs that accept meaningful objects and still do not passivise while expletives do turn up as subjects of passive verbs.

Sag observe that (like Modern Greek MWEs) several English MWEs with fixed NPs fail the relativisation and *Which*-question objecthood diagnostics; however, they note that the failure can be explained by semantic or pragmatic constraints on the diagnostics. Passivisation cannot be considered a semantics sensitive diagnostic because expletives and Fixed_NP turn up as subjects of passivised MWEs. Therefore, the proposed splitting of verbs into transitive and pseudo-transitive ones draws on passivisation ability solely and membership in each of the two groups is a lexical property of the verb.

The Kay & Sag (2014) approach that we have discussed so far relies on the verb predicate in order to explain the non-uniform behavior of "objects". Doug Arnold (University of Essex, personal communication) has suggested an alternative approach, namely that the Fixed_NP could be blamed for the scarcity of MWE passives. The two approaches, the verb predicate oriented and the Fixed_-NP oriented one, can be transcribed in LFG in one of the four ways below:

1. (verb predicate oriented): Some feature of the type +/-PASSIVISES is defined in the lexical entry of the verb and the OBJ GF is assigned to Fixed_NP

2. (verb predicate oriented): The verb does not select an OBJ; rather it selects some other GF and this is why the passivisation lexical rule that requires an OBJ cannot be applied

3. (Fixed_NP oriented): The head of the Fixed_NP is associated with the inside-out constraint (OBJ^) in the lexicon (Doug Arnold's proposal); the result of the constraint is that the Fixed_NP is able to realise only the OBJ GF and no other GF.

4. (Fixed_NP oriented): The case of the Fixed_NP is fixed to ACC (accusative).

Hypotheses 3 and 4 seem to be equivalent in the case of Modern Greek and English where subjects of main clauses are marked with the nominative case. As a result, an NP inherently marked as ACC cannot instantiate a SUBJ GF. Consequently, this NP cannot participate in alternations that result in a change of case, such as passivisation and causative-inchoative alternation. The inside-out constraint (OBJ^) of hypothesis 3 has the same effect. However, there are passivisable verbs in Modern Greek that head non-passivisable MWEs with a non-causative counterpart where the Fixed_NP is the subject. For instance, the MWE ανάβω τα λαμπάκια κάποιου (anavo ta labakia kapiu) 'I make somebody angry' does not have a passive counterpart (49a) although it is headed by a causative verb that has a passive counterpart in compositional language. However, the expression has a non-causative counterpart (49b) where the Fixed_NP *τα λαμπάκια* (ta labakia) turns up as a subject in the nominative case.

(49) a. * *Ανάφτηκαν   τα λαμπάκια   του   Πέτρου   από εμένα.*
          Anaftikan   ta labakia   tu   Petru   apo emena.
          turn.on.PASS the lights.ACC the.GEN Petros.GEN by   me

          'I made Petros angry.'

      b. *Άναψαν   τα λαμπάκια   του   Πέτρου.*
          Anapsan   ta labakia   tu   Petru.
          turn.on.ACT the lights.NOM the.GEN Petros.GEN

          'Petros got angry.'

In addition, there are causative/non-causative MWE pairs that are headed by different verbs such as the causative MWE (50a) and its non-causative counterpart (50b). Such examples suggest that the hypothetical constraint (OBJ^) originates from the causative form of the verb and not from the Fixed_NP. Furthermore, the use of Fixed_NP in titles as illustrated with example (51b)[6], in particular, the use of Fixed_NP that feature in verb MWEs that have no non-causative counterpart (51a), suggests that the Fixed_NP oriented approach should be abandoned.

(50) a. *Ρίχνω   τα μούτρα   μου.*
          Riχno   ta mutra   mu.
          drop.1SG the face.ACC mine

          'I suppress my dignity. '

      b. *Πέφτουν τα μούτρα   μου.*
          Peftun ta mutra   mu.
          fall.3SG the face.NOM mine

          'My dignity is suppressed .'

(51) a. *Πίνω το πικρό   ποτήρι.*
          Pino to pikro   potiri.
          drink the bitter.ACC glass.ACC

          'I have a difficult time.'

---

[6] The conjunction in (51b) ensures the NOM case of the Fixed_NP.

b. *το πικρό ποτήρι, ο   Αλέξης   και ο   Κυριάκος*
   to pikro potiri, o   Alexis   kie o   Kiriakos
   the bitter glass,   the Alexis.NOM and the Kiriakos.NOM

'the difficult time, Alexis and Kiriakos'
http://www.logiastarata.gr/2016/01/blog-post_194.html

We now turn to the verb predicate oriented hypotheses. Hypothesis 2 suggests that the verb assigns to the Fixed_NP some GF other than the OBJ GF. It would make sense to assume that Fixed_NP instantiates OBJ$_\theta$ if Fixed_NP occurred in ditransitive constructions exclusively, but it occurs with a large variety of verbs. In addition, OBJ$_\theta$ is restricted to themes; it would be risky to apply semantic roles on the idiomatic meanings of Fixed_NP and of verbs in MWEs. Furthermore, OBJ$_\theta$ cannot be replaced with a clitic but it can be omitted (Kordoni 2004). For all these reasons, the OBJ$_\theta$ GF is an unattractive hypothesis for Fixed_NP.

Hypothesis 1 suggests that OBJ is assigned to Fixed_NP and some feature of the type +/-PASSIVISES is defined on the lexical entry of the verb. This is not a semantic feature because a robust theory that attributes passivisation to verbal semantics is not available yet. On the other hand, such a feature is needed anyway in LFG, otherwise the passivisation lexical rule will apply to verbs like *σπάω* (spao) 'break' (1) that select a SUBJ and an OBJ.

However, hypothesis 1 is less principled than a GF-based approach. Features are dedicated to specific phenomena while GFs avail themselves to wider generalisations, for instance OBJ$_\theta$ has been used to encode the behavior of ditransitives and applicatives cross-linguistically (Bresnan & Moshi 1990). In the case of Fixed_NP, apart from passivisation there is a need to encode two more facts that do not characterise OBJ and cannot be stated as a property of non-passivisable verbs: first, only Fixed_NP introduced with a definite article can be replaced with a clitic in Modern Greek while the English Fixed_NP cannot be replaced with *it*, and second, Fixed_NP are obligatory in both languages.

In the light of the discussion above, one could be tempted to define a new GF that would be instantiated by Fixed_NP. Let us call this GF FIX. The facts we have seen so far that favor the new GF approach, and would be the defining features of FIX, are the following:

- Distributional/semantic: Fixed_NP can be found only with MWEs

- No passivisation: Fixed_NP do not appear as subjects of passive MWEs (very strong tendency)

- Replacement with a clitic: it is restricted to definite Fixed_NP only

- Optionality: Fixed_NP is hardly optional

- Cross-linguistic evidence: Similar behavior is observed in at least two languages, English and Modern Greek.

We have already alluded to the fact that the combined effect of the OBJ_θ and the proposed FIX is not enough to model the range of non-passivisable verbs. FIX could be assigned to Fixed_NP and, probably, to the objects of measurement verbs as well as, generally, to verbs whose object cannot be assigned some clear semantic role. However, it would seem awkward to lump the Modern Greek typically transitive but non-passivisable change of state verbs like *σπάω* (spao) 'break' (1) together with MWEs and measurement verbs; change of state verbs clearly assign the Proto-Patient semantic role to their objects while it is hard to pin down the role that is assigned by measurement verbs and MWEs to the accusative NPs that we discuss here. A clearly unwelcome feature of the GF approach is that it leaves room for more object-like GFs that block passivisation and are selected by rather specific types of predicate, given that OBJ_θ is selected by ditransitives and applicatives and FIX by MWE verbal heads only. Certainly, it would be preferable to keep the GF population small in size because GFs are primitive concepts of LFG (Dalrymple 2001).

Despite the problems discussed above, we would opt for FIX, because it is more principled since it generalises over properties of English and Modern Greek MWEs. Below, we will attempt to support our preference with more facts drawn from Modern Greek MWEs.

6 Words_With_Spaces and the FIX

Fixed_NPs comprise more complex phrasal structures than the ones we have seen so far. These may be of the type DETERMINER+ADJECTIVE+NOUN (51), NP.GEN+NOUN[7], or NOUN+NP.GEN or NOUN+PP (35). These MWEs do not passivise. (51), (52) can be replaced with a clitic within the same predication because Fixed_NP is introduced with the definite article while the NP in (35) is not.

(52) Έφαγαν τη σκόνη του Διαμαντίδη.
      Efayan ti skoni tu Διamantiδi.
      ate.3PL the dust.ACC the Diamantidis.GEN

      'They were overtaken by Diamantidis.'

---

[7]NP.GEN+NOUN can be free or fixed; (50) exemplifies a free genitive NP.

In fact, a wider range of fixed strings behave as single complements of the MWE verb (Samaridi & Markantonatou 2014). Here we will exemplify the idea with a predication structure.

The compositional equivalent of the fixed string in (53a) is that of an object that controls a predicative complement. The string *το ψωμί ψωμάκι* (to psomi psomaki) (53a) is fixed because its parts cannot be separated (53b) and no free XP can intervene (53c). At the same time, constituency diagnostics show that it is a constituent ((53a)-word order permutations, (53d)-temporal adverb interpolation) and can be questioned (53e). The fixed string is introduced with a definite article and can be replaced with a clitic in the context of the same MWE (53f). Therefore, *το ψωμί ψωμάκι* (to psomi psomaki) behaves like a Fixed_NP.

(53)   a.   *Λέμε   το   ψωμί   ψωμάκι.   / To   ψωμί   ψωμάκι   λέμε.*
            Leme   [to psomi psomaki].   / [To psomi psomaki] leme.
            call.1PL the bread little.bread

            'We are starving.'

       b.   * To psomi leme psomaki. / *Psomaki leme to psomi.

       c.   * *Λέμε   το   γλυκό ψωμί   καημένο   ψωμάκι.*
            Leme to   γliko psomi kaimeno   psomaki
            say   the sweat bread poor   little-bread

       d.   *Λέμε τώρα το   ψωμί   ψωμάκι.*
            Leme tora to   psomi psomaki.
            call   now the bread little-bread

            'We are starving now.'

       e.   *Τί   λέμε   τώρα; Το   ψωμί   ψωμάκι.*
            Ti   leme   tora? To psomi psomaki.
            what do.we.say now? the bread little-bread

       f.   *Λέμε   το   ψωμί   ψωμάκι;   Ναι, το λέμε.*
            Leme   to   psomi psomaki?   Ne, to leme.
            do.we.say the bread little-bread? yes, it we.say

            'Are we starving? Yes, we are.'

The fixed string *το ψωμί ψωμάκι* (to psomi psomaki) is a Word_With_Spaces (WWS) (Sag et al. 2002) that satisfies constituency diagnostics. If *το ψωμί ψωμάκι* (to psomi psomaki) is not treated as a WWS, additional constraints to block (53b) would be needed. Similar ideas have been discussed in Green et al. (2013), where the fixed parts of MWEs are represented as flat structures. In the examples above, the idiomatic predicate λέω (leo) 'call' assigns the FIX GF. Lack of a passive counterpart and clitic replacement follow from FIX normally.

To represent structures like (52), where a free genitive NP occurs as part of the fixed structure of the MWE, the WWS τη_σκόνη (ti_skoni) selects for a POSS Grammatical Function. The POSS function will allow for the representation of binding phenomena that are often found with MWEs. For instance, (50a) is an example of a MWE where the possessive pronoun that complements the WWS τα μούτρα (ta_mutra) is necessarily bound by the free subject of the idiomatic verb.

In a nutshell, the FIX GF seems to be instantiated exclusively by phrases headed by fixed strings, such as (53a), that may or may not be generated with the phrase structure rules devised for compositional structures. Along with other work on MWEs within the LFG framework (Attia 2006) we list fixed strings in the lexicon. Treating WWSs as lexical entries deals with the problem of generating noncompositional fixed strings while FIX captures passivisation and replacement with a clitic.

7 Conclusion

We have argued that verbal MWEs that contain direct complements of verbs headed by fixed strings cannot be captured with exactly the same syntactic machinery that has been developed for compositional structures. Despite appearances, fixed complements do not behave as direct or indirect objects with respect to a number of classical objecthood diagnostics. We argued that this special syntactic behaviour is identifiable at a syntactic functional level. If we are right, the syntactic apparatus that has been developed in LFG to represent the notion of "objecthood" in compositional structures has to be expanded to accommodate a new GF that we called FIX. The new GF is necessary for modeling a wide-spread type of MWEs.

Certainly, several issues are left for future research: the range of syntactic phenomena involving the strings that instantiate FIX (modification, alternations as they are illustrated in (49b), (50b) and (51b) and pose questions concerning the treatment of MWEs with a fixed subject), control phenomena and, probably, the modeling of the switch from MWE to compositional contexts that gives rise to joke/irony/pun effects –a phenomenon that might be modeled more easily in terms of WWSs and FIX.

Abbreviations

GF	grammatical function	NLP	Natural Language Processing
HPSG	Head-driven Phrase Structure Grammar	NP	noun phrase
		OBJ	object
LFG	Lexical Functional Grammar	OBJ$_\theta$	OBJECT$_\theta$
		POSS	possessive grammatical function
MWE	multiword expression		

References

Anastasopoulos, Antonis, Stella Markantonatou & Yanis Maistros. 2013. *Using object noun and clitic frequencies in the study of transitivity in Modern Greek*. The relative frequencies of nouns, pronouns, & verbs in discourse: an international workshop organised in the framework of the 10th Biennial Conference of the Association for Linguistic Typology, Leipzig, August 12-13.

Ariel, Mira. 2001. Accessibility theory: an overview. In Ted Sanders, Joost Schilperoord & Wilbert Spooren (eds.), *Text representation: Linguistic and psycholinguistic aspects*. Amsterdam: John Benjamins.

Attia, Mohammed A. 2006. Accommodating multiword expressions in an Arabic LFG Grammar. In Tapio Salakoski, Filip Ginter, Tapio Pahikkala & Tampo Pyysalo (eds.), *Advances in Natural Language Processing. Lecture Notes in Computer Science*, vol. 4139, 87–98. Berlin, Heidelberg: Springer.

Baker, Mark C. 2001. Phrase structure as a representation of "primitive"grammatical relations. In William Davies & Stanley Dubinsky (eds.), *Objects and other subjects: Grammatical functions, functional categories and configurationality*, vol. 52, 21–51. Dordrecht: Springer.

Bargmann, Sascha & Manfred Sailer. 2018. The syntactic flexibility of semantically non-decomposable idioms. In Manfred Sailer & Stella Markantonatou (eds.), *Multiword expressions: Insights from a multi-lingual perspective*, 1–29. Berlin: Language Science Press. DOI:10.5281/zenodo.1182587

Bresnan, Joan & Lioba Moshi. 1990. Object asymmetries in comparative Bantu syntax. *Linguistic Inquiry* 21(2). 147–185.

Cardinaletti, Anna & Micheal Starke. 1999. The typology of structural deficiency: A case study of the three classes of pronouns. In Henk van Riemdijk (ed.), *Clitics in the languages of Europe*, 273–290. Berlin: Mouton de Gruyter.

Dalrymple, Mary. 2001. *Lexical Functional Grammar* (Syntax and Semantics 34). San Diego, CA: Academic Press.

Dowty, David. 1990. Thematic Proto-Roles and argument selection. *Language* 67(3). 547–619.

Green, Spence, Marie-Catherine de Marneffe & Christopher D. Manning. 2013. Parsing models for identifying multiword expressions. *Computational Linguistics* 39(1). 7–23.

Gross, Maurice. 1998a. Les limites de la phrase figée. *Langage* 90. 7–23.

Gross, Maurice. 1998b. Sur les phrases figées complexes du français. *Langue française* 77. 47–70.

Hudson, Richard. 1992. So-called "double objects" and grammatical relations. *Language* 68(2). 251–276.

Joseph, Brian J. 1989. The benefits of morphological classification: On some apparently problematic clitics in Modern Greek. In Wolfgang U. Dressler, Hans Christian Luschützky, Oskar E. Pfeiffer & John Rennison (eds.), *Contemporary Morphology*, 171–181. Berlin: Mouton de Gruyter.

Kay, Paul & Ivan A. Sag. 2014. A lexical theory of phrasal idioms. http://www1.icsi.berkeley.edu/~kay/idioms-submitted.pdf, accessed 2018-4-19.

Kordoni, Valia. 2004. Modern Greek ditransitives in LMT. In Miriam Butt & Tracy Holloway King (eds.), *Proceedings of the 9th International Lexical Functional Grammar Conference (LFG 2004)*. Stanford, CA: CSLI Publications.

Kotzoglou, George. 2001. First notes on Greek subjects. *Reading Working Papers in Linguistics* 5. 175–199.

Pollard, Carl & Ivan A. Sag. 1994. *Head-Driven Phrase Structure Grammar*. Chicago & London: University of Chicago Press.

Radford, Andrew. 1988. *Transformational grammar: A first course* (Cambridge Textbooks in Linguistics). Cambridge, UK: Cambridge University Press.

Raskin, Victor. 1985. *Semantic mechanisms of humor*. Dordrecht & Boston & Lancaster: D. Reidel Publishing Company.

Sag, Ivan A., Timothy Baldwin, Francis Bond, Ann Copestake & Dan Flickinger. 2002. Multiword expressions: A pain in the neck for NLP. In *Proceedings of the 3rd International Conference on Intelligent Text Processing and Computational Linguistics (CICLing-2002)*, 1–15.

Samaridi, Niki & Stella Markantonatou. 2014. Parsing Modern Greek verb MWEs with LFG/XLE grammars. In *The 10th Workshop on Multiword Expressions (MWE 2014), Workshop at EACL 20*, 33–37. Gothenburg, Sweden.

Shi-Ching, Olivia Lam. 2008. *Object functions and the syntax of double object constructions in Lexical Functional Grammar*. Oxford: University of Oxford dissertation.

Thomas, Victoria Joanne. 2012. *Double object constructions and "bill" verbs in English*. University of Oxford Thesis for the MPhil in General Linguistics and Comparative Philology.

Tsimpli, Ianthi M. & Maria Mastropavlou. 2007. Feature interpretability in L2 acquisition and SLI: Greek clitics and determiners. In Helen Goodluck, Juana Liceras & Helmut Zobl (eds.), *The role of formal features in Second Language Acquisition*, 143–183. New York: Routledge.

Tsimpli, Ianthi M. & Stavroula Stavrakaki. 1999. The effects of a morphosyntactic deficit in the determiner system: The case of a Greek SLI child. *Lingua* 108. 31–85.

Chapter 8

Derivation in the domain of multiword expressions

Verginica Barbu Mititelu

Romanian Academy Research Institute for Artificial Intelligence

Svetlozara Leseva

Institute for Bulgarian Language, Bulgarian Academy of Sciences

Multiword expressions and derivation have rarely been discussed together, even though analyzing the interaction between them is of great importance for the study of each topic and, in general, for the study of the language and for Natural Language Processing. Derivation is a means of enriching the lexicon with both words and multiword expressions. Various types of derivation (suffixation, prefixation or both, as well as other derivational devices) can act upon either words or multiword expressions. The focus of our work here is the formation of multiword expressions from other multiword expressions via derivation. We analyze the morphological, syntactic and semantic aspects of this process, providing examples from Romanian and Bulgarian, languages, which belong to different families but have been in contact throughout their history. The study can be further extended with data from other languages. The perspective adopted here is paradigmatic, but the syntagmatic approach, which can only be mentioned as further work, will add to the quality of the analysis of facts: corpus data will contextualize the phenomena discussed here and offer quantitative information about them.

1 Introduction

Widely accepted as a difficult task to deal with, the identification of multiword expressions (MWEs) in processing natural languages becomes even more difficult when the MWEs are new creations in the language or even ad-hoc creations in

Verginica Barbu Mititelu & Svetlozara Leseva. 2018. Derivation in the domain of multiword expressions. In Manfred Sailer & Stella Markantonatou (eds.), *Multiword expressions: Insights from a multi-lingual perspective*, 215–246. Berlin: Language Science Press. DOI:10.5281/zenodo.1182601

the text as a result of the linguistic creativity of speakers, usually carrying an emotional load (1):[1]

(1) *a băga de seamă – băgător de seamă*   (RO)

'to pay attention to' – '(the one) who only watches without playing any role (in the action)'

In example (1) the latter MWE is derived from the former and carries a negative connotation.

While the interest in the origin of MWEs has been manifested in all languages, specialists have normally investigated the social, economic, ethnographic, and other aspects motivating the process of turning certain word combinations into MWEs. When the origins cannot be found in the national background, MWEs are attributed to other languages, so they are borrowings or linguistic calques. Another (language internal) source of MWEs can be found in the inventory of already existing MWEs. In this paper we focus on one type of MWE formation: derivation from other MWEs, as shown in (1). We put together two topics that have rarely been discussed together in the same study.

On the one hand, MWEs have been classified and characterized according to syntactic and morphological variability (Nunberg et al. 1994; Sag et al. 2002; Baldwin et al. 2003; Baldwin & Kim 2010, among others) and/or semantic decomposability (Nunberg et al. 1994; Baldwin et al. 2003, among others), as well as according to types of idiomaticity (Baldwin 2004; 2006, among others). From a morphological perspective, only inflection and the reflexive form of verbs were discussed for each type of MWE (Sag et al. 2002; Savary 2008).

On the other hand, derivation is a process defined as involving words (Marouzeau 1933): it is the process of creating new words out of existing ones, by means of attaching or detaching affixes to or from a stem respectively, the latter type being better known as back-formation. An example of derivation is the word *survival*, created by attaching the suffix *–al* to the stem *survive*. An example of back-formation is the verb *to back-form*, obtained from *back-formation* by removing the suffix *–ation*. However, derivation can act both on words and MWEs.

---

[1]As convention of writing:

(i) We adopt the use of the international two letter code of the country in which the language is spoken in front of each example to mark the language to which it belongs: RO for Romanian, BG for Bulgarian.

(ii) We show the base MWEs on the left and the derived MWEs on the right.

In the former case, it always results in a new word; in the latter, it creates either a new word or a new MWE, as we will show below.

In the literature dedicated to either of the two topics (derivation, MWEs), one can identify two predominant trends: on the one hand, the discussion about derivation has always implied that words are the output and only rarely MWEs; on the other hand, the discussion about MWEs has implied, from time to time, reference to derivation: this interest has also been expressed, although sporadically, in studies on phraseology, particularly in analyzing the behavior of idioms with respect to their derivational morphology.

In this chapter, we describe the way derivation affects MWEs, providing examples from Romanian and Bulgarian, languages which belong to different language families (Romance and Slavic, respectively) but have had a long history of contact. We focus on MWEs derived from other MWEs, highlighting morphological, syntactic and semantic modifications triggered by these transformations.

In both Romanian and Bulgarian, derivation is much more productive than compounding or other internal means of enriching the vocabulary. Moreover, progressive derivation is more frequent than back–formation. In both languages suffixation is the prevalent derivational means. Prefixation in Romanian is much less productive. Bulgarian has a very developed deverbal verb formation as verbal prefixes express aktionsart and the language has a rich Aktionsart system. Cases of prefixation were not found in our data involving cross–part–of–speech derivation. Derivation affects all content word classes, simple or compound words.

2 Types of lexemes derived from MWEs

When subject to derivation, MWEs can serve as bases for the creation of either other MWEs or words. We discuss these types in the subsections below. In our discussion, we will use the term BASE MWE to denote the MWE that serves as the input to the derivation process.

2.1 MWEs derived from MWEs

We offer here some examples of MWEs derived from MWEs, in both Romanian and Bulgarian:

(2) *a mustra cugetul*   (*pe cineva*)   – *mustrare de cuget*   (RO)
     to chide   the.conscience (on someone) – chiding   by conscience
     'to have remorse' – 'having remorse'

(3) *съвестта   гризе (някого)   – гризене на съвестта*   (BG)
     săvestta   grize (nyakogo) – grizene na săvestta
     the.conscience gnaws (someone) – gnawing of the.conscience
     'to have remorse' – 'having remorse'

(4) *cronică literară – cronicar literar*   (RO)
     'literary review' – 'literary reviewer'

(5) *моден дизайн – моден дизайнер*   (BG)
     moden dizayn – moden dizayner
     'fashion design' – 'fashion designer'

These examples show that different types of MWEs can feed derivations: idioms in (2) and (3), terms in (4) and compounds in (5).

One content word (usually the syntactic head) of the base MWE is subject to affixation: e.g. in (2) above *mustrare* (noun) is derived from the verb *a mustra* with the suffix *–re*; in (4) *cronicar* is derived from *cronică* (the head of the base MWE noun phrase) with the agentive suffix *–ar*. Likewise, in (3) the process of derivation is carried out by means of suffixation of the verb *гриза* (griza) 'gnaw' with the suffix *–не*, thus obtaining the deverbal noun *гризене* (grizene) 'gnawing', and in (5) the head noun *дизайнер* (dizayner) 'designer' is obtained from the noun дизайн, dizayn, 'design' by means of the agentive suffix *–ep*.

2.2 Words derived from MWEs

When one content word of the MWE is subject to affixation and the derived word has the semantic content of the base MWE, we regard this as words being derived from MWEs; the other words of the base MWE simply do not occur in the result of the derivation:

(6) *a face un lucru mușama – a mușamaliza*   (RO)
     to make a   thing oilcloth
     'to cover something up'

(7) *извадя (бизнес,   ...) на светло – изсветля*   *(бизнес,   ...)*   (BG)
     izvadya (biznes,   ...) na svetlo – izsvetlya   (biznes,   ...)
     bring.v (business, ...) to light   – make.brighter.v (business, ...)
     'to legalize (business, ...)'

(8) *a face la rotisor – rotisa*   (RO)
     'to cook in a rotisserie'

(9) *instalator de gaze – gazist*   (RO)
     'gas installer'

(10) *въздух под налягане – въздухар*   (BG)
     văzduh pod nalyagane – văzduhar

     'air under pressure' – 'an unreliable or incompetent person (especially
     one who pretends otherwise)'

This type of derivation involves semantic condensation as one of the content
words of the MWE, the one that carries most of the semantic load, takes up the
meaning of the whole. The word may be adapted morphologically to express
the relevant part of speech, for example by means of suffixation with a verbal
suffix, e.g. RO *–iza* (6), where the noun *muşama* 'oilcloth' yields the derivative
verb *muşamaliza*, by means of back–formation, e.g. (8) where the verb *rotisa* is
created from *rotisor*, or parasynthetically, e.g. BG *из–, –я* (7), where the nominalized adjective светло, svetlo, 'light' gives the verb *из–светл–я* (iz–svetl–ya)
'make brighter'. In addition, noun suffixes, such as the agentive suffixes RO *–ist*
(9) and BG *–ар* (10), express the semantic role of the derived noun.

These types of derivation seem to affect collocations (8), terms (9) and idioms
(6), (7), (10) alike. In Romanian linguistics, the phenomenon has been described
as very frequent and systematic (Groza 2011). However, no quantitative support
has been offered for these claims and, as a consequence, we will not adhere to
this estimation. In the Bulgarian literature, the specialists have remarked that
while dephraseologization (and semantic condensation) is a productive process
in the contemporary language, word–formation processes, including derivation,
are relatively rare (Blagoeva 2011). We will not investigate this phenomenon here.

3 Data selection and processing

In order to study the behavior of MWEs with respect to derivation, we worked
with an inventory of MWEs extracted from big Romanian and Bulgarian dictionaries containing MWEs.

For Romanian, this inventory was created starting from DELS (Dictionary of
Expressions, Idioms and Collocations) (Mărănduc 2010). The dictionary was automatically parsed, MWEs were extracted and those marked as archaic were eliminated, along with expressions, as they are unproductive with respect to deriva-

tion; for the remaining 11,158 MWEs (collocations and idioms) we looked for derivationally related MWEs by searching the web and manually inspecting the results. Only for about 500 MWEs could we find derivationally related MWEs. So, a first remark is the relatively low impact that derivation has on MWEs, at least judging from the Romanian data. This may be a reason why the two phenomena have rarely been discussed together.

The Romanian MWEs were preprocessed and annotated morphosyntactically: they were automatically tokenized, lemmatized, tagged for part-of-speech (PoS) and chunked using the TTL web service (Ion 2007). Each word form in the MWE was identified, lemmatized and a PoS tag containing information about its part of speech and morphosyntactic characteristics (number, gender, case, etc., depending on the PoS) was attached to it. Syntactic groups were identified and marked as such, they are called chunks and are useful for the analysis in §6.

The Bulgarian data were excerpted from a large electronic dictionary of MWEs (Stoyanova & Todorova 2014). Named entities were removed since they are unproductive with respect to the phenomena explored in this work. The remaining MWEs were inspected and other unproductive types, such as proverbs, sayings and other expressions, were also filtered out automatically, using as a filter the code of the relevant type of MWE. Finally, obsolete and dialect entries were manually removed. The resulting dictionary of 4,039 entries consists predominantly of verb idioms and support verb constructions. The number of entries reflects two facts: (i) many Bulgarian verbs form aspectual pairs, whose members are distinct lexemes with their own inflectional and derivational morphology; therefore, unless there are semantic restrictions to the contrary, two MWE entries (one headed by a perfective aspect verb and one by an imperfective aspect verb) were encoded in the dictionary; (ii) (to a lesser degree) prefixation is a regular process which creates new verbs. Although the prefixed verbs meaning is modified to a lesser or to a greater extent, a variant of the MWE headed by a prefixed verb is often formed, thus the word family of a verb idiom may include a number of derived verb idioms. In the dictionary we kept only the more frequent MWEs, derived through prefixation, basically those bearing resultative meaning, e.g. (15). We found derivational MWEs for 2,612 entries in the dictionary, with a great prevalence of deverbal MWEs. The data were additionally supplemented with examples collected by the authors, adding up to 2,725 pairs.

The MWEs were automatically tokenized, lemmatized and PoS-tagged using the Bulgarian Language Processing Chain (LPC) (Koeva & Genov 2011), which is available as a web service, and subsequently chunked using a stand-alone tool which uses the LPC output (Stoyanova et al. 2015). As a result, all the words in each MWE were marked with the relevant grammatical information, and the basic syntactic structure of the MWEs (head, dependent syntactic groups) was identified and marked explicitly.

4 Derivation types in the domain of MWEs

In this section we present the types of derivation detected in the domain of MWEs: progressive derivation by means of suffixes, prefixes or both, back-formation and zero-derivation.

4.1 Progressive derivation

The vast majority of derivation cases are **progressive** (i.e., MWEs are created by adding affixes to a word in a previously existent MWE). In Bulgarian and Romanian, these affixes can be suffixes, prefixes or both. Each subtype will be discussed in the subsections below.

4.1.1 Suffixation

In Romanian all 339 cases of progressive derivation are represented by **suffixation**. In Bulgarian almost all of the 2,704 instances of progressive derivation are accounted for by suffixation, with the exception of 10 cases of parasynthetic derivation. The productivity of the suffixes in the two languages is represented in Table 1.[2]

Other Romanian suffixes (*–a*, *–ime*, *–iza*) are much less productive in the set of pairs we dealt with, with only one or a maximum of two occurrences. In Bulgarian, other suffixes denoting events or results of events are instantiated with only a few examples in the data: *–еж* (three cases), *–ов* (one case), *–ица* (one case). The noun suffix *–ост*, which denotes properties, is found in three cases. Other agentive suffixes are *–ант/–ент* (two cases), *–ия* (two cases), *–ик* (one case). The suffixes *–ура*, *–ище*, *–ция* are found with institutions (one example per suffix).

There are cases when the same MWE serves as a derivational base for two different MWEs. There are two ways in which this can be achieved. The first one is through separate derivational paths. The derivative MWEs in (11) and (12) are formed through independent derivational processes:

---

[2] Abbreviations used in Table 1: Ag: Agent; Ev: Event; Instn: Institution; Instr: Instrument; L: Language; Re: Result; SVs: Semantic Values; St: State.

Table 1: Suffixes. Their productivity and semantics.

L	Suffix	P	SVs	Examples
RO	*–re*	305	Ev	*a–şi băga minţile în cap*, to insert one's minds into head, 'to come to reason' – *băgare a minţilor în cap*, inserting one's minds into head, 'coming to reason'
RO	*–(ă)tor*	18	Ag	*a face rele* 'to do bad things' – *făcător de rele* 'wrongdoer'
RO	*–ie*	7	St	*sărac lipit* 'dog poor' – *sărăcie lipită* 'extreme poverty'
			Ev	*călători de plăcere* 'to travel for pleasure' – *călătorie de plăcere* 'travelling for pleasure'
			Instn	*judecător de pace* 'justice of the peace' – *judecătorie de pace* 'the court of a justice of the peace'
RO	*–ătură*	4	Ev	*a–ţi arunca ochii* 'to cast a glance' – *aruncătură de ochi* 'glance'
BG	*–ne*	2,604	Ev, Re	*pisha istoriya*, to write history, 'to make history' – *pisane na istoriya* 'making of history'
BG	*–ba*	5	Ev, Re	*prodam na edro*, to sell in bulk, 'to wholesale' – *prodazhba na edro* 'a wholesale'
BG	*–ach*	42	Ag	*svalyam zvezdi*, to take down stars, 'to promise the moon' – *svalyach na zvezdi* 'one who promises the moon'
			Instr	*hvashtam brimki* 'to mend ladders/stitches (e.g. in stockings)' – *hvashtach na brimki* 'a tool for mending ladders'
BG	*–or/–er/–ir*	13	Ag	*komandvam parada*, to command the parade, 'to call the shots' – *komandir na parada* 'one who calls the shots'
BG	*–tel*	10	Ag	*stroya văzdushni kuli* 'to build castles in the air' – *stroitel na văzdushni kuli* 'one who builds castles in the air'
BG	*–ets*	4	Ag	*tărguvam na edro* 'to deal wholesale' – *tărgovets na edro* 'wholesaler'

(11) a. *a aduce laudă – aducere de laudă*   (RO)
         'to give praise' – 'giving praise'

      b. *a aduce laudă – aducător de laudă*   (RO)
         'to give praise' – 'the one who gives praise'

(12) a. *разбивам сърца – разбиване на сърца*   (BG)
         razbivam sărtsa – razbivane na sărtsa
         'to break hearts' – 'breaking of hearts'

      b. *разбивам сърца – разбивач на сърца*   (BG)
         razbivam sărtsa – razbivach na sărtsa
         'to break hearts' – 'heartbreaker'

The verb MWEs in (11) and (12) undergo suffixation and yield either an eventive noun (by means of the suffixes *–re* and *–не*, respectively) or an agentive one (by the suffixes *–tor* and *–ач*, respectively) in the derivationally related MWEs.

The second way to form two or more MWEs from the same source follows several steps along a single derivational path. We spotted six such instances in the Romanian data and three in Bulgarian (Table 2). Typologically, the examples are different: in Romanian, the noun–to–noun derivation yields antonyms. In Bulgarian, the derived nouns lexicalize different semantic roles in the eventuality denoted by the corresponding verb. Due to the small number of instances, no conclusions can be reached for either of the languages. More examples from

Table 2: Multiple derivations.

Language	Pattern	Productivity	Example
RO	V–N–N	3	*a şti carte*, to know book, 'to be educated' *ştiinţă de carte* 'education' *neştiinţă de carte* 'lack of education'
RO	V–A–A	3	*a şti carte*, to know book, 'to be educated' (*ştiutor de carte*, 'educated') *neştiutor de carte* 'uneducated'
BG	V–N$_{AGENT}$–N$_{LOCATION}$	3	*pera pari* 'to launder money' *perach na pari* 'money launderer' *perachnitsa na pari* 'a business involved in money laundering'

these languages (as well as from others) would help to better understand possible derivations.

Besides, as the verbs belonging to a given aspectual pair in Bulgarian are characterized by their own derivational morphology and derivational patterns, MWEs (just like single words) headed by different members of an aspectual pair may serve as a base for derived MWEs with similar semantics, e.g. the imperfective aspect verb gives rise to an eventive nominalization (13a) , while the perfective aspect counterpart yields a different deverbal MWE with an eventive (and possibly resultative) interpretation (13):

(13) a. *побеждавам по точки – побеждаване по точки* (BG)
pobezhdavam po tochki – pobezhdavane po tochki

'to outpoint, to outscore' – 'outpointing'

b. *победя по точки – победа по точки* (BG)
pobedya po tochki – pobeda po tochki

'to outpoint, to outscore' – 'outpointing'

4.1.2 Parasynthetic derivation

Another derivational device detected only in the Bulgarian data is parasynthetic derivation, when both a suffix and a prefix are attached to an existing word. All ten cases we found in the data represent derivations of verbs from adjectives:

(14) *гладен като вълк – огладнея като вълк* (BG)
gladen kato vălk – ogladneya kato vălk

'as hungry as a wolf' – 'to become as hungry as a wolf'

4.1.3 Prefixation

Prefixation alone rarely serves as a means for deriving new MWEs in Romanian (see the examples of consecutive derivation in Table 2). In the Bulgarian data MWEs resulting from verb to verb derivation (15), where prefixation is a productive process, were included as separate entries in the dictionary and will not be discussed further below:

(15) *пера пари – из–пирам пари* (BG)
pera pari – iz–piram pari

'to launder money' – 'to launder money up' (resultative meaning)

We made this decision because the derivationally related verb MWEs have different (although related) meanings and can themselves be subject to derivation, e.g. *пера пари* (pera pari) 'to launder money' – *пра–не на пари* (pra–ne na pari) 'money laundering', *из–пирам пари* (iz–piram pari) 'to launder money up' – *из–пира–не на пари* (iz–pira–ne na pari) 'money laundering', resultative meaning.

4.2 Back-formation

We found only one case of back-formation in Romanian, in which the verb *lucra* is derived from the noun *lucru* (16), and six cases in Bulgarian (17), all of which are neologisms:

(16)   *lucru de mână – a lucra de mână*   (RO)
       'handiwork' – 'to work by hand'

(17)   *промиване на мозъци – промивам мозъци*   (BG)
       promivane na mozătsi – promivam mozătsi

       'brainwash(ing))' – 'to brainwash' (example from Blagoeva 2008)

These data reflect a tendency noted in works on Bulgarian terminology and neology (Baltova 1986; Kolkovska 1993/1994; Kostova 2013, among others) concerning the creation of eventive nouns, in particular nouns ending in *–не* or ending in a verbal suffix followed by *–не* that do not have a verb counterpart. The corresponding verbs are often formed by back-formation (17) and the newly created verbs or verb MWEs can be subject to further derivations:

(18)   *промивам мозъци – промивач на мозъци*   (BG)
       promivam mozătsi – promivach na mozătsi

       'to brainwash' – 'brainwasher'

4.3 Zero-derivation (conversion)

Fifteen cases in the Bulgarian data represent the process of conversion (also called zero-derivation) in which the derived MWE is formed without the attachment of a suffix and/or a prefix and usually involves detachment of a grammatical affix such as the inflection:

(19) *ударя под кръста – удар под кръста*   (BG)
      udarya pod krăsta – udar pod krăsta
      'to hit below the belt' – 'a hit below the belt'

With Romanian MWEs, conversion manifests itself in two ways: (i) the participle form functions as an adjective with more than 150 verb MWEs; (ii) the supine form of several verb MWEs functions as a noun. The participle and the supine are homonymous non-finite verb forms. However, the discussion below will exclude such cases (and therefore zero-derivation) and will focus only on affixal derivation.

5 The morphological classes of the MWE heads involved in MWE derivation

The formal description and analysis of the basic syntactic structure of MWEs and their representation in the lexicon are important for the encoding and prediction of some of the major morphological and syntactic properties of the MWEs, such as: the components that are likely to inflect; the possibilities for modification by optional elements (optional elements are placed in brackets), e.g. BG *пера (мръсни) пари* (pera (mrăsni) pari) 'launder (dirty) money'; the possibility for eliding modifiers with no change in meaning (placed in square brackets in this example), e.g. *вдигам летвата [високо]* (vdigam letvata [visoko]) 'raise the bar [high]'; paradigmatic restrictions on agreement, on singular/plural forms, and so forth. Among others, the syntactic analysis makes it possible to predict the potential of MWEs for derivation and the structural changes that may take place in this process (see §6).

The majority of the Romanian pairs extracted from the DELS involve verbs as bases for derivation. The most frequent type is represented by pairs of MWEs displaying verb nominalization, while derivative pairs involving other parts of speech are much rarer (see Table 3).

For Bulgarian 2,725 derivative pairs were found. The difference in the number of pairs as compared with the initial set of 4,039 entries is due largely to the fact that the perfective aspect verbs in the set are very unproductive with respect to the derivational processes discussed. Deverbal noun formation accounts for the majority of cases (2,663), with much smaller numbers for the opposite noun to verb pattern, verb to adjective, adjective to verb, noun to noun, adjective to noun (see Table 3).

Table 3: Morphological alternations occurring in MWE derivations.

Stem PoS–derived word PoS	#RO examples	#BG examples	Example from the RO data	Example from the BG data
V–N	349	2,663	*a depune jurământul* 'to take the oath' *depunerea jurământului* 'taking the oath'	*potrivam rătse* 'to rub (one's) hands' *potrivane na rătse* 'rubbing of (one's) hands'
V–A	2	16	*a sări în ochi*, to jump into eyes, 'to be straightforward' *săritor în ochi*, jumping into eyes, 'straightforward'	*mălcha kato păn*, to keep silent like a log, 'to be as mute as a maggot/fish' *mălchaliv kato păn*, silent like a log, '(as) mute as a poker'
N–V	4	8	*semnal luminos* 'light signal' *a semnaliza luminos* 'to signal with lights'	*igra na nervi* 'a battle of nerves' *igraya na nervi* 'to lead a battle of nerves'
N–N	5	18	*judecător de pace* 'justice of the peace' *judecătorie de pace* 'the court of a justice of the peace'	*voenen prokuror* 'military prosecutor' *voenna prokuratura* 'military prosecutor's office'
A–N	4	10	*sărac lipit* 'dog–poor' *sărăcie lipită* 'extreme poverty'	*nisht duhom* 'poor in spirit' *duhovna nishteta* 'spiritual poverty'
A–V	–	10	–	*byal kato platno* 'as white as a sheet' *pobeleya kato platno* 'to become as white as a sheet'

6 Syntactic reorganizations resulting from derivations

Dependency Grammar is used as a syntactic framework for our discussion. In this framework, verbs admit subjects, complements and adjuncts, nouns (even those derived from verbs) admit modifiers and adjectives admit complements. Syntactic functions are understood as in Quirk et al. (1985).

Out of the total number of 414 Romanian pairs, fifty do not undergo any internal reorganization in the process of derivation; in Bulgarian this holds true for 54 out of the 2,725 pairs:

(20)   *agent de publicitate – agenție de publicitate*   (RO)
       'advertising agent' – 'advertising agency'

(21)   *военен прокурор – военна прокуратура*   (BG)
       voenen prokuror – voenna prokuratura

       'military prosecutor' – 'military prosecutor's office'

In (20), *de publicitate* receives the same syntactic analysis in both MWEs: it is a modifier of the nouns *agent* and *agenție*, respectively. In (21) the adjectives *военен* (voenen) 'military' and *военна* (voenna) 'military' which modify the head noun *прокурор* (prokuror) 'prosecutor' and *прокуратура* (prokuratura) 'prosecutor's office', respectively, have the same analysis.

The cases without syntactic reorganization include the noun to noun, verb to adjective and adjective to verb patterns. In the following sections we will deal with the other two structural types of MWEs found in the data, that is: verb to noun and noun to verb MWEs.

The syntactic structure of the base MWE determines whether the syntactic expression of a dependent phrase is obligatory. For instance, a direct object NP_{DO} ($_{DO}$ stands for direct object) that is not a fixed part of a base MWE but is licensed by a transitive verb, as illustrated below, is not an obligatory dependent of the derived MWE, while an internal argument that is a fixed part of the base MWE is an obligatory component of the derived MWE. For example, in BG, *пъхвам (някого) зад решетките* (păhvam (nyakogo) zad reshetkite) 'put (someone) behind bars', the internal argument position (NP_{DO}) is not a fixed part of the idiom; rather, it is an open position that is filled by a suitable entity. In the nominalization *пъхване (на някого) зад решетките* (păhvane (na nyakogo) zad reshetkite) 'putting (of someone) behind bars' the position corresponding to the direct object may be left empty. On the contrary, if the NP_{DO} is a fixed part of the MWE, it cannot be omitted, e.g. *кърша ръце* (kărsha rătse) 'wring hands' – *кършене на рьце* (kărshene na rătse) 'wringing of hands'. The syntactic structure of the base MWE also determines the word order of obligatory and non–obligatory components in the derived MWE (e.g. typically the object of the base MWE is closer to the deverbal noun than other base MWE components).

Next, we present the syntactic reorganizations observed in derived MWEs, as we found them in the available data for Romanian and Bulgarian. Their documentation facilitates text processing. Given the limited MWE dictionaries available, all knowledge facilitating the automatic morphosyntactic analysis of text is considered valuable. Below we offer rules that algorithms can use to process new MWEs which are derived from existing ones.

6.1 Verb PP or AdvP complement or adjunct – noun modifier

This pattern is observed when a verb MWE is related with a noun MWE via derivation (see (i1) below) or the other way round (i2). It accounts for 260 Romanian and 792 Bulgarian pairs:[3]

(i) (1) VP [V PP/AdvP] > NP [$N_{V-derived}$ PP/AdvP]
(2) NP [N PP/AdvP] > VP [$V_{N-derived}$ PP/AdvP]

The verb admits a prepositional phrase (PP) or an adverbial phrase (AdvP) functioning as a complement or an adjunct in the MWE, but it can also admit other modifiers placed out of the MWE. Through derivation, the constituents, except for the head word, preserve their syntactic category and internal structure, as can be noticed in (i), where the form of the modifying phrase is the same. Although semantically the dependent functions similarly in the NP and the VP, its syntactic role is different according to our analysis: when the head is a verb, we analyse the particular dependent as a complement or an adjunct and, when the head is a noun, we analyse it as a modifier.

Below we indicate the syntactic category (PP, AdvP) and the status (complement, adjunct, modifier) of the dependent phrases. Complement or adjunct status is determined with respect to the argument structure of the verb that heads the respective MWE.

In the verb MWE in (22), *de credință* is the prepositional object (i.e., a complement) of the reflexive verb *a se lepăda*, whereas in the noun MWE the same PP is a modifier of the noun *lepădare* derived from *a se lepăda* with the suffix *–re*. Likewise, in the BG verb MWE in (23) the Goal PP *в джоба* (v dzhoba) 'in the pocket' is the prepositional object of the verb *бъркам* (bărkam) 'thrust

---

[3]Patterns are enumerated in the text with Roman numbers.

one's hand', whereas, in the noun MWE, it functions as a modifier of the noun *бъркане* (bărkane) 'thrusting one's hand', derived from the verb *бъркам* (bărkam) by means of the suffix –*не*.

(22) *a se lepăda de credință – lepădare de credință* (RO)
      'to depart from the faith' – 'departing from the faith'

(23) *бъркам   в джоба   (на някого) – бъркане в джоба* (BG)
      bărkam   v dzhoba   (na nyakogo) – bărkane v dzhoba
      thrust.one's.hand.v in the.pocket (of someone)

      'to incur expenses (on someone)' – 'incurring of expenses'

The PP *în peniță* (24) is a modifier in the first MWE, and an adjunct of the verb in the second MWE and the verb is derived from the noun in the former MWE. In (25), the PP *под кръста* (pod krăsta) 'below the belt' is an adjunct of the verb in the first MWE and a modifier of the noun *удар* (udar) 'hit' in the second MWE and the noun is derived from the verb *ударя* (udarya) 'hit'.

(24) *desen în peniță – a desena în peniță* (RO)
      'pen drawing' – 'to draw in pen'

(25) *ударя под кръста – удар под кръста* (BG)
      udarya pod krăsta   – udar pod krăsta

      'to hit below the belt' – 'a hit below the belt'

In (26) the adverb *aminte* is a complement of the verb in the former MWE and a noun modifier in the latter. In (27) the adverb *отвисоко* (otvisoko) 'from above' is an adjunct of the verb *гледам* (gledam) 'look' in the former MWE and a noun modifier in the latter.

(26) *a lua aminte – luare aminte* (RO)
      'to take into consideration' – 'taking into consideration'

(27) *гледам отвисоко (някого / нещо) – гледане отвисоко* (BG)
      gledam otvisoko (nyakogo / neshto) – gledane otvisoko

      'to look down on (someone / something)' – 'looking down on (someone / something)'

In both languages derivation from a noun MWE to a verb MWE is much rarer:

(28) *игра   на нерви – играя на нерви*   (BG)
      igra   na nervi – igraya na nervi
      a.play of nerves – play.v   nerves
      'a battle of nerves' – 'to lead a battle of nerves'

6.2 Subject complement or object complement – noun modifier

In the Bulgarian data we detected a small number of verb MWEs that have a subject complement or an object complement (Quirk et al. 1985; Downing 2014) as part of their structure.[4] Syntactically, these complements are expressed as NPs, PPs or APs. We use the notation ($_{CS}$) for subject complements and ($_{CO}$) for object complements.

With this type of derivation, the verb MWE subject complement turns up as a modifier in the derived noun MWE (12 cases altogether). The derivation may be represented as in (ii).

(ii) VP [V NP$_{CS}$/PP$_{CS}$/AP$_{CS}$] > NP [N$_{V-derived}$ NP$_{CS}$/PP$_{CS}$/AP$_{CS}$]

The derivation involves a copular verb, such as *съм* (săm) 'be', *ставам* (stavam) 'become', *оставам* (ostavam) 'remain' or a verb that is not a typical copula (e.g., *отивам* (otivam) 'go') and admits a subject complement in the MWE. The deverbal noun (N$_{V-derived}$) derived from this verb heads the noun MWE, and the subject complement turns up as a post–modifier that preserves both its syntactic category and the type of syntactic linking to the head word. The examples below illustrate subject complements – PP$_{CS}$ (29), AP$_{CS}$ (30), N$_{CS}$ (31).

(29) *ставам   за смях   – ставане   за смях*   (BG)
      stavam   za smyah   – stavane   za smyah
      to.become for ridicule – becoming for ridicule

      'to become a laughing stock' – 'becoming a laughing stock'

(30) *ставам   разноглед – ставане   разноглед*   (BG)
      stavam   raznogled – stavane   raznogled
      to.become cross–eyed – becoming cross–eyed

      'to become confused or overwhelmed (by something)'

---

[4]A subject or an object complement is a constituent that does not represent a new participant but completes the predicate by adding information about the subject or the object referent, respectively (Downing 2014), e.g. *a separate notion* in *The country became a separate notion*, *young* in *He died young* (subject complement); *a genius* in *People considered Picasso a genius* (object complement).

(31) *отивам войник – отиване войник*   (BG)
       otivam voynik – otivane voynik
       go.v a.soldier – going a.soldier
       'to go into the army' – 'going into the army'

Derivations involving an object complement are exemplified with 44 cases in the data. It typically applies on transitive verbs (but verbs admitting PP–object do occur, see (iv), (34) below). The direct object (NP_{DO}) is licensed by the verb that heads the MWE but it is not a fixed part of the MWE. In the formal representation this NP_{DO} is enclosed in curly brackets "{}". As we are particularly concerned with the way the structure of the MWE is reorganized, we do not consider the expression of the MWE–external NP_{DO} if it occurs, although it obeys the rules applying to any direct object:

(iii) VP [V {NP_{DO}} $NP_{CO}/PP_{CO}/AP_{CO}$] > NP [$N_{V–derived}$ {PP [P NP_{DO}]} $NP_{CO}/$ PP_{CO}/AP_{CO}]

Here are examples of an MWE headed by a transitive verb with different realizations of the object complement: an AP_{CO} (32) and a PP_{CO} (33):

(32) *дера (някого) жив – дране жив (на някого)*   (BG)
       dera (nyakogo) zhiv – drane zhiv (na nyakogo)
       skin.v (someone) alive – skinning alive (of someone)
       'to cause great trouble (to someone)'

(33) *правя (някого / нещо) на решето – правене на решето*   (BG)
       pravya (nyakogo / neshto) na resheto – pravene na resheto
       make.v (someone / something) a riddle – making a riddle
       (на някого / нещо)
       (na nyakogo / neshto)
       (of (someone / something)
       'to make a lot of holes in someone/something, to riddle someone/something'

The lack of preposition insertion is a structural difference between the derivations involving subject/object complement NPs and direct object NPs, since the latter normally turn up as prepositional modifiers of the corresponding deverbal nouns. We leave aside the marginal cases of direct objects (not introduced by a preposition) that occasionally co–occur with the canonical form in formal administrative language.

The derivation involving an MWE headed by a verb that admits a prepositional object (PP$_O$) has the following representation (iv):

(iv) VP [V PP$_O$ AP$_{CO}$/NP$_{CO}$/PP$_{CO}$] > NP [N$_{V-derived}$ PP$_O$ AP$_{CO}$/NP$_{CO}$/PP$_{CO}$]

(34) exemplifies an MWE with a verb admitting a PP–object. The prepositional object retains its syntactic expression when it turns up as an NP modifier.

(34) *казвам на черното бяло – казване на черното бяло* (BG)
      kazvam na chernoto byalo – kazvane na chernoto byalo
      call.v   to the.black white – calling   to the.black white

      'to call black white' – 'an instance of calling black white'

6.3 Subject or direct object – noun modifier

This particular derivation pattern concerns fixed subject verb MWEs or fixed direct object verb MWEs. Unlike the cases discussed in §6.1 and §6.2, in this category nominalization triggers either insertion of a preposition (in both languages) that introduces the former subject or direct object as a prepositional noun modifier (see §6.3.1), or mapping of the former subject or direct object into a genitive modifier (only for Romanian) (see §6.3.2). We will reserve the term 'genitive modifier' for modifiers whose head noun is marked with the genitive case.

6.3.1 Subject or direct object – prepositional modifier

A subject (v) or a direct object (vi) in a verb MWE turns up as a prepositional modifier of the corresponding deverbal noun that heads the corresponding noun MWE. In (v1) and (vi1) a noun MWE is derived from a verb MWE, while in (v2) and (vi2) a verb MWE is derived from a noun MWE.

(v) (1) NP$_S$ V > NP [N$_{V-derived}$ PP[P NP$_S$]]
     (2) NP [N PP[P NP$_S$]] > NP$_S$ V$_{N-derived}$

(vi) (1) VP [V NP$_{DO}$] > NP [N$_{V-derived}$ PP [P NP$_{DO}$]]
      (2) NP [N PP [P NP$_{DO}$]] > VP [V$_{N-derived}$ NP$_{DO}$]

There are eight pairs in Romanian and seventy-five in Bulgarian involving the subject, and thirty-two pairs in Romanian and 1,732 in Bulgarian involving the direct object.

In Romanian the preposition *de* is always used and Bulgarian usually adds the preposition *на*. Both prepositions can be glossed in English with *of*. In Bulgarian, other prepositions may occur, generally when the noun is derived with a suffix other than *–не* or *–ние* (the prevalent suffixes for eventive and/or resultative deverbal nouns) or by other derivational means, e.g. zero-derivation, *обичам* (obicham) 'to love' – *обич* (obich) 'love'.

We repeat (2) and (3) as (35) and (36), respectively, in order to exemplify a case where the subject of a verb MWE corresponds to a prepositional modifier of the deverbal noun that heads the derived noun MWE. The subjects of the verb MWEs (*cugetul* and *съвестта* (săvestta)) correspond to the prepositional modifiers of the deverbal nouns *mustrare* and *гризене* (grizene) which are derived from the verbs *mustra* and *гриза* (griza) respectively.

(35)   *a mustra cugetul*   *(pe*   *cineva)*   – *mustrare de*   (RO)
     to chide   consciousness (ObjMarker somebody) – chiding   by
     cuget
     consciousness
     'to have remorse' – 'having remorse'

(36)   *съвестта*   *гризе (някого)*   – *гризене на съвестта*   (BG)
     săvestta   grize (nyakogo) – grizene   na săvestta
     the.consciousness gnaws (someone) – gnawing of the.consciousness
     'to have remorse' – 'having remorse'

(37) and (38) exemplify the case where the direct object of the verb MWE corresponds to a prepositional modifier of the deverbal noun that heads the derived noun MWE (derived from the verb) of the noun MWE. The direct objects *carte* and *локуми*, lokumi correspond to the prepositional modifiers of the (negative) adjective *(ne)știutor* and the noun *разтегач* (raztegach) respectively, which have been derived from the verbs *ști* and *разтягам* (raztyagam) respectively.

(37)   *a ști*   *carte – (ne)știutor*   *de carte*   (RO)
     to know book – (not)knowing of book
     'to be educated' – '(un)educated'

(38)   a. *разтягам локуми*   (BG)
       raztyagam lokumi
       'to spin yarn, to tell tales'

b. *разтегач на локуми* (BG)
   raztegach na lokumi
   spinner   of yarn
   'yarnspinner'

As noted in §6.2, when the direct object is not a fixed part of the MWE, it may be left unexpressed. This is not the case with direct objects that are fixed parts of base MWEs: they are neither left out nor replaced with a possessive pronoun.

Apart from a direct object, the MWEs in this and in other categories may have other constituents, e.g. (an)other complement(s), such as a prepositional object or an adjunct. These constituents preserve their syntactic category and the syntactic link to the head word, but assume a different syntactic status (similarly to what was presented in §6.1.).

(39) *a despica firul   în patru – despicarea firului   în patru* (RO)
     to split   the.hair in four – splitting   of.a.hair in four
     'to make small and overly fine distinctions'

(40) *цепя   стотинката на две – цепене   на стотинката на две* (BG)
     tsepya stotinkata   na dve – tsepene na stotinkata   na dve
     split.v the.penny   in half – splitting of the.penny   in half
     'to be very stingy'

In (39) and (40), *în patru* 'in four' and *на две* (na dve) 'in half' are PPs functioning as adjuncts in the VP and as modifiers in the derived NPs.

In the Bulgarian data we found MWEs headed by verbs that take a direct object and an object complement that are both part of the MWE (three pairs). The construction has the following form (vii):

(vii) VP [V NP$_{DO}$ AP$_{CO}$/NP$_{CO}$/PP$_{CO}$] > NP [N$_{V-derived}$ PP [P NP$_{DO}$] AP$_{CO}$/NP$_{CO}$/PP$_{CO}$]

The syntactic status of the MWE constituents in the derived structure is predictable: in the noun MWE, the NP$_{DO}$ constituent of the base verb MWE corresponds to a modifier introduced by a preposition (*на*) and the object complement phrase of the base MWE turns up as a modifier of the derived MWE that is expressed in the same way: as an AP in (41) – *развързани* (razvărzani) 'untied', as an NP in (42) *бяло* (byalo) 'white' and as a PP in (43) – *с истинските им имена* (s istinskite im imena) 'by their proper names':

Verginica Barbu Mititelu & Svetlozara Leseva

(41) *оставям ръцете (на някого) развързани – оставяне на* (BG)
ostavyam rătsete (na nyakogo) razvărzani – ostavyane na
leave.v the.hands (of someone) untied – leaving of
ръцете (на някого) развързани
rătsete (na nyakogo) razvărzani
the.hands (of someone) untied

'to untie someone's hands' – 'untying someone's hands'

(42) *наричам черното бяло – наричане на черното бяло* (BG)
naricham chernoto byalo – narichane na chernoto byalo
call.v the.black white – calling of the.black white

'to call black white' – 'an instance of calling black white'[5]

(43) *наричам нещата с истинските им имена – наричане на* (BG)
naricham neshtata s istinskite im imena – narichane na
нещата с истинските им имена
neshtata s istinskite im imena

'call things by their proper names' – 'calling things by their proper names'

6.3.2 Subject or direct object – genitive modifier

In this case the subject or the direct object of the verb MWE corresponds to a genitive modifier in the derived MWE. The reorganization may be represented as (viii) and (ix) for the subject and the object, respectively:

(viii) $NP_S\ V > NP\ [N_{V-derived}\ NP_{S-Genitive}]$

(ix) $VP\ [V\ NP_{DO}] > NP\ [N_{V-derived}\ NP_{DO-Genitive}]$

We encountered 12 MWEs described by (viii) in our data. As shown in (44), the subject *întunericul* corresponds to the genitive modifier of the noun *lăsarea* derived from the verb *lăsa*:

---

[5]The expression in (42) is synonymous to the one in (34). The structural difference is due to the different syntactic properties of the synonymous verbs казвам, kazvam, 'call' and наричам, naricham, 'call': казвам takes a PP-object in the respective sense, while наричам takes an NP object.

(44) *se   lasă   întunericul   – lăsarea   întunericului*   (RO)
      REFL lower the.darkness – lowering of.the.darkness
      'it is getting dark' – 'the fact of getting dark'

Forty–six pairs display the type of derivation where the direct object of the verb MWE corresponds to a genitive modifier in the noun MWE (45):

(45) *a băga zâzanie   – băgarea   zâzaniei*   (RO)
      to insert dissension – insertion of.dissension
      'to sow dissent' – 'the sowing of dissent'

The direct object *zâzanie* corresponds to a genitive modifier of the noun *băgarea*, derived from the verb *a băga*.

6.4 Adjunct – adjectival modifier

In this case, the adjunct (either a prepositional or an adverb phrase) modifying the verbal head of an MWE corresponds to an adjectival phrase in a noun MWE derived from a verb MWE (see (x1) below) or vice versa – a verb MWE is derived from a noun MWE and the adjective modifier in the noun MWE corresponds to an adjunct (either a prepositional or an adverb phrase) in the verb MWE (see (x2) below). This structure, represented in (x), was detected in six Romanian and sixteen Bulgarian pairs.

(x) (1) VP [V PP/Adv(P)] > NP [$N_{V-derived}$, A(P)]
     (2) NP [$N_{V-derived}$, A(P)] > VP [V PP/Adv(P)]

In Romanian the modifying adjective usually occurs after the modified noun. The normal position of the modifier in Bulgarian is to the left of the modified noun. The comma in (x) is used for signalling the possibility of having the modifier and the modified noun in either order with respect to each other.

Here are some examples of this type of syntactic reorganization:

(46) *arest preventiv – a aresta preventiv*   (RO)
      'preventive detention' – 'to subject to preventive detention'

(47) *честна игра – играя честно*   (BG)
      chestna igra – igraya chestno
      'a fair play' – 'to play fairly'

In (46) *preventiv* is an adjective modifying the noun *arest* in the first MWE and an adverb modifying the verb *aresta*, derived from *arest*. Likewise, in the BG example (47), честна (chestna) 'fair' is the adjectival modifier of the noun игра (igra) 'play' and честно (chestno) 'fairly' is the adverb modifier of the verb играя (igraya) 'play'.

An example of a derivation of a noun MWE with an adjective modifier (*трезва* (trezva) 'straight') from a verb MWE with an adverb (*трезво* (trezvo) 'straight') is shown in (48):

(48)   мисля трезво – трезва мисъл   (BG)
        mislya trezvo – trezva misăl
        'to think straight' – 'straight thinking'

Examples (46), (47) and (48) involve an adverb modifier in the verb MWE. The other type of construction presented in (x) (involving a PP adjunct) is exemplified by (49):

(49)   търгувам на едро – едра търговия   (BG)
        tărguvam na edro – edra târgoviya
        'to deal wholesale' – 'wholesaling'

The PP modifier *на едро* (na edro) 'big/in bulk' of the verb MWE *търгувам на едро* (tărguvam na edro) 'to deal wholesale' corresponds to the adjective modifier *едра* (edra) 'big' of the noun MWE *едра търговия* (edra târgoviya) 'wholesaling'. Note that variants are possible where the PP adjunct of the verb MWE becomes a PP post-modifier in the noun MWE; these cases fall under §6.1.

Table 4 sums up the data presented in §6, along with their share (in percentage) in the overall number of cases that undergo syntactic reorganization (364 for Romanian and 2,671 for Bulgarian).

Several conclusions can be drawn. The MWEs in which the fixed base MWE subject corresponds to a fixed PP modifier in the derived MWE or vice versa (§6.3.1) have a very similar share in the two languages and, as the numbers show, the construction is relatively rare. The same holds for verb MWE adjuncts that turn up as adjectival modifiers or vice versa (§6.4). The cases involving subject complements or object complements (§6.2) are found only in Bulgarian. Still, this pattern is potentially productive as the head verbs involved in it are very common (e.g. *make/do*). In Romanian, the correspondence between a subject or an object and a genitive modifier (§6.3.2) is more common than the correspondence to a PP modifier (§6.3.1).

Table 4: Distribution of Romanian and Bulgarian MWEs across types.

Type	No. of RO examples	No. of examples	RO data %	BG data %
§6.1 PP/AdvP	260	792	71.2%	29.65%
§6.2 Subject/object complement	0	56	0%	2.1%
§6.3.1 Subject	8	75	2.5%	2.81%
§6.3.1 Object	32	1,732	8.8.%	64.84%
§6.3.2 Subject	12	0	3.3%	0%
§6.3.2 Object	46	0	12.63%	0%
§6.4 Adjunct	6	16	1.65%	0.6%

There is a striking difference with respect to the prevalent base MWE structure in each of the languages. In Romanian the most frequent construction is verb–prepositional object/adjunct (§6.1), while the verb–direct object construction is quite uncommon (§6.3.1). In Bulgarian the most frequent type is verb–direct object (§6.3.1); verb–prepositional object/adjunct (§6.1) is also typical, although there are twice as many verb–direct object constructions. This points to a significant difference in the syntactic expression of complements (as reflected in the structure of MWEs); PP objects are by far the preferred choice in Romanian, while in Bulgarian both direct objects and PP objects are common, with a marked preference for the former.

7 Semantics of the derivational patterns

In this section we present the semantic aspects of the MWEs that involve derivation. Although we refer to the semantics of the base MWE, we are more interested in the semantics of the derived MWEs. Tables 5 and 6 offer an overview of the derived MWE semantics.[6]

In Romanian, the great majority of the base MWEs (349) designate events. This remark correlates with the data in Table 4, where most base MWEs are verbs. Furthermore, the derived nominalizations (mostly with the suffix –*re*) also denote events (322 cases); this correlates with the number of V–N pairs in Table 3.

---

[6]For verb–noun pairs we used the inventory of morpho–semantic relations from PWN (Fellbaum et al. 2009), but we added to it some roles whenever they proved necessary.

Table 5: Semantics of the base and the derived MWEs. Frequencies and examples.

Language	Base MWE	Derived MWE	Occurrences	Examples
RO	Event	Event	322	*a cădea în păcat* 'to fall into sin' *cădere în păcat* 'falling into sin'
BG	Event	Event	2,590	*promivam mozătsi* 'to brainwash' *promivane na mozătsi* 'brainwash'
RO	Event	Agent	18	*a vâna zestre* 'to hunt dowry' *vânător de zestre*, hunter of dowry, 'fortune hunter'
BG	Event	Agent	53	*promivam mozătsi* 'to brainwash' *promivach na mozătsi* 'one who does brainwashing'
RO	State	State	11	*a mustra cugetul (pe cineva)* 'to have remorse' *mustrare de cuget* 'having remorse'
BG	State	State	12	*zhiveya po tsarski* 'to live regally' *zhivot po tsarski* 'a regal life'
RO	Event	Instrument	3	*arunca flăcări* 'to throw flames' *aruncător de flăcări*, thrower of flames, 'flamethrower'
BG	Event	Instrument	3	*razbărkvam karti* 'to shuffle cards' *razbărkvach na karti* 'card shuffler'
RO	State	Experiencer	3	*a voi binele* 'to wish well' *voitor de bine*, wisher of well, 'well–wisher'
RO	Event	Distance	3	*arunca cu băţul* 'to throw with a stick' *aruncătură de băţ* 'as far as the stick can be thrown'
BG	Event	Institution	5	*kova zakoni*, forge laws, 'to create and promulgate laws' *kovachnitsa na zakoni*, smithy of laws, 'the parliament'

Table 6: Semantics of the base and the derived MWEs. Frequencies and examples.

Language	Base MWE	Derived MWE	Occurrences	Examples
RO	Job	Institution	8	*judecător de pace* 'justice of the peace' *judecătorie de pace* 'the court of a justice of the peace'
BG	Job	Institution	3	*voenen prokuror* 'military prosecutor' *voenna prokuratura* 'military prosecutor's office'
RO	Event	Vehicle	1	*a vâna submarine* 'to hunt for submarines' *vânător de submarine*, hunter of submarines, 'a vessel for locating and attacking submarines'
RO	Result	Action	1	*lucru de mână* 'handiwork' *a lucra de mână* 'to work by hand'
RO	Artefact	Event	2	*desen în peniță* 'pen drawing' *a desena în peniță* 'to draw in pen'
RO	Event	Characteristic	2	*a sări în ochi*, to jump into eyes, 'to be straightforward' *săritor în ochi*, jumping into eyes, 'straightforward'
BG	Event	Characteristic	8	*rabotya kato vol*, work like an ox/horse, 'to work hard' *rabotliv kato vol*, as hard–working as an ox, 'very hard–working'
BG	State	Characteristic	8	*mălcha kato păn*, keep silent like a log, 'to be as mute as a maggot/fish' *mălchaliv kato păn*, silent like a log, '(as) mute as a maggot/fish'
BG	Inchoative state	Characteristic	10	*gladen kato vălk* 'as hungry as a wolf/bear' *ogladneya kato vălk* 'to become as hungry as a wolf/bear'
BG	Job	Agent	18	*softuerno inzhenerstvo* 'software engineering' *softueren inzhener* 'software engineer'

The Bulgarian data also support the productivity and regularity of the derivation of eventive nominalizations (2,590) predominantly with the suffix *–не*. Another interesting tendency (though represented by few examples), especially with respect to neologisms, is the back–formation of verbs from nouns. The other semantic types encountered with derived MWEs constitute a small number of the overall data. The derivatives such as agents, experiencers, instruments and locations are derived primarily from VP [V NP_{DO}] MWEs, and less frequently from VP [V PP/AdvP]. No examples were found for such nouns derived from MWEs with the following syntactic structure: NP_S V or VP [V $NP_{CS}/PP_{CS}/AP_{CS}$].

The productivity of event nominalization is not unexpected, because in the process of MWE-to-MWE derivation the majority of cases account for idiomatic (partial) predicate–argument structures. As the structure of eventive nominalizations may reflect the argument structure of the base verb (Grimshaw 1990), it readily renders these idiomatic structures. The frequency of use of eventive nominalizations, whether single words or MWEs, is substantiated by the fact that they make it possible to refer to an action/event regardless of its doer and the time of occurrence (as expressed by verbal categories) (Pometkova 2006), and hence they may be used interchangeably with the verb-headed construction, or even may be preferred contextually in certain cases or in certain registers, such as scientific discourse.

In Romanian, the number of nominalizations increases greatly (by almost 200 cases in our data) when taking into account supine forms of verbs which, via conversion, become nouns; and the rest of the MWE behave, in these cases, similarly to the cases displaying affixal derivation, i.e. almost the same types of syntactic changes occur. Moreover, supine nouns are (for more than 150 cases in our data) alternatives to derived nominalizations, with a semantic difference: Cornilescu (2001) maintains that *–re* nominalizations tend to express results, while supines express events.

As the data show, other types of verb–noun derivational patterns, such as the ones resulting in agents, experiencers, instruments, locations and so forth, are significantly fewer in number. In our opinion, the semantic grounds for this phenomenon is that the situations described by the respective verb MWEs frequently do not conceptualize a particular type of agent, experiencer or instrument and so forth that needs to be lexicalized. Moreover, in terms of their semantic and syntactic properties, these types of nouns do not as readily inherit and express the base verb arguments and/or adjuncts. This is supported by the fact that when the need arises for expressing the relevant agentive or instrumental, etc. meaning, participle–headed constructions are preferred, at least in Bulgarian (50).

(50) *вземам решение – вземащ решение*   (BG)
      vzemam reshenie – vzemasht reshenie

      'to make a decision' – '(the one) making a decision'

These participial constructions may be either contextually used or may undergo nominalization and lexicalization.

Besides, another word-formation device that is also frequent is compounding, in which case the arguments/adjuncts are incorporated in the word structure. Here are some examples of one-word compounds that have MWE counterparts in the data e.g. *сърцеразбивач* (sărtserazbivach) 'heartbreaker', *миторазбивач* (mitorazbivach) 'mythbuster', *кодоразбивач* (kodorazbivach) 'codebreaker', *монетосекач* (monetosekach) 'coiner/minter', etc.

8 Conclusions

Putting MWEs and derivation together, we notice that derivation affects MWEs, creating either words or other MWEs. The productivity of this phenomenon seems to depend on language characteristics: Bulgarian, a language with aspect, allows for more cases of derivation than Romanian, which lacks aspect. Another factor influencing productivity is the data set: Romanian DELS lacks terms, which do occur in the Bulgarian dictionary and are productive in terms of derivation, serving the need for expressing different actors, instruments, objects, places, etc. within a domain of activity.

We have presented data from Bulgarian and Romanian. However, derivation has been reported to act upon MWEs in other languages: Piela (2007) discusses examples of words created from idioms and argues that this process is productive in Polish; in Russian, the process of creating MWEs from MWEs seems to be the most productive internal means of MWE formation (Ermakova et al. 2015). We can conclude that MWEs are subject to derivation in more languages and comparing and contrasting them from such a perspective can be of linguistic interest.

9 Acknowledgements

Most part of the work reported here has been carried out within the project PARSing and Multiword Expressions (PARSEME) IC1207 COST Action. Another part has been carried out within the joint project "Enhanced Knowledge Bases for Bulgarian and Romanian" of the Institute for Bulgarian Language, Bulgarian

Academy of Sciences, and the Research Institute for Artificial Intelligence, Romanian Academy.

We would like to thank Ivelina Stoyanova and Maria Todorova for providing the Bulgarian MWE dictionary in electronic form, Ivelina Stoyanova for the automatic processing of the Bulgarian data, Cătălina Mărănduc for kindly providing us with the electronic version of DELS and Cătălin Mititelu for the automatic processing of the Romanian data.

Last but not least, we are grateful to the anonymous reviewers of the paper and to the editors for their comments on the previous versions of the paper and for their suggestions that helped us to improve its quality. We also thank Judith Elver for being kind enough to proofread this paper on very short notice.

Abbreviations

AG	Agent	INSTR	Instrument
BG	Bulgarian	L	Language
LPC	Bulgarian Language Processing Chain	POS	part of speech
		RE	Result
DELS	Dictionary of Expressions, Idioms and Collocations	RO	Romanian
		SVS	Semantic Values
EV	Event	ST	State
INSTN	Institution	V	Verb (in the glosses)

References

Baldwin, Timothy. 2004. *Multiword expressions. Advanced course.* Australasian Language Technology Summer School (ALTSS 2004). Sydney, Australia.

Baldwin, Timothy. 2006. *Compositionality and multiword expressions: Six of one, half a dozen of the other.* Invited talk given at the COLING/ACL'06 Workshop on Multiword Expressions: Identifying & Exploiting Underlying Properties.

Baldwin, Timothy, Colin Bannard, Takaaki Tanaka & Dominic Widdows. 2003. An empirical model of multiword expression decomposability. In *Proceedings of the ACL 2003 Workshop on Multiword Expressions: Analysis, Acquisition and Treatment*, vol. 18, 89–96. Sapporo.

Baldwin, Timothy & Su Nam Kim. 2010. Multiword expressions. In Nitin Indurkhya & Fred J. Damerau (eds.), *Handbook of Natural Language Processing*, 2nd edn., 267–292. Boca Raton: CRC Press.

Baltova, Yulia. 1986. Za nyakoi yavleniya i tendentsii v izgrazhdaneto na leksi-kalnata sistema na savremenniya balgaski knizhoven ezik. In *Vaprosi na savre-mennata balgarska leksikografiya i leksikologiya*, 74–80. Sofia: BAS Publishing House.

Blagoeva, Diana. 2008. Novi frazeologichni kalki v balgarskiya ezik (v sapostavka s drugi slavyanski ezitsi). In *Izsledvaniya po frazeologiya, leksikologiya I leksiko-grafiya*, 149–153. Sofia: Prof. M. Drinov Publishing House.

Blagoeva, Diana. 2011. Defrazeologizatsiyata kato iztochnik na leksikalni i seman-tichni inovatsii v savremenniya balgarski ezik. In *Ezikovedski izsledvaniya v chest na Prof. Siyka Spasova-Mihaylova*, 139–151. Sofia: Prof. M. Drinov Pub-lishing House.

Cornilescu, Alexandra. 2001. Romanian nominalizations: Case and aspectual structure. *Journal of Linguistics* 37(3). 467–501.

Downing, Angela. 2014. *English grammar: A university course*. London & New York: Routledge.

Ermakova, Elena Nicolayevna, Natalia Nikolaevna Zolnikova, Guzel Chakhva-rovna Faizullina, Milyausha Sakhretdinovna Khasanova & Tatiana Nikolaevna Khlyzova. 2015. Derivation and the derivational space in Phraseology as a prob-lem of contemporary language development. *Mediterranean Journal of Social Sciences* 6. 335–340.

Fellbaum, Christiane, Anne Osherson & Peter E. Clark. 2009. Putting semantics into WordNet's "morphosemantic"links. In Zygmunt Vetulani & Hans Uszko-reit (eds.), *Human Language Technology. Challenges of the Information Society: Third Language and Technology Conference, LTC 2007. Revised selected papers*, 350–358. Poznan, Polland.

Grimshaw, Jane. 1990. *Argument structure*. Cambridge, MA: MIT Press.

Groza, Liviu. 2011. *Probleme de frazeologie: studii, articole, note*. Editura Univer-sității din București.

Ion, Radu. 2007. *Word Sense Disambiguation Methods Applied to English and Ro-manian*. Romanian Academy, Bucharest dissertation.

Koeva, Svetla & Angel Genov. 2011. Bulgarian language processing chain. In *Pro-ceedings of Integration of Multilingual Resources and Tools in Web Applications. Workshop in conjunction with GSCL*, vol. 26.

Kolkovska, Siya. 1993/1994. Slovoobrazuvane na imena za deystviya ot otimenni glagoli (s ogled na terminologiyata). *Balgarski ezik* 4. 478–480.

Kostova, Nadya. 2013. Novite imena za deystviya v balgarskiya ezik i tyahnoto leksikografsko predstavyane. In Diana Blagoeva, Sia Borisova Kolkovska &

Margarita Lishkova (eds.), *Problemi na neologiyata v slavyanskite ezitsi*, 77–108. Sofia: Prof. M. Drinov Publishing House.

Mărănduc, Cătălina. 2010. *Dicționar de expresii, locuțiuni și sintagme ale limbii române*. București: Corint.

Marouzeau, Jules. 1933. *Lexique delà terminologie linguistique*. Paris: Librairie orientaliste Paul Geuthener.

Nunberg, Geoffrey, Ivan A. Sag & Thomas Wasow. 1994. Idioms. *Language* 70(3). 491–538.

Piela, Agnieszka. 2007. Od Frazeologizmu do derywatu. *LingVaria* II 1(3). 41–48.

Pometkova, Yana. 2006. Spetsifikatsiya na konstruktsiite s otglagolno sashtestvitelno ime vav funktsiyata na podlog v nauchnata rech. In *Sbornik Yordanka Marinova. Izsledvaniya po sluchay neyniya sedemdesetgodishen yubiley*, 276–284. V. Tarnovo: Sv. sv. Kiril i Metodiy University Press.

Quirk, Randolph, Sidney Greenbaum, Geoffrey Leech & Jan Svartvik. 1985. *A comprehensive grammar of the English language*. Longman.

Sag, Ivan A., Timothy Baldwin, Francis Bond, Ann Copestake & Dan Flickinger. 2002. Multiword expressions: A pain in the neck for NLP. In *Proceedings of the 3rd International Conference on Intelligent Text Processing and Computational Linguistics (CICLing-2002)*, 1–15.

Savary, Agata. 2008. Computational Inflection of MultiWord Units. A contrastive study of lexical approaches. *Linguistic Issues in Language Technology* 1(2). 1–53.

Stoyanova, Ivelina, Svetlozara Leseva & Svetla Koeva. 2015. *Partial syntactic analysis of Bulgarian*. Paisievi chetenia, Plovdiv, 30–31 October 2015.

Stoyanova, Ivelina & Maria Todorova. 2014. Razrabotvane na rechnitsi ot sastavni edinitsi za balgarski. In Svetla Koeva & Diana Blagoeva (eds.), *Ezikovi resursi i tehnologii za balgarski ezik*, 185–201. Sofia: Prof. M. Drinov Publishing House.

Chapter 9

Modelling multiword expressions in a parallel Bulgarian-English newsmedia corpus

Petya Osenova

Linguistic Modelling Department, IICT-BAS

Kiril Simov

Linguistic Modelling Department, IICT-BAS

The paper focuses on the modelling of multiword expressions (MWE) in Bulgarian-English parallel news corpora (SETimes; CSLI dataset and PennTreebank dataset). Observations were made on alignments in which at least one multiword expression was used per language. The multiword expressions were classified with respect to the PARSEME lexicon-based (WG1) and treebank-based (WG4) classifications. The non-MWE counterparts of MWEs are also considered. Our approach is data-driven because the data of this study was retrieved from parallel corpora and not from bilingual dictionaries. The survey shows that the predominant translation relation between Bulgarian and English is *MWE-to-word*, and that this relation does not exclude other translation options. To formalize our observations, a catenae-based modelling of the parallel pairs is proposed.

1 Introduction

This work proposes a catenae-based modelling of aligned pairs in parallel Bulgarian-English news corpora. A representation is suggested that handles bilingual pairs comprising at least one MWE. Our main aim is to offer a representation that deals equally well with cross-language symmetries and asymmetries.

In each language, MWEs were annotated independently from the alignments in the corpus. Then, using the alignments, we examined how MWEs were trans-

Petya Osenova & Kiril Simov. 2018. Modelling multiword expressions in a parallel Bulgarian-English newsmedia corpus. In Manfred Sailer & Stella Markantonatou (eds.), *Multiword expressions: Insights from a multi-lingual perspective*, 247–269. Berlin: Language Science Press. DOI:10.5281/zenodo.1182603

lated between the two languages. The following general alignment types of examples are considered: MWE-to-MWE; MWE-to-word; MWE-to-phrases. This general typology is not exhaustive since, and in most of the cases, another translation option could have been used. Thus, it is interesting to observe the lexical choices actually made in the parallel data.

In our work we refer to the classifications of MWEs developed within PARSEME (PARSing and Multiword Expressions)[1] in Working Groups 1 and 4 – WG1: Lexicon-Grammar Interface and WG4: Annotating MWEs in Treebanks. The first one focuses on the linguistic properties of MWEs (structure, reflexes to alternations such as passivisation, etc.) and is more detailed, while the second one is treebank-related and thus focuses on a different set of MWE features such as the structural correspondences among MWEs across languages and the distributions observed in corpora.

The results from the empirical study highlight at least the following issues: (1) realization options of different MWE types in two languages with different morphological complexity and word order; (2) a data-driven typology of alignment possibilities among various types of MWEs; (3) modelling the bilingual data with a catenae-based approach.

The paper is structured as follows: §2 outlines the related work; §3 introduces catenae in a more formal way and also describes the main operations that can be applied on them; §4 presents bilingual catenae; §5 describes the parallel data and its classification; and §6 concludes the paper.

2 Related work

This section comprises two parts: a discussion on MWE classification and a presentation of catenae. Concerning the former, there is extensive literature regarding the study of MWEs within a language and across languages, theoretical issues on MWE modelling, etc. Here only some of them will be mentioned. To the best of our knowledge, this is the first attempt to use catenae for modelling bilingual or multilingual MWE correspondences.

2.1 MWE classifications

There is no widely accepted classification of MWEs (Villavicencio & Kordoni 2012). For the task of automatic recognition of MWEs in Bulgarian Stoyanova

---

[1]PARSEME is an interdisciplinary scientific network devoted to the role of multiword expressions in parsing – IC1207 COST Action.

(2010) adopts the classification of Baldwin et al. (2003). This classification could be characterized as a semantically oriented division, since the MWEs are classified as non-decomposable by meaning, idiosyncratically decomposable and simple decomposable.

In Sag et al. (2002) another classification is proposed. The MWEs are divided into lexicalized phrases and institutionalized phrases. Here we do not consider institutionalized phrases (semantically and syntactically compositional, but statistically idiosyncratic) as a distinct group. Lexicalised phrases are further subdivided into fixed expressions, semi-fixed expressions and syntactically flexible expressions. Fixed expressions are said to be fully lexicalized and undergoing neither morphosyntactic variation nor internal modification. Semi-fixed expressions have a fixed word order, but "undergo some degree of lexical variation, e.g. in the form of inflection, variation in reflexive form, and determiner selection," Sag et al. (2002: 4) including non-decomposable idioms and proper names. Syntactically flexible expressions allow for some variation in their word order (light verb constructions, decomposable idioms).

On the multilinguality front, there are various approaches to different MWE-related problems. For example, in Rácz et al. (2014) the multilingual annotation of light verb constructions is discussed for English, Spanish, German and Hungarian. The specific annotation properties of these elements are described for each language. Another popular task is the construction of bi- or multilingual MWE lexicons on the base of parallel or comparable corpora. In Seo et al. (2014) a context-oriented method is proposed for French and Korean.

The WG4 classification was specially tailored to reflect the typology of MWEs in syntactically annotated corpora (treebanks). It divides MWEs into the following groups on the basis of the parts-of-speech (PoS) of the head word:

1. Nominal MWEs

2. Verbal MWEs

3. Prepositional MWEs

4. Adjectival MWEs

5. MWEs of other categories

6. Proverbs

Some of these groups are further subdivided into subtypes: *Nominal MWEs* including named entities (NEs), nominal compounds as well as other nominal

MWEs and *verbal MWEs* including phrasal verbs, light verb constructions, VP idioms and other verb MWEs. Thus, the WG4 classification is syntax-based.

WP1 classification elaborates the typology by studying idiomaticity and flexibility on the basis of a large set of morphosyntactic diagnostics. With respect to flexibility, the WG1 approach differs from Sag et al. (2002) in providing a coarser division between semi-flexible and flexible MWEs. With respect to idiomaticity, the classification is based on Baldwin & Kim (2010). It handles five types: lexical, syntactic, semantic, pragmatic and statistical idiomaticity. Our work deals with the syntactic and semantic idiomaticity in a bilingual context.

2.2 Catena

The notion of catena "chain" was introduced in O'Grady (1998: 284) as a mechanism for representing the syntactic structure of idioms. He shows that for this task there is need for a definition of syntactic patterns not coinciding with constituents. A variant of this definition was offered by Osborne (2006):

> The words A, B, and C (order irrelevant) form a chain if and only if A immediately dominates B and C, or if and only if A immediately dominates B and B immediately dominates C. (Osborne 2006: 258)

In recent years the notion of catena revived again and was applied to dependency representations. Catenae have been used successfully for the modelling of problematic language phenomena. Gross (2010) presents the morphological and syntactic problems that have led to the introduction of the subconstituent catena level. Constituency-based analysis has to deal with non-constituent structures in ellipsis, idioms, and verb complexes.

Apart from the linguistic modelling of language phenomena, catenae have been used in a number of NLP applications. Maxwell et al. (2013), for example, present an approach to Information Retrieval based on catenae. The authors consider the catena as a mechanism for semantic encoding which overcomes the problems of long-distance paths and elliptical sentences. Also, Sanguinetti et al. (2014) present a catena-related approach for syntactic alignments in multilingual treebanks. In translation research, catenae are best known as "treelets" (Quirk & Menezes 2006). We employ catenae, which have already been used in NLP applications, to model the interface between the treebank and the lexicon.

A first attempt to formalise MWE information with catenae is discussed in Simov & Osenova (2015). In the next section we present the main notions of our proposal.

3 Definition of catena. Operations on catenae

We follow the definition of catena provided by O'Grady (1998) and Gross (2010): a CATENA is a word or a combination of words directly connected with dominance relations. In fact, in the domain of dependency trees, this definition is equivalent to a subtree definition. Figure 1 shows a complete dependency tree and some of its catenae. Notice that the complete tree is also a catena. Individual words are catenae, too. With "root$_C$" we mark the root of the catena that might be identical with the root of the complete tree, but it also might be different as in the case of *John* and *an apple* in Figure 1.

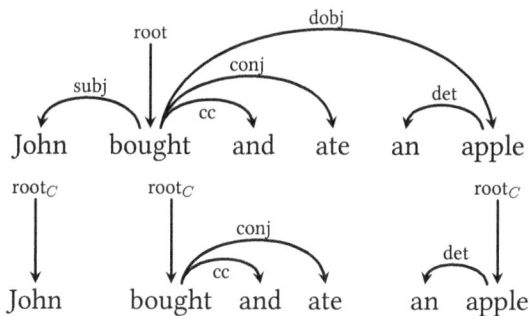

Figure 1: A complete dependency tree and some of its catenae.

A catena as an object on its own is a tree in which the nodes are decorated with various labels including word forms, lemmas, and parts-of-speech; the grammatical features and the arcs are augmented with dependency labels. The labeling function is partial. Thus, some nodes or arcs remain non-decorated in the catena and allow for different mappings to dependency trees. When the catenae are not mapped on dependency trees, they are considered part of the lexicon or the grammar of a given language.

We call the mapping of a catena onto a given dependency tree the *realization of the catena in the tree*. We consider the realization of the catena as a fully specified subtree including all the nodes and arc labels. Each realization of a catena has to agree with its labeling outside of the dependency tree. For example, the catena for *(to) spill the beans* will allow for any realization of the verb form like in: *they spilled the beans* and *he spills the beans*. Thus, the catena in the lexicon will be underspecified with respect to the grammatical features and word forms for the corresponding lexical items.

Lexical catena:

Realization 1:

Realization 2:

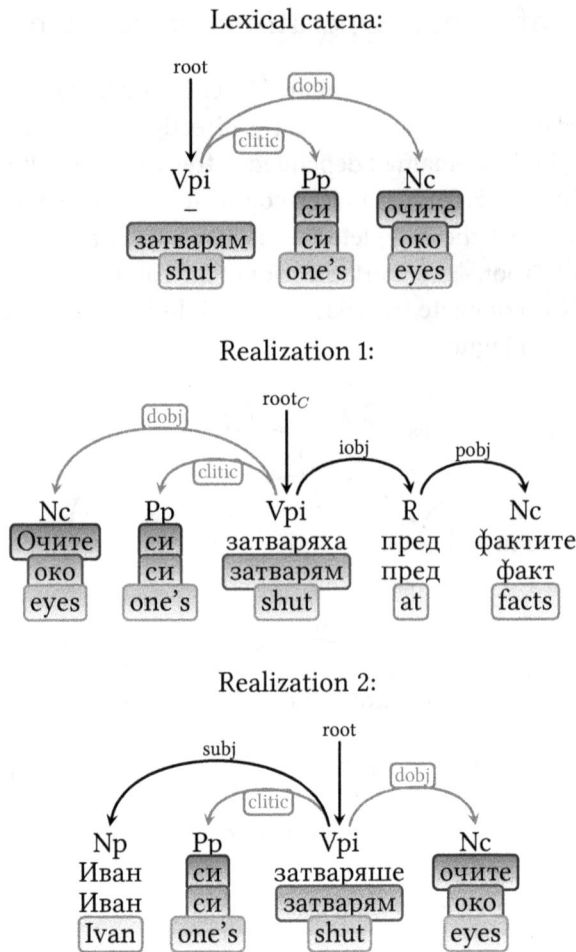

Figure 2: Catena realization.

In this paper, the underspecified catena is called a *lexicon catena* (LC) and it is stored in the lexical entries. Figure 2 shows a lexical catena for the idiom *затваря-м си оч-и-те* (zatvarya-m si ochite) close-PRS.1SG REFL eye-PL-DEF shut one's eyes,[2] and two of its realizations. Catenae in the lexicon do not specify any particular word order.[3] The word order of the catena realization reflects the

---

[2]Examples contain the Bulgarian string in Cyrilic, its latin transcription placed in brackets and the gloss. A literal translation may follow in the form of an English text while translations are always enclosed in inverted commas (").

[3]Formalisation of the word order within the catena remains an open question for future work.

rules of the grammar, therefore, the realisation of the same catena in different dependency trees could materialise with different word orders.

The upper part of the image in Figure 2 represents the lexicon catena for the idiom. It determines the fixed elements of the catena: arcs and their labels as well as nodes and their labels. More precisely, the following information is included: extended part of speech (PoS),[4] word forms, and lemmas.[5] The translations of the word form are presented, too. A dash (–) under a node indicates that the corresponding element is not defined for the given node. In Figure 2, the dash represents the fact that the word form for the verb node is underspecified, therefore the idiom can be marked with a variety of tense, person and other values.

In the two realizations, the fixed elements of the catena are represented as in the lexicon catena. Thus, the lemmas are the same as the word forms, the parts-of-speech and the grammatical features for the direct object and for the clitic are also the same. The realizations are different from the lexicon catenae with respect to the word forms and the grammatical features of the verb node: in both examples the verb is in past tense while in the first realization it is in plural and in the second in singular number. The word order in the two realizations is different. Thus, the underspecified catenae representation allows for various levels of morphosyntactic and semantic flexibility within the multiword expressions.

The catena representation of the lexical items explicitly denotes their properties that constrain their interaction. We proceed to show how we model the selectional restriction of a given lexical unit with respect to a catena in a sentence. The main operation for modelling the interactions among the catenae is called COMPOSITION. For example, let us assume that the verb *to read* requires that its subject denotes a human and that its object denotes an information object. In Figure 3 we present how the catena for *I read* is combined with the catena *a book* in order to form the catena *I read a book*. The figure represents the level of word forms and the level of semantics (specified only for the node, on which the composition is performed). The catena for *I read* ... specifies that the unknown direct object has the semantics of an *Information Object* (InfObj). The catena for *a book* represents the fact that the book is an Information Object. Thus the two catenae are composed on the two nodes marked as InfObj. The result is represented at the lower part of Figure 3. We have defined the composition operation for catenae that agree with each other on one node; the operation can be defined

---

[4]The extended parts of speech are defined as prefixes of the tags in the BulTreeBank tagset: http://www.bultreebank.org/TechRep/BTB-TR03.pdf

[5]In some examples we give the important information only, thus, some of these rows are missing. In some examples new rows are used to introduce additional information.

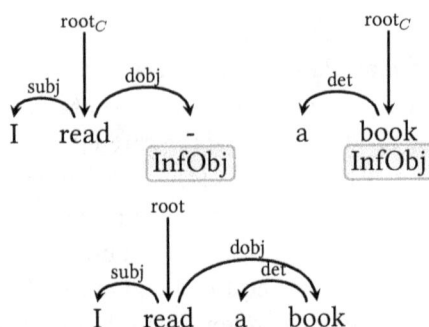

Figure 3: Composition of catenae.

on more agreeing nodes.

In Figure 4 the structure of the lexical entry for the verb *бяга-м* (byaga-m) run-PRS.SG 'run' is presented in the sense 'run away from facts'. The verb selects an indirect object in the form of a prepositional phrase introduced with the preposition *om* (ot) 'from'. In Figure 5 we give the catena for the synonymous MWE *затварям си очите* (zatvaryam si ochite) close.PRS.1SG REFL eye.PL 'I close my eyes'.

The lexical entry of a MWE uses the format: a **lexicon-catena**, **semantics** and **valency**.[6] Lexicon-catenae for the MWEs are stored in their canonical form. The semantics part of a lexical entry is represented with a logical formula comprising elementary predicates. The role of possible modifiers has to be specified in the lexicon-catena, if modification of the MWE is possible, for instance when structures with modifiers of the noun can be attested in the data. For example, the MWE *затварям си очите* (zatvaryam si ochite) close.PRS.1SG REFL eye.PL.DEF, which is synonymous to the verb *бягам* (byagam) run.PRS.1SG, is presented in Figure 5.[7] The valency level is built as follows: the root of the valency catena is marked with the identifier of the node in the lexical catena for which the particular valency representation is applicable. In Figure 5 the valency representation is applicable to the root node CNo1 of the lexical catena. The two catenae are composed on this node. The composition is applied to the semantics of the lexical catena and of the valency catena. Note that the nodes No1 and No2 are different from the nodes CNo1 and CNo2.

---

[6]The corresponding fields in the lexical entry (rows in the tables below) are marked as: LC, SM, Fr (for valency frames).

[7]The grammatical features are: 'poss' for possessive pronoun, 'plur' for plural number and 'def' for definite noun.

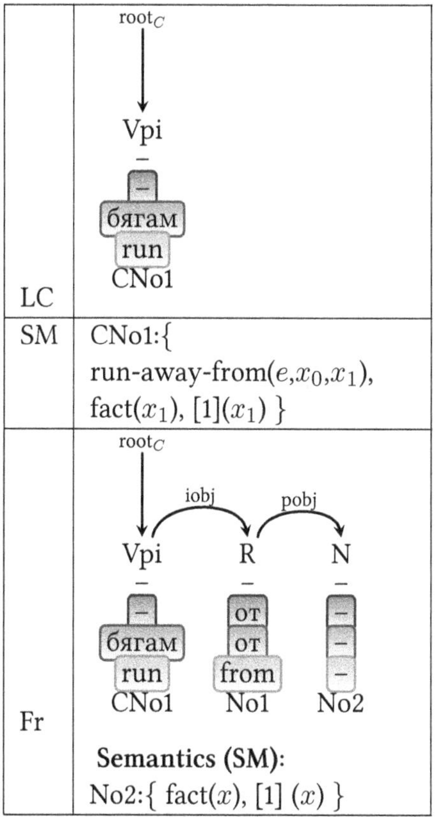

LC	root$_C$ → Vpi − [бягам / run / CNo1]
SM	CNo1:{ run-away-from(e,x_0,x_1), fact(x_1), [1](x_1) }
Fr	root$_C$ → Vpi (iobj) R (pobj) N Vpi − [бягам / run / CNo1] R − [от / от / from / No1] N − [/ / / No2] **Semantics (SM):** No2:{ fact(x), [1] (x) }

Figure 4: Lexical entry for the verb *run*.

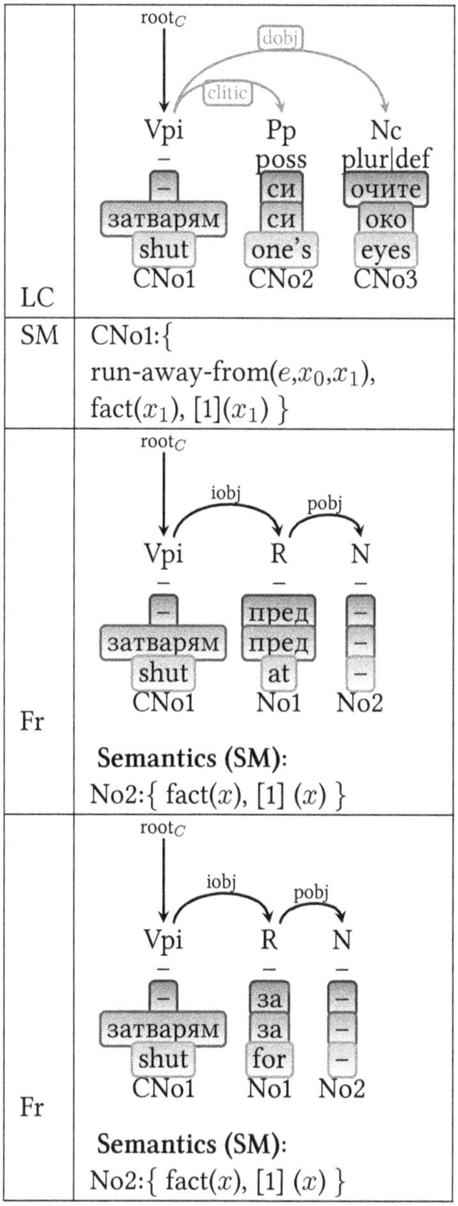

LC	root$_C$ (dobj) (clitic) → Vpi / Pp poss / Nc plur|def Vpi − [затварям / shut / CNo1] Pp poss [си / си / one's / CNo2] Nc plur|def [очите / око / eyes / CNo3]
SM	CNo1:{ run-away-from(e,x_0,x_1), fact(x_1), [1](x_1) }
Fr	root$_C$ → Vpi (iobj) R (pobj) N Vpi − [затварям / shut / CNo1] R − [пред / пред / at / No1] N − [/ / / No2] **Semantics (SM):** No2:{ fact(x), [1] (x) }
Fr	root$_C$ → Vpi (iobj) R (pobj) N Vpi − [затварям / shut / CNo1] R − [за / за / for / No1] N − [/ / / No2] **Semantics (SM):** No2:{ fact(x), [1] (x) }

Figure 5: Lexical entry for *I close my eyes*.

We use catenae to represent both single words and MWEs because single words are also catenae by definition.

We can specify all the grammatical features of a lexical item using the formal definition of catena given above. The semantics defined in the lexical entry can be attached to each node in the lexicon-catena. In Figure 4 there is just one node of the lexicon-catena. In this paper, we present only the set of elementary predicates rather than providing their full semantic structures because we focus on the principles of the representation.[8] In Figure 4 the verb introduces three elementary predicates: *run-away-from*(e, x_0, x_1), *fact*(x_1), $[1](x_1)$. The predicate *run-away-from*(e, x_0, x_1) represents the event and its main participants: x_0, x_1. The predicate *fact*(x_1) is part of the meaning of the verb in the sense that the agent represented by x_0 will run away from some (unpleasant) situation. The underspecified predicate $[1](x_1)$ has to be compatible with the predicate *fact*(x_1). This predicate is used for incorporating the meaning of the indirect object *at something* in the frame *shut one's eyes at something*. The valency frame is given as a set of valency elements defined as a catena with a semantic description. The catena describes the basic structure of the valency element including the necessary lexical information, grammatical features, and the syntactic relation to the main lexical item. The semantic description determines the main semantic contribution of the frame element and is incorporated in the semantics of the whole lexical item with structural sharing. In Figure 4 there is only one frame element. It is introduced with the preposition *om* (ot) 'from'. The semantics originates in the dependent noun that has to be compatible with the predicate *fact*(x) and in the underspecified predicate $[1](x_1)$, that may introduce a specific predicate. Via the structure sharing index [1], this specific predicate is copied on the semantics of the main lexical item.

The lexical entry in Figure 5 is similar to the one shown in Figure 4. The main differences are: the lexicon-catena represents a MWE and not a single word. The semantics is the same, because the verb and the MWE are synonyms. The valency frame contains two alternative elements for indirect object introduced by two different prepositions. The conclusion that the two descriptions are alternatives follows from the fact that the verb has only a free indirect object slot. If a direct object slot was free as well then the valency set would contain elements to fill also this slot; however, in the MWE presented, the direct object slot is occupied by a fixed element.

In a nutshell, catenae are an appropriate mechanism for the representation of MWEs because they adequately encode the grammatical flexibility of some

---

[8]For a full semantic representation we employ *Minimal Recursion Semantics*, introduced by Copestake et al. (2005).

elements within the MWEs and also allow for the informative representation of single words.

In the rest of the paper we extend the above lexicon model in order to handle correspondences among translation pairs with at least one MWE as a member.

4 Bilingual catena modelling

In this section we show the treatment of the following bilingual types of pairs in Bulgarian and English: MWE-to-MWE and MWE-to-word. Our survey is corpus-driven and we have chosen to discuss the most frequent pairs in our data (see next section for data statistics).

4.1 MWE-to-MWE

Let us consider the example:

(1)   EXAMPLE RD:[9] *взема решение* (vzema reshenie) take.PRS.1SG decision 'reach a decision'.

The two MWEs are flexible in several ways. First, the verb *reach* (and the corresponding one in Bulgarian *взема* (vzema) 'take, get') allow for morphological variation, including tense, person, etc. The noun *decision* allows for pre- and post-modifiers as in: *we reached an important decision* or *they will reach a decision about us tomorrow*. The Bulgarian MWE presents the same behavior. Figure 6 shows the lexical entry for the parallel MWEs that are modeled as catenae. In the lexical entries we can see the catenae for both MWEs. In the next row, the semantics of the parallel MWEs is represented with a set of elementary predicates coupled with a coindexation strategy between the semantics of the MWE and its frame semantics.

In Figure 6, the indices [1] and [2] represent the unknown semantics of the modifying nouns. If no modification phrases exist, these predicates are assumed to express the most general one, namely *everything(x)*. Thus, the set {take-decision(e,x_0,x_1), decision(x_1,x_2), $[1](x_1)$, problem(x_2), $[2](x_2)$} represents the meaning of the MWE[10]: event "take-decision" e with two participants x_1 and x_2. The participant x_0 is the agent who takes the decision. The participant x_1 is

---

[9]We use a special notation after each example: RD, IG and CH for ensuring the correct connection with the corresponding pictures in Figures 6, 7, and 8.

[10]The examples present light verb constructions that are translational equivalents between Bulgarian and English.

the main argument of the predicate for the relational noun *decision* that, being a two-argument predicate, introduces a third participant in the event, namely the problem that the decision is about, denoted with the variable x_2. If along with the lexicon catena the frame catena is also realized in the sentence, then the new predicates introduced by the corresponding nouns are added to the semantics of the new bigger catena. This mechanism of representing bilingual lexicon entries is suitable for the processing of the bilingual information including the shared representation of the semantics and correspondences between the grammatical features of the parallel realisations of the catenae in the different languages.

In some cases the lexical entry of the parallel MWEs might be quite simple, as in the following example:

(2) EXAMPLE IG: *като цяло* (kato tsyalo) as whole 'in general'.

In Figure 7 the adverbials share the same semantics. They do not have frames and they allow for no modification. Only the PoS assigned to their elements may be different.

4.2 MWE-to-word

Concerning the relation MWE-to-word irrespectively of the language direction, two main cases can be observed. The first one relates to functional PoS, such as the English preposition *after* and the Bulgarian complementiser *след като* (sled kato) after when, that are translational equivalents and have identical semantics but differ in PoS and some selectional properties.

A challenging problem occurs when non-functional counterparts are considered. For example, the term

(3) EXAMPLE CH: the English term *chemicals* translates into the Bulgarian MWE *химическ-и продукт-и* (himichesk-i produkt-i) chemical-PL product-PL 'chemical products'.

Both expressions might be modified by adjectives, PPs or clauses: **dangerous** *chemicals*, *chemicals* **from airplanes**, and *chemicals* **that are used by the pharmaceutical industry**. We find similar examples in Bulgarian like *отровни химически продукти* (otrovni himicheski produkti) poisonous.PL chemical.PL product.PL 'poisonous chemical products'.

In Figure 8 a part of the parallel lexical entry for this example is presented. It can be seen that in the English part of the lexical entry there is a catena for a single word while in the Bulgarian part there is a catena for a noun phrase of

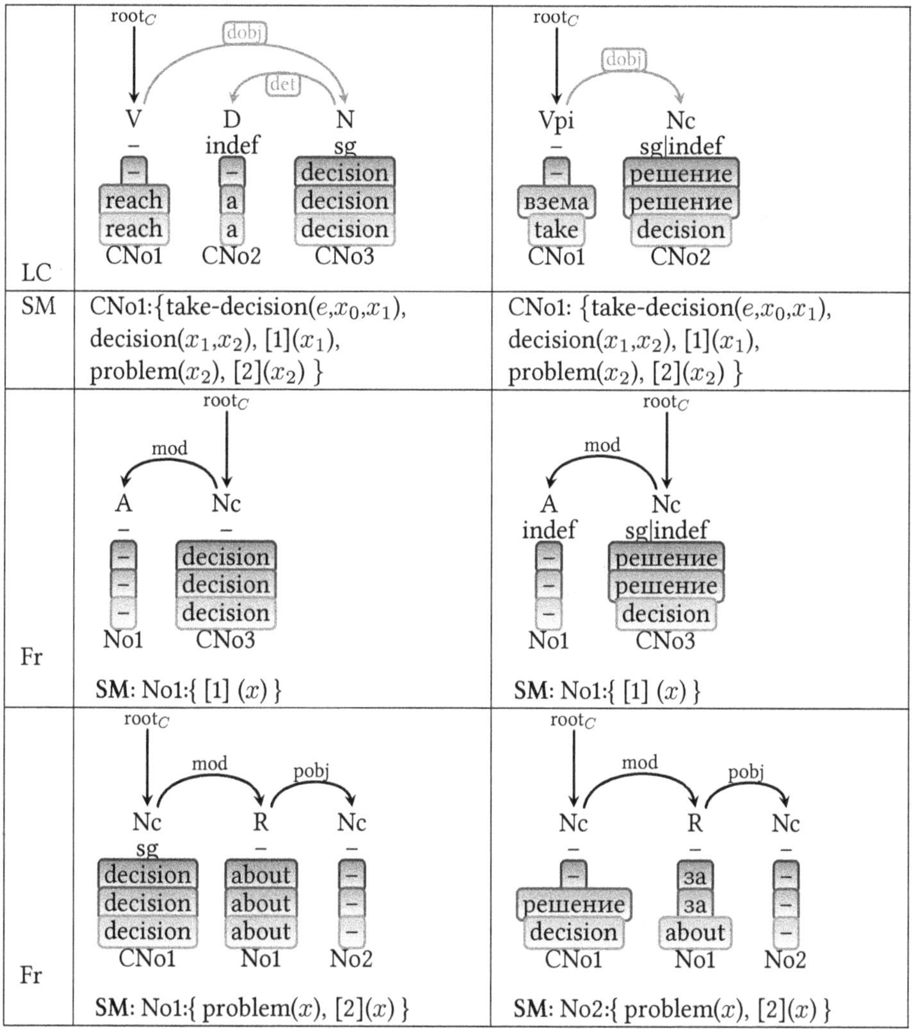

Figure 6: Parallel Lexical Entries for the parallel MWEs: **example RD.**

type adjectival modifier - head noun. The catena for the Bulgarian MWE is underspecified for the word form and the grammatical features because the whole phrase might be definite: *химическите продукти* (himicheskite produkti) '**the** chemicals'. The English and the Bulgarian entries are specified for the same semantics. In the frame part of the lexical entries all possible modifications have to be defined (in the example just one of them is given, namely left modification with adjectives; however, modification with PPs has been encountered in the

	root$_C$		root$_C$	
	R ⟶ A (pobj)		R ⟶ Dm (pobj)	
	in / in / in — general / general / general CNo1 CNo2		като / като / as — цяло / цяло / whole CNo1 CNo2	
LC				
SM	CNo1:{ generally(e,e_1) }		CNo1:{ generally(e,e_1) }	
Fr				

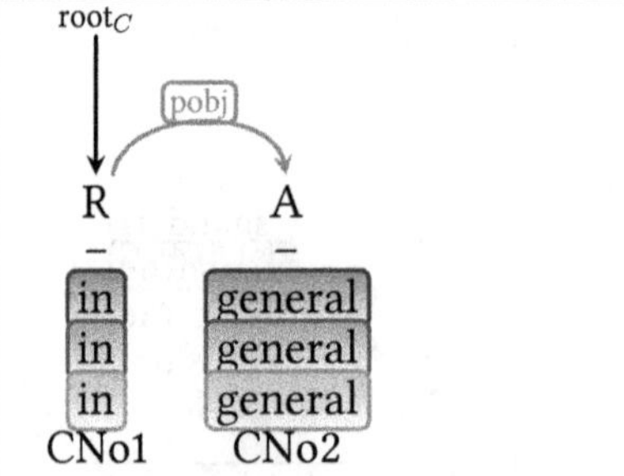

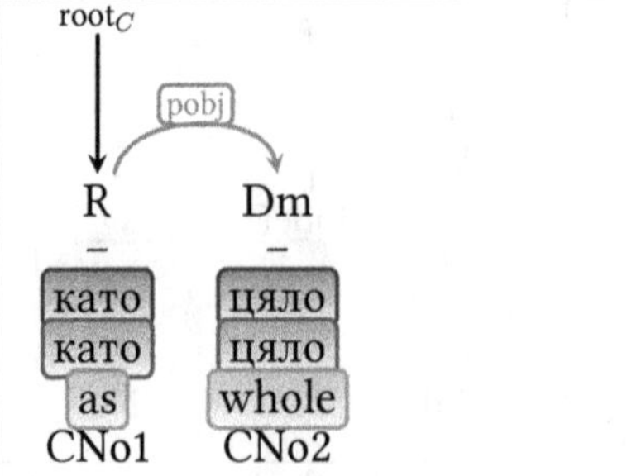

Figure 7: Parallel Lexical Entries for the parallel MWEs: **example IG.**

data, etc.). The important point here is that the lexicon catenae for the two languages have to contain appropriate correspondences of the frames in order to be proper translations of each other. The correspondences of the frames have to be established on semantic grounds – the corresponding frames in the English and the Bulgarian part have to define the same semantic contributions to the lexical catenae.

The frame catena in Figure 8 marks the fact that the lexical catena can be modified by an adjectival modifier. The realization of such a modifier is additional to the realization of the adjectival modifier *химическ-и* (himichesk-i) chemical-PL that is a fixed part of the MWE. In the frame catena we mark only the nominal head of the MWE.

Note that we do not aim at an exhaustive analysis of all the bilingual pairs. Our aim is to present a mechanism which would deal with both—symmetric (MWE-to-MWE) and asymmetric (MWE-to-word) relations in translations. Our hypothesis is that the correspondences between the two languages in the lexicon have to be governed by the semantics of the lexical catenae and the semantic contribution of the possible frames. A consequence of this hypothesis is that, in the lexicon, we have to allow for correspondences not only between MWEs, but also between MWEs and words, and between words/MWEs in one of the languages and compositional phrases in the other.

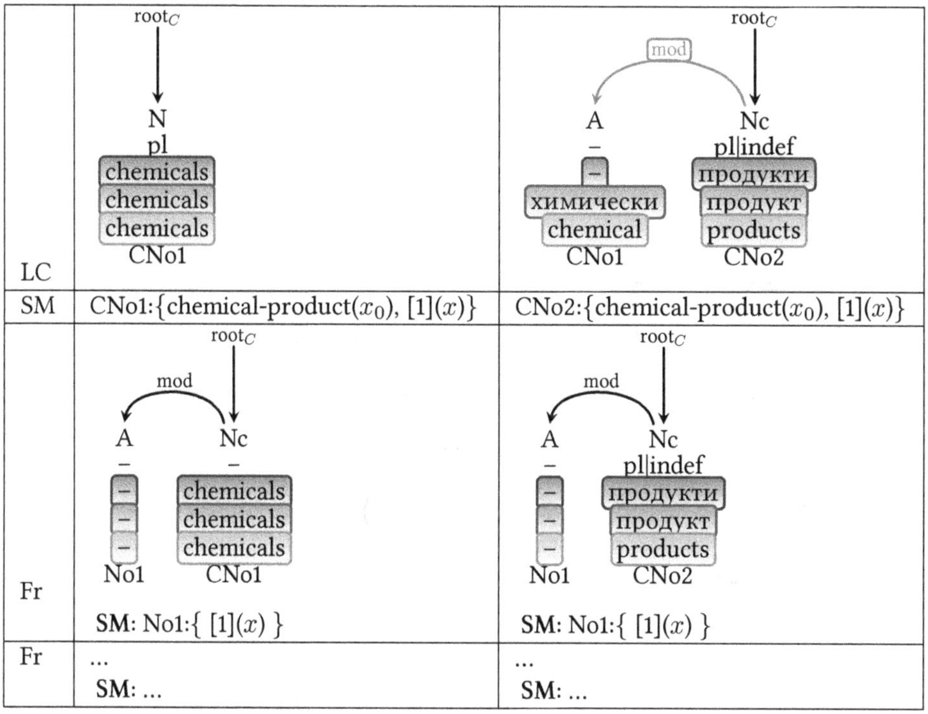

Figure 8: Parallel Lexical Entries for the parallel MWEs: **example CH**.

5 Classification of the parallel data

In this section we provide a classification of parallel pairs that consist of two MWEs or an MWE and a word. For each class of correspondences the minimum information to be included in the lexical entries has been specified. The parallel Bulgarian-English newsmedia corpus consists of two parts: SETimes plus CSLI dataset (920 sentences, or 9308 tokens); PenTreebank dataset (838 sentences, or 21949 tokens). Thus, our final dataset consists of: 1758 sentences or 31 257 tokens.

The data was aligned according to Simov et al. (2011). However, the alignments did not mark the MWEs. For that reason, additional annotation was performed for detecting the alignments with MWEs in at least one of the two languages.

Our aim was to extract various types of alignments with at least one MWE as a member. Thus, our data included the following general types: MWE-to-word; MWE-to-MWE and MWE-to-compositional phrase in both language directions.

As shown in Table 1, 510 occurrences of MWEs were detected within these data. 370 MWEs of these occurrences are of type MWE-to-word (for example

Table 1: General Classification.

	Occurrences
MWE-to-MWE	126
MWE-to-word	370
MWE-to-phrase	14
Total	510

Table 2: MWE-to-Word classification.

	MWE-to-word
Bulgarian MWE	220
English MWE	150
Total	370

the English *within* is translated as *в рамките на* (v ramkite na) in frame.PL of); 126 MWEs are of type MWE-to-MWE (for example the English *with respect to* is translated as *що се отнася до* (shto se otnasya do) as far as relate.PRS.3SG to), and 14 MWEs are of type MWE-to-phrase (for example, the English *take-it-or-leave it* is translated as *приемаш или се отказваш* (priemash ili se otkazvash) accept.PRS.2SG or refuse.PRS.2SG).

Table 2 shows the distribution of MWEs in the largest set, namely the set of the type MWE-to-word: 220 Bulgarian and 150 English MWEs were detected.

Two types of classification are applied. First, the aligned pairs are classified into three groups: MWE-to-MWE, MWE-to-word and MWE-to-phrase (see Tables 1 and 2). This classification offers a coarse picture of the bilingual situation. Then, the classification methods developed in PARSEME WG1 and WG4 are applied. These classifications draw on the structural and the semantic features of MWEs.

When mapped to the PARSEME WG1/WG4 typologies, both languages showed very similar MWE properties. Thus, the most frequent MWE types in both languages are: *verbal MWEs; noun MWEs; other categories of MWEs.* The language specific features are evident in the subtypes. Thus, phrasal verbs and reflexive (formally or semantically) *се*-verbs seem to be the most frequently used verb MWEs in the English and Bulgarian data respectively. Both languages feature light verb constructions and VP idioms. Lastly, compounds are the most frequent type of noun MWEs in English while adjective-noun phrases are in Bulgarian.

To present a slightly more detailed analysis of the correspondence type MWE-to-MWE, we use the WG1 classification (predominantly the syntactic and semantic dimensions), that focuses on the internal structure of the MWEs.

Within the set of the *MWE-to-MWE pairs*, correspondences are grouped to straightforward mappings and to cross-language specific types. A presentation of these two groups follows.

5.1 Straightforward mappings

The class of straightforward mappings includes: verb MWEs (light verb constructions, VP idioms) and other categories (adverbs, prepositions), etc.

In this group of translation equivalent, two main classes of Bulgarian–English MWE pairs are identified: pairs with cross-lingual variance that have to be considered in the lexicons, and MWEs with no cross-lingual variance that are trivially handled in the lexicon. In the first case, the grammatical behavior of the MWE elements in both languages has to be taken into account, such as the possibility of inflection for number, or of accepting modifiers. In the second case, the MWE elements hardly undergo inflection or modification, so the translational equivalents are registered in the lexicon without further elaboration on the behavior of their elements.

The first case includes verb and noun MWEs and the second one complex PoS and non-inflecting MWEs.

Examples for the first group are given below:

- Light verbs in one language often correspond to similar constructions in the other. For instance,

  - 'reach a decision' *взем-а решение* (vzem-a reshenie) take-PRS.3SG decision

  where V NP in English translates to V NP in Bulgarian,

  - 'take effect' *влез-е в сила* (vlez-e v sila) enter-PRS.3SG in power,

  - 'take control' *влез-е във владение* (vlez-e vav vladenie) enter-PRS.3SG in possession

  where V NP translates to V PP.

  In this group the MWEs are assigned identical semantics, but they might differ in the elements and in valence selection.

- Noun MWEs of the type A N that are translational equivalents, often are literal translations of each other:

  – 'tough line' *твърда позиция* (tvarda pozitsiya) tough position,

  – 'free market' *свободни-я пазар* (svobodni-ya pazar) free-DEF market,

  – 'real estate' *недвижимо-то имущество* (nedvizhimo-to imushtestvo) nonmoving-DEF property.

  The MWEs in this group share the same semantics and the same modification mechanisms.

- The structure V NP tends to characterise both members in pairs consisting of verb MWE translational equivalents:

  – 'is drawing fire' *привлич-а критик-и-те* (privlich-a kritik-i-te) attract-PRS.3SG critic.PL-DEF,

  – 'haven't got a clue' *няма-т представа* (nyama-t predstava) not.have.PRS.3PL idea.

  The MWEs in this group are assigned the same semantics, but vary in their elements and valence selection.

Examples for the second group are given below:

- Multiword adverbial constructions:

  – 'on the other hand' *от друга страна* (ot druga strana) from other side,

  – 'of course' *разбир-а се* (razbir-a se) understand-PRS.3SG REFL,

  – 'more and more' *все повече и повече* (vse poveche i poveche) even more and more,

  – 'in particular' *в частност* (v chastnost) in detail.
  Here, however, the prepositional complement varies in the PoS across the two languages. For example, in the last translational equivalent the English prepositional complement is the adjective *particular*, while in Bulgarian it is the noun *частност* (chastnost).

  The MWEs in this group are assigned the same semantics, but may vary in the elements. However, this difference is not taken into consideration, because the elements hardly inflect and do not allow for insertion of additional elements.

- Complex prepositions in English tend to have structurally similar counter-parts in Bulgarian. For instance,

  – 'with respect to' *по отношение на* (po otnoshenie na) at relation to.

  The MWEs in this group are assigned the same semantics, but since, presumably, they are assigned the same PoS and do not inflect, the element variance is not relevant.

- Conjunctions composed of multiple words:

  – 'as well as' *както и* (kakto i) as and.

Like the complex preposition group, this group also contains MWEs that are assigned the same semantics and the same PoS; these MWEs do not inflect, therefore the element variance is not relevant.

5.2 Cross-language specific types

Here we include English phrasal verbs having Bulgarian reflexive *ce*-verbs, as translational equivalents and English nominal compounds having Bulgarian other NP MWEs, mainly adjective-noun or noun-preposition-noun, as translational equivalents. In this group, translational equivalents are assigned the same semantics, but they may present systematic structural differences due to language specific constructions. The elements in the MWEs always differ across languages.

- English phrasal verbs often correspond to Bulgarian *ce*-verbs:

  – 'give up' *ce откаж-е* (se otkazh-e) REFL decline-PRS.3SG,

  – 'move back' *ce върна-т* (se varna-t) REFL return-PRS.3SG.

  Bulgarian and English MWEs in this group may differ in valency and in the way meaning is constructed. Thus, Bulgarian uses the lexical aspect and the reflexive *ce* (se) to construct MWE meanings, while English uses the verb in combination with the phrasal affix.

- English N N compounds can map to A N compounds in Bulgarian:

  – 'face amount' *номинална стойност* (nominalna stoynost) nominal value.

  The MWEs in this group differ in the PoS of the modifier of the head noun: with Bulgarian A N MWEs the head noun is modified by an adjective and with English N N MWEs by a noun.

- English N N can also be translated as N PP in Bulgarian. The first N in the English MWEs and the PP in the Bulgarian MWEs make the same semantic contribution:

  – 'law enforcement' *сил-и-те на ред-а* (sil-i-te na red-a) force-PL-DEF of order-SG.DEF.

  The MWEs in this group differ in the PoS of the modifier of the head noun: with Bulgarian N NP MWEs the head noun is modified by a PP and with English N N MWEs by a noun.

- English N and N constructions can apparently be translated with coordinated constructions in Bulgarian; however, the PoS of the coordinated constituents differs across the two languages:

  – 'pros and cons' *доводи за и против* (dovodi za i protiv) argument.PL for and against
  (N and N / N p and p).

  The MWEs in this group differ in the head obligatoriness. In Bulgarian the head noun is present, while in English a head noun is only inferred.

- An English idiomatic clausal construction (V NP PP) can be translated with a light verb construction in Bulgarian:

  – 'putting pen to paper' *предприел действие* (predpriel deystvie) take.PTSP.3SG action.

  The MWEs in this group differ with respect to modification and selectional properties. The English MWE does not seem to admit any modifiers, while its Bulgarian translational equivalent allows for them (for example, *предприел **важно** действие* (predpriel vazhno deystvie) taken.PTSP.3SG **important** action.

- English V AP can be translated in Bulgarian with minimal changes into V AdvP:

  – 'broke even' *са излезли начисто* (sa izlezli nachisto) are come.out.PRST.3SG clean.

  The English adjective *even* translates into the Bulgarian adverb *начисто* (nachisto) 'clean'.

- English V PP can be translated as V NP in Bulgarian:

– 'will be priced of a job' *ще загубя-т работа-та си* (shte zagubya-t rabota-ta si) will lose-PRS.3SG job DEF.

It is interesting to observe that an English passive construction can be translated with a Bulgarian active construction. In such cases the valency parts will differ with respect to both the predicate and the participants.

Our work on the Bulgarian-English lexicon aims to provide representations for all these types of correspondence: the representations will be bilingual catena-based lexical entries.

6 Conclusions

The paper has argued that the catena approach can be extended to model pairs of translational equivalents retrieved from parallel English-Bulgarian corpora with at least one MWE as a member. In this way, cross-language asymmetries are handled. Our frequency counts have shown that the *MWE-to-MWE* and *MWE-to-word* correspondences are prevalent. In contrast, the *MWE-to-phrase* correspondence was not found to have a wide distribution. It would be interesting to perform a detailed analysis of more examples in order to uncover persistent correspondences between the two languages. Such knowledge can be used in designing automatic translation systems and in identifying best practices in human translation. Furthermore, these correspondences can possibly illuminate the different ways employed by the two languages to express meaning.

The proposed catena model takes into consideration both flexibility and idiomaticity when representing MWEs and words in the lexicon. These dimensions can be detailed further depending on the available specific subclassifications in a cross-lingual aspect.

Acknowledgments

This research has received support by the EC's FP7 (FP7/2007-2013) under grant agreement number 610516: "QTLeap: Quality Translation by Deep Language Engineering Approaches" and by European COST Action IC1207: "PARSEME: PARSing and Multiword Expressions. Towards linguistic precision and computational efficiency in natural language processing"

Abbreviations

def	definite noun	poss	possessive pronoun
LC	lexicon catena	SM	semantics
POS	part of speech	Fr	valency frames
plur	plural number		

References

Baldwin, Timothy, Colin Bannard, Takaaki Tanaka & Dominic Widdows. 2003. An empirical model of multiword expression decomposability. In *Proceedings of the ACL 2003 Workshop on Multiword Expressions: Analysis, Acquisition and Treatment*, vol. 18, 89–96. Sapporo.

Baldwin, Timothy & Su Nam Kim. 2010. Multiword expressions. In Nitin Indurkhya & Fred J. Damerau (eds.), *Handbook of Natural Language Processing*, 2nd edn., 267–292. Boca Raton: CRC Press.

Copestake, Ann, Dan Flickinger, Carl Pollard & Ivan Sag. 2005. Minimal recursion semantics: An introduction. *Research on Language & Computation* 3(4). 281–332.

Gross, Thomas. 2010. Chains in syntax and morphology. In Ryo Otoguro, Kiyoshi Ishikawa, Hiroshi Umemoto, Kei Yoshimoto & Yasunari Harada (eds.), *Proceedings of the 24th Pacific Asia Conference on Language, Information and Computation*, 143–152. Tohoku University, Sendai, Japan: Institute of Digital Enhancement of Cognitive Processing, Waseda University. http://www.aclweb.org/anthology/Y10-1018, accessed 2018-4-19.

Maxwell, K. Tamsin, Jon Oberlander & W. Bruce Croft. 2013. Feature-based selection of dependency paths in ad hoc Information Retrieval. In *Proceedings of the 51st Annual Meeting of the Association for Computational Linguistics (Volume 1: Long Papers)*, 507–516. Sofia, Bulgaria: Association for Computational Linguistics. http://www.aclweb.org/anthology/P13-1050, accessed 2018-4-19.

O'Grady, William. 1998. The syntax of idioms. *Natural Language and Linguistic Theory* 16. 279–312.

Osborne, Tim. 2006. Beyond the constituent – A Dependency Grammar analysis of chains. *Folia Linguistica* 39. 251–297.

Quirk, Christopher & Arul Menezes. 2006. Dependency treelet translation: The convergence of statistical and example-based machine-translation? *Machine Translation* 20(1). 43–65. DOI:10.1007/s10590-006-9008-4

Rácz, Anita, Istvan Nagy T. & Veronika Vincze. 2014. 4FX: Light verb construc-
tions in a multilingual parallel corpus. In Nicoletta Calzolari, Khalid Choukri,
Thierry Declerck, Hrafn Loftsson, Bente Maegaard, Joseph Mariani, Asuncion
Moreno, Jan Odijk & Stelios Piperidis (eds.), *Proceedings of the Ninth Interna-
tional Conference on Language Resources and Evaluation (LREC'14)*. Reykjavik,
Iceland: European Language Resources Association (ELRA).

Sag, Ivan A., Timothy Baldwin, Francis Bond, Ann Copestake & Dan Flickinger.
2002. Multiword expressions: A pain in the neck for NLP. In *Proceedings of the
3rd International Conference on Intelligent Text Processing and Computational
Linguistics (CICLing-2002)*, 1–15.

Sanguinetti, Manuela, Cristina Bosco & Loredana Cupi. 2014. Exploiting cate-
nae in a parallel treebank alignment. In Nicoletta Calzolari, Khalid Choukri,
Thierry Declerck, Hrafn Loftsson, Bente Maegaard, Joseph Mariani, Asuncion
Moreno, Jan Odijk & Stelios Piperidis (eds.), *Proceedings of the Ninth Interna-
tional Conference on Language Resources and Evaluation (LREC'14)*. Reykjavik,
Iceland: European Language Resources Association (ELRA).

Seo, Hyeong-Won, Hong-Seok Kwon, Min-ah Cheon & Jae-Hoon Kim. 2014. Constructing bilingual multiword lexicons for a resource-poor language pair. *Advanced Science and Technology Letters* 54. 95–99.

Simov, Kiril & Petya Osenova. 2015. Catena operations for unified dependency
analysis. In *Proceedings of the Third International Conference on Dependency
Linguistics (Depling 2015)*, 320–329. Uppsala, Sweden: Uppsala University, Uppsala, Sweden. http://www.aclweb.org/anthology/W15-2135, accessed 2018-4-
19.

Simov, Kiril, Petya Osenova, Laska Laskova, Aleksandar Savkov & Stanislava
Kancheva. 2011. Bulgarian-English parallel treebank: Word and semantic level
alignment. In *Proceedings of the Second AEPC Workshop*, 29–38. http://www.
aclweb.org/anthology/W11-4305, accessed 2018-4-19.

Stoyanova, Ivelina. 2010. Factors influencing the performance of some methods
for automatic identification of multiword expressions in Bulgarian. In *Proceedings of the 7th FASSBL Conference*, 103–108.

Villavicencio, Aline & Valia Kordoni. 2012. *There is light at the end of the tunnel:
Multiword expressions in theory and practice, course materials*. Tech. rep. Tech-
nical report, Erasmus Mundus European Masters Program in Language and
Communication Technologies (LCT).

Chapter 10

Spanish multiword expressions: Looking for a taxonomy

Carla Parra Escartín

ADAPT Centre, SALIS/CTTS, Dublin City University

Almudena Nevado Llopis

Universidad de San Jorge

Eoghan Sánchez Martínez

Universidad de San Jorge

In this article, we analyze Spanish multiword expressions (MWEs) and describe their linguistic properties. The ultimate goal of our analysis is to find an MWE taxonomy for Spanish which is suitable for Natural Language Processing purposes. As a starting point of our study, we take the MWE taxonomy proposed by Ramisch (2012; 2015). This taxonomy distinguishes between morphosyntactic classes and other classes which cannot be considered morphosyntactic and he calls "difficulty classes". To carry out our research, a data set of Spanish MWEs was built and subsequently analyzed. We also added a new axis to Ramisch's (2012; 2015) taxonomy, namely the flexibility one introduced by Sag et al. (2002). In the light of our analysis, we modified and adapted the taxonomy to Spanish MWEs. The different types of MWEs in Spanish are analyzed and described in this article. Flexibility tests for Spanish MWEs are also discussed.

1 Introduction

Research on multiword expressions (MWEs) has a long history both in linguistics and in Natural Language Processing (NLP). Many researchers have addressed the MWE challenge from different perspectives (Mel'čuk & Polguère 1987; Church & Hanks 1990; Sinclair 1991; Smadja 1993; Moon 1998; Lin 1999).

Carla Parra Escartín, Almudena Nevado Llopis & Eoghan Sánchez Martínez. 2018. Spanish multiword expressions: Looking for a taxonomy. In Manfred Sailer & Stella Markantonatou (eds.), *Multiword expressions: Insights from a multi-lingual perspective*, 271–323. Berlin: Language Science Press. DOI:10.5281/zenodo.1182605

MWEs are part of the lexicon of native speakers of a language and thus are interesting from a theoretical linguistics point of view. Researchers working on language acquisition also assess the acquisition of MWEs (Devereux & Costello 2007; Villavicencio et al. 2012; Nematzadeh et al. 2013); and they have also been researched in psycholinguistics (Rapp 2008; Holsinger & Kaiser 2013; Holsinger 2013; Schulte im Walde & Borgwaldt 2015), among other theoretical fields. In the case of NLP applications, MWEs need to be correctly detected and processed. In addition, when NLP applications deal with two or more languages, the treatment of MWEs needs to deal with multilingual aspects.

A lot of research has focused on specific subclasses of MWEs (e.g. *idioms, collocations, light verb constructions*). More general works studying the MWE phenomenon as such have focused on English, or have taken prior research on English as a starting point. However, this English-driven analysis needs to be further investigated taking other languages into account. As the intrinsic characteristics of a language vary, it seems necessary to use broad, general taxonomies that allow for the classification, description and analysis of MWEs notwithstanding the language they are applied to. In this article, we test this by analyzing Spanish MWEs using an existing taxonomy.

As a starting point of our study, we take the MWE taxonomy proposed by Ramisch (2012; 2015). He distinguishes three morphosyntactic classes and three additional so-called "difficulty classes". The three morphosyntactic classes are *nominal expressions, verbal expressions* and *adverbial and adjectival expressions*. Nominal expressions are further subdivided in *noun compounds, proper names* and *multiword terms*, and verbal expressions in *phrasal verbs* and *light verb constructions*. Finally, he distinguishes three difficulty classes: *fixed expressions, idiomatic expressions*, and *"true" collocations*.

We created a data set of Spanish MWEs with the aim of finding examples of each type of MWE proposed by Ramisch (2012; 2015). Then, we reviewed our data set and the features of the different MWEs gathered. As a result of this study, we revised the taxonomy and modified it to make it conform with the Spanish language.

The remainder of this article is structured as follows: §2 summarizes existing MWE taxonomies and §3 discusses MWE fixedness tests applicable to Spanish and used in our study. §4 explains the creation of our initial data set of Spanish MWEs. In §5, we present the taxonomy we propose for Spanish MWEs based on the results of our research. We also update the information about our data set, expanded to cover all types of MWEs in our new taxonomy. §6 is devoted to the description of the linguistic properties of each MWE type for Spanish. Finally, §7 summarizes our work.

2 Multiword expression typologies

There seems to be a lack of a commonly used taxonomy of MWEs, both in theoretical linguistics and in NLP. In fact, several MWE taxonomies have been proposed throughout the years. Most of them have focused on English MWEs, but as we will point out later in this section, there also exist other taxonomies based on different languages. While it is not the purpose of this section to discuss all existing MWE taxonomies and assess their applicability to the Spanish language and NLP, we think that a brief overview of the state-of-the-art as regards the classification of MWEs is needed. This will not only illustrate the task at hand – finding an MWE taxonomy suitable for Spanish from an NLP point of view – but it will also illustrate the great existing variety of approaches and perspectives.

2.1 MWE taxonomies in theoretical linguistics

As mentioned earlier, several researchers have worked on the analysis and classification of MWEs from a theoretical linguistics point of view. Some of them, such as Moon (1998) worked on specific types of MWEs, while others like Mel'čuk & Polguère (1995) and Fillmore et al. (1988) addressed more general issues. As mentioned by Moon (1998), there is a lack of agreement as far as the terminology on the topic is concerned and she reported the extended discussions of the problem as proof of it. We will not discuss her work here, as her taxonomy – despite being a reference – only focuses on English fixed expressions and idioms and leaves out other important MWE classes such as compound words because they were beyond the scope of her study.

Fillmore et al. (1988) proposed a typology based on the predictability of a construction with respect to the syntactic rules. They distinguished three classes: *unfamiliar pieces unfamiliarly combined*, *familiar pieces unfamiliarly combined*, and *familiar pieces familiarly combined*. While *familiar pieces familiarly combined* are formed following the rules of grammar, they have an idiomatic interpretation. *Familiar pieces unfamiliarly combined* require special syntactic and semantic rules, and *unfamiliar pieces unfamiliarly combined* are unpredictable.

Mel'čuk & Polguère (1995), on the other hand, used as their criterion the relevance of an expression as a dictionary entry. Their taxonomy is thus mainly based on the semantics of MWEs, and they distinguished between *complete phrasemes*, *semi-phrasemes* and *quasi-phrasemes*. In their approach, *complete phrasemes* are fully non-compositional and would constitute an independent dictionary entry. *Semi-phrasemes* would be those in which at least one of the elements preserves its meaning, and could be listed in the dictionary entry of the base word of the phraseme. Finally, *quasi-phrasemes* are expressions in which all elements keep their original meaning but their combination adds an extra element of meaning, constituting independent dictionary entries.

2.2 MWE taxonomies in Natural Language Processing

MWEs are not only a topic of interest in theoretical linguistics. In NLP research they constitute a major bottleneck for various applications and tools and thus have also been extensively investigated. Sag et al. (2002) and Baldwin & Kim (2010) proposed MWE taxonomies from the point of view of NLP.

Sag et al. (2002) discuss strategies for processing MWEs in NLP applications and thus proposed a taxonomy mainly based on their syntactic fixedness, as this is what needs to be modeled to deal with MWEs in a successful way. Figure 1 summarizes their taxonomy. They first distinguish between *lexicalized* and *institutionalized phrases* and then they further divide lexicalized phrases into *fixed* (e.g. *by and large*), *semi-fixed* and *syntactically flexible*. Semi-fixed MWEs include *non-decomposable idioms* (e.g. *to spill the beans; to kick the bucket*), *compound nominals* (e.g. *attorney general; car park*), and *proper names* (e.g. *San Francisco; Oakland Raiders*). Syntactically-flexible MWEs, on the other hand, include *verb-particle constructions* (e.g. *to look up; to break up*), *decomposable idioms* (e.g. *to let the cat out of the bag; to sweep under the rug*), and *light verbs* (e.g. *to make a mistake; to give a lecture*). According to Sag et al. (2002), lexicalized phrases are explicitly encoded in the lexicon, whereas institutionalized phrases are only statistically idiomatic.[1]

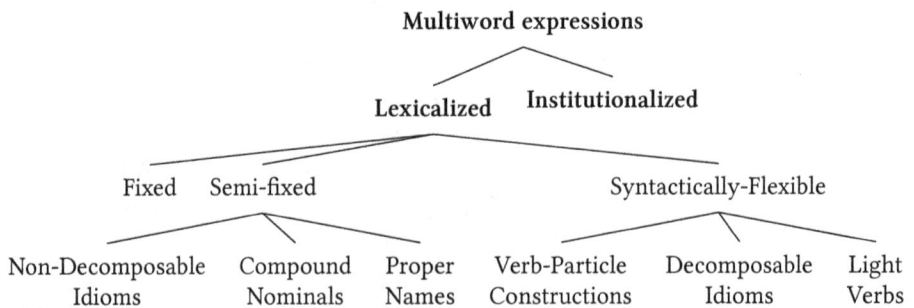

Figure 1: Taxonomy proposed by Sag et al. (2002).

---

[1]All examples are taken from Sag et al. (2002).

Baldwin & Kim (2010) carry out a twofold classification. They make a morphosyntactic classification and, additionally, they propose an MWE classification based on syntactic variability, which in turn is based on that of Sag et al. (2002). In their taxonomy, illustrated in Figure 2, they group compound nominals and proper names into a broader category named *nominal MWEs*. From a morphosyntactic point of view, they distinguish *nominal, verbal* and *prepositional MWEs*. Verbal MWEs are further classified into *verb-particle constructions, prepositional verbs,*[2] *light-verb constructions* and *verb-noun idiomatic combinations,* and prepositional MWEs are classified into *determinerless-prepositional phrases* (PP-DS, e.g. *on top*) and *complex prepositions* (complex PPS, e.g. *in addition to*).

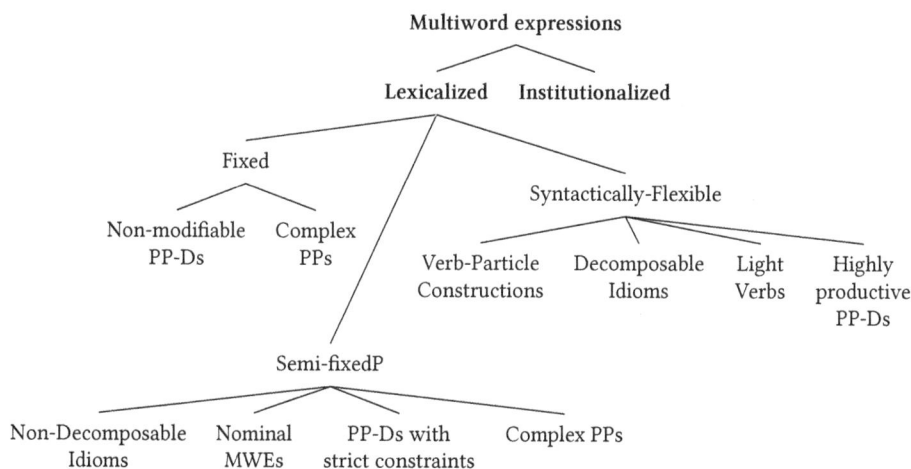

Figure 2: Taxonomy proposed by Baldwin & Kim (2010).

Ramisch (2012; 2015) proposed a simplified typology based on the morphosyntactic role of the whole MWE in a sentence and its difficulty from an NLP perspective. As illustrated in Figure 3, he identifies three *morphosyntactic classes* (*nominal expressions, verbal expressions,* and *adverbial and adjectival expressions*) and three additional so-called *difficulty classes* (*fixed expressions, idiomatic expressions,* and *"true" collocations*). Nominal expressions are further subdivided into *noun compounds* (e.g. *traffic light; Russian roulette*), *proper names* (e.g. *United Na-*

---

[2]For Baldwin & Kim (2010) *verb-particle constructions* are "a verb and an obligatory particle, typically in the form of an intransitive preposition (e.g. *play around, take off*), but including adjectives (e.g. *cut short, bund together*) and verbs (e.g. *let go, let fly*)". *Prepositional verbs* are "a verb and a selected preposition, with the crucial difference that the preposition is transitive (e.g. *refer to, look for*)". Although they do not discuss it further, there are cases such as *look forward to*, which would fall into both categories.

tions; *Alan Turing*) and *multiword terms* (e.g. *profit and loss account*; *myocardial infarction*). Verbal expressions are further subdivided into *phrasal verbs*, which in turn are subdivided into *transitive prepositional verbs* (e.g. *to agree with*; *to rely on*) and *more opaque verb-particle constructions* (e.g. *to give up*; *to take off*); and *light verb constructions* (e.g. *to take a walk*; *to give a talk*).

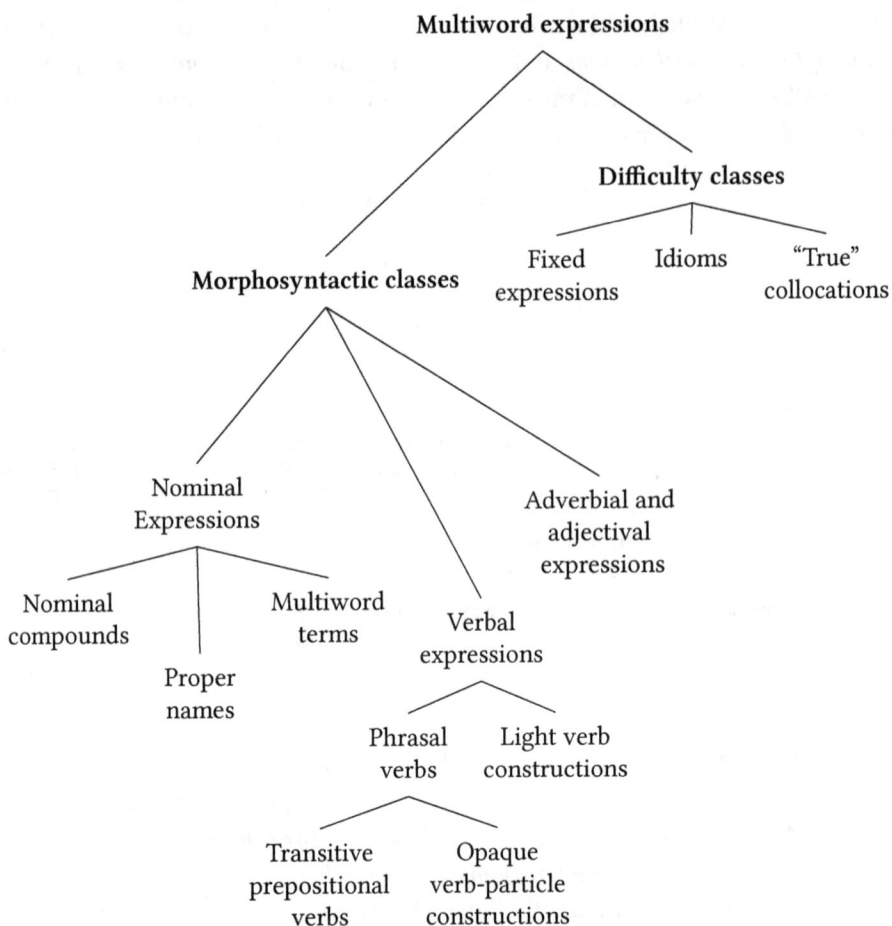

Figure 3: Simplified taxonomy proposed by Ramisch (2012; 2015).

2.3 Spanish MWE taxonomies

Although Spanish is a widely researched language, few researchers have worked on taxonomies of Spanish MWEs. The main reference for our study could be the seminal work by Corpas Pastor (1996) in Phraseology, who studied Spanish phraseological units, revised previous work and proposed a new taxonomy to classify them. Her taxonomy attempted to establish a classification of Spanish phraseological units based on a set of criteria that should help classify any unit under a specific type. Her taxonomy, summarized in Figure 4, has three major categories subsequently subdivided in more fine-grained subclasses. While *collocations* are classified following their possible part-of-speech patterns (e.g. subject_noun+verb, adjective+noun, etc.), *expressions* are classified according to the syntactic role they may have in a sentence (e.g. *nominal expressions, verbal expressions, prepositional expressions...*). Finally, *phraseological expressions* are divided into *sentences with a specific value, quotes* and *proverbs*.

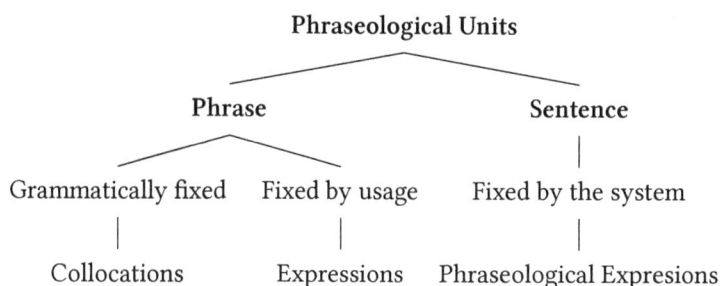

Phraseological Units

- Phrase
  - Grammatically fixed
    - Collocations
  - Fixed by usage
    - Expressions
- Sentence
  - Fixed by the system
    - Phraseological Expresions

Figure 4: Taxonomy of Spanish phraseological units by Corpas Pastor (1996).

From an NLP point of view, the work by Corpas Pastor (1996) cannot be easily adapted for NLP usage because many classes could be difficult to distinguish from one another. Nominal expressions, for instance, are further subdivided into types following a determined part-of-speech pattern. However, some of these patterns are identical to the ones used to classify collocations. Thus, to automatically determine whether a "noun+adjective" sequence shall be classified as a collocation (e.g. *enemigo acérrimo* 'archenemy'), or a nominal expression (e.g. *mosquita muerta* 'two-faced person') could be challenging.

Finally, it is also worth mentioning the work by Leoni de León (2014), who also attempted to propose a typology of phraseological units based on the lexical status and the syntactic phenomena of MWEs. In his taxonomy, he first distinguishes between *multi-member lexical units*, which are "units of meaning without necessarily being lexical units", and *collocations*, which are "a lexical choice probably motivated by communication style, with no semantic implications". *Multi-member lexical units* are further divided into lexicalized units (*multi-*

member lexemes) and non-lexicalized ones. According to Leoni de León (2014), multi-member lexemes can be characterized by the procedures used to create them. Thus, he distinguishes between those undergoing morphological procedures (*poly-lexemic lexemes*), and those undergoing syntactic procedures (*combined lexemes*). Non-lexicalized units can either be *phrasemes* or *thematic fusions*. He defines *thematic fusions* as "the result of the combination of a supporting verb and a predicative nominal", and *phrasemes* as "unit(s) of meaning formed from at least two open-class lexical morphemes, one of which constitutes the nucleus of the unit and bears the category V". As far as *phrasemes* are concerned, he distinguishes between "continuous expressions that extend across a sentence" (*complete phrasemes*), and "discontinuous expressions that can be replaced by a verb"(*syntagmatic phrasemes*). Figure 5 illustrates his taxonomy.

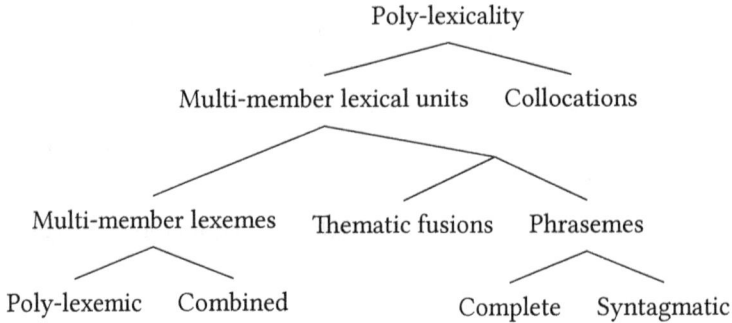

Figure 5: Taxonomy of Spanish phraseological units by Leoni de León (2014).

In this article, we use the taxonomy proposed by Ramisch (2012; 2015) as a starting point for a taxonomy of Spanish MWEs and we combine it with the approach taken by Sag et al. (2002) and Baldwin & Kim (2010) based on syntactic flexibility. This decision was made because these two taxonomies are widely spread among the research community and we wanted to test whether an English-driven taxonomy could be applied to the Spanish language.

3 MWE fixedness tests for Spanish

As one of our objectives was to classify MWEs according to their degree of syntactic flexibility, it is important to determine how this flexibility is going to be measured. Here, we will consider *fixed expressions* those which admit no alteration of their form. *Semi-fixed expressions* will be those which have a certain degree of morphosyntactic variability. This variability, however, is due to the need to conform with the grammatical and orthographical rules of the Spanish language and thus is controlled to a certain extent. From an NLP point of view, these expressions could be easily processed. In the case of fixed MWEs, the words-with-spaces approach proposed by Sag et al. (2002) could be used, while in the case of semi-fixed MWEs, this approach could be used adding pointers to the in-flected parts of the MWE, just as Sag et al. (2002) also propose. Finally, flexible MWEs will be those presenting a high degree of variability in their usage (e.g. non-contiguousness, free slots, etc.), which makes their form difficult to predict.

Based on previous work by Nunberg et al. (1994), where they try to determine the fixedness of MWEs, we designed a set of potential tests to establish the degree of flexibility of Spanish MWEs. This list may be expanded upon further research and, as pointed out by Laporte (2018 [this volume]), it needs further testing to be supported with statistics. However, we believe that it is a valid starting point for any work on the flexibility of Spanish MWEs and their further linguistic descrip-tion.

3.1 Inflection

Spanish is a rich morphological language. Thus, the first test that can be used to determine whether an MWE has some degree of flexibility is to check its inflec-tion. In the case of nouns and adjectives, whether or not these can be inflected for number, and in some cases for gender, shall be checked. Generally, adjectives agree in number and gender with the nouns they complement. Thus, their inflec-tion will be dependent on the possibility to inflect their head noun. Examples (1a)–(1b), (2a)–(2b) and (3a)–(3d) exemplify this.

(1)   a.   *anillo*   *de*   *compromiso*   b.   *anillos*   *de*   *compromiso*
       N.MASC.SG PREP N.MASC.SG   N.MASC.PL PREP N.MASC.SG
       ring   of   engagement   rings   of   engagement
       'engagement ring'   'engagement rings'

(2)   a.   *raíz*   *cuadrada*   b.   *raíces*   *cuadradas*
       N.FEM.SG ADJ.FEM.SG   N.FEM.PL ADJ.FEM.PL
       root   square   roots   square
       'square root'   'square roots'

(3) a. *lobo*   *con*   *piel*   *de*   *cordero*
      N.MASC.SG   PREP N.FEM.SG PREP N.MASC.SG
      wolf.MASC.SG with   skin   of   lamb

      'wolf.MASC.SG in sheep's clothing'

     b. *loba*   *con*   *piel*   *de*   *cordero*
      N.FEM.SG   PREP N.FEM.SG PREP N.MASC.SG
      wolf.FEM.SG with   skin   of   lamb

      'wolf.FEM.SG in sheep's clothing'

     c. *lobos*   *con*   *piel*   *de*   *cordero*
      N.MASC.PL   PREP N.FEM.SG PREP N.MASC.SG
      wolves.MASC.PL with   skin   of   lamb

      'wolves.MASC.PL in sheep's clothing'

     d. *lobas*   *con*   *piel*   *de*   *cordero*
      N.FEM.PL   PREP N.FEM.SG PREP N.MASC.SG
      wolves.FEM.PL with   skin   of   lamb

      'wolves.FEM.PL in sheep's clothing'

When the MWE includes a pronominal reference to a person, this can also have some variance to agree with the reference. Additionally, when the MWE includes a verb, this can also be inflected for person, tense and mode. Examples (4a)–(4d) and (5a)–(5c), respectively, exemplify this.

(4) a. ***el***   *que*   *corta*   *el*   *bacalao*
      DET.MASC.SG PRON V.3RD.SG.PRES.IND DET.MASC.SG N.MASC.SG
      the   who   cuts   the   cod

      'big fish.MASC.SG'

     b. ***la***   *que*   *corta*   *el*   *bacalao*
      DET.FEM.SG PRON V.3RD.SG.PRES.IND DET.MASC.SG N.MASC.SG
      the   who   cuts   the   cod

      'big fish.FEM.SG'

     c. ***los***   *que*   *cortan*   *el*   *bacalao*
      DET.MASC.PL PRON V.3RD.PL.PRES.IND DET.MASC.SG N.MASC.SG
      the   who   cut   the   cod

      'big fishes.MASC.PL'

d. *las*   *que*   *cortan*   *el*   *bacalao*
DET.FEM.PL PRON V.3RD.PL.PRES.IND DET.MASC.SG N.MASC.SG
the   who   cut   the   cod

'big fishes.FEM.PL'

(5)   a. *Vives*   *a*   *cuerpo*   *de*   *rey.*
V.2ND.SG.PRES.IND PREP N.MASC.SG PREP N.MASC.SG
live.you   by   body   of   king

'You live high on the hog.'

b. *Vivieron*   *a*   *cuerpo*   *de*   *rey.*
V.3RD.PL.PAST.IND PREP N.MASC.SG PREP N.MASC.SG
lived.they   by   body   of   king

'They lived high on the hog.'

c. *Hubiera vivido*   *a*   *cuerpo*   *de*   *rey.*
V.1ST/3RD.SG.PAST.SUBJ   PREP N.MASC.SG PREP N.MASC.SG
would have lived.I/he/she by   body   of   king

'I/he/she would have lived high on the hog.'

As the variation of this type of MWEs is controlled, in our study all MWEs which only undergo inflection are classified as semi-flexible MWEs.

3.2 Change of determiner

In some cases, the determiner appearing in an MWE is flexible in the sense that there are several items that can occupy that spot within the MWE. Examples (6a)–(6c) illustrate some of the variations of two of the MWEs in our data set.

(6)   a. *Nos*   *hicimos*   **varias**   *fotos.*
PRON.1.PL V.1.PL.PAST.IND ADJ.FEM.PL N.FEM.PL
Ourselves took.1ST.PL   several   pictures

'We took several pictures.'

b. *Nos*   *hicimos*   **muchas**   *fotos.*
PRON.1.PL V.1.PL.PAST.IND ADJ.FEM.PL N.FEM.PL
Ourselves took.1ST.PL   many   pictures

'We took many pictures.'

c. *Nos*   *hicimos*   **una**   *foto.*
PRON.1.PL V.1.PL.PAST.IND ADJ.FEM.SG N.FEM.SG
Ourselves took.1ST.PL   a   picture

'We took a picture.'

In our study, if an MWE *only* undergoes a change of determiner, it is classified as a semi-flexible MWE because this feature can be modeled computationally.

3.3 Pronominalisation

Another useful test to check the degree of flexibility of an MWE is to test whether part of it can be pronominalized. This is only possible for the Noun Phrase and Complementizer Phrase parts of verbal MWEs. Examples (7) and (8) illustrate such cases.[3]

(7) *Habíamos quedado   para **hacer las fotos**   el   lunes,   pero al*
     Agreed.to.meet.1ST.PL to   make the pictures the Monday, but in.the
     *final **las**   hicimos   el   martes.*
     end   them made.1ST.PL the Tuesday

     'We had agreed to **take the pictures** on Monday, but in the end we took **them** on Tuesday.'

(8) *Después de cenar **dimos**   **un** largo **paseo** por   el   campo y*
     After   of dinner went.1ST.PL a   long walk   through the field   and
     ***lo** disfrutamos   mucho.*
     it   enjoyed.1ST.PL a lot

     'We **went for a** long **walk** through the field after dinner and we enjoyed **it** greatly.'

When part of a Spanish MWE can be pronominalized, we classify such MWE as a flexible MWE because the fact that not all lexical elements are together in the same clause makes its identification and processing more difficult. While in example (7) the object of the MWE (*las fotos* 'the pictures') is pronominalized and the same verb is used in the second occurrence of the MWE, in example (8) the object is used as the object of a different verb (*disfrutar* 'to enjoy').

3.4 Topicalization

In some cases, it is possible to alter the order in which the elements of an MWE appear. Similarly to what happens with the pronominalisation of MWEs, topicalization is only possible for the Noun Phrase and Complementizer Phrase parts of verbal MWEs. Example (9) shows how the prepositional phrase (*de política* 'about

---

[3]From here on, we omit the morphological analysis of the examples as it is not needed to illustrate the flexibility issues described.

politics') of a verb with a governed prepositional phrase (*hablar de* 'talk about') may be fronted and appear before the verb itself. Example (10) illustrates how in interrogative sentences the noun phrase of a light verb construction (*qué trato* 'what deal') may also be placed prior to the verb it refers to (*harán*, 'make').[4]

(9) **De   política** no **hablaban** nada   más que los domingos.
     About politics   not talked.3RD nothing more than the Sundays

     'They only talked about politics on Sundays.'

(10) *¿Qué trato* crees   que *harán*   las empresas?
     What deal   think.2ND that will make.3RD the companies

     'What deal do you think the companies will make?'

When an MWE allows for the topicalization of part of it, we classify it as a flexible MWE. An additional reason is that when topicalization occurs, the MWE appears separated in the clause. As it is not possible to determine how many other phrases (and of which type) can appear between the elements of the MWE, its successful processing requires more than just a morphosyntactic analysis.

3.5 Subordinate clauses

MWEs can also appear in complex sentences which have subordinate clauses. In this case, two phenomena may occur. First, the MWE can be partially embedded in a subordinate clause because the element appearing outside of the subordinate clause is also the antecedent of the subordinating conjunction. Example (11) shows this: *el trato* 'the deal' is the antecedent of the subordinating conjunction *que* 'that/which'.

(11) *El   trato que hizo* mi hermana consistía en ...
     The deal that made my sister   consisted in ...

     '**The deal** my sister **made** involved ...'

Second, part of the MWE can be the antecedent of a subordinate clause, as illustrated in (12).

(12) *Mi hermana hizo un trato que* consistía en ...
     My sister   made a deal that consisted in ...

     'My sister **made a deal that** involved ...'

---

[4]In this example, a second phenomenon occurs, as the verb is part of a subordinate clause whereas the noun phrase is part of the main clause. This is discussed in the next flexibility test in §3.5.

When a part of an MWE can be embedded in a relative clause or be the antecedent of a relative clause, we classify it as a flexible MWE.

3.6 Passivization

A frequent way of testing the flexibility of English MWEs is to test whether or not their passivization is possible. As the passive voice is not as frequent in Spanish as in English, this test may not be very informative for testing Spanish MWEs. Moreover, in Spanish there are two passivization mechanisms:

1. Passives using the auxiliary verb *ser* 'to be'; and

2. passives using the pronoun *se*, also called 'passive *se*'.

Passives using the auxiliary verb *ser* are not very frequent, and it is common to find 'passive *se*' sentences.

In the case of MWEs, this test can still be used, and in some cases, such as the one in example (13), it will be possible to find an MWE appearing in a passive voice construction. In some cases, both types of passives are possible. Example (14), shows how the passivization of example (13) could be also done by means of the Spanish pronoun *se*.

(13) **La decisión fue tomada** el   lunes.
      The decision was taken   the Monday
      '**The decision was made** on Monday.'

(14) **La decisión se   tomará**   el   lunes.
      The decision itself will be taken.3RD.SG the Monday
      '**The decision will be made** on Monday.'

If an MWE can *only* undergo passivization (i.e. all other tests are negative), we classified it as semi-flexible. Else, we classified it as a flexible MWE.

3.7 Appearance of other elements

In some cases, other elements such as adjectives, adverbs or pronouns which do not belong to the MWE appear embedded in the MWE. The number of elements that can appear embedded in the MWE also varies. There could be only one element, or several. Examples (15) to (17) illustrate this.

(15) *dar   un **largo** paseo*
     to take a   long   walk

     'to take a **long** walk'

(16) *dar   un **largo** y   **agradable** paseo*
     to take a   long   and nice   walk

     'to take a **long and nice** walk'

(17) *echar **profundamente** la   siesta*
     to take deeply   the nap

     'to take a nap **deeply**'

When other elements can appear embedded within the elements of an MWE we classified it as a flexible MWE.

3.8 Ellipsis

Finally, part of an MWE can sometimes be omitted. This is usually the case when, for instance, the object of an MWE has been mentioned earlier and then it is referred to at a later stage. Example (18) illustrates this. In the example, the complement of the verb *hacer* 'to do' is elided but *qué* 'what' is used to refer to it 'what deal'.

(18) *¿**Qué** crees   que **harán**?*
     What think.2ND.SG that do.3RD.PL

     '**What (deal)** do you think they will **do**?'

Ellipsis may also occur when there is coordination. Example (19) illustrates this by showing two coordinated main clauses that share the same predicate (*quedarse* 'to keep for oneself') with a change both of the subject (*María–Juan*), and of the complement of the prepositional phrase governed by the verb (*el libro* 'the book' vs. *el disco* 'the disc').

(19) *María **se**   **quedó con** el   libro y   Juan **con** el   disco.*
     María herself kept   with the book and Juan with the disc

     'María kept the book and Juan the disc.'

In those cases in which an MWE allows for the omission of part of it, we classified the MWE as a flexible MWE.

4 Creating a data set to analyze Spanish MWEs

As a starting point for our study, we took the MWE taxonomy proposed by Ramisch (2012; 2015) and created a preliminary data set of Spanish MWEs. It was not compiled by doing a corpus analysis and subsequently trying to analyze and classify the MWEs detected, but rather by taking the English examples from Ramisch (2012; 2015) and trying to find similar ones in Spanish. The preliminary data set consisted of 150 Spanish MWEs classified according to Ramisch's taxonomy (Parra Escartín et al. 2015).

Figure 6 exemplifies all of the MWE types distinguished in Ramisch's taxonomy with Spanish examples and their translations into English. As may also be observed, there is no example for *phrasal verbs*. This is because Spanish lacks such a type of MWE, although there are verbs with a governed prepositional phrase (e.g. *acordarse de* 'to remember') which, to a certain extent, have a similar behavior to that of English phrasal verbs.[5]

We then analyzed and classified the MWEs by their degree of difficulty for NLP purposes. To this aim, we used the "fixed, semi-fixed, flexible" classification proposed in the papers by Sag et al. (2002) and Baldwin & Kim (2010).

The Spanish Grammar[6] (Real Academia Española 2010) was also used to detect additional MWE types not present in the taxonomy, describe MWE subclasses, and gather further examples for our data set. As we aimed at having a number of entries for each MWE type that allowed us to properly describe its features, additional new entries were also added to the data set. Appendix A, Appendix B, and Appendix C comprise our data set classified in fixed, semi-fixed and flexible MWEs respectively.

5 Our Spanish MWE taxonomy

When creating our data set, we realized that the taxonomy we had started to work with was not completely matching the Spanish MWEs we were gathering. Thus, we started to modify the taxonomy and adapt it to the Spanish language. This

---

[5]As pointed out in the annotation guidelines for the PARSEME shared task on automatic detection of verbal multiword expressions (Vincze et al. 2016), VERB PARTICLE CONSTRUCTIONS (also called phrasal verbs), "are pervasive in English, German, Hungarian and possible other languages but irrelevant to or very rare in Romance and Slavic languages or in Farsi and Greek for instance". As Vincze et al. (2016) also point out, contrary to inherently prepositional verbs (referred to in this paper as *verbs with a governed prepositional phrase*), the particle present in phrasal verbs cannot introduce a complement.

[6]In this article, we use italics to refer to the Spanish grammar written by the *Real Academia de la Lengua Española* (RAE, Royal Spanish Language Academy) used as a reference in our work.

		Noun compounds	*sacacorchos* *ruleta rusa*	bottle opener Russian roulette
	Nominal expressions	Proper names	*Nueva York* *Unión Europea* *Barack Obama*	New York European Union Barack Obama
		Multiword terms	*cuenta de resultados* *infarto de miocardio*	profit and loss account myocardial infarction
Morphosyntactic classes	Verbal expressions	Phrasal verbs		
		Light verb constructions	*tener fe* *hacer una foto* *dar un paseo*	to have faith to take a picture to go for a walk
	Adverbial and adjectival expressions		*más o menos* *en líneas generales*	more or less by and large
	Fixed expressions		*ad hoc* *en lo que respecta a*	ad hoc with regard to
Difficulty classes	Idiomatic expressions		*estirar la pata* *poner la antena* *ponerse las pilas* *cargar las pilas*	to kick the bucket to listen without being invited to to get one's act together to recharge one's batteries
	"True" collocations		*escribir una carta* *firmar un acuerdo*	to write a letter to sign an agreement

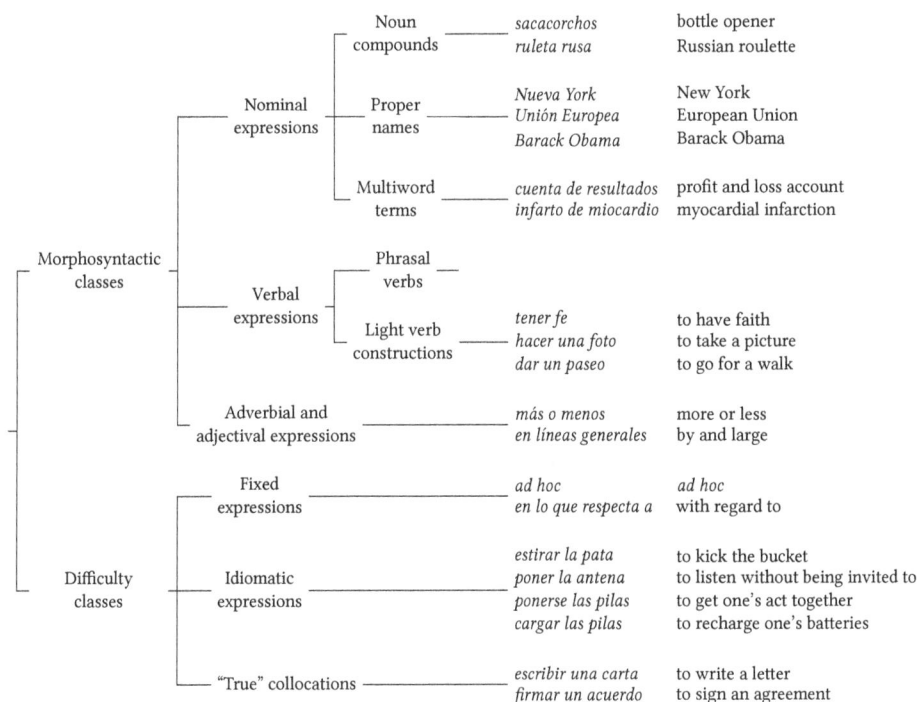

Figure 6: Spanish MWEs classified following Ramisch (2012; 2015) taxonomy.

confirms the common criticism against current MWE taxonomies claiming they are based on the English language and that other languages cannot be classified in the same way.

After revising our data and discussing the different categories we had encountered, we first decided to eliminate the types *compound nouns* and *multiword terms* and add a new category, *complex nominals*, to account for single-token compound nouns in Spanish such as *abrebotellas* 'bottle opener', and syntagmatic compounds such as *botella de vino* 'wine bottle'.

The concept of complex nominals was already introduced by Atkins et al. (2001) to account for complex nominal constructions in languages other than English that can be considered MWEs. While compounds in Germanic languages such as English or German are created by appending several nouns together in either several tokens (e.g. English) or one (e.g. German, Norwegian), in Spanish (and other Romance languages such as Italian or French), these expressions require the usage of prepositions and articles and show a different structure.

Multiword terms were eliminated as an MWE type in our taxonomy because the different types of terms could be actually classified within other MWE types in our taxonomy. Terms might be either single words (e.g. *fideicomiso* 'trust') or more complex structures, ranging from complex nominals (e.g. *cuenta de resultados* 'profit and loss account') to verbal MWEs (e.g. *fallar a favor* 'to rule in favor') and idiomatic MWEs (e.g. *a tenor de lo dispuesto en* 'in accordance with/under the stipulations of'), which justified their reclassification into other categories in our new taxonomy. Moreover, terminology is a different research field with its own taxonomies for classifying terms. The terms gathered in our data were thus redistributed in the other MWE types in our taxonomy.

Adjectival and adverbial MWEs had to be split in two different categories as they do not share the same features. Moreover, a closer look at *adjectival expressions* revealed that in Spanish we can distinguish between three different main subclasses: *compounds, adjectival phrases* and *adjectives with a governed prepositional phrase*.

In the case of *verbal expressions*, we deleted *phrasal verbs* because, as explained earlier (cf. §4), Spanish does not have such type of verbs. In order to cover other MWE types in Spanish, we had to add three new subclasses: *periphrastic constructions, verbal phrases* and *verbs with a prepositional phrase*.

We also decided to eliminate the *fixed expressions* from the taxonomy as this refers to a type of flexibility rather than a type of MWE. According to Ramisch (2015), "they correspond to the fixed expressions of Sag et al. (2002), that is, it is possible to deal with them using the words-with-spaces approach. Such expressions often play the role of functional words (*in short; with respect to*), contain foreign words (*ad infinitum; déjà vu*) or breach standard grammatical rules (*by and large; kingdom come*)". The fixed expressions present in our data set could easily be redistributed across two additional MWE types added to the morphosyntactic types: *conjunctional phrases* and *prepositional phrases*. Foreign MWEs have been excluded of our study because their classification and characterization is beyond the scope of this article.

As far as the other two *"difficulty classes"* in the taxonomy proposed by Ramisch (2012; 2015), we also eliminated them as they did not comply with our aim of classifying MWEs by morphosyntactic types and rather constituted categories based on semantic criteria (*idioms*), or statistical co-occurrence (*"true" collocations*). We reclassified all items in those categories across several of the morphosyntactic types: *complex nominals, light verb constructions* and *verbal phrases*. To accommodate the remaining few items that could not be reclassified, we created a new and broader category: *sentential expressions*.

Our taxonomy comprises two different axes: *MWE morphosyntactic type* and *flexibility degree*. The MWE *morphosyntactic type* axis is based on Ramisch's (2012; 2015) taxonomy with the modifications explained above. The *flexibility degree* axis is based on the three levels of MWE flexibility identified by Sag et al. (2002) and Baldwin & Kim (2010). Thus, all MWEs in our data set are classified according to their morphosyntactic type and flexibility.

Figure 7 shows our taxonomy and its two main axes: the MWE type and the flexibility degree. It also quantifies the number of samples in our data set per morphosyntactic type and flexibility.

6 The linguistic properties of Spanish MWEs

In what follows we analyze the Spanish MWEs in our data set per type and describe their main linguistic properties. The analysis was carried out manually and complemented by making searches in Spanish written corpora when we needed to verify our linguistic intuition of a particular MWE.[7] Specifically, we used two contemporary Spanish corpora: CREA[8] and CORPES XXI.[9]

All entries in our data set were manually analyzed.[10] Our manual study, combined with the grammar study and the corpus queries, allowed us to identify and verify the specific linguistic features of Spanish MWEs described here.

6.1 Adjectival expressions

6.1.1 Adjectival compounds

Adjectival compounds in Spanish are one typographic word (e.g. *drogadicto* 'drug addicted'; *pelirrojo* 'redheaded'). They are usually formed by joining two adjectives together, or a noun and an adjective. Although they constitute one typographic word, we consider them multiwords because they are composed of sev-

---

[7]A deeper corpus study of the MWEs gathered in our data is planned as future work.

[8]Corpus de referencia del español actual (Reference Corpus for Current Spanish): http://corpus.rae.es/creanet.html.

[9]Corpus del español del siglo XXI (Corpus for 21st Century Spanish): http://web.frl.es/CORPES/view/inicioExterno.view.

[10]As mentioned earlier, the inflectional morphology of Spanish is richer than the morphology of English and therefore it requires a more detailed linguistic analysis. A similar observation was made in Savary (2008) and Graliński et al. (2010), who studied the complexity of encoding MWEs in morphologically rich languages such as Polish and French. Testing the formalisms they propose is beyond the scope of this article.

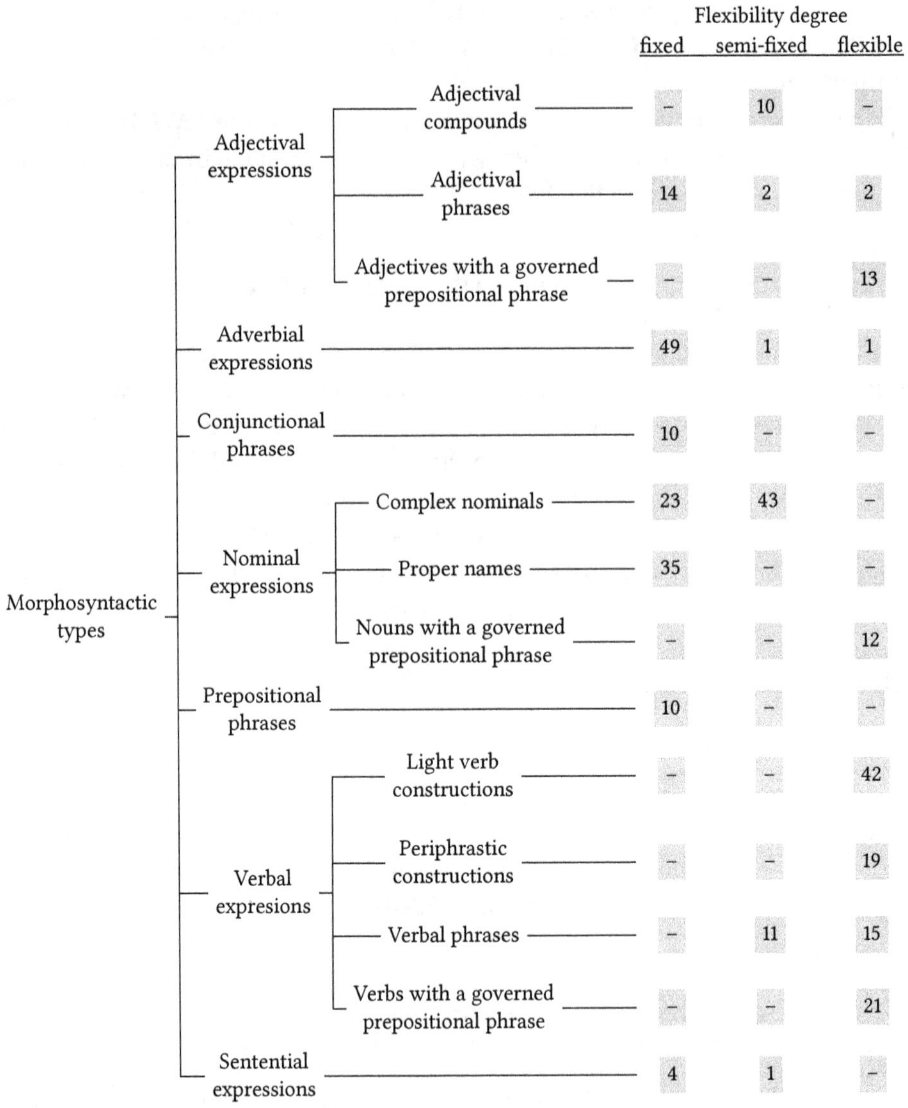

Morphosyntactic types			fixed	semi-fixed	flexible
Adjectival expressions	Adjectival compounds		–	10	–
	Adjectival phrases		14	2	2
	Adjectives with a governed prepositional phrase		–	–	13
Adverbial expressions			49	1	1
Conjunctional phrases			10	–	–
Nominal expressions	Complex nominals		23	43	–
	Proper names		35	–	–
	Nouns with a governed prepositional phrase		–	–	12
Prepositional phrases			10	–	–
Verbal expresions	Light verb constructions		–	–	42
	Periphrastic constructions		–	–	19
	Verbal phrases		–	11	15
	Verbs with a governed prepositional phrase		–	–	21
Sentential expressions			4	1	–

(Flexibility degree: fixed, semi-fixed, flexible)

Figure 7: New MWE taxonomy for Spanish.

eral words and might need to be processed in a special way in some NLP applications (like Machine Translation), as German compounds, for instance.

In our data set, all adjectival compounds are semi-flexible.[11] They inflect either in gender (masculine/feminine) and number (singular/plural), or only in number (singular/plural).[12] In some cases, these adjectival compounds are nominalized in usage, despite them being adjectives. For instance, *drogadicto* can occur in a sentence as an adjective or a nominalized adjective. Examples (20) and (21) illustrate this.

(20) *Ella está ayudando a un hombre drogadicto.*
       She is   helping   to a man.N drug.addicted.ADJ
       'She is helping a drug addicted man.'

(21) *Ella está ayudando a un drogadicto.*
       She is   helping   to a drug.addicted.N
       'She is helping a drug addict.'

6.1.2 Adjectival phrases

According to *the Spanish Grammar* (2010: 261), adjectival phrases are lexicalized phrases that behave syntactically like adjectives. Many have the structure of a prepositional phrase which complements a head noun, and sometimes are equivalent to adverbial collocations complementing predicates (e.g. *juramento **en falso*** 'a lie under oath' vs. *jurar **en falso*** 'to lie under oath'). Alternatively, they can also be of the form *como* 'as' followed by a nominal phrase (e.g. *como una catedral* 'huge'). Finally, it is also possible to find adjectival phrases formed by adjectives in coordination (e.g. *corriente y moliente* 'plain ordinary').

The majority of the adjectival phrases gathered in our data set are fixed (14), although we also registered 2 semi-fixed phrases and 2 flexible ones. The 2 flexible phrases are of the type "preposition + noun", whereas in the semi-fixed ones one has the Part-of-Speech (PoS) pattern "preposition + adjective + noun" and the other one is of the type "adjective + conjunction + adjective". Moreover, all these PoS patterns are also present among the 14 fixed ones, which suggests that there is not a preferred form that flavors flexibility.[13] This seems to be in line with the fact that these phrases are lexicalized, and thus show a tendency to be invariable.

---

[11]Cf. Figure 7.

[12]See Appendix B.

[13]This shall however be confirmed by undergoing a corpus based analysis of all items in our data set and new ones.

6.1.3 Adjectives with a governed prepositional phrase

Adjectives with a governed prepositional phrase are adjectives that are always followed by a certain preposition. The preposition is not predictable, since it is due to both semantic and historical reasons. Moreover, in some cases the prepositional phrase has to be explicit (e.g. *carente de* 'deprived of'), whereas in other cases where the information is considered to be implicit, the prepositional phrase can be omitted (e.g. *ser fiel a* 'to be loyal to').

We gathered 13 adjectives with a governed prepositional phrase in our data set. All of them are fully flexible, as they can be modified not only according to number (singular/plural) and gender (masculine/feminine), but also allow for other elements such as adverbs to be inserted between the adjective and the prepositional phrase.

6.2 Adverbial expressions

According to *the Spanish Grammar* (2010: 599), adverbial expressions are fixed expressions formed by several words that account for a single adverb. They might not have the form of an adverb, but they function as such. Some can be substituted by adverbs ending in *-mente* (e.g. *en secreto* 'in secret' and *secretamente* 'secretly'), but most of them have a more specific or slightly different meaning from the adverbs which are morphologically similar to the adverbial expression.

There are some very exceptional cases in Spanish in which adverbial expressions can be slightly modified (Real Academia Española 2010: 600) by adding a suffix to the main noun (e.g. *a golpes/a golpetazos*,[14] 'violently'; lit. 'by hits/by thumps') or introducing an adjective between two elements of the expression (e.g. *a mi entender/a mi modesto entender* 'by my understanding/by my modest understanding').

There are three different types of adverbial expressions in Spanish:

- "Preposition + noun phrase", where the noun phrase may be a single noun (e.g. *por descontado* 'of course'), or a noun modified by other elements such as determiners or adjectives (e.g. *a la fuerza* 'by force');

- "preposition + adjective/participle" (e.g. *a escondidas* 'behind somebody's back'; *por supuesto* 'of course'); and

---

[14]In Spanish, the suffix *-azo* is a very productive suffix with different meanings. Here, it is used as an augmentative to indicate the size or strength of the blow.

- "lexicalized phrase" which typically expresses quantity, manner and/or degree (e.g. *una barbaridad* 'quite a lot'; *codo con codo* 'elbow to elbow').

We gathered a total of 51 adverbial expressions in our data set. 28 of them are of the type "preposition + noun phrase" (12 in which the noun phrase is a single noun and 16 in which the noun phrase includes modifiers); 11 are of the type "preposition + adjective/participle", and the remaining 12 are lexicalized phrases expressing quantity, manner or degree. A manual analysis of these 51 items revealed that adverbial expressions in Spanish are mostly fixed in their structure, which confirms what is stated in *the Spanish Grammar* (2010: 601).

6.3 Conjunctional phrases

Conjunctional phrases are groups of words containing a conjunction that function as a single conjunction (e.g. *a fin de que* 'in order to'). In Spanish, once identified, this type of MWEs is easy to deal with from an NLP perspective. They are invariable and do not allow the inflection of any of its parts, which would allow to process them successfully using the words-with-spaces approach used with other fixed expressions. 10 conjunctional phrases were included in our data set.

6.4 Nominal expressions

6.4.1 Complex nominals

We have defined this category similarly to what Atkins et al. (2001) propose. Thus, it accounts for noun compounds in Spanish, and includes other nominal phrases that usually behave as nominal compounds in other languages such as English. *The Spanish Grammar* (2010) accounts for several types of compounds in Spanish:

- **Noun compounds of one typographic word**: *cascanueces* 'nutcracker'; *limpiacristales* 'window cleaner'; *aguafiestas* 'spoilsport'.

- **Noun compounds of two typographic words**: two nouns after one another as in *mesa camilla* 'round table'; *hombre lobo* 'werewolf'; or a noun followed by an adjective as in *guerra civil* 'civil war'.

- **Syntagmatic compounds**: nominal phrases typically including a prepositional phrase as in *goma de borrar* 'eraser'; *café con leche* 'coffee with milk'; *el día a día* 'everyday life'; *ley de la jungla* 'law of the jungle'.

We gathered a total of 66 complex nominals in our data set. A manual analysis of these 66 items revealed that complex nominals in Spanish are either fixed in their structure (23), or semi-fixed (43).

We further classified our data according to the three types described above. 11 items were noun compounds of one typographic word, 19 items were noun compounds of two typographic words, and the rest (36) were syntagmatic compounds. All compounds of one typographic word in our data but one are fixed and do not experience any kind of morphosyntactic variation in their usage. However, this does not hold true for all Spanish noun compounds of one typographic word. In our data, most of the noun compounds we gathered end in -*s*, which means that both the singular and the plural forms of such noun compounds are the same. Other noun compounds, such as the only one we gathered as semi-fixed (*bocacalle* 'side-street') do inflect in plural (*bocacalles*).

19 items were noun compounds of two typographic words. In 2 cases these noun compounds are fixed and do not show any kind of variance: *vergüenza ajena* 'the feeling of being embarrassed for somebody', and *gripe aviar* 'avian influenza'. The remaining items can be inflected in either singular or plural and thus are semi-fixed. We gathered 13 items of the type "noun + adjective" and 6 of the type "noun + noun". While the compounds of the type "noun + adjective" seem to require that both the noun and the adjective are inflected and agree in number, in the case of the "noun + noun" compounds this does not always hold true. In some cases, only the head of the compound can be inflected in the plural forms (e.g. *ciudad dormitorio* 'dormitory town' vs. *ciudades dormitorio* 'dormitory towns'; and *niño prodigio* 'child prodigy' vs. *niños prodigio* 'child prodigies'). The *Spanish Grammar* (2010) points out that when the modifier of the compound adopts an adjectival function (e.g. *disco pirata* 'pirated CD'; *momento clave* 'key moment'), the plural form of the compound can be formed by only inflecting the head of the compound[15] (e.g. *discos pirata* 'pirated CDs'; *momentos clave* 'key moments') or both nouns, the head and the modifier (e.g. *discos piratas*; *momentos claves*).

Finally, the remaining 36 items in our data set were *syntagmatic compounds*. 11 of them are fixed, while the other 25 are semi-fixed.

Complex nominals in Spanish can only inflect in terms of number. Although there seems to be a pattern in which only the head of the compound is inflected (e.g. *ciudad/ciudades dormitorio* 'dormitory town/towns'), it is not always the case.

---

[15] In Spanish, the head of a compound is the left-most element in the compound.

For NLP purposes, an easy strategy to test whether a complex nominal is fixed or allows for inflection would be to inflect the complex nominal in number and check whether that form can be found in a monolingual corpus. If it is not the case, the complex nominal is fixed. Otherwise, it is semi-fixed.

6.4.2 Proper names

Proper names identify a being among others without providing information of its features or its constituent parts. These nouns do not express what things are, but what their name is as individual entities. Proper names have referring capacity, do not participate in lexical relations and, strictly speaking, cannot be translated (*Spanish Grammar* 2010: 209–210).

The *Spanish Grammar* (2010: 219) identifies two types of proper names: anthroponyms and toponyms. However, it also argues that names that account for festivals or celebrations, celestial bodies, allegorical representations, works of art, foundations, religious orders, companies, clubs, corporations and other institutions share the same characteristics.

We gathered a total of 35 proper names in our data set. A manual analysis of these 35 items revealed that proper names in Spanish cannot be morphologically modified.

We classified our data according to the three types listed above. 12 items were toponyms, 11 items were anthroponyms, and 12 were classified under "others", which include celestial bodies, works of art, foundations, companies, clubs, corporations, etc. All those items do not have any kind of morphological variation.

6.4.3 Nouns with a governed prepositional phrase

Nouns with a governed prepositional phrase are nouns that are always followed by a certain preposition. Occasionally, more than one preposition is possible (e.g. *actitud con/hacia/respecto de* 'attitude with/towards/regarding'). This is usually the case when the phrase following the preposition indicates matter, direction or addressee. In some cases, two prepositions with exactly the same meaning are valid (e.g. *asalto a/de* 'assault to/on'; *solución a/de* 'solution to/of').

Some nouns followed by a prepositional phrase derive from the verbal form, maintaining the same preposition (e.g. *oler a/olor a* 'to smell like'/'smell of'; *eximir de/exento de* 'to exempt from'/'exempt from'). There are cases, though, where the preposition changes (e.g. *amenazar con/amenaza de* 'to threaten to'/'threat of'; *interesarse por/interesado en* 'to be interested in'/'interested in').

We gathered 12 nouns with a governed prepositional phrase. As the adjectives with a governed prepositional phrase, all of them are fully flexible. They can be modified according to number (singular/plural) and gender (masculine/feminine), and they admit an adverb and/or an adjective between the noun and the preposition.

6.5 Prepositional phrases

Prepositional phrases are groups of words containing a preposition that function as a single preposition (e.g. *en detrimento de* 'at the expense of'). Similarly to conjunctional phrases (cf. §6.3), these MWEs are fixed in Spanish and thus none of its parts can inflect. Our data set includes 10 prepositional phrases.

6.6 Verbal expressions

6.6.1 Light verb constructions

Light verb constructions (LVC) in Spanish are semi-lexicalized verb constructions formed by a verb with a supporting role or semantically weak complemented by an abstract noun[16] (Real Academia Española 2010: 14). *The Spanish Grammar* (Real Academia Española 2010: 14) identifies the following light verbs in Spanish: *dar* 'to give'; *tener* 'to have'; *tomar* 'to take'; *hacer* 'to do' or 'to make'; and *echar* 'to throw'. In some cases, the noun is preceded by an article. Many LVCs can be paraphrased using another single verb with similar meaning (e.g. *dar un paseo*: *pasear* 'to take a walk': 'to walk'; *hacer alusión*: *aludir* 'to make an allusion': 'to allude').

This definition thus differs from the one offered by Laporte (2018 [this volume]), as well as with the one specified in the annotation guidelines for the PARSEME shared task on automatic detection of verbal multiword expressions (Vincze et al. 2016). Vincze et al. (2016) identify the following six general characteristics of LVCs:

1. They are formed by a verb and its argument containing a noun. The argument is usually a direct object, but sometimes also a prepositional complement or a subject.

2. Both the verb and the noun (included in the complement) are lexicalized.

---

[16] *The Spanish Grammar* (2010: 210) defines abstract nouns as those nouns which refer to something of a non-material nature such as actions, processes and attributes that we assign to beings when we think of them as independent entities (e.g. beauty, dirt).

3. The verb is "light", i.e. it contributes to the meaning of the whole only to a small degree.

4. The noun has one of its regular meanings.

5. The noun is predicative, and in LVCs one of its arguments becomes also a syntactic argument of the verb. Moreover, the subject is usually an argument of the noun.

6. The noun typically refers to an action or event.

Bearing in mind that our ultimate goal is to find a taxonomy of Spanish MWEs that can be used from an NLP point of view, we took here a rather comprehensive approach and combined both definitions. Thus, the LVCs in our data set include both expressions including the light verbs identified by *The Spanish Grammar*, and other verbs that in combination with certain nouns can be considered light because their meaning is bleached to a certain extent.

We gathered a total of 42 LVCs in our database. The verbs contained in light verb expressions always inflect in person (1st, 2nd, 3rd / singular or plural), tense (present, past or future) and mode (indicative, subjunctive or imperative), just as any other verb. Most of the times, the other elements of the expression (article and noun) can also be modified without changing the meaning of the expression (e.g. *dar un beso* 'to give a kiss'; *dar dos besos* 'to give two kisses').[17] In our data set, the noun phrases of 10 of the 42 LVCs can appear either in singular or plural. There are some exceptional cases in which the meaning of the expression changes when the noun is singular or plural (e.g. *tener gana*, 'to be hungry' vs. *tener ganas* 'to feel like'; *hacer ilusión* 'to look forward to' vs. *hacerse ilusiones* 'to get one's hope up').[18] Finally, adjectives and adverbs can be included between the different elements of the expression (e.g. *echar **profundamente** la siesta*, 'to take a nap **deeply**'; *echar una **larga** siesta*, 'to take a **long** nap'), which means that they are flexible MWEs.

Regarding other flexibility tests such as pronominalisation, topicalization, subordinate clauses and passivization,[19] further research in large Spanish corpora would be required. It seems that most constructions do allow for the pronominalization of the noun (cf. example (8)) and the appearance of subordinate clauses (e.g. *El paseo que dimos ayer* 'The walk we took yesterday'), while they do not seem so prone to allow for topicalization or passivization.

---

[17] For more examples of changes in the determiner, see Examples (6a) to (6c).

[18] These cases are registered in our data set as different MWE entries.

[19] Cf. §§3.3–3.6.

From an NLP perspective, light verb expressions are challenging in Spanish. While some issues such as the verb tenses can be targeted specifically, some other issues require the usage of other processing strategies. Thus, a change in the determiner or the insertion of adjectives and adverbs between the different elements of the expression will require the design of specific strategies to successfully identify and process these MWEs.

6.6.2 Periphrastic constructions

Verbal periphrastic constructions in Spanish are syntactic combinations in which an auxiliary or semi-auxiliary verb is used in combination with a past participle, an infinitive or a gerund and both verbs constitute a unique predicate (Real Academia Española 2010: 529). The verb used as an auxiliary can also appear in non-periphrastic constructions having its full meaning. In some cases, these constructions include the usage of a preposition (e.g. *empezar a* ... 'to begin to ...'; *acabar de* ... 'to have just finished to ...').

The first verb in the periphrastic construction is the one which undergoes inflection, whereas the second one always appears in the same non-finite form, and it is the one which varies and constitutes the main verb of the clause. Sometimes, as example (22) shows, an element such as an adverb can appear between the first element of the periphrasis and the second one. The subject can also appear in between the main verb and the auxiliary or semi-auxiliary verb (example (23)).

(22) *Tuvo*   ***casi***   *que saltar para no caerse.*
      Had.3RD.SG.MASC/FEM almost that jump for   not fall.himself/herself.
      'He/she almost had to jump to avoid falling down.'

(23) *No podía **yo** creérmelo, pero ...*
      Not could I   believe.it, but ...
      'I could not believe it, but ...'

We gathered a total of 19 periphrastic constructions in our data set. Due to their variability in inflection and the allowance of other elements, we have tentatively classified them as flexible. However, further research is needed to determine if certain types could be considered semi-flexible (i.e. those in which the MWE only undergoes inflection) because these structures do not seem to allow for pronominalization, topicalization, subordination or passivization.

(24) *Prometió*   *comprar el*   *libro.*
     Promised.3RD.SG.MASC/FEM buy   the book
     'He/she promised to buy the book.'

(25) *Pudo*   *comprar el*   *libro.*
     Could.3RD.SG.MASC/FEM buy   the book
     'He/She could have bought the book.'

One problem of this type of construction is that sometimes it has the same structure as a non-periphrastic one. There are cases, in which a full verb is followed by another verb in a non-finite form, and is the head of the predicate, while the non-finite form is introducing a subordinate clause which complements the main verb. In such cases, there is no periphrasis. In other cases, the same structure ("inflected verb + verb in non-finite form") act as a single unit. In such cases, the inflected verb acts as an auxiliary or semi-auxiliary verb, while the main verb is the one in non-finite form. Examples (24) and (25) illustrate this. In (24), *comprar el libro* 'buy the book' would be a subordinate infinitive clause that is the direct object of the predicate (*prometió* 'promised') of the main clause. In (25), however, *pudo comprar* 'could have bought' is the predicate of the clause and *el libro* 'the book' is its direct object. This makes this type of constructions particularly tricky to detect and to process.[20]

6.6.3 Verbal phrases

Verbal phrases are those MWEs whose head is a verb and which cannot be classified as any other type of verbal MWEs. All of them share the feature that to a certain extent they are idiomatic expressions whose semantics are non-compositional. As we aimed at classifying Spanish MWEs from a morphosyntactic point of view, many of the items that we originally had classified as idioms following Ramisch's taxonomy (2012; 2015) are classified as verbal phrases in our data set.

In total, 26 items of our data set were classified as verbal phrases. 11 of them were classified as semi-fixed MWEs and the remaining 15 as flexible MWEs. In all the verbal phrases classified as semi-fixed the verb appearing in the MWE inflects (e.g. *coger el toro por los cuernos* 'to take the bull by the horns'; *empezar la casa por el tejado* 'to put the cart before the horse').

---

[20]This type of structure is worth researching within a larger project including large corpus searches. This is beyond the scope of this article, where we only aim at detecting MWE types in Spanish that are not covered in the current MWE taxonomies explained in §2.

Carla Parra Escartín, Almudena Nevado Llopis & Eoghan Sánchez Martínez

Finally, we detected cases in which it was also possible for other words to appear within the MWE to modify its meaning. In these cases, besides the verb inflection and the noun singular/plural and masculine/feminine alternations, the MWE could include other modifying elements. For example, *entrar al trapo* 'to respond to provocations', can be modified by elements referring to its frequency (e.g. *entrar **siempre** al trapo* 'to respond to provocations **always**').

Another special type of flexibility is the one created by the presence of reflexive pronouns as part of the verb in the MWE, because depending on the overall structure of the sentence the pronoun may appear in different parts of it. Examples (26a) to (26c) below show this phenomenon with the MWE *irse de la lengua* 'to let the cat out of the bag'.

(26) a. *No   tienes   que   irte   de   la*
ADV V.2ND.SG.PRES.IND PRON V.INF+PRON.2ND.SG PREP DET.FEM.SG
not   have(.you)   that   go.yourself   of   the
lengua
N.FEM.SG
tongue

'Do not let the cat out of the bag.'

   b. *No te   tienes   que   ir de la*
ADV PRON.2ND.SG V.2ND.SG.PRES.IND PRON V.INF PREP DET.FEM.SG
not yourself   have(.you)   that go of the
lengua
N.FEM.SG
tongue

'Do not let the cat out of the bag.'

   c. *Prometió   que no se   iría   de*
V.3RD.SG.PAST.IND PRON ADV PRON.3RD.SG V.3.SG.COND.IND PREP
Promised.MASC/FEM that not himself/herself would go   of
la   lengua
DET.FEM.SG N.FEM.SG
the   tongue

'He/she promised not to let the cat out of the bag.'

As MWEs in which a reflexive verb appears also allow for other types of flexibility such as the apparition of modifiers, we classified them as flexible MWEs. However, most of these verbal phrases do not occur undergoing other types of flexibility such as topicalization or passivization and further research is needed to confirm their flexibility degree.

6.6.4 Verbs with a governed prepositional phrase

Verbs with a governed prepositional phrase are verbs that are always followed by a certain preposition.[21] The preposition is not predictable, since it is due to both semantic and historical reasons. Usually, only one preposition governs the phrase, though occasionally more than one is possible, especially in those cases where the phrase following the preposition indicates matter, direction or addressee (e.g. *hablar de/sobre/acerca de* 'to talk of/about'; *viajar a/hacia/hasta* 'to travel to/towards').

Spanish reflexive verbs usually have a governed prepositional phrase (e.g. *arrepentirse de* 'to regret'; *referirse a* 'to refer to'), and a few show a possible alternation between the governed prepositional phrase and a direct object (e.g. *quedarse algo/quedarse con algo* 'to keep something'). Finally, some verbs require a governed prepositional phrase for some of their meanings. In such cases, the meaning of the verb is determined by the occurrence of a governed prepositional phrase (e.g. *entender algo/entender de algo* 'to understand something'/'to know about something').

We gathered a total of 21 verbs with a governed prepositional phrase. A manual analysis revealed that the verb can always inflect in terms of person, tense and mode. As other elements may intervene between the verb and the prepositional phrase, and the prepositional phrase can sometimes undergo topicalization (see example (9)), we tentatively classified all of them as flexible.

6.7 Sentential expressions

Some of the MWEs that we included in our data set constitute full clauses. They all share the fact that they are idiomatic expressions as well. However, as we aimed at classifying MWEs from a morphosyntactic point of view, we have classified them as "sentential expressions".

In our data set, only 5 MWEs of this type have been gathered. 4 of them are fixed, whereas 1 is semi-fixed: *la gota que colma el vaso* 'straw that breaks the camel's back'. Their main difference is that while the fixed ones are fully lexicalized (e.g. *cuando el río suena, agua lleva* 'when there is smoke, there is fire'), the semi-fixed allows for verb inflection.

---

[21]They are similar in this sense to the adjectives and nouns with a governed prepositional phrase described in Sections 6.1.3 and 6.4.3.

If we consider Spanish proverbs as sentential expressions, this class of our data set could be expanded greatly. However, at this point we do not aim at finding a way of automatically identifying such exceptional cases and characterizing them.[22]

7 Conclusion

In this article, we have analyzed the different types of Spanish MWEs we identified. The starting point of our research was a data set created on the basis of an existing taxonomy for MWEs. Upon our linguistic analysis, we realized that such taxonomy was not adequate for describing Spanish MWEs and we modified it to accommodate our findings.

One interesting finding is the fact that in Spanish there seem to be some MWE categories that are only fixed (*conjunctional phrases, prepositional phrases* and *proper names*), or only flexible (*light verb constructions, adjectives, nouns and verbs with governed prepositional phrases* and *verbal periphrastic constructions*). Only *adjectival compounds* are exclusively semi-flexible. The other MWE types having semi-flexible MWEs are either also fixed (*complex nominals* and *sentential expressions*), also flexible (*verbal phrases*) or both fixed and flexible (*adjectival expressions* and *adverbial phrases*).

It also seems clear that MWE typologies should be adapted to the language under research, and classic typologies mainly based on the English language do not seem adequate to describe and classify MWEs in other languages. Our research is proof of this fact. Moreover, the taxonomy proposed here has also shown ways of integrating the traditionally considered "difficulty class" of *idioms* within the morphosyntactic classes.

We believe that our work is novel in the sense that we have tested an existing MWE taxonomy to classify Spanish MWEs. In future work we intend to validate our data set asking other linguists whether they agree or not with our classification. We also intend to expand it for the categories underrepresented and carry out further corpus searches to validate our analyses.

Another possible path to explore would be to evaluate the extent to which the flexibility tests discussed in §3 are valid and whether specific types of MWEs require specific tests. It would also be interesting to explore the word-span between the different parts of MWEs and whether discontinuous MWEs in Spanish share

---

[22]The *Centro Virtual Cervantes* (Instituto Cervantes), has a collection of Spanish proverbs translated to other languages and with useful information about their variants and synonyms that could be used for further research (http://cvc.cervantes.es/lengua/refranero/Default.aspx).

some features. This would enable their automatic identification and processing in NLP applications.

From a multilingual perspective, it would be interesting to further compare our data set with the translations of its entries into other languages. This is interesting from a traductological point of view, as it would allow to further compare MWEs and their behavior in different languages. Our data set includes the translations into English of all the items. Many Spanish MWEs translate as English MWEs. In fields such as translation studies or Machine Translation, a further study of these correspondences would be highly relevant.

Finally, it would also be interesting to see if language families share a common MWE taxonomy. We have argued here the need of a language-specific MWE taxonomy. However, it could be that languages belonging to the same language family share a taxonomy and thus instead of language-specific taxonomies there is a need for language-family specific taxonomies.

Acknowledgments

The authors wish to thank the anonymous reviewers for their valuable feedback.

Carla Parra Escartín was supported by the People Programme (Marie Curie Actions) of the European Union's Framework Programme (FP7/2007-2013) under REA grant agreement n° 317471, the European Union's Horizon 2020 research and innovation programme under the Marie Skłodowska-Curie grant agreement N° 713567, and the Science Foundation Ireland in the ADAPT Centre (Grant 13/RC/2106) (www.adaptcentre.ie) at Dublin City University.

Abbreviations

1/2/3	first/second/third person	N	noun
ADJ	adjective	NLP	natural language processing
ADV	adverb	PAST	past tense
CONJ	conjunction	PL	plural
DET	determiner	POS	part of speech
FEM	feminine	PREP	preposition
IND	indicative	PRES	present tense
INF	infinitive	PRON	pronoun
GER	gerund	SG	singular
LVC	light verb construction	SUBJ	subjunctive
MASC	masculine	V	verb
MWE	multiword expression		

Carla Parra Escartín, Almudena Nevado Llopis & Eoghan Sánchez Martínez

Appendix

List of abbreviations used in the appendix

1/2/3 PERS	1st/2nd/3rd person	PAST	past tense
ADJ	adjective	PL	plural
ADV	adverb	POS	possessive
CONJ	conjunction	PP	past participle
DET	determiner	PRES	present tense
FEM	feminine	PREP	preposition
GER	gerund	REFL V	reflexive verb
IND	indicative	PRON	pronoun
INF	infinitive	SG	singular
MASC	masculine	SUBJ	subjunctive
N	noun	V	verb

The following three appendices present the Spanish data set used in this article classified according to our taxonomy. It shall be noted that the translations of MWEs not always result in MWEs in the target language, nor in the same syntactic class.

Appendix A Spanish Fixed MWEs data set

Table 1: Adjectival phrases.

	Spanish MWE	PoS pattern in Spanish	English translation
1	*a cuadros*	prep + n	plaid
2	*a rayas*	prep + n	striped
3	*como puños*	adv + n	like daggers
4	*como una catedral*	adv + det + n	huge
5	*contante y sonante*	adj + conj + adj	hard cash
6	*corriente y moliente*	adj + conj + adj	plain ordinary
7	*de gala*	prep + n	gala
8	*de pared*	prep + n	wall
9	*de segunda mano*	prep + adj + n	second hand
10	*en directo*	prep + n	live
11	*en falso*	prep + adj	lie
12	*en jarras*	prep + n	on hips
13	*en vivo*	prep + adj	live
14	*mondo y lirondo*	adj + conj + adj	plain and simple

Table 2: Adverbial expressions.

Spanish MWE	PoS pattern in Spanish	English translation
1 *a bote pronto*	prep + n (masc; sg) + adj (masc; sg)	out of the blue
2 *a caballo*	prep + n (masc; sg)	on horseback
3 *a escondidas*	prep + pp (fem; pl)	behind somebody's back
4 *a fondo*	prep + n (masc; sg)	in depth
5 *a grito pelado*	prep + n (masc; sg) + adj (masc; sg)	at the top of one's lungs
6 *a gusto*	prep + n (masc; sg)	at ease
7 *a la carrera*	prep + det (fem; sg) + n (fem; sg)	in a rush
8 *a la fuerza*	prep + det (fem; sg) + n (fem; sg)	by force
9 *a la perfección*	prep + det (fem; sg) + n (fem; sg)	to perfection
10 *a la vez*	prep + det (fem; sg) + n (fem; sg)	all at once
11 *a la vista*	prep + det (fem; sg) + n (fem; sg)	in sight
12 *a las mil maravillas*	prep + det (fem; pl) + adj + n (fem; pl)	perfectly
13 *a manos llenas*	prep + n (fem; pl) + adj (fem; pl)	hand over fist
14 *a medias*	prep + adj (fem; pl)	halfway
15 *a oscuras*	prep + adj (fem; pl)	in the dark
16 *a secas*	prep + adj (fem; pl)	plainly
17 *a tientas*	prep + n (fem; pl)	blindly
18 *a toda velocidad*	prep + adj (fem; sg) + n (fem; sg)	at full speed
19 *al por mayor*	prep + det (masc; sg) + prep + adj (masc; sg)	wholesale
20 *codo con codo*	n (masc; sg) + prep + n (masc; sg)	elbow-to-elbow
21 *con las manos en la masa*	prep + det (fem; pl) + n (fem; pl) + prep + det (fem; sg) + n (fem; sg)	red-handed
22 *contra reloj*	prep + n (masc; sg)	against the clock
23 *con una mano delante y otra detrás*	prep + det (fem; sg) + n (fem; sg) + adv + conj + adj (fem; sg) + adv	from hand to mouth
24 *de buenas*	prep + adj (fem; pl)	with all one's heart
25 *de cabo a rabo*	prep + n (masc; sg) + prep + n (masc; sg)	head to tail
26 *de golpe y porrazo*	prep + n (masc; sg) + conj + n (masc; sg)	all of a sudden
27 *de reojo*	prep + n (masc; sg)	out of the corner of one's eye

28 *en breve*	prep + adj (masc; sg)	shortly/in due course
29 *en consecuencia*	prep + n (fem; sg)	consequently
30 *en definitiva*	prep + adj (fem; sg)	in conclusion
31 *en el acto*	prep + det (masc; sg) + n (masc; sg)	in the act
32 *en líneas generales*	prep + n (fem; pl) + adj (fem; pl)	by and large
33 *en pocas palabras*	prep + adj (fem; pl) + n (fem; pl)	in a nutshell
34 *en secreto*	prep + n (masc; sg)	in secret
35 *en suma*	prep + n (fem; sg)	in short
36 *en un santiamén*	prep + det (masc; sg) + n (masc; sg)	in a flash
37 *más o menos*	adv + conj + adv	more or less
38 *ni más ni menos*	conj + adv + conj + adv	no more, no less
39 *para colmo*	prep + n (masc; sg)	to top it all
40 *por casualidad*	prep + n (fem; sg)	by chance
41 *por cierto*	prep + adj (masc; sg)	by the way
42 *por consiguiente*	prep + adj (masc; sg)	hence
43 *por descontado*	prep + pp (masc; sg)	needless to say
44 *por el contrario*	prep + det (masc; sg) + adj (masc; sg)	on the contrary
45 *por supuesto*	prep + adj (masc; sg)	of course
46 *sin embargo*	prep + n (masc; sg)	nevertheless
47 *sin más ni más*	prep + adv + conj + adv	just like that
48 *sin ton ni son*	prep + n (masc; sg) + adv +n (masc; sg)	without rhyme or reason
49 *una barbaridad*	det (fem; sg) + n (fem; sg)	quite a lot

Table 3: Conjunctional phrases.

	Spanish MWE	PoS pattern in Spanish	English translation
1	*a fin de que*	prep + n (masc; sg) + prep + conj	in order to
2	*a medida que*	prep + n (fem; sg) + conj	as
3	*a menos que*	prep + adv + conj	unless
4	*así que*	adv + conj	consequently
5	*con tal de que*	prep + adv + prep + conj	as long as
6	*mientras que*	adv + conj	while
7	*siempre que*	adv + conj	whenever
8	*tan pronto como*	adv + adv + conj	as soon as
9	*visto que*	adj + conj	since
10	*ya que*	adv + conj	because

Table 4: Complex nominals.

	Spanish MWE	PoS pattern in Spanish	English translation
1	*abrebotellas*	n (masc; sg/pl)	bottle opener
2	*aguafiestas*	n (masc/fem; sg/pl)	spoilsport
3	*cascanueces*	n (masc; sg/pl)	nutcracker
4	*correveidile*	n (fem/masc; sg)	tell-tale
5	*lavavajillas*	n (masc; sg/pl)	dishwasher
6	*limpiacristales*	n (fem/masc; sg/pl)	window cleaner
7	*rascacielos*	n (masc; sg/pl)	skyscrapper
8	*sacacorchos*	n (masc; sg/pl)	bottle opener
9	*soplagaitas*	n (fem/masc; sg/pl)	dumbbell
10	*pinchadiscos*	n (masc/fem; sg/pl)	disc jockey
11	*complejo de Edipo*	n (masc; sg) + prep + n (masc; sg)	Oedipus complex
12	*el día a día*	det (masc; sg) n (masc; sg) + prep + n (masc; sg)	everyday life
13	*el día del juicio final*	det (masc; sg) + n (masc; sg) + prep + det (masc; sg) + n (masc; sg) + adj (masc; sg)	doomsday
14	*gripe aviar*	n (fem; sg) + adj (fem; sg)	avian influenza
15	*la flor y la nata*	det (fem; sg) + n (fem; sg) + conj + det (fem; sg) + n (fem; sg)	cream of the crop
16	*la gran pantalla*	art (fem; sg) + adj (fem; sg) + n (fem; sg)	the big screen
17	*la teoría de la relatividad*	det (fem; sg) + n (fem; sg) + prep + det (fem; sg) + n (fem; sg)	theory of relativity
18	*mucho ruido y pocas nueces*	adj (masc; sg) + n (masc; sg) + conj + adj (fem; pl) + n (fem; pl)	much ado about nothing
19	*perro ladrador, poco mordedor*	n (masc; sg) + adj (masc; sg) + adv + adj (masc; sg)	his bark is worse than his bite
20	*sentido del ridículo*	n (masc; sg) + prep + n (masc; sg)	self-concious
21	*síndrome de down*	n (masc; sg) + prep + n (masc; sg)	Down Syndrome
22	*vergüenza ajena*	n (fem; sg) + adj (fem; sg)	feel embarrassment for
23	*síndrome de Estocolmo*	n (masc; sg) + prep + n (masc; sg)	Stockholm Syndrome

Table 5: Proper names.

	Spanish MWE	PoS pattern in Spanish	English translation
1	*Air Jordan*	n (masc; sg) + n (masc; sg)	Air Jordan
2	*Al Capone*	n (masc; sg) + n (masc; sg)	Al Capone
3	*América Latina*	n (fem; sg) + adj (fem; sg)	Latin America
4	*Amnistía Internacional*	n (fem; sg) + adj (fem; sg)	Amnesty International
5	*Banco Central Europeo*	n (masc; sg) + adj (masc; sg) + adj (masc; sg)	European Central Bank
6	*Billy el Niño*	n (masc; sg) + det (masc; sg) + n (masc; sg)	Billy the Kid
7	*Buenos Aires*	adj (masc; pl) + n (masc; pl)	Buenos Aires
8	*Costa Rica*	n (fem; sg) + adj (fem; sg)	Costa Rica
9	*Cruz Roja*	n (fem; sg) + adj (fem; sg)	Red Cross
10	*el Cordobés*	det (masc; sg) + adj (masc; sg)	el Cordobés
11	*El Greco*	det (masc; sg) + adj (masc; sg)	El Greco
12	*El Pelusa*	det (masc; sg) + n (fem; sg)	el Pelusa
13	*El Principito*	det (masc; sg) + n (masc; sg)	The Little Prince
14	*Gran Bretaña*	adj (fem; sg) + n (fem; sg)	Great Britain
15	*José María*	n (masc; sg) + n (fem; sg)	José María
16	*La Paz*	det (fem; sg) + n (fem; sg)	La Paz
17	*La sombra del viento*	det (fem; sg) + n (fem; sg) + prep + det (masc; sg) + n (masc; sg)	The Shadow of the Wind
18	*Lawrence de Arabia*	n (masc; sg) + prep + n (fem; sg)	Lawrence of Arabia
19	*Lord Byron*	n (masc; sg) + n (masc; sg)	Lord Byron
20	*Los Ángeles*	det (masc; pl) + n (masc; pl)	Los Angeles
21	*Manchester United*	n + adj	Manchester United
22	*María José*	n (fem; sg) + n (masc; sg)	María José
23	*Médicos Sin Fronteras*	n (masc; pl) + prep + n (fem; pl)	Doctors Without Borders
24	*Mona Lisa*	n (fem; sg) + n (fem; sg)	Mona Lisa
25	*Nueva York*	adj (fem; sg) + n (fem; sg)	New York
26	*Nueva Zelanda*	adj (fem; sg) + n (fem; sg)	New Zealand
27	*Osa Mayor*	n (fem; sg) + adj (fem; sg)	Ursa Major
28	*Países Bajos*	n (fem; sg) + adj (fem; sg)	the Netherlands
29	*Papá Noel*	n (masc; sg) + n (masc; sg)	Father Christmas
30	*Real Academia Española*	adj (fem; sg) + n (fem; sg) + adj (fem; sg)	Royal Spanish Language Academy
31	*Real Madrid*	adj (masc; sg) + n (masc; sg)	Real Madrid
32	*Reino Unido*	n (masc; sg) + adj (masc; sg)	United Kingdom
33	*República Dominicana*	n (fem; sg) + adj (fem; sg)	Dominican Republic
34	*San Salvador*	adj (fem; sg) + n (masc; sg)	San Salvador
35	*Unión Europea*	n (fem; sg) + adj (fem; sg)	European Union

Table 6: Prepositional phrases.

	Spanish MWE	PoS pattern in Spanish	English translation
1	*por culpa de*	prep + n (fem; sg) + prep	because of
2	*a pesar de*	prep + n (masc; sg) + prep	in spite of
3	*al margen de*	prep + det (masc; sg) + n (masc; sg) + prep	apart from
4	*con miras a*	prep + n (fem; sg) + prep	looking to
5	*de conformidad con*	prep + n (fem; sg) + prep	according to
6	*en contra de*	prep + n (fem; sg) + prep	in opposition to
7	*en cuanto a*	prep + adverb + prep	with regard to
8	*en detrimento de*	prep + n (masc; sg) + prep	at the expense of
9	*en relación con*	prep + n (fem; sg) + prep	in relation to
10	*respecto a*	n (masc; sg) + prep	in relation to

Table 7: Sentential expressions.

	Spanish MWE	PoS pattern in Spanish	English translation
1	*cuando el río suena, agua lleva*	conj + det (masc; sg) + n (masc; sg) + v (3rd pers; sg) + n (fem; sg) + v (3rd pers; sg)	where there's smoke, there's fire
2	*cuando las ranas críen pelo*	adv + det (fem; pl) + n (fem; pl) + v (3rd pers; pl) + n (masc; sg)	when pigs fly
3	*dime con quién andas y te diré quién eres*	v (2nd pers; sg) + prep + pron + v (2nd pers; sg) + conj + pron + v (1st pers; sg) + pron + v (2ª pers; sg)	birds of a feather flock together
4	*más vale tarde que nunca*	adv + v (3rd pers; sg) + adv + conj + adv	better late than never

Appendix B Spanish Semi-fixed MWEs data set

Table 8: Adjectival compounds.

	Spanish MWE	PoS pattern in Spanish	English translation
1	*agridulce*	adj (masc/fem; sg)	sweet-and-sour/bittersweet
2	*boquiabierto*	adj (masc; sg)	open-mouthed
3	*cabizbajo*	adj (masc; sg)	downcast
4	*cejijunto*	adj (masc; sg)	unibrow
5	*drogadicto*	adj (masc; sg)	drug addict
6	*hispanohablante*	adj (masc/fem; sg)	Spanish-speaking
7	*narcotraficante*	adj (masc/fem; sg)	drug dealer/drug trafficker
8	*patidifuso*	adj (masc; sg)	astonished
9	*pelirrojo*	adj (masc; sg)	redheaded
10	*vasodilatador*	adj (masc; sg)	vasodilator

Table 9: Adjectival phrases.

	Spanish MWE	PoS pattern in Spanish	English translation
1	*de primera mano*	prep + adj + n (fem; sg)	first hand
2	*sano y salvo*	adj + conj + adj	safe and sound

Table 10: Adverbial expressions.

	Spanish MWE	PoS pattern in Spanish	English translation
1	*a golpes*	prep + n (masc; pl)	violently

Carla Parra Escartín, Almudena Nevado Llopis & Eoghan Sánchez Martínez

Table 11: Complex nominals.

	Spanish MWE	PoS pattern in Spanish	English translation
1	*la ley de la jungla*	det (fem; sg) + n (fem; sg) + prep + det (fem; sg) + n (fem; sg)	law of the jungle
2	*anillo de compromiso*	n (masc; sg) + prep + n (masc; sg)	engagement ring
3	*bicicleta estática*	n (fem; sg) + adj (fem; sg)	exercise bike
4	*bocacalle*	n (fem;sg)	side-street
5	*bomba nuclear*	n (fem; sg) + adj (fem; sg)	nuclear bomb
6	*café con leche*	n (masc; sg) + prep + n (fem; sg)	coffee with milk
7	*campo de concentración*	n (masc; sg) + prep + n (fem; sg)	concentration camp
8	*centro de salud*	n (masc; sg) + prep + n (fem; sg)	health center
9	*cinta de correr*	n (fem; sg) + prep + inf	treadmill
10	*ciudad dormitorio*	n (fem; sg) + n (masc; sg)	dormitory town
11	*complejo de inferioridad*	n (masc; sg) + prep + n (fem; sg)	inferiority complex
12	*crema de manos*	n (fem; sg) + prep + n (fem; pl)	hand cream
13	*cuenta de débito*	n (fem; sg) + prep + n (masc; sg)	debit account
14	*cuenta de resultados*	n (fem; sg) + prep + n (masc; pl)	profit and loss account
15	*cuento chino*	n (masc; sg) + adj (masc; sg)	a tall tale
16	*deporte de aventura*	n (masc; sg) + prep + n (fem; sg)	adventure sport
17	*diente de león*	n (masc; sg) + prep + n (masc; sg)	dandelion
18	*disco pirata*	n (masc; sg) + n (masc; sg)	pirate CD
19	*fin de semana*	n (masc; sg) + prep + n (fem; sg)	weekend
20	*goma de borrar*	n (fem; sg) + prep + inf	eraser
21	*guerra civil*	n (fem; sg) + adj (fem; sg)	civil war
22	*hombre lobo*	n (masc; sg) + n (masc; sg)	werewolf
23	*hueso duro de roer*	n (masc; sg) + n (masc; sg) + adj (masc; sg) + prep + inf	hard nut to crack
24	*impuesto revolucionario*	n (masc; sg) + adj (masc; sg)	revolutionary tax
25	*infarto de miocardio*	n (masc; sg) + prep + n (masc; pl)	myocardial infarction

26	*la gallina de los huevos de oro*	det (fem; sg) + n (fem; sg) + prep + det (masc; pl) + n (masc; pl) + prep + n (masc; sg)	cash cow
27	*la ley del más fuerte*	det (fem; sg) + n (fem; sg) + prep + det (masc; sg) + adv + adj (masc; sg)	survival of the fittest
28	*lobo con piel de cordero*	n (masc; sg) + prep + n (fem; sg) + prep + n (masc; sg)	wolf in sheep's clothing
29	*mesa camilla*	n (fem; sg) + n (fem; sg)	round table
30	*momento clave*	n (masc; sg) + n (fem; sg)	key moment
31	*niño mimado*	n (masc; sg) + adj (masc; sg)	blue-eyed boy
32	*niño prodigio*	n (masc; sg) + n (masc; sg)	child prodigy
33	*patata caliente*	n (fem; sg) + adj (fem; sg)	hot potato
34	*perro de caza*	n (masc; sg) + prep + n (fem; sg)	hunting dog
35	*raíz cuadrada*	n (fem; sg) + adj (fem; sg)	square root
36	*realidad virtual*	n (fem; sg) + adj (fem; sg)	virtual reality
37	*renta per cápita*	n (fem; sg) + prep + n (fem; sg)	income per capita
38	*ruleta rusa*	n (fem; sg) + adj (fem; sg)	Russian roulette
39	*salto mortal*	n (masc; sg) + adj (masc; sg)	somersault
40	*sentimiento de culpa*	n (masc; sg) + prep + n (fem; sg)	guilt
41	*tarjeta de crédito*	n (fem; sg) + prep + n (masc; sg)	credit card
42	*tortilla de patata*	n (fem; sg) + prep + n (fem; sg)	Spanish omelette
43	*zumo de naranja*	n (masc; sg) + prep + n (fem; sg)	orange juice

Table 12: Verbal phrases.

	Spanish MWE	PoS pattern in Spanish	English translation
1	*coger el toro por los cuernos*	v + det (masc; sg) + n (masc; sg) + prep + det (masc; pl) + n (masc; pl)	to take the bull by the horns
2	*echar por tierra*	v + prep + n (fem; sg)	to upset the applecart
3	*empezar la casa por el tejado*	v + det (fem; sg) + n (fem; sg) + prep + det (masc; sg) + n (masc; sg)	to put the cart before the horse
4	*estar como unas castañuelas*	v + adv + det (fem; pl) + n (fem; pl)	to be tickled pink
5	*ir de guatemala a guatepeor*	v + prep + n (fem; sg) + prep + n (masc; sg)	out of the frying pan and into the fire
6	*ni pinchar ni cortar*	conj + v + conj + v	to cut no ice
7	*ser de armas tomar*	v + prep + n (fem; pl) + verb	to be someone to be reckoned with
8	*ser el ojito derecho*	v + det (masc; sg) + n (masc; sg) + adj (masc; sg)	to be the apple of one's eye
9	*ser harina de otro costal*	v + n (fem; sg) + prep + adj (masc; sg) + n (masc; sg)	to be a horse of a different colour
10	*ser la crème de la crème*	v + det (fem; sg) + n (fem; sg) + prep + det (fem; sg) + n (fem; sg)	to be crème de la crème
11	*vivir a cuerpo de rey*	v + prep + n (masc; sg) + prep + n (masc; sg)	to live high on the hog

Table 13: Sentential expressions.

	Spanish MWE	PoS pattern in Spanish	English translation
1	*la gota que colma el vaso*	det (fem; sg) + n (fem; sg) + conj + v (3rd pers; sg) + det (masc; sg) + n (masc; sg)	straw that breaks the camel's back

Appendix C Spanish Flexible MWEs data set

Table 14: Adjectival phrases.

	Spanish MWE	PoS pattern in Spanish	English translation
1	*de cuidado*	prep + n (masc; sg)	dangerous
2	*de ensueño*	prep + n (masc; sg)	fantastic

Table 15: Adjectives with a governed prepositional phrase.

	Spanish MWE	PoS pattern in Spanish	English translation
1	*adicto a*	adj (masc; sg) + prep	addicted to
2	*aficionado a*	adj (masc; sg) + prep	fond of
3	*apto para*	adj (masc; sg) + prep	suitable for
4	*aspirante a*	adj (masc/fem; sg) + prep	candidate for
5	*carente de*	adj (masc/fem; sg) + prep	deprived of
6	*casado con*	adj (masc; sg) + prep	married to/with
7	*celoso de*	adj (masc; sg) + prep	jealous of
8	*culpable de*	adj (masc/fem; sg) + prep	guilty of
9	*dependiente de*	adj (masc/fem; sg) + prep	dependent on
10	*exento de*	adj (masc; sg) + prep	exempt from
11	*interesado en*	adj (masc; sg) + prep	interested in
12	*preocupado por*	adj (masc; sg) + prep	worried about
13	*sospechoso de*	adj (masc; sg) + prep	suspected of

Table 16: Adverbial expression.

	Spanish MWE	PoS pattern in Spanish	English translation
1	*a mi/tu/su/nuestro/vuestro entender*	prep + pos + n (masc; sg)	by my/your/her/his/our/their understanding

Table 17: Nouns with a governed prepositional phrase.

	Spanish MWE	PoS pattern in Spanish	English translation
1	*actitud con/hacia/respecto de*	n (fem; sg)+ prep	attitude with/towards/regarding
2	*amenaza de*	n (fem; sg) + prep	threat of
3	*asalto a/de*	n (masc; sg) + prep	assault to/on
4	*confianza en*	n (fem; sg) + prep	trust in
5	*esperanza de*	n (fem; sg) + prep	hope to
6	*interés por*	n (masc; sg) + prep	interest in
7	*olor a*	n (masc; sg) + prep	smell of
8	*prohibición de*	n (fem; sg) + prep	prohibition of
9	*sabor a*	n (masc; sg) + prep	taste of
10	*salida de*	n (fem; sg) + prep	exit of
11	*traducción a*	n (fem; sg) + prep	translation to
12	*veto a*	n (fem; sg) + prep	ban on

Table 18: Light verb constructions.

	Spanish MWE	PoS pattern in Spanish	English translation
1	*cantar las cuarenta*	v + det (fem; pl) + adj (fem pl)	to haul over the coals
2	*comer la olla*	v + det (fem; sg) + n (fem; sg)	to talk someone into something
3	*cortar el bacalao*	v + det (masc; sg) + n (masc; sg)	to be the big cheese/big fish
4	*dar acidez*	v + n (fem; sg)	to produce heartburn
5	*dar ánimos*	v + n (masc; pl)	to cheer up
6	*dar calor*	v + n (masc; sg)	to keep warm
7	*dar carpetazo*	v + n (masc; sg)	to put an end to
8	*dar esquinazo*	v + n (masc; sg)	to give the slip
9	*dar la palabra*	v + det (fem; sg) + n (fem; sg)	to give the floor to
10	*dar la tabarra*	v + det (fem; sg) + n (fem; sg)	to pester
11	*dar plantón*	v + n (masc; sg)	to stand [sb] up
12	*dar suerte*	v + n (fem; sg)	to give [sb] luck

13	*dar un beso*	v + det (masc; sg) + n (masc; sg)	to give a kiss
14	*dar una patada*	v + det (fem; sg) + n (fem; sg)	to kick
15	*dar un paseo*	v + det (masc; sg) + n (masc; sg)	to go for a walk
16	*dar un puñetazo*	v + det (masc; sg) + n (masc; sg)	to punch
17	*despertar el apetito*	v + det (masc; sg) + n (masc; sg)	to awaken one's apettite
18	*echar la siesta*	v + det (fem; sg) + n (fem; sg)	to take a nap
19	*echar un cable*	v + det (masc; sg) + n (masc; sg)	to give a hand
20	*empinar el codo*	v + det (masc; sg) + n (masc; sg)	to bend one's elbow
21	*hacer alusión*	v + n (fem; sg)	to make an allusion
22	*hacer añicos*	v + n (masc; pl)	to break into pieces
23	*hacer gracia*	v + n (fem; sg)	to be funny
24	*hacer ilusión*	v + n (fem; sg)	to look forward to
25	*hacer la compra*	v + det (fem; sg) + n (fem; sg)	to do the shopping
26	*hacer la pelota*	v + det (fem;sg) + n (fem; sg)	to suck up to
27	*hacer un trato*	v + det (masc; sg) + n (masc; sg)	to make a deal
28	*hacer una foto*	v + det (fem; sg) + n (fem; sg)	to take a picture
29	*hacer una oferta*	v + det (fem; sg) + n (fem; sg)	to make an offer
30	*hacerse ilusiones*	refl v + n (fem; pl)	to get one's hopes up
31	*levar anclas*	v + n (fem; pl)	to weigh anchor
32	*llamar la atención*	v + det (fem; sg) + n (fem; sg)	to attract one's attention
33	*pasar la pelota*	v + det (fem; sg) + n (fem; sg)	to pass the buck
34	*ponerse las pilas*	refl v + det (fem; pl) + n (fem; pl)	to get one's act together
35	*sacar pecho*	v + n (masc; sg)	to stick your chest out
36	*sufrir las consecuencias*	v + det (fem; pl) + n (fem; pl)	to suffer the consequences
37	*tener gana*	v + n (fem; sg)	to be hungry
38	*tener ganas*	v + n (fem; pl)	to feel like
39	*tomar el pelo*	v + det (masc; sg) + n (masc; sg)	to tease [someone]
40	*tomar el sol*	v + det (masc; sg) + n (masc; sg)	to sunbathe
41	*tomar partido*	v + n (masc; sg)	to take sides
42	*tomar una decisión*	n + det (fem; sg) + n (fem; sg)	to make a decision

Table 19: Periphrastic constructions. Periphrastic constructions do not have straightforward English translations. The ones give here are an indication of what the usually mean but the translations will depend on the verb appearing in a non-finite form in the periphrasis.

	Spanish MWE	PoS pattern in Spanish	English translation
1	*acabar de + inf*	v + prep + inf	to finish to
2	*andar + ger*	v + ger	to be doing
3	*deber + inf*	v + inf	to have to
4	*deber de + inf*	v + prep + inf	to may have
5	*empezar a + inf*	v + prep + inf	to begin to
6	*estar por + inf*	v + prep + inf	to be about to
7	*haber de + inf*	v + prep + inf	to have to
8	*haber que + inf*	v + pron + inf	to have to
9	*ir + ger*	v + ger	to begin/be doing
10	*ir a + inf*	v + prep + inf	to go to
11	*llegar a + inf*	v + prep + inf	to manage to
12	*llevar + ger*	v + ger	to have been doing
13	*llevar + pp*	v + pp	to have done
14	*poder + inf*	v + inf	to be able to
13	*sacar a + inf*	v + prep + inf	to take someone out to
15	*seguir + ger*	v + ger	to continue doing
16	*tener que + inf*	v + pron + inf	to have to
17	*venir + ger*	v + ger	to have been doing
18	*venir a + inf*	v + prep + inf	to be
19	*volver a + inf*	v + prep + inf	to do something again

Table 20: Verbal phrases.

	Spanish MWE	PoS pattern in Spanish	English translation
1	*dar por sentado*	v + prep + adj (masc; sg)	take for granted
2	*entrar al trapo*	v + prep + det (masc; sg) + n (masc; sg)	to respond to provocations
3	*estar al pie del cañón*	v + prep + det (masc; sg) + n (masc; sg) + prep + det (art; sg) + n (masc; sg)	to be ready and waiting
4	*estar en Babia*	v + prep + n (fem; sg)	to be daydreaming
5	*estar en las nubes*	v + prep + det (fem; pl) + noun (fem; pl)	to be in the clouds
6	*hacer una montaña de*	v + det (fem; sg) + n (fem; sg) + prep + det (masc; sg) + n (masc; sg) + prep + n (fem; sg)	make a mountain out of a molehill
7	*irse de la lengua*	refl v + prep + det (fem; sg) + n (fem; sg)	to let the cat out of the bag
8	*irse de rositas*	refl v + prep + n (fem; pl)	to get off scot free
9	*irse por las ramas*	refl v + prep + det (fem; pl) + n (fem; pl)	to beat around the bush
10	*llamar a la puerta equivocada*	v + prep + det (fem; sg) + n (fem; sg) + adj (fem; sg)	to bark up the wrong tree
11	*salir al paso*	v + prep + det (masc; sg) + n (masc; sg)	to refute
12	*salir de cuentas*	v + prep + n (fem; pl)	to be due
13	*salir de marcha*	v + prep + n (fem; sg)	to go partying
14	*saltar a la comba*	v + prep + det (fem; sg) + n (fem; sg)	to skip rope
15	*ser fiel a*	v + adj (masc/fem; sg) + prep	to be loyal to

Table 21: Verbs with a governed prepositional phrase.

	Spanish MWE	PoS pattern	English translation
1	*abstenerse de*	refl v + prep	to refrain yourself from
2	*acordarse de*	refl v + prep	to remember
3	*amenazar con*	v + prep	to threaten to
4	*arrepentirse de*	refl v + prep	to regret
5	*atenerse a*	refl v + prep	to stick to
6	*confiar en*	v + prep	to trust in
7	*contribuir a*	v + prep	to contribute to
8	*creer en*	v + prep	to believe in
9	*cuidar de*	v + prep	to take care of
10	*empeñarse en*	refl v + prep	to insist on
11	*engancharse a*	refl v + prep	to get hooked on
12	*entender de*	v + prep	to know about
13	*eximir de*	v + prep	to exempt from
14	*gozar de*	v + prep	to enjoy
15	*hablar de/sobre/acerca de*	v + prep	to talk about/of
16	*interesarse por*	refl v + prep	to be interested in
17	*oler a*	v + prep	to smell like
18	*pelear por*	v + prep	to fight for
19	*quedarse con*	refl v + prep	to keep
20	*referirse a*	refl v + prep	to refer to
21	*viajar a/hacia/hasta*	v + prep	to travel to/towards

References

Atkins, Beryl T., Núria Bel, Pierrette Bouillon, Thatsanee Charoenporn, Dafydd Gibbon, Ralph Grishman, Chu-Ren Huan, Asanee Kawtrakul, Nancy Ide, Hae-Yun Lee, Paul J. K. Li, Jock McNaught, Jan Odijk, Martha Palmer, Valeria Quochi, Ruth Reeves, Dipti Misra Sharma, Virach Sornlertlamvanich, Takenobu Tokunaga, Gregor Thurmair, Marta Villegas, Antonio Zampolli & Elizabeth Zeiton. 2001. *Standards and Best Practice for Multiligual Computational Lexicons. MILE (the Multilingual ISLE Lexical Entry) Deliverable D2.2-D3.2.* ISLE project: ISLE Computational Lexicon Working Group. http://www.w3.org/2001/sw/BestPractices/WNET/ISLE_D2.2-D3.2.pdf, accessed 2018-4-19.

Baldwin, Timothy & Su Nam Kim. 2010. Multiword expressions. In Nitin Indurkhya & Fred J. Damerau (eds.), *Handbook of Natural Language Processing*, 2nd edn., 267–292. Boca Raton: CRC Press.

Church, Kenneth Ward & Patrick Hanks. 1990. Word association norms, mutual information, and lexicography. *Computational Linguistics* 16(1). 22–29.

Corpas Pastor, Gloria. 1996. *Manual de fraseología española.* Madrid: Gredos.

Devereux, Barry & Fintan Costello. 2007. Learning to interpret novel noun-noun compounds: Evidence from a category learning experiment. In *Proceedings of the Workshop on Cognitive Aspects of Computational Language Acquisition*, 89–96. Prague, Czech Republic: Association for Computational Linguistics.

Fillmore, Charles J., Paul Kay & Mary Catherine O'Connor. 1988. Regularity and idiomaticity in grammatical constructions: The case of *let alone. Language* 64(3). 501–538.

Graliński, Filip, Agata Savary, Monika Czerepowicka & Filip Makowiecki. 2010. Computational lexicography of multi-word units: How efficient can it be? In *Proceedings of Multiword Expressions: from Theory to Applications (MWE 2010). Workshop at COLING 2010.* Beijing, China.

Holsinger, Edward. 2013. Representing Idioms: Syntactic and Contextual Effects on Idiom Processing. *Language and Speech* 56(3). 373–394.

Holsinger, Edward & Elsi Kaiser. 2013. Effects of context on processing (non)-compositional expressions. *Journal of Experimental Psychology: Learning, Memory, and Cognition* 39(3). 866–878.

Laporte, Éric. 2018. Choosing features for classifying multiword expressions. In Manfred Sailer & Stella Markantonatou (eds.), *Multiword expressions: Insights from a multi-lingual perspective*, 143–186. Berlin: Language Science Press. DOI:10.5281/zenodo.1182597

Leoni de León, Jorge Antonio. 2014. Lexical-syntactic analysis model of Spanish multi-word expressions. In Brian Nola & Carlos Periñán-Pascual (eds.), *Language Processing and Grammars. The role of functionally oriented computational models*, 39–77. John Benjamins Publishing Company.

Lin, Dekang. 1999. Automatic identification of non-compositional phrases. In *Proceedings of the 37th Annual Meeting of the Association for Computational Linguistics*, 317–324. College Park, Maryland, USA: Association for Computational Linguistics.

Mel'čuk, Igor & Alain Polguère. 1987. A formal lexicon in the Meaning-Text Theory: (or how to do lexica with words). *Computational Linguistics* 13(3–4). 261–275.

Mel'čuk, Igor & Alain Polguère. 1995. *Introduction à la lexicologie explicative et combinatoire*. Louvain-la-Neuve: Duculot.

Moon, Rosamund. 1998. *Fixed expressions and idioms in English: A corpus-based approach*. Oxford University Press.

Nematzadeh, Aida, Afsaneh Fazly & Suzanne Stevenson. 2013. Child acquisition of multiword verbs: A computational investigation. In *Cognitive Aspects of Computational Language Acquisition. Theory and Applications of Natural Language Processing* (Theory and Applications of Natural Language Processing), 235–256. Heidelberg: Springer.

Nunberg, Geoffrey, Ivan A. Sag & Thomas Wasow. 1994. Idioms. *Language* 70(3). 491–538.

Parra Escartín, Carla, Almudena Nevado Sánchez, Eoghan Sánchez Martínez & María Pilar Cardos Murillo. 2015. *Spanish multword expressions: Typology and cross-lingual analysis from a traductological viewpoint*. Poster. PARSEME 4th general meeting, 19-20 March 2015, Valletta, Malta.

Ramisch, Carlos. 2012. *A generic and open framework for multiword expressions treatment: From acquisition to applications*. Grenoble, France: University of Grenoble (France) & Federal University of Rio Grande do Sul (Brazil) dissertation. 246 p. Available on request.

Ramisch, Carlos. 2015. *Multiword expressions acquisition: a generic and open framework* (Theory and applications of Natural Language Processing series XIV). Springer.

Rapp, Reinhard. 2008. The computation of associative responses to multiword stimuli. In *Proceedings of the COLING 2008 Workshop on cognitive aspects of the lexicon (COGALEX 2008)*, 102–109. Manchester.

Real Academia Española. 2018a. *Banco de datos (CORPES XXI). Corpus del Español del Siglo XXI (CORPES)*. on-line. Real Academia Española. http://www.rae.es, accessed 2018-4-19.

Real Academia Española. 2018b. *Banco de datos (CREA). Corpus de referencia del español actual*. on-line. Real Academia Española. http://corpus.rae.es/creanet. html, accessed 2018-5-8.

Real Academia Española. 2010. *Manual de la nueva gramática de la lengua española*. Madrid: Espasa.

Sag, Ivan A., Timothy Baldwin, Francis Bond, Ann Copestake & Dan Flickinger. 2002. Multiword expressions: A pain in the neck for NLP. In *Proceedings of the 3rd International Conference on Intelligent Text Processing and Computational Linguistics (CICLing-2002)*, 1–15.

Savary, Agata. 2008. Computational Inflection of MultiWord Units. A contrastive study of lexical approaches. *Linguistic Issues in Language Technology* 1(2). 1–53.

Schulte im Walde, Sabine & Susanne R. Borgwaldt. 2015. Association norms for German noun compounds and their constituents. English. *Behavior Research Methods*. 1–23. DOI:10.3758/s13428-014-0539-y

Sinclair, John. 1991. *Corpus, concordance, collocation*. Oxford: Oxford University Press.

Smadja, Frank. 1993. Retrieving collocations from text: Xtract. *Computational Linguistics* 19(1). 143–177.

Villavicencio, Aline, Marco A. P. Idiart, Carlos Ramisch, Vítor Araújo, Beracah Yankama & Robert Berwick. 2012. Get out but don't fall down: verb-particle constructions in child language. In *Proceedings of the EACL 2012 workshop on computational models of language acquisition and loss*, 43–50. Avignon, France: Association for Computational Linguistics.

Vincze, Veronika, Agata Savary, Marie Candito & Carlos Ramisch. 2016. Annotation guidelines for the PARSEME shared task on automatic detection of verbal Multi-Word Expressions. Version 5.0. http://typo.uni-konstanz.de/parseme/ images/shared-task/guidelines/PARSEME-ST-annotation-guidelines-v5.pdf.

Name index

Language index

Subject index

Accessibility Theory, 198
adjectival compound, 289, 311
affix
    prefix, 217, 224–225
    suffix, 216, 218–219, 221, 229–230
alternation
    causative-inchoative, 77, 206
    syntactic, 77–79
    transitive-intransitive, 78
antipassive, 123

c-structure, xvii
catena, 132–133, 250–251
    composition, 253
    lexicon catena, 253
classification of MWEs, *see* taxonomy
clitic, 41, 53–56, 198
compositionality, xx
compound nominal, 274–276, 287, 293–295, 308
compound nominals, 311
Construction Grammar, v, xix, 94, 136
Corpus Pattern Analysis, ix, 93, 96
CPA, *see* Corpus Pattern Analysis
cross-linguistic, 72
cross-linguistic parallelism, 1, 4^3, 10, 70, 71, 83, 85–88

Deep Structure, xv

Dependency Grammar, 228
    dependency tree, 251
dictionary, 163^{28}, 170, 171, 177
ditransitive verb, 188
diversity, 105

emotion
    aspect of emotion event, 80
    aspect of the emotion event, 83
    classification, 71–83, 88
    Emotion Lexicon, 70–83
    intensity, 71, 72, 80–84
    polarity, 80–81, 84
entropy, 105, 108
event nominalisation, 239–242
expletive pronoun, 7, 9–11, 11^{10}, 12, 18–20, 23

f-structure, xvii
feature
    clear-cut, 144–146, 150–155
    correlated, 155, 159, 173
    fuzzy, 144, 146–155
frequency
    of collocation, 114

Generalized Phrase Structure Grammar, vii, xix
Generative Grammar, xv–xvi, 137
genitive, 129

Head-driven Phrase Structure Grammar, xix–xx, 12, 155, 170